# *Practice Issues for the Beginning Counselor*

D0206869

# Practice Issues for the Beginning Counselor

**Harold Hackney**

*Fairfield University*

*Allyn and Bacon*

*Boston • London • Toronto • Sydney • Tokyo • Singapore*

**Vice President, Education:** *Paul A. Smith*
**Senior Editor:** *Virginia Lanigan*
**Editorial Assistant:** *Karin Huang*
**Marketing Manager:** *Brad Parkins*
**Editorial-Production Administrator:** *Annette Joseph*
**Editorial-Production Coordinator:** *Holly Crawford*
**Editorial-Production Service:** *Lynda Griffiths, TKM Productions*
**Composition Buyer:** *Linda Cox*
**Electronic Composition:** *TKM Productions*
**Manufacturing Buyer:** *Suzanne Lareau*
**Cover Administrator:** *Jenny Hart*
**Cover Designer:** *Suzanne Harbison*

Copyright © 2000 by Allyn & Bacon
A Pearson Education Company
160 Gould Street
Needham Heights, MA 02494

Internet: www.abacon.com

Between the time Website information is gathered and then published, it is not unusual for some sites to have been closed. Also, the transcription of URLs can result in unintended typographical errors. The publisher would appreciate notification where these occur so that they may be corrected in subsequent editions. Thank you.

**Library of Congress Cataloging-in-Publication Data**

Hackney, Harold
    Practice issues for the beginning counselor / Harold Hackney.
      p.    cm.
    Includes bibliographical references and index.
    ISBN 0-205-30649-7
    1. Counseling.   I. Title.
    BF637.C6H255   1999
    158'.3--dc21                      99-36234
                                                CIP

Printed in the United States of America

10  9  8  7  6  5  4  3  2       04  03  02  01  00

# Contents

# *Preface*

As is often the case, this book began in a discussion among colleagues about how to present the material of a course on counseling issues and professional identity. The teaching of that core area of the Council for Accreditation of Counseling and Related Educational Programs (CACREP) standards has tended to emphasize professional ethics. And yet, there are so many other issues that affect the emerging counselor's performance at least as much as ethics. So, the project was begun with the question: What professional topics would you most want the graduating professional counselor to have considered? This resulted in a list of 10 topics, all related to the CACREP standard 1: *Professional Orientation*.

Next came the selection of a group of counselor educators whose expertise included those 10 topics. When each was invited to contribute, the question was posed: What final message on this topic would you most want the graduating counselor to hear? It was at this time that we realized the developmental nature of professional issues, and how new issues would emerge as existing issues were being assimilated into professional practice. So, an examination of newer issues was initiated. It quickly became apparent that there were enough issues to fill two books, not one. We then decided to present two emerging issues that could be considered representative of *emerging* but not yet fully defined professional issues. The issues we chose were *spirituality and counseling* and the *Internet and counseling*. Neither of these topics has been assimilated into professional thinking as yet. Even so, both topics are receiving increasing attention in the professional literature. Finally, in the process of writing this book, the contributors became aware of the immense riches of the Internet that could be used as resources for the exploration of topics. We have included those websites that proved most helpful.

## *The Plan of the Book*

The overall purpose of this book is to provide the emerging professional counselor with a more concrete sense of what the practice of professional counseling means. Further, the issues and topics that help define the character of professional counseling will be examined, both from the context of how they contribute to that definition and how they affect the practice of counseling.

The book begins with an examination of the meanings attached to the label *professional counselor*. In a world of constructed realities, Dr. Brooke B. Collison, counselor educator at Oregon State University, asks in Chapter 2: How do clients construct the identity of a counselor? What information, insights, and expectations contribute to that construction? How do our colleagues construct our identity? And how do those constructions impact our psyche? What is the public's perception of who we are? From where does that amorphous public draw its information and impressions of us? Is there a "profession's view" of the profession? How honest is that construction? Finally, Collison speaks to perhaps the most meaningful reality—the individual counselor's self-view. Clearly, it has been molded by the individual's aspirations and training, and even more so by his or her experiences. But how does the practicing counselor ensure that those moments of insight and inspiration keep coming? How can that self-view of professionalism reflect both reality and idealism? Long a national leader in the counseling profession and past president of the American Counseling Association, Collison is eminently qualified to discuss the professional counselor's identity.

In Chapter 3, two realities are introduced: people are their pasts as well as their presents and as people think, so they are. The chapter title is History and Philosophy of Professional Counseling. In some respects, this is a nature/nurture experience. There are certain evolved *givens* that may constitute the *nature* of counseling. But equally important, there are other agendas and issues that constitute the *nurture,* or environment, of counseling practice. Professional counseling has evolved through the influence of both. Professor Samuel T. Gladding of Wake Forest University, one of the foremost writers and educators in our profession today, provides a historical perspective of the counseling profession. His message is clear. We are, in part, our history.

Next, the book will examine the nature of counselor preparation and how it contributes to the definition of the profession. The comparison of training standards to similar standards of social workers and marriage and family therapists provides a way to consider how sister professions are both similar and different in their philosophies, values, and areas of emphasis. In fact, the training standards are significantly different from one another, even though the amount of time and effort to become a professional counselor, a social worker, or a family therapist are remarkably similar.

At the point of completion of one's training, new agendas arise. The first is a validation process that the newly hatched counselor is both a legitimate and a valid player in the delivery of mental health services. How does the emerging professional counselor become licensed or certified to practice, and what is involved in maintaining the license to practice? Dr. John M. Sutton Jr. of the University of Southern Maine authors this important chapter. Sutton's qualifications for this task are impressive. He was an active player in Maine's successful effort to obtain professional counselor licensure. He then served as a member and then Chairman of the Licensure Board for the State of Maine, and most recently has served as Chair of the Board of the American Association of State Licensure Boards.

Just beyond validation, one must jump into the practice. In Chapter 6, two experienced and successful mental health counselors discuss the world of the private practitioner. As colleagues in a successful joint private practice, Lynn E. Brueske and Robert S. Walton are unusually well qualified to provide this introduction to the private practice world. They also reinforce the message that the counselor must work to avoid becoming isolated in that world through professional involvement. Both have been active locally, within their state, and nationally. Brueske currently serves on the Board of the National Board for Certified Counselors, Inc.

Brueske and Walton raise the question of both ethical and legal practice. The chapters that follow examine both topics in depth. In Chapter 7, Dr. Robert H. Pate Jr. of the University of Virginia considers what constitutes the ethical practice of counseling. A widely acknowledged scholar on counseling practice and preparation, Pate presents both the ethical constraints and ethical ideals of professional counseling practice. Pate has written widely on ethical and spiritual values in counseling and has served as Chair of the Board of the National Board for Certified Counselors, Inc.

It is difficult to discuss professional ethics in today's litigious environment without also examining the legal issues related to delivery of mental health services. In Chapter 8, Carolyn B. Woodworth, a professional counselor and practicing attorney in Maine and a visiting associate professor of law at the University of Maine Law School, examines the intricacies of counseling practice from the context of the law. She describes how litigation is a part of every counselor's practice, either explicitly or implicitly, and discusses ways that the professional counselor can protect himself or herself through practice guidelines of an ethical code as well as a thorough grounding in case law.

If ethics and the law are the social structure of counseling practice, clinical supervision is the means by which that structure may be addressed and facilitated. Increasingly, practicing counselors are realizing how important it is to seek and utilize clinical supervision from peers or mentors. Indeed, the need for clinical supervision is so important that it is addressed in most state licensure laws. Its utility, however, goes beyond licensure to include wise practice, client rights, and ethical behavior. In Chapter 9, Professor Janine M. Bernard addresses what constitutes quality clinical supervision and how one might go about contracting for, or providing to another peer, quality clinical supervision. Bernard is a professor of counselor education at Fairfield University and a prolific writer on clinical supervision. She is well grounded in counselor preparation through her service as past chair of the National Board for Certified Counselors, Inc., and through her consultation to other universities on CACREP training standards.

You will find a common theme running through these chapters. That theme addresses the need for professional counselors to be ready and constant advocates for their clients, for themselves, and for the profession. Brueske and Walton make the point that if it were not for the efforts of counselors, state legislatures would not have passed licensure laws covering the practice of counseling. And if it were not for such laws, the movement of the health delivery system toward managed care today would not have included professional counselors. Furthermore, the current environment requires that practitioners of all varieties keep a constant eye on legislatures, insurance companies, and sister professions to maintain access to the health delivery system. In Chapter 10, Dr. Howard B. Smith, Senior Director of Professional Affairs at the American Counseling Association, examines the need for and effective practice of professional advocacy. As past president of the American Mental Health Counselors Association, a longtime counselor educator, and a leader in the professional advocacy movement, Smith is superbly qualified to bring this topic to the forefront.

Finally, two emerging social/professional issues are addressed, both of which are beginning to affect counseling practice in significant, albeit vastly different, ways. In Chapter 11, Professor Oliver J. Morgan, counselor educator at the University of Scranton and member of the CACREP Board, examines the role that spirituality plays in human problems and the increasing role it plays in the resolution of those problems. Contrasting spirituality with established religion, Morgan goes on to explore how psychology has traditionally excluded spiritual matters from the process of psychotherapy. There is a growing trend toward reintegration of the spiritual self with other aspects of human existence, and it is proposed that this trend will have an increasing impact on the theoretical conceptualization and practice of counseling.

In the last chapter, Professor John W. Bloom, who was instrumental in the development of ethical guidelines for web counseling, describes the rapidly expanding technology scene and the potential strengths and hazards that accompany such practices as web counseling, Internet supervision, and so on. As you read about the impact of the Internet on delivery of services to clients, you will realize how much the paradigm of counseling is shifting. Bloom is a counselor educator at Butler University in Indianapolis, Indiana.

## *Acknowledgments*

Counseling and teaching about counseling are two wonderful callings. The rewards that come from teaching and mentoring new counselors are legion. But it has been most rewarding for me to have the experience of working with real scholars, the likes of whom fill these pages with their experience and wisdom. Thank you to the 11 authors who so graciously acceded to my haranguing invitations to contribute. All are very busy professional counselors. More than that, they are among the leaders in our profession today, representing association presidents, board chairs, corporation directors, and already acclaimed authorities on the topics. None really needed another project, yet each one responded with enthusiasm and goodwill to the opportunity. I am deeply indebted and thank them very much.

I also want to thank my students in Professional Issues, who read and reacted to each chapter. Their perspective was, after all, the one I was most interested in reaching.

Finally, I extend my appreciation to the National Board of Certified Counselors for granting free and unrestricted permission to publish its several codes of ethical conduct as appendices. Thank you to my editors at Allyn and Bacon, Ray Short and Virginia Lanigan, for their warm support and encouragement, and to Karin Huang for her gentle nudges and support. Thanks also to my wife and colleague, Janine Bernard, who willingly read manuscripts and offered valuable suggestions. In fact, after I had struggled through a fruitless search for a fitting title, Janine offered one more suggestion that found its way to the cover of this book.

H. H.

# 1

# *Exploring Topics of Consequence*

## Harold Hackney

*Harold (Dick) Hackney's career as counselor began in the public schools of northern Virginia, where he was both a middle school and high school counselor and later a director of guidance. After receiving his doctorate in counselor education from the University of Massachusetts, he was a professor at Purdue University for 15 years. Hackney also holds a B.S. degree from West Virginia University and an M.A. in counseling and psychology from George Washington University. Hackney has been a professor of counselor education at Fairfield University, a Jesuit university in Connecticut, since 1984. He has coauthored several counseling texts with Sherry Cormier, including* Counseling Strategies and Interventions *(Allyn and Bacon) and* The Professional Counselor—A Process Guide to Counseling *(Allyn and Bacon), and numerous professional articles. Hackney has been given many opportunities for professional service, including both regional and national president of the Association for Counselor Education and Supervision, member of the Governing Council of the American Counseling Association, and member of the Board of Directors of the Association for Spiritual, Ethical and Religious Values in Counseling. He lives with his wife and colleague, Janine Bernard, in Stratford, Connecticut. His interests and pastimes include writing, cooking, the seashore, and occasional golfing.*

## *In This Chapter ...*

- Who determines the counselor's professional identity?
- How does the counselor's professional identity affect his or her counseling practice?
- Why is it important that counseling specialties find common ground with each other?
- What role do *topics of consequence* play in the professional counselor's work?
- What are some emerging topics that will affect the counselor's practice?

The legislative chamber where the proposed counselor licensure bill was being debated was strangely out of proportion. A massive rectangular desk dominated the room. On three sides, the 15 members of the joint Public Health Committee sat, some listening to the testimony, some absorbed in their reading, and some milling about, talking to other members or visitors. A small, rather uncomfortable visitor gallery surrounded the hearing table on three sides. It was filled with observers, individuals who were there to give testimony, and a few lobbyists. The latter popped in and out of their seats as new arrivals entered through the heavy wooden doors at the end of the chamber, clearly working their way through the morning.

Testimony was being heard on why the state needed a strong professional counselor licensure law. Midway through the first speaker's presentation, the Chair of the Public Health Committee, an ageless woman, interrupted the speaker with a question.

"Just what *is* a professional counselor?"

The question provoked a moment of stunned silence. As the speaker gathered his wits and began to respond, other legislators sat up to listen, observers squirmed in their uncomfortable seats, and lobbyists came to life in riveted attention to what the answer would be. It seemed like a make-or-break kind of moment.

Even though I had been a practicing counselor for a number of years when I first confronted this question, I had several reactions. They varied from "Why don't you already know?" to "Isn't it obvious?" to "How can I possibly answer this question?" The fact is that a large number of the public do not have a clear idea of who professional counselors are, what their professional training is like, how they differ from other mental health professionals, and why people need counselors, in addition to psychologists, social workers, family therapists, and so forth. I have heard this question asked by agency directors, state legislators, physicians, and school board members, among many others. There is no malice in the question. Their intent is merely to clarify confusion that exists in their own minds.

Peterson and Nisenholz (1999) document how other helping professionals also have difficulty defining the professional counselor: "If those who consider themselves to be mental health experts have difficulty recognizing and describing all those who are actively working in the field, then it should not be surprising that the general public is also confused about the similarities and differences between each profession." They lay out the challenge that "as an aspiring counselor, this means that you will have to educate the public as you pursue your professional work" (p. 39).

The purpose of this book is to provide you with a structure for thinking about and clarifying topics of consequence that will affect your practice of counseling. Most of the topics will not be new to you. But the underlying issues and complexities of these topics may not have been so obvious in your studies. Thus, this book addresses the issues that influence, shape, and challenge both your practice and your identity. As you read, it will become apparent that the professional counselor is not a static role. Rather, it is an identity that is always in process of change.

What makes a professional topic an *issue?* When a set of conditions begins to influence how the professional practices, or with whom the professional practices, or limits a professional's realm of practice, that set of conditions has become a professional issue. Professional issues have a developmental life span. When an issue first emerges on the professional scene, it attracts much attention and concern. As the issue evolves in its complexity, the profession responds with answers, strategies, or concessions, depending on the nature of the demand. Further along in the issue's life span, it begins to be eclipsed by newly emerging issues. This is not to say that the original issue has been satisfactorily resolved or has receded in importance. It means that the original issue receives less attention by the profession, either because it has been assimilated into the profession (e.g., professional ethics) or because it has been pushed to the side by new issues arising. Thus, professional issues are not necessarily solved or resolved. Most professions have a closet full of issues in various stages of resolution and assimilation.

And so it is with professional issues. Some issues sit in our professional closets, unsettled and occasionally interrupting our activities with their rude presence. Typically, the mature issue has a considerable history. A good example is the professional counselor's identity. Although this issue has been around for at least 30 years, it tends to make its presence known when the counseling profession (or the individual counselor) interfaces with sister helping professions (e.g., through licensure efforts or employment in noncounselor settings). A professional issue that has less history than the identity issue, but enough history to reveal its complexity and importance to the profession, is the matter of multiculturalism and counseling. In the past 10 years, this topic has received significant and deserved attention by the counseling profession. That attention is reflected in the prolific literature on multicultural counseling, the establishment of multicultural counseling competencies, and the continuing call to be educated, enlightened, and empowered to provide ethical multicultural counseling services to clients. Then there are the *new* professional issues—ones that have not yet established their impact on the profession. Indeed, such topics might not even be accepted as professional issues by all counselors. Certainly, their complexity has not yet revealed itself.

Such is the nature of this book. From each author's frame of reference, all of the selected topics are professional issues. Some of these issues are mature, closet issues (e.g., professional history and identity, training, and perhaps certification and licensure); others are in the process of revealing their complexity (e.g., ethics, the law, private practice, and professional advocacy). Also included are two topics that are considered to be emerging professional issues, not yet revealed in their full complexity, not yet demanding a full professional response, but, nevertheless, not likely to recede or disappear in the next 5 to 10 years. These issues are (1) the integration of spirituality as a component of wellness into the practice of counseling, a void that has existed since Freud's explicit exclusion of spiritual matters from the treatment of patients, and (2) the explosion of technology and the Internet on the public's daily functioning and the potential impact that explosion will have on professional counselors and existing clinical services (e.g., web counseling), as well as distance learning and the preparation of professional counselors. These are not offered as the *two* definitive new issues, but rather as examples of issues in early stages of development and impact.

There is one remaining ambient professional issue that lurks within the pages of this and many other counseling books. That issue reflects the degree to which counselors of all types and persuasions consider themselves to be similar or different, close relatives or merely neighbors. Is there a reason to treat all professional helpers as the same species? Or are our differences more important than our similarities?

## The Present Scene

For a variety of reasons, the mental health delivery system reflects a divided field, made up of school counselors, mental health counselors, rehabilitation counselors, pastoral counselors, social workers, family therapists, psychologists, and other specialists. This condition is exemplified in the paradoxical role of the school counselor. Trained as a developmental specialist who works with children to help them meet and successfully resolve life challenges (including learning), many school counselors still do not view themselves as part of the *mental health team.* Similarly, the college student personnel counselor may see little relationship between his or her activities and those of the community mental health counselor, even though they both are dealing with similar problems, using similar skills, and often trained in the same program.

## Realities of the Problem

Perhaps the most practical aspect of this problem is that there is not a consensus on what the problem actually is, or even that there is a problem. The training of professional counselors suggests that all counselors, regardless of their settings, share a common identity. The Council for Accreditation of Counseling and Related Educational Programs (CACREP) standards outline a core curriculum shared by all counseling specialties, combined with a specialization that consumes roughly one-third of the total program. Thus, the school counselor is a *counselor* who works with youth in educational institutional settings. The mental health counselor is a *counselor* who works with people in a community agency or private practice setting. The career counselor is a *counselor* who works with clients in a school, community, corporate, or private practice setting. The alternative to this line of thinking is that while all counselors share some qualities in common, it is really the work setting that defines who the counselor is. This latter position has produced a kaleidoscopic view of counseling and has, in the opinion of many, made the quest for counselor licensure and identity a more contentious issue.

This division of services affects the professional counselor in numerous ways. Access to third-party payment by insurance companies, competition for employment in schools and in public and private agencies, status within the mental health field, and, occasionally, even something as basic as acknowledgment of one's existence are factors in this dilemma.

A dramatic example of this latter point was played out in the winter of 1995. The highly respected publication, *Consumer Reports,* noted for its appraisal of goods and services and on its insistence for nonbiased reporting, printed an article on the topic, "Mental Health: Does Therapy Work?" (November 1995). As part of the article, the magazine included a table titled "The Types of Therapies and Therapists" that identified psychiatrists, psychoanalysts, psychologists, social workers, marriage and family therapists, and psychiatric nurses as providers.

Where were professional counselors in the listing? How could such a reputable publication overlook counselors? The answer to this reflects the fact that an identity problem continues to plague the profession. In response to this oversight, the presidents of the American Counseling Association and the American Mental Health Counselors Association wrote a joint letter to the editor, noting, "The November report on mental health therapy failed to identify one of the key disciplines within the mental health profession—the nation's 70,000 licensed and 24,000 board-certified professional counselors, who hold at least a master's degree" (*Consumer Reports*, January 1996, p. 4).

This identity problem has manifested itself in other ways. Although more than 90 percent of the states have enacted licensure bills for professional counselors, one common theme has repeated itself in state after state. During the legislative process, advocates found that legislators did not know who professional counselors were and had to be educated as to their similarities and differences with other helping professions.

The legislators were not alone in their confusion. Many states have reported experiences where *professional counselor* legislation led to significant disagreement among professionals. Under the threat of licensure legislation, it is not uncommon for many nontraditional helping groups to emerge, claiming a position in the legislation. In some cases, practitioners who are clearly professional counselors (e.g., school counselors) are intentionally excluded from licensure efforts or choose to be excluded. (School counselors often believe, perhaps erroneously, that their biggest battles are within the education establishment rather than in the larger public community.)

The public, users of professional services, also experiences a lack of awareness of these differences. In a world where the label *counselor* is often used in lieu of the more appropriate title of *advisor* or *consultant,* it is easy to see why *counselor* may be an ambiguous term. Thus, the profession has attempted to respond through the identifier, *professional* counselor. Whether this is an adequate clarification is debatable. It remains the case, however, that even the local telephone company's yellow pages rarely include a specific category called *Counselors (Mental Health).* This is complicated by the fact that state licensure laws across the 46 licensable states contain eight different titles referring to the professional counselor (discussed in Chapter 5).

Over the years, the counseling profession, through the leadership of the American Counseling Association, has attempted to provide a consensus definition of *professional counseling.* Because there are variations on professional counseling, such as school counseling, mental health counseling, rehabilitation counseling, marriage and family counseling, career counseling, and others, this has proven to be a long drawn-out task. However, the Governing Council of the American Counseling Association, representing all 16 divisions and 4 regions, finally was able to adopt a definition of professional counseling at its October 1997 meeting. That definition and how it evolved is provided in the discussion of advocacy in Chapter 10.

Having a consensus definition of professional counseling can go a long way toward addressing such matters as enlightening the public, school boards, legislators and regulators of professional practice, and underwriters of health insurance. But this may not adequately address the dynamics of the problem—namely, that counselors themselves need to know who they are and how they can communicate this identity. In fact, it has been argued that the agreed-upon definition serves most professional counselors, except for counselors in educational settings. In this case, the final decision on a definition of professional counseling might actually widen the rift among counseling specialties.

## *Implications for Professional Counselors*

Counselors neglect their own well-being in numerous ways. First, it is important to know our history. Such knowledge will prove helpful in understanding why and how we interact with the public and with our clients. Since we draw so heavily on psychological principles, why are we not psychologists? Similarly, since we draw on educational contexts in our evolution, why are we not educators? How are we different? How does training affect our identity? What are our unique qualities and how did we come to have them? These are the types of questions that help a professional group to coalesce, to function with one another, and to serve the public efficiently and effectively.

It is no less important for our sister professions to know us well. The fact that so many professional identities are represented in the mental health community suggests a need to be continually interacting with one another, referring clients to one another, and consulting, assisting, and supporting one another.

## *Contingencies of Counseling Practice*

In addition to the core issue of identity, there are many other topics of consequence that present themselves. Typically, these topics arise in the practice of counseling. They begin at the threshold of one's career, when certification and/or licensure become a concern and a goal. Although national certification is available (the *National Certified Counselor* designation of the National Board for Certified Counselors, Inc.), certification, licensure, or registry is mostly a state-by-state matter and can vary widely in practice. If you plan to live out your life in one state, you should know the processes as well as the criteria for that state's licensure, certification, or registry. If you see yourself as mobile, then you may need to know those processes and criteria for multiple states.

### *Title and Practice Restrictions*

A title restriction means that only those individuals who have met certain practice criteria may use the title (e.g., certified pastoral counselor). A practice restriction is much more controlling. With a practice restriction, only those people who have met certain criteria may *perform the types of activities* that are prescribed by the specialty. (In a state that has a practice restriction on professional counseling, only those people who hold the certification or license may perform the activities that a professional counselor normally does). So, imbedded in most registry, certification, and licensure systems is a title or a practice provision.

### *Licensure*

"A license is a credential authorized by a state legislature that regulates either the title, practice, or both of an occupational group. As a result, there are title acts, and title/practice acts" (Brown & Srebalus, 1996, p. 251). If your state has a title licensure law for professional counselors, only those individuals holding that license may call themselves professional counselors. Similarly, if the law is a title/practice law, only those who hold the license may identify themselves as professional counselors *or may perform the services* prescribed in the law as professional counseling services.

### *Certification*

Certification means that the candidate (you) has met certain minimal training and experience criteria to be included in a list of *qualified* practitioners. Generally speaking, the decision process is administered by a board or association of similarly qualified practitioners, and the criteria are generally accepted standards by the profession. Certification can be both specialty based and geographically based. Examples of specialty certification include school counseling, rehabilitation counseling, alcoholism counseling, and pastoral counseling. Most of these examples are national in scope, but school counseling certification is determined by individual state departments of education. (There is a current movement to make teaching and other related educational specialties, including counseling, a national certification.) Specialty certification is a way to restrict practice to include only those who have met the established criteria. For example, state departments of education have absolute power to determine who will practice school counseling in the public schools (only those who are certified) and what criteria will be used to establish certification standards. In practice, the school counselor certification is a title/practice restriction.

### *Registry*

Registry is another way of allowing an occupational group to designate individuals who have met a set of specified standards (Brown & Srebalus, 1996). It is usually established as a title restriction rather than a practice restriction.

## *Additional Counselor Practice Topics*

Just beyond the entry point into the profession, a number of issues arise. If you are not a school counselor, should you aim your career toward private practice or would it be more fitting to practice within the context of a public or private agency? How do you make such decisions? How do you set up a private practice? What are the pitfalls and problems of such a course of action? How do you prepare for *successful* private practice? What is the conventional wisdom of private practice? Can you dabble in private practice, carrying only two or three clients, while working at a full-time job? How much do you need to know to dabble successfully? Should you pursue licensure or registry if it is not required for you to function professionally?

Regardless of work context, what about all the stories one hears about lawsuits and ethics violations? Do you need to be concerned about such things, given that you would always use the highest ethics in your counseling practice? How much of this kind of reality would it take to scare you away? These are the kinds of questions, issues, and concerns that this book will address.

Finally, what about emerging issues? Of the many that might be suggested, two seem ready to have an impact on the profession. The first of these, spirituality and the human condition, affects the process of counseling. The second, web counseling, affects the practice of counseling and raises significant concerns regarding licensure, ethics, liability, and accepted practices.

## *Summary*

The counseling profession has been influenced and shaped by many forces during its brief history. As we have struggled to define and communicate our uniqueness to other helping professions, to the public, and to ourselves, we have encountered many topics of consequence that have contributed and continue to contribute to that uniqueness. From our earliest days, the profession has identified itself with two sources: the public education establishment and the community.

As the world has grown more complex, so has its people. Counseling has evolved from a service to a profession within the twentieth century. By taking that step into "professionalism," we have had to accept other realities, such as competition for employment, standards of practice, a legal system that both protects us and makes us vulnerable, the opportunity for independent practice, the need to advocate for ourselves in the political and public arenas, and the need for credentialing and licensure, and we continue to face new issues.

The purpose of this book is to identify some of those topics that shape our present and will affect our future as counselors. The book begins by raising the question: Who is the professional counselor? It is my hope that you will examine the issues inherent in each of the chapters, look for the implicit messages that contribute to the question of identity, and consider the alternatives that each issue provides.

# 2

# *The Counselor's Professional Identity*

## Brooke B. Collison

*Brooke B. Collison has been a public school teacher as well as a junior high and a senior high school counselor, and has been a counselor educator for the past 30 years, first at Wichita State University and more recently at Oregon State University. He has had a distinguished career of service to the counseling profession, which included president of the American Counseling Association during 1988–1989 and numerous other assignments by the profession. Collison received his doctorate in counseling psychology from the University of Missouri—Columbia, and his M.Ed. in counseling and guidance and B.S. in education from the University of Kansas. He anticipates retirement soon, after 43 years in education. In his retirement, he looks forward to enjoying the great Oregon outdoors—mountains, beaches, rivers, lakes, trees, and wildlife. He fully expects to find ways to stay connected with his lifelong passion—education—but probably as a volunteer in a nearby elementary school. He also expects to find ways to continue to speak out for justice issues in his community and beyond. Collison is an avid fly fisherman and intends to "wet a line" in as many Oregon rivers and lakes as nature will allow.*

## In This Chapter ...

- What constitutes *professionalism?*
- What is *culturally appropriate* counseling?
- What is a *professional counseling environment?*
- What is probably the real impact of the media on professional counseling?
- How does the counseling profession define *professional?*
- How do you define *professional?*

Consider the following client statements:

- "I was treated very professionally."
- "She is a professional counselor."
- "He is a very professional counselor."
- "It is a very professional-looking office."
- "What is your professional opinion?"

Now consider the following statements from professional counselors:

- "He is my professional colleague."
- "She is a very professional counselor."
- "I'm attending a professional counseling association meeting next week."
- "I've been in this profession for a long time."
- "My professional opinion is . . . . "
- "Yes, I do carry professional liability insurance."
- "Well, the standards of the profession say . . . . "
- "That's a very professional-looking dress."
- "Personally, I would say . . . , but professionally, I would say . . . . "

The word *professional* is frequently used in statements about counselors. To grasp the significance of the word, I ask you to reflect on each of the quotations above from four perspectives: What would the statements mean to a client? Another counselor? The public? The counseling profession? Professional identity takes on a different nuance when viewed from other points of view. This chapter takes the position that it is important for professional counselors to examine issues of their own identity from the view of the clients they serve, from the view of the colleagues with whom they work, from the view of the public in whose eyes they are visible, and from the view of the profession of which they are a part.

*Professional identity* can be defined very simply in terms of the following:

1. How the counselor treats clients
2. The surroundings of the place the counselor works
3. How the counselor was trained
4. What licenses or credentials the counselor presents to the public
5. How the counselor appears to other counselors
6. How the counselor decides what to do in different situations
7. What the counselor uses to guide decisions
8. How the counselor is supervised
9. To whom the counselor is accountable

These issues will be interwoven in the presentation of the four perspectives stated earlier: clients, colleagues, public, and profession. A fifth dimension that is critically important is the self-view that the counselor holds. Although illustrations of errors or distorted perspectives will be presented in this chapter, the effort will be to present a positive professional image of what a truly professional counselor is. Because of their importance in the picture, the first perspective examined will be that of the clients served by professional counselors.

## The Clients' View

What do clients see when they contact a professional counselor? What do they mean when they are having coffee with a friend and say about the counselor whose office they just left, "She is a very professional counselor" or "I was treated very professionally"? Like most interpersonal evaluations, the impressions made in the first few moments (or in the first session) probably have a significant effect on the client's definition of professionalism that he or she carries away from the session.

A professional office of a professional counselor is probably described initially by clients as friendly, inviting, attractive, clean, orderly, and designed with the client in mind, with assurances of privacy and respect—terms that could apply to either the physical environment of the counselor's office or the counselor personally. Certainly, a client who finds a messy waiting room and a receptionist or reception area that is not comfortable, who overhears voices or sounds from clients who are already in session, or who has to wait for the counselor to clean off a chair so there will be a place to sit does not leave the office with a sense of professionalism about the environment.

Some clients who have seen the inside of several counselor offices may have a sophisticated set of assessment criteria that they apply to their definition of professionalism. For every client, at some time or other, there is a first meeting, a first appointment, a first contact of some kind. I encourage counselors to call their own offices and wade through the morass of phone message commands or listen anonymously to a receptionist's communication to determine what the impression would be for a first-time caller. And I strongly urge counselors to delete forever the phone message machines that leave the caller with a degree of uncertainty about who, exactly, is going to hear the message.

Physical appearance and dress are also important aspects of a counselor's professionalism. A counselor I know was in the habit of wearing the same clothes on the same day of the week over a period of time. He cycled through his wardrobe with clean garments each day, but Mondays always meant the same shirt and the same tie, Tuesdays were likewise. A client, who always had an appointment on the same day of the week, finally demonstrated some discomfort in a session and, after being invited to share what it was that troubled him, said, "Don't you have any other clothes to wear?" Certainly, the counselor's professionalism was suffering in the eyes of a client who saw what was considered to be a very limited wardrobe.

Assuming that new clients make it through their initial sessions, their feelings about the professionalism of their counselor would be enhanced if they could leave that first session knowing that they had been heard, that there was someone who had a degree of understanding of their issues, that there was a sense on the part of the counselor about what their issues were, and that there was some hope for solutions in continued sessions.

Clients can be thought of as either voluntary (they wish to see a counselor) or involuntary (they have been sent against their wishes). For the most part, the counseling literature talks about the work of the counselor with voluntary clients. The question of what voluntary clients look for in a counselor they label as professional has been studied in a number of different forms. The literature says that clients are most pleased when they find a counselor they believe can help them, who can understand the feelings that they have about themselves and counseling, and with whom they can develop a sense of mutual respect. Further, clients who quickly develop a sense of agreement with the counselor on how to work together on goals and with whom they can develop an emotional connection seem to evaluate their counseling more highly. On the other hand, the same research indicates that dissatisfied clients following initial sessions were those who had been looking for expert diagnoses, advice, recommendations, and action to resolve their problems. This leads counselors to speculate on the potential failure of early sessions when the counselor and client have different ideas about what counseling is but fail to share those ideas early on—especially if the counselors do not consider such things as giving advice and providing solutions as part of their roles.

Egan (1990) explains that the working alliance—the quality of the relationship between client and counselor—is critical to the success of counseling as perceived by the client. Fine and Glasser (1996) emphasize that those important client perceptions happen very early in initial counseling sessions—perhaps in the first few minutes. They identify mutuality of client and counselor, client confidence in the counselor, and a view of professional competence as critical for the client to have if counseling is going to be successful. Fine and Glasser also emphasize that a professional's responses to a client are not like those of everyone else the client knows—a potential source of comfort to the client if their world is full of people who respond inappropriately to them, but a source of consternation if the counselor's response is atypical or incomprehensible. This leads to one of Fine and Glasser's characterizations of the counselor as teacher of counseling process, especially for naive clients.

Clients should see the counselors they work with as people who can help them reach their goals. Those goals and the means to reach them should be mutually understood by client and counselor if counseling is to be effective. Clients will know that they are understood if the counselor can respond to them in a culturally appropriate fashion. *Cultural intentionality* (Ivey, Ivey, and Simek-Morgan, 1997) is described as ways counselors find to broaden their scope of effectiveness with more diverse client groups. Clients have a right to expect that they will be treated and understood within an appropriate cultural context.

Of course, any degree of counselor effectiveness can be demolished by an inadvertent comment from a receptionist or an inappropriate phone message left with the wrong person. A friend of mine recently expressed her fury at a professional's office staff member who called her home and left an important message about an office appointment with her spouse—not that she was hiding something from her spouse, but her sense of professional ethics and protocol was so high that she could only conclude that her client privacy had been violated. She subsequently wrote a scathing letter to the group's administrator.

Office decorations also speak loudly to clients about topics that may or may not be acceptable to discuss. Diplomas, pictures, books on the shelf, framed quotations, and posters all carry messages—perhaps some that the counselor does not intend to send. A counselor's office decorated with only posters of male basketball stars and basketball accessory may open topics for some but will certainly close the topic door for others. Books on the shelf with titles that carry messages about how homosexuality can be "cured" carry one set of messages; titles that convey open dialogue about homosexual relationships carry another. I encourage counselors to sit in the client chair, look around, and ask themselves what they see that says what topics are and are not OK? When I asked this question in a recent seminar, two distinct points of view were expressed by experienced counselors— one, that the office should be so topic neutral that clients would take no cues at all about what topics were OK or not OK, and two, that there should be explicit messages displayed in the office to tell clients that some topics were OK (in this instance, that it was a gay-affirming office). In either case, is the message sent in a professional manner? And is the message that is sent the one that is intended?

Diplomas, licenses, certificates, and awards on the counselor's office wall are very revealing. They tell clients the counselor's full name and when and where he or she went to school. They can be displayed with ostentatious flair or they can be background verification. During those moments when individuals are alone in an office or when they are distracted from the content of their session, many have had the experience of studying the framed documents in offices. Based on those documents, most people will draw conclusions about the professional they are seeing. Are those conclusions the ones the counselor wants to convey?

Clients can sense a counselor's discomfort around fee negotiation—a common condition for many counselors. The manner in which fees are established and clients are asked to pay can set a quality around professional tone for many clients. If fee negotiation is left for a secretary or receptionist to handle—perhaps in a waiting room where other clients can hear the transaction—it does not make for a professional environment. Licensing boards in many states require that fees be a part of a professional disclosure statement. Counselors should examine their own professional disclosure statements to see who they are written for—clients, as a vehicle for informing them about what is likely to happen in counseling, or counselors, as a means of protecting themselves against potential suits from unhappy clients? Perhaps a professional disclosure statement does both, but the statement should not be handed to the client with a "read this some time" nor should the wording be so technically complex as to not provide the client with needed information.

It may be that our litigious society has driven many service industries and service providers to present detailed explanations of services and costs in advance. States that have counselor licensure laws generally require counselors to make professional disclosure statements available to clients. Automobile service departments present a worksheet with a written statement of probable work and estimated costs to the owner before the work is done; television ads are full of offers for free estimates; and public schools develop individual educational plans (IEPs) that describe what will be done, who will do it, and how often it will be done in order to attain a desired outcome. The same concept of providing information in advance for counseling clients does a great deal to increase the sense of professionalism that clients should experience in their interactions with counselors. The statements should not become inflated or unrealistic predictions of cures or change that oversell the counselor's service. Rather, professional disclosure statements and realistic descriptions of process and outcome can enhance the probability that the person will be a more informed client who can participate more fully in his or her own therapeutic process.

Supervision and accountability can also be hallmarks of professionalism in the eyes of the client. To be informed that a counselor is involved in regular supervision sessions and that a counselor's work is accountable to some group—either a professional colleague group, a licensed body, or both—lets a client know that the standard of care he or she receives is of high quality. Even clients unfamiliar with the nature of professional relationships may understand the concept of a built-in second opinion on their issues and concerns.

## *The Colleagues' View*

How is one's professionalism seen by one's colleagues? If you separated your colleagues into two groups—the ones about whom you easily use the word *professional* and the ones whom you are hesitant to call professional—what would differentiate the two groups? This question, of course, implies a qualitative evaluation of the person called a counselor or the services that person provides—the implication is that in some way, professional counselors do it better.

Vacc and Loesch (1994, p. 38) point out that the title *professional counselor* is grounded in law. It may be used with those who have completed the appropriate education and have been licensed by their states as professional counselors. This may be the same use that most colleagues use when they refer to a counselor as a professional counselor. The term infers but does not guarantee quality. According to Vacc and Loesch, professional counselors "are, simply, professionals whose primary vocational activity is the provision of counseling and closely related mental-health services" (p. 38). The authors then provide descriptions of many different specialty groups, each of which would use the word *professional* as a modifier in its label.

More likely, counselors would use the word *professional* with a colleague whose service met a standard of quality that meets the criteria that a particular colleague holds as essential for application of the descriptive label. Those criteria may include such things as quality and reputation of the person's preparation program, licenses or credentials held, the manner in which the person presents himself or herself in both the public and the lay community, and the kinds of personal and professional interactions the person has.

Other criteria that colleagues in the profession may hold could be much more individualistic. For example, because of my position on a personnel committee, I had occasion to read evaluation reports prepared by a person I assumed to be a qualified professional. To my chagrin, I found the reports full of typographical errors, misspelled words, and poor sentence structure. I was left with questions about the conclusions that had been drawn by the report writer based on my own inference (appropriate or not) that the sloppiness of the written report may have indicated an equal amount of sloppiness in the personnel evaluation. My assessment of the person's professionalism was that this individual was less qualified than I had originally thought.

The tendency to equate competence with professionalism is rather natural. Neukrug (1999) states that "being competent is our professional responsibility " (p. 14). He also cites Swenson (1993), who has said that the function of lawsuits is to encourage competent therapy. The frequency of discussion among a group of counseling colleagues about protection from legal action or appropriate response to legal action seldom includes reference to the goal of having litigation function to improve competency. Instead, discussions in textbooks about counseling competence usually include lists of essential requirements, such as "(1) being empathic, (2) being genuine, (3) being accepting, (4) being open-minded and non-dogmatic, (5) striving for internality, (6) being mentally healthy, (7) being capable of building alliances, and (8) being competent" (Neukrug, 1999, p. 15). Gladding (1996) summarizes a number of different studies about characteristics of effective counselors. Included in that list are results from a study by Cormier and Cormier (1985, pp. 11–12) that include seven qualities of effective counselors: (1) intellectual competence, (2) energy, (3) flexibility, (4) support, (5) goodwill, (6) self-awareness, and (7) awareness of cultural experiences.

None of the standard lists of effectiveness characteristics include the ability to spell correctly or write a complete sentence. The lists of characteristics tend to be written for people in the profession or for people in counselor education who look for criteria for admission or graduation decisions. In addition to qualitative indicators that the literature describes, I believe that clients and colleagues alike will add their own implicit and explicit criteria for making decisions about counselor competence—and, subsequently, counselor professionalism.

More serious colleague distinctions about professionalism surround the continuing issues of training, licensing, definition, and status with third-party payers. Colleague respect—or the lack of it—is often attached to identification labels such as *counselor, professional counselor, counseling psychologist, clinical psychologist,* or *social worker*. This chapter does not intend to explore the differences among these professional groups. Within any one of the groups there are variations of professionalism that affect the way that colleagues interact. The list of criteria mentioned at the start of this chapter—how the counselor treats clients, the surroundings, training, credentials, appearance, decision making, supervision, and accountability—apply to each of the professional groups. In addition, legal status within each state may be a significant determiner of professional status and professional image.

If one group works within the legal system to retain access to client populations and to deny access to the same client population by another professional group, the result will surely be one that builds resentment between groups and works to affect the definition of professional for clients and the public. In order for one group to retain access and deny another that same access, differences must be more sharply defined and public discussions of qualifications must be conducted so that law makers and rule makers can have a basis for the decisions they make. To open access and collaboration, differences must be diminished and intergroup respect must increase (Osborne & Collison, 1998).

## The Public's View

What does the public think when the words *professional counselor* are used? There is no single answer to this question, but a number of responses can be listed—some of which are not complimentary to those in the profession. For the large number of public members who have no direct experience with counselors, the image that they have is most likely formed by the media and from indirect contact with people who are willing to share the experiences they have had with counselors. Unfortunately in that respect, those who are willing to share their counselor experiences may be the disgruntled or dissatisfied.

Counselors are often praised by advice columnists. Both Ann Landers and "Dear Abby" frequently advise letter writers to find a good counselor. Some of their columns also reflect bad experiences from writers who have tried and failed in their efforts to find help.

I often ask my students to develop a list of images about counselors that they can draw from movies, television, novels, and the news. Their answers are predictable: The news carries more reports about unprofessional conduct than it does about success. Adolescent shooter stories carry mention of counselors who did not recognize blatant signs of dysfunction. Reports in news stories cover sordid details of counselors who have been brought up on charges by clients. A few scattered human-interest stories carry good news, but the number is small and seldom of great magnitude.

Counselors on television and in the movies tend to be lumped together as ineffectual bores or even as bumbling fools. The majority of movie therapists in recent years have had inappropriate relationships with clients, as have the counselors in many novels. The rare exceptions often include such subtleties in the plot that the issue of professionalism slides by unnoticed. For example, in the recent movie *Good Will Hunting,* Robin Williams portrayed a counselor who was eventually able to reach his client. In making that break-through, the counselor that Williams portrayed revealed indirectly that his own past contained parental abuse and other dysfunctions. He also revealed his own family and community similarity to that of the client. In addition, he had one episode of near violence when the client provoked the emergence of the counselor's own issues in the session. In spite of these flaws, Williams portrayed a counselor who was patient, respected the client, believed the client could grow, was tremendously empathic, and was able to stay with the client through the most exasperating of session conditions—all points that may have been missed by many viewers. Those viewers probably did see the several other therapists in the movie who were touted as highly credible but who were easily hoodwinked by a bright and manipulative client. What image did the average viewer take away from that movie?

The media image of counselors has, until recently, been presented through radio, television, and the press. Counseling is available on a call-in basis in nearly every city. Cell phones in cars make counseling available from the highway. The long-time image of Dr. Joyce Brothers has been multiplied many multifold. Whether members of the public are or are not inclined to seek professional counseling, their image of what professional counselors do is being shaped by what they hear—both from the actual or pretend counselors, who are on the air and from Dr. Frasier Crane—the Kelsey Grammer character who metes out advice to others while unable to manage his own life. As Dr. Crane advises callers with serious vocal tones, his facial expression conveys that he has mostly contempt for the listeners who call. Is this what the public believes counselors do? Similarly, in the movie *Ordinary People,* Judd Hirsch portrayed an effective therapist whom many audience members could not understand because the client's "problem" was obvious to all those watching but the therapist never "told" the client what was wrong. Hirsch's character let the client figure it out for himself. I recall audience members saying that he was a pretty stupid counselor, whereas counselors were admiring his ability to work through his client's insights rather than imposing the truth on him.

The Internet has added a new source of information about counselors (I hesitate to use the word *professional* in this sense). As I write this, I am aware of an Internet counseling system that will be implemented in the next month. Advent of live counseling on the

Net has generated significant discussion among counselor educators and others—also on the Net. The touted program is supposed to feature a real counselor and a real client who have a counseling session that anyone with a Net link and the proper software will be able to watch. Supposedly, these sessions will be in "real time," thus eliminating even the possibility of censoring comments or information that would best be left in the counseling session. One could argue that clients in such a situation enter it with full knowledge that what they say can be viewed by countless observers glued to their terminals. I have less concern about the counselor's public disclosure; although I must confess chagrin at this behavior by a member of the profession. Having said that, I also confess that I will be among those who dial in to watch—just to see how counseling will be portrayed to the thousands or millions who may watch. I will raise questions such as What training prepares the counselor for this format? What credentials cover this situation? What codes of ethics guide decision making for an Internet counselor? How is this counselor supervised? and To whom is the counselor accountable?

An additional image of counselors is formed by those who employ them for service to others. In a recent conversation with a municipal financial manager who must develop the contract with an employee assistance program (EAP) that serves several hundred employees, the manager described what *professional* meant and also explained how counselor effectiveness was assessed. *Professional* took on meanings attached to having a license—because "a license means that the profession has identified that you can do the job, that the profession is policing itself, and that there is a formal process for complaints." The financial manager went on to explain that professional licenses were good because they were set up by the profession itself rather than by governmental agencies.

The same financial manager is responsible for evaluating the services of the EAP and deciding if the contract should be renewed or replaced. Criteria for assessing quality (e.g., professional service) included clear expectations of what would happen when different kinds of calls were made (e.g., crisis calls, urgent calls, or convenient appointment requests); that there would be clear goals and objectives of the EAP for employees; and that everyone would know what information would be released by whom and to whom under different conditions (e.g., mandated referrals or self-referred employees). Frequent and accurate feedback was identified as an important criterion—always with respect for the confidential nature of information. Finally, the financial manager said that word-of-mouth comments were used to evaluate effectiveness—that is, if someone in the coffee room said that he had used the EAP counselor and that she had been helpful, that sort of comment was counted heavily by both employees and managers. Unprofessional behavior was described by the same financial manager as sloppy appearance, uninviting office space, breaking confidentiality, and not referring when a client was more troubled than the counselor was able to work with effectively.

The public image of counselors is also shaped by the advertisements that counselors use to promote themselves. As an exercise, I ask students to peruse the yellow pages of their phone books and describe the resulting impressions they have about counselors. One of the more common responses students make is that the counselors seem to be able to do nearly anything and everything. Further examination of yellow page ads reveals that counselors may have long lists of their specialties—to which students always comment: "Do you really think the person has been prepared in each of these different areas?" My response to them—and to counselors who promote themselves in this fashion—is to ask whether their professional image is enhanced or diminished by listing so many different areas of focus as areas of expertise or specialty. To the unsophisticated client who is seeking counseling services, finding an ad that lists every possible condition as an area of expertise for a single counselor may be attractive; however, there is a bit of a department store metaphor that applies—There may be a lot of different items, but the quality of the specialty store may also be missing.

## The Profession's View

The counseling profession also has a view of the image of the professional counselor. If the profession is thought of as the association that represents professional counselors, then a professional counselor would be one who (1) has met the educational and licensing criteria for membership, (2) has maintained continuing membership in good standing while engaged in practice, (3) has worked within the professional association for those items that advance the profession and benefit the professionals who are in it, and (4) has not violated the ethical standards of the profession while being a member.

A major responsibility of the profession is to provide leadership in developing standards for preparation programs that are then codified and implemented through accreditation processes. Those standards are continually revised based on input from the professional counselor, who is affected by them through established channels of discussion and debate. Similarly, standards of practice are defined through certification and licensing regulations. The profession has worked to develop codes of ethics and to assure that ethical violations are processed in a judicious manner. These standards are presented to the public and to consumers through various media.

From the standpoint of the profession itself, a *professional counselor* is one who practices according to the accepted standards of the profession. This clearly implies that there are professional standards and that they are known and practiced by the counselors who call themselves professionals. My comment to students has always been that the courtroom defense to charges of malpractice is that "this individual practiced according to the standards of the profession." Subsequently, the question becomes: Can you define the standards of the profession in the situations in which you will work?

It is expected that the professional counselors will participate in a planned program of continuing professional development. This is based on the assumption that knowledge within a profession is not static, nor are the laws that have an impact on professional practice. Professional counselors would be expected to maintain or advance their level of knowledge through a variety of activities, such as workshops, attendance and participation in professional association activities, courses of study, and periodic self-examination.

Professional counselors are expected to have an ongoing supervisory relationship—a position advocated by professional counseling associations. Codes of ethics describe the conditions under which a counselor should seek consultation—continual and regular supervision is an expected method of addressing consultation needs. Beginning counselors, familiar with supervision from their graduate preparation programs, sometimes believe that once established in practice, that they will no longer need supervision. Experienced counselors who know themselves well know that regular supervision is one of the ways that they maintain the quality of their professional practice.

The profession demands accountability from professional counselors. Although there are times when it appears that people who call themselves counselors can practice with impunity, for licensed or certified counselors who are members of their professional associations, there is always the penalty of being publicly listed as being in violation of some ethical code or law such that the public should be warned. Short of felonious behavior, however, there are few practice restrictions for many of the kinds of public notice penalties that do exist. Certainly, members of the profession who know that another member has been publicly censured or had a license or certificate revoked, would probably not use the censured individual in the same way that they would if that individual was in good standing. The small legal penalties of certain censure actions (e.g., being forbidden to use initials or other indicators of certificate or license status) may not deter naive members of the public who seek counseling and expect to pay for it out of pocket.

The accoutrements of professional membership should be evident in the offices of professional counselors. Clients and members of the public should be alert to those signs and symbols—they do not guarantee quality, but they are another assurance that quality service is more likely from the professional member who takes his or her profession seriously.

## The Self-View

How should professional counselors view themselves? One would hope that professional counselors see themselves as working for their clients, as highly trained and educated and equipped with the tools to do their jobs well, and as people who hold licenses and feel good about the certifications and licenses that they do hold. It would be good if professional counselors also saw themselves as members of a professional community with which they enjoyed high-quality relationships and that they held the other members of that community in high respect just as the other members held them in high respect. I would hope that the professional counselor utilized a consistent theoretical orientation and a standard ethical foundation in making the kind of decisions that must be made concerning clients. Professional counselors would also see themselves as persons who profited from the continuing supervision sessions that are part of their practice, and would always know that they were accountable for their work—first to their clients, and then to the tenets of the profession and the license body that they identify as theirs.

Professional counselors should also see themselves as reflective practitioners with enough self-assurance and ego strength to be a solid source of security and calm for the clients in various states of distress. To this end, it would be important for professional counselors to see themselves as mentally healthy—but not to hold to the self-demand to be so mentally healthy that they would deny any inadequacies that exist or that would occur because of situational stresses. Professional counselors should be able to accept input from others about their appearance and the way that they work with clients, but be secure enough in their own identities that any decision to change would be based on a sound rationale for change rather than a change just to please someone else. A student of mine recently cut her hair—the long hair that had been a part of who she was for several years was gone and in its place was a new look. A supervisor remarked that she must have cut her hair in order to take on a more professional look. The decision to cut her hair was something that had been considered for some time, and the reaction of others that it was an attempt to become more professional was moderately distressing. Whether the new look made her appear more professional was not her goal and she was not pleased that others made inferences about her reasons. The situation was a bit of a catch-22 for her, but at least she had not cut her hair because someone else told her she would look more professional if she did.

Counselors should feel good about the education they received in preparation to be professional counselors. Even so, reflective practitioners should be able to assess their own strengths and weaknesses in order to develop specific plans of continuing professional development. Professional counselors know that their education does not stop with completion of a degree. Unfortunately, those of us who have provided continuing professional development courses for licensed professionals have identified those who come to seminars or preparation workshops and will state openly that they are there merely to complete the number of required hours for license renewal. Observation of these individuals during lectures or workshop activities will bear out that they have no interest in acquiring new or enhanced skills. As a workshop director, I have been inclined to hand the person a financial refund and ask him or her to leave. My own biases about self-assessment have entered interview and other personnel issues when I have asked a person: "What do you believe you would need to do to become a better counselor (or teacher, or other professional title)"? I have always assumed that the astute professional would have an answer to that question based on having done a thorough self-assessment. I am similarly concerned when the person answers that there is nothing he or she needs to do to improve. I believe that professional counselors should always know where their knowledge and skills could be enhanced.

Maintenance of license status is also important for professional counselors. Furthermore, they should be active in those organizations that work to refine the license regulations in the state or region where they are employed. To confess that they do not know the license regulations that apply to them is an admission of ignorance that does not fit the word *professional* when applied to counselors. Since licensing is designed to protect the public, counselors especially should know how their licenses provide that protection. Professional counselors should also know how the license regulations could be enhanced through legislative change or modification of administrative rule so that the licenses do what they should do. Counselors must also know which of their colleagues are licensed and which ones have had license penalties resulting from their practice behaviors. To know this requires that counselors keep abreast of actions against their colleagues—not for morbid curiosity but because it is important to know what is happening to one's colleagues in the profession. Being part of a professional colleague community is consistent with being a professional counselor.

The sense of a professional colleague community is probably best illustrated in the professional associations that respond to counselor concerns and interests. It is interesting to observe membership statistics of counseling associations. The general conclusion from these data is that only a minority of eligible members maintain active membership in their counseling professional associations. Unlike trade organizations that require membership in order to practice, volunteer membership organizations for counselors have membership because counselors decide to join. In one sense, refusal to be a member is rejection of the professional colleague group of which one is a part. If a professional association has invested resources to develop the professional knowledge base, ethical codes, professional standards of practice, licensing procedures, and legislative lobbying efforts that make the counselor's day-to-day activities possible, it seems incumbent on the professional counselor that he or she would continue to be a member in order to support those same efforts for self as well as colleague community. Unfortunately, the absence of many from membership roles ultimately weakens one of the core elements of the profession that they wish to practice.

Remaining open to new ideas and information from relevant research projects is also a part of the professional counselor's responsibility. Counselors practice according to a theoretical framework that guides their decision making; however, as new information becomes available, theory needs to be reexamined and practice needs to be questioned. As a part of the professional counselor's continuing education, examination of theory and related practice is a natural process. Examples of change could be dramatic (e.g., the decision to remove homosexuality from a pathological status) or they could be minor (e.g., the subtle refinements of a counseling approach that follow publication of a new or revised textbook). Change as it affects practice can be slow or fast—for example, information about AIDS changes almost daily, and counselors who work with persons with AIDS or related family members must find ways to stay on top of treatment information and related counseling processes. Regardless of the degree of change, professional counselors need to be informed about the cutting edge issues that relate to their areas of practice. To do otherwise is to border on malpractice.

Counselors should see themselves as culturally competent. It is not possible for a counselor's cultural background to match that of every client, nor can the counselor have had experiences with every culture represented by every client if the counselor's practice is in a diverse population such as a school, community agency, or a culturally rich community. The counselor's self-view, however, should be such that the counselor knows and understands self within a cultural context and that the counselor has expanded personal experiences as much as possible in order to be a more appropriate counselor with clients who represent other lives. A good rationale for having counselors work on diversity issues as a broader concept than multicultural issues is found in Ivey, Ivey, and Simek-Morgan (1997).

## *Summary*

The image of the professional counselor changes, depending on the perspective of the person who looks—the client, professional colleagues, the public, the counseling profession itself, or the counselor who takes a self-view. The ideal would be that several images are consistent and complementary. Ideally, clients should see a professional counselor who is competent, who cares about them, and who will work with them to resolve the problems or issues that the client brings. Professional colleagues should see a competent colleague that they respect because of the quality of preparation that they received and the licenses and certificates that they hold. In addition, professional colleagues should see someone who works with clients in an effective manner and to whom they can refer clients with confidence.

The public should see a professional counselor who projects the outward appearance of a consummate professional and about whom there is no hint of ethical or professional violation. Because the public often sees counselors through the media, the hope would be that there would be many more stories of professional counselors who do good work than there would be of those who have ethics or license charges or who are in the public eye because of inappropriate behavior in or out of the counseling setting.

The counseling profession should see a professional counselor who upholds the standards of the profession and who is an active member of the professional associations that work with the issues of their practice concern. A counselor who contributes to the counseling profession through added knowledge, activity on behalf of other counselors, and sustained membership contributions is the desirable picture of a professional.

The counselor's self-view should reveal a person who is knowledgeable about the profession he or she practices. A self-view should show a person who is confident about and enjoys his or her work as well as life away from work. The professional counselor's self-image should acknowledge that his or her own life has its difficulties but does not regard work as a counselor as the means to resolve those personal difficulties. Similarly, counselors should not hold themselves to unreasonable standards of mental health to the end that they deny problems or issues that need personal work.

There should be a sense of accomplishment about their counseling practice and, at the same time, enough self-confidence and ego strength to sustain them through those times when little progress has been noted. The counselor's self-view should be one that relishes the kind of critique that comes from good supervision and from timely and appropriate consultation on problematic clients.

Finally, the counselor's self-view should be one of a person who is culturally competent and who continually seeks to broaden or extend personal knowledge of the diverse populations of the world so that he or she works with cultural intentionality. That culturally competent counselor should serve clients well and, in the process, should serve the community in which they live and work well. The culturally competent professional counselor would be a voice for equity and justice—through empowering clients and through addressing inequities where they are found. That counselor is one that clients, colleagues, the public, and the profession would easily call a professional.

# 3

# *History and Philosophy of Professional Counseling*

## Samuel T. Gladding

*Samuel T. Gladding has had a rich career as a counselor. Early on, he was director of children's services for the Rockingham County (NC) Mental Health Center. From there, he began a succession of teaching positions, first at Fairfield University, then at the University of Alabama (Birmingham). Today, he is professor of counselor education at Wake Forest University. Gladding has also had a most active career of service in the counseling profession. He has been president of the Association for Counselor Education and Supervision, the Association for Specialists in Group Work, and the counseling honorary society Chi Sigma Iota. He has also been a prolific author over a wide range of professional topics, including* Community and Agency Counseling; Counseling: A Comprehensive Profession; Group Work: A Counseling Specialty; *and* Family Therapy: History, Theory, and Practice, *all published by Merrill/Prentice Hall. Gladding received his doctorate from the University of North Carolina at Greensboro. Prior to that, he received a Master of Arts in religion from Yale and a B.A. and M.A. from Wake Forest. His interests and pastimes include swimming, tennis, poetry, and travel. Gladding finds humor to be a solution as well as a pleasure. His preferred moments are with his family—Claire, Ben, Nate, Tim, and Maggie the Dog.*

## *In This Chapter...*

- What does Gladding consider to be the origins of counseling?
- How have societal conditions added to the historical development of counseling?
- How have counseling "theories" shaped the historical development of counseling?
- How have professional organizations shaped the historical development of counseling?
- How have program accreditation and certification/licensure shaped the historical development of counseling?

According to the American Counseling Association, the practice of *professional counseling* is "the application of mental health, psychological or human development principles, through cognitive, affective, behavioral or systemic interventions, strategies that address wellness, personal growth, or career development, as well as pathology" (www.counseling. org/consumers_media). Although this definition may appear straightforward, behind it is a history of debate about the nature of counseling as well as how counseling associations should be organized and counseling services delivered.

Thus, counseling should be conceptualized like a fabric composed of many threads woven together. Some of the strands have had a greater impact on the profession than others. However, there is no one person or event that marks the beginning of the profession. There is also no uniform agreement on the emphasis that should be given to most aspects of counseling. Rather, numerous people, activities, and thoughts have contributed to the whole of the profession and the strength of counseling lies in the intermingling and uniting of its elements. The profession is richly textured and deep. It is also still evolving.

In this chapter, the historical and philosophical fibers of counseling will be examined in context. Historically, counseling can best be viewed as the coming together of different people and forces that were both preventive and clinical. Planned and happenstance events helped shape the profession, too. Philosophically, counseling can be seen most completely through the ideas that those within the profession either borrowed or generated. Three philosophical ideas—the nature of reality, human nature, and the goals of individuals—will be stressed in the second part of this chapter. Through the intermingling of its history and philosophy, the parts as well as the whole of counseling emerge as a dynamic mixture. The background of counseling is interesting as well as important for contemporary professionals to know. For without knowledge of the past, counselors will repeat mistakes of their predecessors, reinvent ideas, and fail to contribute to the future of the profession.

## *History of Counseling*

Counseling as a broad-based activity has been a part of human existence since antiquity. There have always been "counselors"—that is, people who were sensitive in listening and wise in responding to the needs of others. Often these individuals were the elders in tribes or clans. They were called by many names, such as *shaman, witch doctors,* and *spiritual guides.* They had experienced life to its fullest or had extraordinary insight into human relationships and were willing to share their knowledge and approaches to living with the less experienced (Gibson & Mitchell, 1995). In remote parts of the world, this type of so-called counseling still occurs. Thus, from a cultural standpoint, broad-based counseling, as represented by this tradition, is a universal phenomenon.

However, in the United States, counseling has a more recent and specific history. It can be dated to the late nineteenth-century social reform movement. In this movement, social activists argued for and urged more humane treatment of the less fortunate in society, whether they be immigrants, the poor, the unemployed, or those who were mentally disturbed. Most of the pioneers in counseling (then called *guidance*) identified themselves as teachers and reformers. They focused on teaching children and young adults. The goal was to help members of these populations be more sensitive and appropriate in regard to themselves, others, the world of work, and civic life. Initially, these helpers were involved primarily in child welfare, vocational guidance, educational instruction, and legal reform. Their work was built on specific information and lessons that they dispensed, such as moral instruction on being good and doing right. They particularly concentrated their efforts on promoting positive intra- and interpersonal relations (Nugent, 1994). Jane Addams and Dorothea Dix stand out as two prime examples of those within the reform movement who engaged in productive and concrete actions to make individuals and society better. However, Addams and Dix were not counselors.

The three individuals usually credited with the genesis of counseling, however, were among the social reformers of the early 1900s. What they did has had a lasting influence on Americans and has even made a global impact. These three pioneers were Frank Parsons, Jesse Davis, and Clifford Beers. Their contributions were in the area of career decision making, educational guidance, and mental health. They established the initial emphases from which counseling would grow. Their ideas and activities affected what later became these three professional specialties as detailed here as well as offshoots from these foundations of counseling. Thus, while counselors in the twenty-first century test, assess, and work with everything from preschoolers to geriatrics, as well as those who search for greater growth and those who struggle with dysfunctionality, the basis from which counseling developed is found in the areas addressed by Parsons, Davis, and Beers.

## Career Counseling

The area of careers will be examined first because it was the initial focus of counseling. Clients have been concerned about work and their vocational identities and fit from the start of the counseling profession. Career counseling is said to have begun with the work of Frank Parsons, who has been called the Father of Guidance. Parsons was a broad scholar, a persuasive writer, a tireless activist, and a great intellect (Davis, 1988; Zytowski, 1985). He outlined a process for choosing a career while founding Boston's Vocational Bureau in 1908. Parsons theorized that choosing a vocation was a matter of relating three factors: a knowledge of work, a knowledge of self, and a matching of the two (Drummond & Ryan, 1995). Parsons devised a number of procedures to help his clients learn more about themselves and the world of work. One of his devices was an extensive questionnaire that asked about experiences ("How did you spend each evening last week?"); preferences ("At a World's Fair, what would you want to see first? second? third?"); and morals ("When have you sacrificed advantage for the right?") (Gummere, 1988, p. 404).

Parsons's book, *Choosing a Vocation* (1909), published one year after his death, was quite influential, especially in Boston. For example, the superintendent of Boston schools, Stratton Brooks, designated 117 elementary and secondary teachers as vocational counselors (Nugent, 1994). The "Boston example" soon spread to other major cities as school personnel recognized the need for vocational planning. By 1910, 35 cities were emulating Boston (Lee, 1966).

A further development in the emphasis on careers in counseling was in 1913 when the National Vocational Guidance Association (NVGA) was established. In 1915, the NVGA began publishing, irregularly a bulletin, which became a regular periodical in 1921: the *National Vocational Guidance Bulletin* (Goodyear, 1984). The periodical evolved in later years to become the *National Vocational Guidance Magazine* (1924–1933), *Occupations: The Vocational Guidance Magazine* (1933–1944), *Occupations: The Vocational Guidance Journal* (1944–1952), *Personnel and Guidance Journal* (1952–1984), and finally the *Journal of Counseling and Development* (1984 to the present). The founding of the NVGA was important because it established an association and published a body of knowledge on guidance and counseling. It also united for the first time, those with an interest in vocations. Now there was more than a single person, Frank Parsons, advocating for systematic and scientific research into choosing a career.

Complementing the founding of the NVGA were two other events. The first was the congressional passage of the Smith-Hughes Act of 1917. This legislation provided funding for public schools to support vocational education. The second was the publication of vocational interest tests. The first major test of this sort (and the grandparent to subsequent tests) was the *Strong Vocational Interest Inventory (SVII),* which Edward Strong published in 1928. The SVII was a well-researched vocational interest test and set the standard for others that followed.

The Great Depression of the 1930s was another major event in the development of career counseling. During the Depression, about one-third of the work force in the United States was unemployed or underemployed. This phenomenon influenced vocational researchers and practitioners to emphasize helping strategies and counseling methods that related specifically to employment (Ohlsen, 1983). A highlight of the decade was the development of a theory of vocational choice by E. G. Williamson and his colleagues at the University of Minnesota. Williamson essentially modified and elaborated on Frank Parsons's theory and used it to work with the unemployed. His pragmatic approach emphasized the teaching, mentoring, and influencing skills of the counselor.

One premise of Williamson's theory was that people had *traits* (e.g., aptitudes, interests, personalities, and achievements) that could be integrated in a variety of ways to form *factors* (constellations of individual characteristics). Counseling was based on a scientific, problem-solving, empirical method that was individually tailored to each client in order to help him or her stop nonproductive thinking and become an effective decision maker (Williamson & Biggs, 1979).

During the 1930s, the U.S. government became involved in career counseling activities. It established the U.S. Employment Service, an agency that not only tried to match the unemployed with jobs but also published the first edition of the *Dictionary of Occupational Titles (DOT)* in 1939. The *DOT,* which became a major source of career information for guidance specialists working with students and the unemployed, described known occupations in the United States and coded them according to job titles.

With the advent of World War II, the U.S. government needed counselors to help select and train specialists for the military and industry (Ohlsen, 1983). The war also brought about a new way of looking at vocations for men and women. Many women worked outside the home during the war, and that situation made a lasting impact. Traditional occupational sex roles began to be questioned, and greater emphasis was placed on personal freedom. However, it was not until the late 1960s and 1970s that the vocational counseling of women and ethnic minorities arose. For example, Public Law (P.L.) 94-482 in 1976 directed states to "develop and implement programs of vocational education specifically to provide equal educational opportunities to both sexes to overcome sex bias and sex stereotyping" (Glosoff & Rockwell, 1997, p. 16). With the women's and civil rights movements as well as the enactment of other federal legislation, the need and demand for more career counseling related to these two groups became more prevalent. By the 1990s, models of career development for women and ethnic minorities had developed (Cook, 1993; Locke & Faubert, 1993).

In the meantime, life-span models of career counseling emerged beginning in the 1950s. Donald Super (1957), who believed that career development was a process of implementing a self-concept, created the strongest of these models. Super conceptualized five stages in the evolution of a person's career. In the first stage, growth (from birth to age 14), a child forms a mental picture of the self in regard to others and becomes oriented to work. In the second stage, exploration (ages 15–24), a young adult explores the world of work and specifies a career preference. The third stage is establishment (ages 25–44), where a person concentrates on becoming established in an appropriate field of work. Next comes the stage of maintenance (ages 45–64), where the focus is on preserving what one has already achieved. Finally, there is decline (age 65 to death), where there is disengagement from work and an alignment with other sources of satisfaction. The refinement of Super's theory continues today.

In the 1970s, trait-and-factor theory became refined once more. The author of this process, John Holland (1973), proposed six types of personalities and environments: realistic, investigative, artistic, social, enterprising, and conventional. Holland's premise, which was backed up with extensive research, is that personal satisfaction in work settings is dependent on the degree of congruence between one's personality type and the work environment.

In the 1980s and 1990s, the passage of federal legislation once again had an impact on career counseling. The Carl D. Perkins Vocational Act of 1984 (reauthorized in 1990) was the strongest piece of career legislation of this time. The Perkins Act was aimed at helping states serve previously underserved people—such as the disabled, single parents, and displaced homemakers—by developing vocational and applied education programs so that people would learn marketable skills. Counseling and career development services were seen as a national priority.

In the new millennium, career counseling is being influenced by many factors. Among these are school-to-work initiatives aimed at helping high school students who do not plan on college move directly from school to the world of work. This initiative is a partnership between educators and businesses and is supported by the School-to-Work Opportunities Act of 1994. Complementing almost all career counseling today is technology. Thus, career testing, scoring, and placement services are either on-line or accessible by a computer. Frank Parsons would be amazed but most likely pleased.

## *School Counseling*

A second historical development that occurred early in the twentieth century was school counseling. Initially, the aim of counselors in schools was to promote citizenship. Jesse B. Davis was the first person to set up a systematized guidance program in the public schools (Aubrey, 1977). As superintendent of the Grand Rapids, Michigan, school system, he suggested in 1907 that classroom teachers of English composition teach their students a lesson in guidance once a week, with the goal of building character and preventing problems. Influenced by progressive U.S. educators such as Horace Mann and John Dewey, Davis believed that proper guidance would help cure the ills of American society. What he and other progressive educators advocated was not counseling in the modern sense but a fore-runner of counseling: *school guidance* (a preventive educational means of teaching students how to deal effectively with life events).

Davis's influence was followed by that of John Brewer, who published a book entitled *Education as Guidance* in 1932. Brewer proposed that every teacher be a counselor and that guidance be incorporated into the school curriculum as a subject. He believed that all education should focus on preparing students to live outside the school environment. Thus, the focus of school counseling initially was on learning and development of the whole person.

This preventive focus was furthered and strengthened in the late 1950s and early 1960s. The reason was the U.S. reaction to the Soviet Union's launching of its first space satellite, *Sputnik I.* The U.S. government feared it would fall behind the Soviets in scientific and mathematic advancements. Therefore, in 1958, Congress passed the National Defense Education Act (NDEA), whose primary purpose was to identify scientifically and academically talented students and promote and encourage their further education. A part of the act provided funds through Title V-A for upgrading school counseling programs. This title established counseling and guidance institutes as well, and provided funds and stipends through Title V-B to train counselors. In 1964, the NDEA was extended to include elementary counseling. The end of the 1950s began a boom in school counseling that lasted through the 1960s, thanks to the Cold War and the coming of school age of the baby boomer generation (Baker, 1996).

In the 1970s and 1980s, more school counselors were hired, especially at the elementary level. Prevention was stressed over treatment and placement. Nevertheless, many school counselors in those decades had difficulty defending their jobs as essential. Those who did conducted needs assessments, established peer helper programs, were active in classroom guidance activities, and stressed parent and community involvement (Stamm & Nissman, 1979). These counselors also used groups and consultation to supplement and complement what they did on individual levels. New role responsibilities for school counselors that were developed by the American School Counselor Association (ASCA) (1981) helped school counselors at all levels define their duties and responsibilities better.

In the 1990s, greater emphasis was placed on having school counselors work more in the remediation of children who were at risk for failure. In addition, school counselors became more involved in working with families. In essence, the role of school counselors broadened even more. All areas of a child's life—personal, social, cognitive, and emotional—remained within the domain of school counselors with the addition of initiating and coordinating services with teachers, parents, principals, and community organizations. In an attempt to try to define itself better, the American School Counselor Association established a looser connection with the American Counseling Association, so individuals who wished could join the ASCA without being a member of the ACA. Jesse Davis would probably not have understood the politics of the latter move and it is doubtful he would have seen school counselors as a separate entity from teachers. Yet, in the evolution of the profession, the special task of working with children in schools became larger than teachers could handle, and school counselors as distinct, full-time professionals became not only necessary but essential.

## *Mental Health Counseling*

The impetus for the mental health counseling in the United States came as a result of the work of Clifford Beers, a former Yale student who was hospitalized for mental illness several times during his life. Beers found conditions in mental institutions deplorable and the treatment harsh and inhumane. He exposed these conditions and treatments in a book, *A Mind That Found Itself* (1908). The text became a popular best-seller and persuaded public officials on many levels to reform both mental health facilities as well as the treatment of the mentally ill. For example, in 1909, leaders of Cook County, Illinois, "decided that counseling services would benefit children" and established "countywide child guidance clinics" (Glosoff & Rockwell, 1997, p. 9). In the same year, the National Committee on Mental Hygiene was established by the United States Congress. These early reforms helped propel mental health to the forefront of American life.

However, as time passed, conditions again deteriorated in the mental health field. Although a number of child guidance clinics were set up, the emphasis within the mental health field focused more on treatment. States invested more in setting up large mental hospitals for individuals with severe disturbances than they did for prevention. To counter this trend, "the National Institute of Mental Health (NIMH) was established just after World War II, and the National Mental Health Act was passed in 1946 authorizing funds for research, demonstration, training, and assistance to states in the use of effective methods of prevention, diagnosis, and treatment of people with mental health disorders (Glosoff & Rockwell, 1997, p. 15). In 1955, the Mental Health Study Act established the Joint Commission on Mental Illness and Health. In the same year, the number of patients housed in large state mental hospitals began declining.

Another major development in the mental health field was the passage of the 1963 Community Mental Health Centers Act. This act authorized the establishment of 2,000 community mental health centers. These centers were to focus on the prevention of mental health problems as well as tend to some aftercare needs of patients returning from mental health institutions. They put new emphasis on mental health counseling, especially as a preventative service, and opened up opportunities for counselor employment outside of vocational and educational settings.

As the number of counselors grew in mental health settings, many counselors found themselves without an association with which to identify. Consequently, the American Mental Health Counselors Association (AMHCA) was founded in 1976, first as an independent association and then later as a division within what would become the American Counseling Association. The AMHCA quickly became a large division and united mental health counselors into a professional organization where they defined their roles and goals.

Other federal initiatives and mandates influenced mental health counseling in the late 1970s and 1980s, as well. For instance, the President's Commission on Mental Health was established by President Carter in 1977. Likewise, the Mental Health Systems Act of 1980, which was passed but then repealed for lack of federal funding, stressed the need for "balancing services in both preventive and remedial mental health programs. The act required the development of new services for children, youth, minority populations, older people, and people with chronic mental illness" (Glosoff & Rockwell, 1997, p. 17). It set a new standard for the delivery of services, although without funding, the standard was not always met.

Overall, mental health counseling has focused on three services throughout its history: primary prevention, secondary prevention, and tertiary prevention. *Primary prevention* is characterized by its intention to stop disorders in individuals, groups, families, and communities. It is a "before the fact" strategy. *Secondary prevention* is aimed at controlling mental problems that have already surfaced but are not severe, and *tertiary prevention* is controlling serious mental health problems to keep them from becoming chronic or life threatening (Gladding, 2000).

In the 1990s, mental health counseling continued to evolve. In some states, such as Florida, counselors are licensed as *mental health counselors*. The Council for the Accreditation of Counseling and Related Educational Programs (CACREP) has set up guidelines for degrees in mental health counseling, too. Likewise, the criteria for becoming a Certified Clinical Mental Health Counselor (CCMHC), a specialty administered by the National Board for Certified Counselors (NBCC), is in place. Medicare, managed care, and employee assistance programs (EAPs) have also had an impact on mental health counseling. To become more active in influencing legislative acts, the American Mental Health Counselors Association loosened its formal ties with ACA in 1998 and began recruiting members who were not necessarily affiliated with the ACA. While maintaining an emphasis on prevention, the AMHCA also began placing considerable focus on diagnosis and the treatment of disorders. Some of this emphasis is due to the influence of managed care and reimbursement based on diagnosis. Some is due to a preponderance of mental health disorders, including considerable addiction problems among the population of the United States. Nevertheless, the tendency for mental health counseling to be global in its emphasis is one of its legacies from Clifford Beers.

## *Development of Counseling Theories*

Regardless of its setting, counseling is theory based (although in the beginning of the profession it was not). E. G. Williamson formulated the first theory of counseling. It was directive in nature and counselor focused. It essentially put the counselor in charge of the counseling session. The approach came to be known by several names, such as the *Minnesota point of view* and *trait-and-factor counseling*. As mentioned previously, it emphasized the teaching, mentoring, and influencing skills of the counselor (Williamson, 1939). The Minnesota point of view dominated counseling in the 1930s and 1940s but came into direct conflict with Carl Rogers's *nondirective theory* in the 1940s.

Rogers's idea was "that individuals had the capacity to explore themselves and make decisions without an authoritative judgment from a counselor. He saw little need to make diagnoses of client problems or to provide information or direction to those he called clients. He emphasized the importance of the relationship between the counselor and client. In his system, the client rather than the counselor was the most important factor" (Glosoff & Rockwell, 1997, p. 13). Rogers published his ideas in *Counseling and Psychotherapy*

(1942), which was followed nine years later with a more definitive work, *Client-Centered Therapy* (1951).

Besides directed and nondirected theories, counselors before 1950 also depended on psychoanalysis and insight theories (e.g., Sigmund Freud's theory) and, to a lesser extent, behavioral theories (e.g., B. F. Skinner's theory). Debates among counselors usually centered on whether directive or nondirective counseling was most effective, and almost all counselors assumed that certain tenets of psychoanalysis (such as defense mechanisms) were true and that behavioral techniques, such as reinforcement and extinction, could be helpful in promoting change.

During the 1950s, new approaches to helping began to emerge. Applied behavioral theories, such as Joseph Wolpe's systematic desensitization, were formulated. Cognitive theories also made an appearance, as witnessed by the growth of Albert Ellis's rational-emotive therapy and Eric Berne's transactional analysis. Learning theory, gestalt theory, existentialism, and advances in developmental psychology made an impact, as well (Aubrey, 1977). Adlerian theory experienced a renaissance, too. By the end of the decade, the number and complexity of theories associated with counseling had grown considerably.

In the 1960s and 1970s, theories were applied to groups and new theories from family work were generated. Counselors became more receptive to considering new theoretical approaches, including those that have evolved from the fields of psychology, sociology, biology, and education, such as general systems theory (Bertalanffy, 1968). Increased attention to gender issues and sexual preferences expanded the scope of theories even more. Carol Gilligan's (1982) landmark study on the development of moral values in females helped solidify feminist theory into the counseling arena and forced counselors to examine the differences between genders. Likewise, the challenges of working with different ethnic and cultural groups received more attention in counseling (Ponterotto & Casas, 1987). In focusing on multicultural issues, multicultural counseling approaches such as those advanced by Allen Ivey, Derald Sue, and Paul Pedersen began to develop.

Since the late 1980s, working with systems (i.e., large community groups) has gained increased emphasis. In addition, eclectic counseling has become pervasive. In both of these approaches, a single theory is not seen as sufficient to address the complexity of the situation. Therefore, procedures from different theories have been selected and used in treatment. This type of approach, called *technical eclecticism,* is premised on the idea that techniques, not theories, are actually used in treating clients (Lazarus, 1967). Thus, counseling theories have not only increased in numbers but they have also been used differently over the years.

## *Professionalism and Counseling*

Counseling as a distinct profession is like other professions, in that it is characterized by a role statement, a code of ethics, accreditation guidelines, competency standards, licensure, certification, and "other standards of excellence" (VanZandt, 1990, p. 243). The way counseling developed into a profession was a result of both planning and chance factors. The seed for the growth of counseling was planted in 1952, when the forerunner of the American Counseling Association began.

## The Founding of the American Counseling Association

Initially, counseling was seen as an applied social science, a branch of psychology. However, much of psychology, with the exception of Counseling Psychology, Division 17 in the American Psychological Association, divorced itself from an emphasis on counseling over a number of years.

Into this vacuum came the forerunners of the American Counseling Association (ACA), first the American Personnel and Guidance Association (APGA) and then the American Association for Counseling and Development (AACD). The APGA grew out of the American Council of Guidance and Personnel Associations (ACGPA), a loose confederation of organizations "concerned with educational and vocational guidance and other personnel activities" (Harold, 1985, p. 4). The ACGPA operated from 1935 to 1951, but its major drawback was a lack of power to commit its members to any course of action. The APGA was formed in 1952 with the purpose of formally organizing groups interested in guidance, counseling, and personnel matters. During its early history, the APGA was an interest group rather than a professional organization because it did not originate or enforce standards for membership (Super, 1955).

However, times changed. During the 1970s, the APGA emerged as a strong professional organization. It built its own headquarters in Alexandria, Virginia. The APGA also began to question its professional identification because guidance and personnel seemed to be an outmoded way of defining the organization's emphases. So in 1983, after considerable debate, the APGA changed its name to the American Association for Counseling and Development (AACD) to "reflect the changing demographics of its membership and the settings in which they worked" (Herr, 1985, p. 395). The name was changed again in 1992 to the American Counseling Association (ACA), which is the largest professional counseling association in the world.

## Counselor Licensure

By the mid-1970s, state boards of examiners for psychologists had become restrictive, such as barring graduates of education department counseling programs from taking the psychology licensure exam. This action caused considerable tension among counseling professionals and led to action that resulted in state licensure for counselors (Ohlsen, 1983). Virginia was the first state to adopt a professional counselor licensure law, doing so in 1976. The state's adoption was based on a landmark case, *Weldon* v. *Virginia State Board of Psychological Examiners, 1972*, where the Virginia State Supreme Court proclaimed that personnel and guidance was a profession separate from psychology and should be recognized and regulated as such (Hosie, 1991). By 1999, 46 states and the District of Columbia had counselor licensure laws (Gladding, 2000). Furthermore, it was estimated that over 50,000 licensed counselors were practicing in the United States (Wedding, 1995).

## Standardization of Counseling Degrees

Simultaneously with the emphasis on state licensure came an emphasis within counseling on standards for degrees in counseling. In 1973, the Association for Counselor Education and Supervision (ACES) outlined the standards for a master's degree in counseling, which was followed in 1977 by the ACES approved guidelines for doctoral preparation in counseling (Stripling, 1978). In 1981, the Council for Accreditation of Counseling and Related Educational Programs (CACREP) was formed as an affiliate organization of the APGA. It refined the standards first proposed by the ACES in the late 1970s and initially accredited four programs and grandparented programs already recognized as accredited by the California state counselor association and the ACES (Steinhauser & Bradley, 1983). In 1987, the CACREP achieved membership in the Council on Postsecondary Accreditation (COPA), bringing it "into a position of accreditation power parallel to" such specialty accreditation bodies as the APA (Herr, 1985, p. 399). Today, the CACREP has standardized counselor education programs for master's and doctoral programs in the areas of school, community, mental health, and marriage and family counseling, as well as for college student affairs services personnel services.

## *The National Board for Certified Counselors*

Complementary to the work of the CACREP, the National Board for Certified Counselors (NBCC), which was formed in 1983, began to certify counselors on a national level. It developed a standardized test and defined eight major subject areas in which counselors should be knowledgeable: (1) human growth and development, (2) social and cultural foundations, (3) helping relationships, (4) groups, (5) life-style and career development, (6) appraisal, (7) research and evaluation, and (8) professional orientation. To become a national certified counselor (NCC), examinees have to pass a standardized test and meet experiential and character reference qualifications. By 1999, there were over 23,000 National Certified Counselors.

Aside from the generalist certified counselor, NBCC also established other specialty areas of certification. These included career, addiction, mental health, gerontology, and school counseling. Counselors who wished to be recognized for their special knowledge and skills acquired these credentials in increasing numbers at the end of the 1990s.

## *Chi Sigma Iota*

Chi Sigma Iota (CSI), an international academic and professional honor society, was formed in 1985 to promote excellence in the counseling profession. It would not be considered so important in the formation of counseling except that it did several unique things. First, it promoted excellence in counseling. Through a variety of means, CSI publicly recognized experienced and beginning counselors whose academic performances and professional commitments were exemplary. Second, CSI held a variety of conferences to promote counseling as a profession. For example, in 1998, it brought the ACA divisions together for an advocacy meeting, a unique idea and one that the ACA was not able to conduct itself. Chi Sigma Iota also made regular and generous contributions to the ACA, such as to its library, in order to strengthen counseling in the United States. Finally, through its international chapters, Chi Sigma Iota promoted and spread counseling abroad. By the end of 1999, Chi Sigma Iota had over 200 chapters in all parts of the world.

## Diversification of Counseling: The Forming of New Divisions

Prior to 1970, seven divisions had composed what would become the American Counseling Association:

1. National Career Development Association (NCDA). Founded in 1913; formerly the National Vocational Guidance Association
2. Association for Humanistic Education and Development (AHEAD). Founded in 1931; formerly the Student Personnel Association for Teacher Education
3. Association for Counselor Education and Supervision (ACES). Founded in 1938; formerly the National Association of Guidance Supervisors and Counselor Trainers
4. American School Counselor Association (ASCA). Founded in 1953
5. American Rehabilitation Counseling Association (ARCA). Founded in 1958; formerly the Division of Rehabilitation Counseling
6. Association for Assessment in Counseling (AAC). Founded in 1965; formerly the Association for Measurement and Evaluation in Guidance
7. National Employment Counselors Association (NECA). Founded in 1966

In the 1970s, counseling began to become more diverse. This diversity was seen most concretely in the formation of new divisions within the APGA. Five new divisions were chartered in the 1970s:

1. Association for Multicultural Counseling and Development (AMCD). Founded in 1972; formerly the Association for Non-white Concerns in Personnel and Guidance
2. International Association of Addiction and Offender Counselors (IAAOC). Founded in 1972; formerly the Public Offender Counselor Association (POCA).
3. Association for Specialists in Group Work (ASGW). Founded in 1973
4. Association for Spiritual, Ethical, and Religious Values in Counseling (ASERVIC). Founded in 1974; formerly the National Catholic Guidance Conference and the Association for Religious and Value Issues in Counseling
5. American Mental Health Counselors Association (AMHCA). Founded in 1976

In the 1980s and 1990s, the trend to establish new divisions continued with the following five being chartered:

1. Association for Counselors and Educators in Government (ACEG). Founded in 1984
2. Association for Adult Development and Aging (AADA). Founded in 1986
3. International Association of Marriage and Family Counselors (IAMFC). Founded in 1989
4. American College Counseling Association (ACCA). Founded in 1991
5. Association for Gay, Lesbian, and Bisexual Issues in Counseling. Founded in 1996

By the end of 1999, there were 17 divisions in the American Counseling Association. The number of divisions was both an asset and liability. The advantage of such a wide variety of divisions to choose from was that the ACA became more attractive as a professional association. The disadvantage was that some of the larger divisions attempted to venture out on their own independently from the ACA, while others were so specialized that they did not attract more than a minimum number of members.

# The Philosophical Basis of Counseling

In addition to history, the philosophy of counseling is important to understand because it is from philosophy that counselors conceptualize and justify what they do. Thus, theory and practice are rooted in philosophy.

Counselors and clients are always asking a number of philosophical questions about themselves and relationships on either an implicit or explicit level. Some of these questions concern the nature of reality, others focus on knowledge, and still others are directed at addressing what is most valued in life. Counseling is not united by a single philosophy. It is far too complex. Rather, a confluence of ideas has flowed together. Some common tenets have surfaced over the years as principles that guide the profession. However, the tendency within the field has been to adopt and adapt philosophical ideas. This practice began early in the history of counseling. For example, Aubrey (1977) observes that, because the vocational guidance movement developed without an explicit philosophy, it quickly embraced psychometrics during and after World War I to gain a legitimate foundation.

The tendency to borrow as well as innovate has guided the counseling profession, but ironically has divided it, too. Thus, some counseling specialties, such as elementary school counseling, focus on preventive and educational services, while others, such as mental health counseling, are prone to focus more on mental disorders and pathologies. There are some general principles on which counseling is based. It is assumed that all counselors, regardless of their special expertise, share some common concerns and perspectives, including the nature of reality, human nature, and the nature of goals.

## Nature of Reality

Reality exists on a number of levels. Two of the most relevant for counselors and their clients are the physical and the psychological. On the physical level, there is empiricism, the belief that what we know is what we have experienced with our senses, (i.e., what we see, hear, taste, touch, or smell). Physical reality surrounds people and is a part of their environments. In contrast to the physical is the psychological. This type of reality occurs as the internal or external experiences of people. For example, psychological reality is the thought or feeling a person gets from being in a particular place or with certain people. There is no way to assess this type of reality objectively unless a counselor is able, with the client's help, to discern the thoughts or feelings a client has in regard to particular stimuli.

The accompanying philosophical approach to the question of knowing the nature of reality is *metaphysics* (the investigation of all types of being) (Baruth & Robinson, 1987). Counselors who believe physical realities are crucial to the well-being of individuals and groups are likely to stress the importance of improving environments through social or political efforts. They are more akin to the early pioneers of counseling and are usually social activists. As such, they are most likely to work with groups that are either discriminated against by being intentionally or unintentionally excluded from services. An example might be helping people in a neighborhood gain adequate access to education opportunities or mental health treatment.

On the other hand, counselors who approach reality as being primarily a psychological phenomenon are less interested in what the physical is and more interested in how it is perceived. Therefore, they are more likely to work with individuals rather than groups, families, or communities. They are prone to stay out of the political arena, where they are less at home than counselors who concentrate on the physical dimensions of reality. Therefore, these counselors emphasize internal change more than they do external change. Social-constructionist and existential counseling are both examples of a psychological approach to counseling.

## *Human Nature*

Counselors have one of three perspectives on the nature of human beings. Some theorists and clinicians see people as basically good. They believe that things that have gone wrong in people's lives are a result of individuals not listening to themselves and being incongruent with themselves. The person-centered approach of Carl Rogers is an excellent example of this philosophy.

A second perspective on human nature sees many human actions as either base or undisciplined. From the Freudian perspective, the id, which is the first system of the psyche to develop, responds principally to self-gratification. If left unchecked by the superego and ego, the id constantly gets a person into trouble within the community in which he or she resides. On the opposite side of treatment, but still holding a philosophy that sees human nature as self-serving unless modified, are those theories involving learning. The idea is that people behave according to how they have been reinforced. They may learn bad or inappropriate behaviors and act accordingly unless they are corrected. Many behavioral approaches to counseling emphasize this point. B. F. Skinner, among others, stressed that people respond to the consequences of their behaviors more than anything else. Therefore, if there is no penalty for an action, it will continue, regardless of how it is viewed by society at large.

A third primary view on the nature of people is that humans are dualistic. People have a tendency to engage in both good and evil acts. That is why some individuals will engage in actions, such as taking unnecessary chances with their lives that they know are wrong. Some practitioners who hold this philosophy are engaged in Albert Ellis's rational-emotive behavior therapy (REBT).

## *Nature of Goals*

What are people's goals? Is life meaningless and merely a matter of survival or are there goals in life? The question of values in counseling is one that is increasingly being asked, especially in light of renewed interests among counselors in spirituality and ethics.

The answer to what goals, values, and ethics are worth embracing, if any, is raised repeatedly. One certain answer to the question is that counseling is not value free (Corey,

Corey, & Callahan, 1998). It is either for better or for worse. An approach to counseling that constantly raises the question of values and ethics in people's lives is existentialism, as exemplified in the writings of Victor Frankl (1969). According to Frankl, people have choices in life. It is the exercising of these choices that leads to meaningfulness or psychopathology. To make choices centered on selfish motives or to refuse to make choices leads to either an existential vacuum or anxiety. However, by doing a deed, experiencing a value, or finding a proper attitude in suffering, life is enhanced.

In opposition to the existential position are those that emphasize learning as the major determinate of goals and values. From the learning perspective, all behaviors and the goals that go with them are learned. Therefore, what one wishes to become or do is dependent on what one is taught. The most radical example of this position can be seen in the radical behaviorist, John B. Watson. In the 1920s, Watson stated that the reinforcement of behaviors was the overriding factor in people's lives and that he could make a child value anything if given enough time to set up a proper reinforcement schedule (Gladding, 2000).

## *Summary*

Counseling began to develop in the early 1900s, when social reformers and educators started addressing the ills of society. Three individuals from that time are particularly noteworthy because they established the early direction of counseling. These individuals were (1) Frank Parsons, who focused the fledgling field on the importance of career development and counseling; (2) Jesse Davis, who emphasized the importance of guidance and counseling services in the schools as a supportive measure for the formation of good citizenship; and (3) Clifford Beers, who started the reform movement in mental health that eventually culminated in the prevention, as well as treatment, of emotionally disturbed individuals.

In addition to these three individuals and their work in particular fields, counseling also became a profession because effective theories were formulated. Initially, counseling depended on four main theories: directive (E. G. Williamson), nondirective (Carl Rogers), psychoanalysis, and behaviorism. However, in the 1950s, a plethora of new approaches was created. Theories gave more credence to counseling and made it more acceptable to the general public.

Finally, counseling developed because of the growth of professionalism both within the American Counseling Association and related organizations. Within the ACA, a number of new divisions were formed beginning in the 1970s until there were 17 divisions by the end of the century. The new breath in counseling helped broaden its appeal and made it more diversified. In addition, new counseling-related organizations, such as the Council for Accreditation of Counseling and Related Educational Programs, the National Board of Certified Counselors, and Chi Sigma Iota developed. They promoted counseling as a profession and set up mechanisms that enhanced counseling. The activities of these organizations as well as legislative initiatives included (1) the development of state licensure and licensure boards for counselors, (2) the accreditation of counseling programs, and (3) the certification of counselors on a general and specialty level.

Philosophically, counseling has flourished because it has examined some of the critical issues in people's lives and has based its ways of helping in these areas. Specifically, counseling has addressed the nature of reality, human nature, and the nature of goals. In each of these domains, counselors have tailored approaches to helping that address client needs at concrete and theoretical levels. Thus, clients' concerns have been met in multiple ways from a variety of developmental perspectives.

What lies ahead for the counseling profession is still unknown, but counseling in the future will be richer because of what has been. Settings, theories, associations, and philosophies continue to evolve and interact. In such an environment, the patterns of practice that take shape in time will become even more distinctive and those who clinically serve clients, as well as clients themselves, will benefit.

# 4

## *Professional Preparation Standards in Counseling*

### Harold Hackney

*In This Chapter...* _____

- Does the emphasis on *separate* helping professions serve a useful purpose?
- What are the major reasons why counseling, social work, and marriage and family therapy are differentiated from one another?
- What is the rationale for preparation program accreditation?
- How is the training of counselors and graduate social workers similar? Different?
- How is the training of counselors and marriage and family therapists similar? Different?
- What organizations oversee the accreditation of counseling, social work, and family therapy?

In Chapter 1, you read that the mental health profession is a divided field, made up of counselors, social workers, family therapists, psychologists, and many others. This reality is both logical and illogical. It is logical, from some points of view, because the division into specialties makes licensure more concrete and public awareness easier; it is illogical because, in practice, the true differences between subspecialties can be murky.

This division into specialties holds a number of ramifications for the counselor-in-training and for the job-seeking counselor. For the prospective mental health worker, there is a need to know the difference between a *counselor* and a *clinical social worker,* or the difference between a *counselor* and a *family therapist*. Who is more employable? What do each do that is distinct? Which would be a better fit for you?

Similarly, when counselors complete their training and begin their job search, they may find that they are competing with other specialties for positions, particularly in the community, but increasingly in the schools, as well. Some community agencies will favor only clinical social workers, even though the job description would appear to describe the skills of a counselor. Sometimes, a school system will replace guidance counselors with social workers, in order to provide direct counseling service to students and parents.

Some of the division can be explained by job security issues. Social workers know social work training best, and are inclined to hire other social workers. And, because social work has a long history, its practice may be better understood by other health services. Similarly, family therapy practitioners have a cohesive professional identity and a strong public awareness initiative, the purpose of which is both to educate the public and to enhance the demand for family therapy services. Professional counselors have only recently begun public awareness initiatives through public advocacy initiatives.

Are professional counselors, social workers, and family therapists really different? How different are they? How are their differences manifested?

## Philosophical Differences

As was noted in Chapter 2, in part, the history of professional counseling traces back to educational roots. Implicit in the educational model is the notion that one prepares for one's future. The better one is prepared, the better one is able to anticipate, cope, adjust, and succeed when confronted by life's challenges. The practical application of this would be acquiring parenting skills before starting a family, or anticipating the demands of a changed life-style prior to retirement. Thus, the individual is able to anticipate needed insights, strengths, and skills, or resolve immediate problems. The counseling process is *preventive* in nature. Now, professional counseling is not exclusively preventive, but its point of first departure is that many of life's problems can be diminished or made more solvable when the individual has acquired basic life skills needed to address those problems. In real life, if one is to be preventive, one must be able to anticipate events or conditions before they happen. And in counseling, in order to be successfully preventive, the profession must have a means of identifying issues before they arise. This is achieved through the second characteristic of professional counseling, its reliance on developmental theory. As it is used in professional counseling, developmental theory provides a roadmap of likely future events or conditions, likely because the whole population experiences them in an orderly sequence or time. Thus, life events (e.g., midlife crisis) achieve some predictability.

The alternative to prevention is *remediation,* correcting that which has already become dysfunctional. Remediation requires skillful assessment and diagnosis, prognosis for correction, and a plan for treatment. The remedial manner of thinking is clearly different from the preventive approach. The clientele will be different, as well.

The reality is that prevention is, in fact, a continuum, ranging from *primary* to *secondary* to *tertiary* prevention. Similarly, remediation is a continuum, ranging from *crisis resolution* to *brief therapy* to *personality adjustment* to *long-term custodial treatment.* Although professional counseling is oriented toward prevention, counselors do become involved in remedial stages of treatment. And although social work is oriented toward remediation, social workers do become involved in preventive treatment, particularly at the *secondary* and *tertiary* levels. Family therapy practice is similar to social work in this regard.

## Theoretical Differences

It has been noted that the roots of professional counseling are in education and developmental theory, with some significant ties to counseling psychology. Social work has its roots in the medical model, primarily as a result of its early association with medical practice, and in community service to immigrant and underprivileged populations. Family therapy has its roots in pastoral care and in communication theory and social systems theory.

## Historical Differences

The contemporary practice of professional counseling traces back to the late 1950s and through the 1960s, when both school guidance and clinical mental health practice received significant funding from federal legislation to provide or improve services to underserved community populations. Social work, on the other hand, can be traced back to the late 1800s, and more prominently, through the early 1900s and the Depression years. Family therapy has a history of over 50 years, but its prominence and public image really began to emerge in the early 1970s, primarily as an alternative response to what was perceived as ineffective treatment methods for family ills.

## Political Differences

Success in a competitive environment often is dictated by the degree to which the public understands a service or a product. In other words, the projected image is a critical factor. Similarly, public services are benefited by positive perceptions of federal agencies, state legislative bodies, and state regulatory boards.

   If one is not projecting an accurate, honest, and positive image to the public, one's services will not be as highly regarded as those of the competition. Social work has a long history of accurate, honest, and positive image building. More recently, family therapy has mounted a highly successful effort to present an accurate, honest, and positive image to the public and to the political arena. Professional counseling is a more recent arrival in this competitive scene. Although it is making significant progress in its political agenda, professional counseling is not as well understood by the public as either social work or family therapy. (This activity is further described in Chapter 10 on professional advocacy.)

## Training and Skills of Professional Counselors

The preparation of professional counselors is dictated by program accreditation standards. Programs must be part of an institution accredited by one of six regional accrediting bodies or by a national accrediting body recognized by the Commission on Recognition of Postsecondary Accreditation. In addition, school counseling programs will meet additional requirements imposed by state Departments of Education for the preparation of school counselors. However, since most states have passed regulatory legislation for the practice of mental health services (either through licensure or certification), the standards established by such legislation can have significant impact on standardization of training.

Training standards have been established for professional counseling by the Council for Accreditation of Counseling and Related Educational Programs (CACREP). These standards dictate the curriculum of preparation programs for school counselors, mental health counselors, college student affairs counselors, family counselors, career counselors, community counselors, and gerontological counselors. The standards also govern the professional staffing of those programs and the practical experiences and outcomes that should be part of the total training package. The master's degree in counselor education requires a minimum of 48 semester credits (or 72 quarter hours) for the program to be accredited. (In the mental health counseling and the marital, couple, and family counseling majors, 60 semester credits are required.)

### *The Core Curriculum Standards*

The CACREP standards define eight curriculum core areas of competency in addition to specialty requirements:

1. Human growth and development
2. Social and cultural foundations
3. The helping relationship
4. Group work
5. Career and life-style development
6. Appraisal
7. Research and program evaluation
8. Professional orientation

Additional standards beyond the core areas are prescribed for specialties in community counseling, community counseling with a concentration in career counseling, community counseling with a concentration in gerontological counseling, marriage and family counseling/therapy, mental health counseling, school counseling, and student affairs practice in higher education.

***Human Growth and Development.***   The core area of human growth and development includes studies that provide an understanding of the nature and needs of individuals at all levels of life development. Studies include theories of individual and family development; transitions across the life span; theories of learning and personality development; human behavior, including developmental crises, disability, addictive behavior, and psychopathology; and environmental factors that affect normal and abnormal behavior. Also included are strategies for facilitating development over the life span and associated ethical issues. Typical courses that might be included in this area are Life Span Human Development, Theories of Counseling and Psychotherapy, Psychopathology, and Substance Abuse Counseling.

***Social and Cultural Foundations.***   The focus of the core area of social and cultural foundations is on issues and trends in a multicultural and diverse society. Content that would be relevant includes multicultural and pluralistic trends as well as characteristics and concerns of diverse populations; attitudes and behavior based on such factors as age, race, religious preference, physical disability, sexual orientation, ethnicity and culture; family patterns; gender; socioeconomic status; and intellectual ability. Generally, this content is covered in courses such as Counseling Diverse Populations, Multicultural Populations, and others.

***The Helping Relationship.*** Content within the core area of the helping relationship addresses the counseling and consultation process, such as counseling and consultation theories (individual and systemic); basic interviewing; assessment and counseling skills; counselor/consultant characteristics and behaviors that influence helping processes, such as age, gender, and ethnic differences; verbal and nonverbal behaviors; and personal characteristics, orientations, and skills. Also included in this area would be studies of client/consultee characteristics that influence the helping process and ethical issues inherent to the helping relationship. This content area is usually covered in a variety of courses ranging from Basic Interviewing and Prepracticum to Group Process and Practicum, in addition to portions of other courses.

***Group Work.*** The emphasis in the core area of group work is on understanding group development, dynamics, counseling theories, group counseling methods and skills, and various group work approaches. Content would include principles of group dynamics, developmental stage theories, group member roles/behaviors, group leader characteristics, theories and research related to group process, group counseling methods, ethical standards, group selection and evaluation criteria, and characteristics of task groups, prevention groups, support groups, and therapy groups. One to two specific courses are usually required in a typical master's degree program to cover group content. Typical course titles include Group Process, Group Behavior, Group Leadership, Group Facilitation, and so on.

***Career and Life-Style Development.*** The study of career and life-style development over the life span includes career development theories and decision-making models; career, vocational, educational, and labor market information resources; visual and print media; and computer-based career information systems. Students are taught how to design a career development program and to examine the interrelationships among work, family, and life roles (including multicultural and gender issues related to career development). This core area also includes career and educational placement, follow-up and evaluation, use of assessment instruments for career planning, career counseling processes, techniques and resources, and ethical issues inherent in career counseling. The typical introductory career course might be called Career Development and Theory, and may be followed by a practicum in Career Development or a course in advanced career counseling.

***Appraisal.*** The appraisal core area involves the understanding of individual and group approaches to assessment and evaluation. It includes theoretical and historical bases for assessment techniques, validity and reliability of assessment instruments, and various appraisal methods such as environmental, performance, individual, and group test and inventory methods; and behavioral, computer-managed, and computer-assisted methods of assessment. This material might be presented in a course called Psychological Testing, Educational and Psychological Measurement, or some similar title.

***Research and Program Evaluation.***    The basis for the core area of research and program evaluation is mastery of types of research methods, basic statistics, and ethical and legal considerations in research. Topics include qualitative and quantitative research design; parametric and nonparametric statistics; principles, practices, and applications of needs assessment and program evaluation; computer-assisted data management; and ethical and legal considerations in research. Typically, this material is communicated through a basic statistics course and a research methodology course, and is reinforced in other counseling courses.

***Professional Orientation.***    The core area of professional orientation includes studies designed to provide an understanding of all aspects of professional functioning, such as history, roles, organizational structures, ethics, standards, and credentialing. Studies in this area include, but are not limited to, the following:

1. History of the helping professions, including significant factors and events
2. Professional roles and functions, including similarities and differences with other types of professionals
3. Professional organizations such as American Counseling Association (ACA) and its divisions, branches, and affiliates, including membership benefits, activities, and current emphases
4. Ethical standards of ACA and related entities, ethical and legal issues, and their application to various professional activities (e.g., appraisal, group work, etc.)
5. Professional preparation standards
6. Professional credentialing (e.g., certification, licensure, and effects of public policy on these issues)
7. Public policy processes, including the role of professional counselors in advocating on behalf of the profession and its clientele

This content may be presented in a specific course (e.g., Professional Issues or Introduction to Counseling) or it may be dispersed through a variety of courses across the counseling curriculum. (*Note:* This book is written to cover all of the areas listed under the heading of Professional Orientation.)

## Clinical Practice

The CACREP standards require a 100-hour practicum experience, followed by a 600-hour counseling internship. Supervision for these clinical experiences is based on a faculty/student ratio of 5 to 1 for all individual clinical supervision. Group supervision seminars may not exceed 10 students. Supervisors at the student's internship site must hold a master's degree in counseling or a closely related field, appropriate certification and/or licensure, and a minimum of two years of pertinent professional experience.

## A Sample Program

Generally speaking, accredited programs will share much in common with one another. The Clinical Counseling concentration at the University of Southern Maine (www.usm.maine.edu/~coe/program/ce.htm) requires 60 semester credit hours, which offer students a comprehensive array of studies and integrates the historical, philosophical, societal, cultural, economic, and political dimensions of the mental health and human services system.

### Core Courses (33 Credits)
- Orientation to the Counseling Profession
- Career Counseling
- Psychological Measurement and Evaluation
- Fundamentals of Counseling Theories
- Fundamentals of Counseling Skills
- Group Process and Procedures
- Group Counseling
- Culture, Tradition, and the Life Cycle
- Human Development
- Individual Counseling Practicum
- Research Methods and Techniques

### Required Specialty Courses (18 Credits)
- HRD in Community Settings
- Crisis Intervention
- Diagnosis and Treatment Planning
- Internship in Counselor Education (9 credits—900 hours)

### Electives (9 Credits)
An individual graduating from this specialty would be eligible to sit for the National Counselor Examination (NCE) and prepared to be licensed as a clinical professional counselor (LCPC) in Maine.

## The Master's Degree in Social Work (MSW)

Preparation standards for social workers are established by the Council on Social Work Education's (CSWE) Commission on Accreditation for bachelor's, master's, and doctoral degree programs. As is the case with professional counseling, the state licensure requirements for a master's degree in social work (MSW) makes it a virtual necessity for training programs to meet the CSWE accreditation standards.

These standards define *social work* as the primary profession committed to the provision of social services for the enhancement of human well-being and to the alleviation of poverty and oppression. Professional social work has four related purposes:

1. The promotion, restoration, maintenance, and enhancement of the social functioning of individuals, families, groups, organizations, and communities by helping them accomplish tasks, prevent and alleviate distress, and use resources
2. Planning, formation, and implementation of social policies, services, resources, and programs needed to meet basic human needs and support the development of human capacities

3. Pursuit of policies, services, resources, and programs through organizational or administrative advocacy and social or political action, to empower groups at risk and to promote social and economic justice
4. Development and testing of professional knowledge and skill related to these purposes. (Council on Social Work Education Accreditation Standards, 1998)

## CSWE Core Curriculum

The CSWE's accreditation standards have eight core areas, some of which are similar to CACREP and some which are unique to social work. These core areas, referred to as the *professional foundation,* include the following:

1. Human behavior and the social environment
2. Diversity
3. Promotion of social and economic justice
4. Populations at risk
5. Social welfare policy and services
6. Social work practice
7. Research
8. Social work values and ethics

***Human Behavior and the Social Environment.***    This area includes theories and knowledge of human bio-psycho-social development, including theories and knowledge of social systems in which individuals live (families, groups, organizations, institutions, and communities), and the impact of social systems and economic forces on the individual and social systems. Within this core area, values and ethical issues related to bio-psycho-social theories are included, and students are taught to evaluate theory and apply theory to client situations.

***Diversity.***    Accredited programs must prepare graduates to practice with diverse populations; the curriculum content must cover differences and similarities in the experiences, needs, and beliefs of people. This curriculum must include content about differential assessment and intervention skills that will enable practitioners to serve diverse populations and involve the study of specific population group characteristics as distinguished by race, ethnicity, culture, class, gender, sexual orientation, religion, physical or mental disability, age, and national origin.

***Promotion of Social and Economic Justice.***    Content in this core area includes the understanding of dynamics and consequences of social and economic injustice, and all forms of human oppression and discrimination. The program must provide students with skills to promote social change and to implement a wide range of interventions that further the achievement of individual and collective social and economic justice. Strategies of intervention leading to the achievement of social and economic justice and for combating the causes and effects of institutional forms of oppression must be included in this core area.

***Populations at Risk.*** This core area addresses patterns, dynamics, and consequences of discrimination, economic deprivation, and oppression. The curriculum must provide content about people of color, women, and gay and lesbian people. Such content must emphasize the impact of discrimination, economic deprivation, and oppression on these groups. In addition to those mandated above, other included groups in this area are people distinguished by age, ethnicity, culture, class, religion, and physical or mental disability.

***Social Welfare Policy and Services.*** This area addresses the history, mission, and philosophy of the social work profession. It includes history and current patterns of provision of social welfare services, the role of social policy in helping or deterring people in the maintenance or attainment of optimal health and well-being, and the effect of policy on social work practice. Content must include the political and organizational processes used to influence policy, the process of policy formulation, and the frameworks for analyzing social policies in light of principles of social and economic justice.

***Social Work Practice.*** Content in this core area emphasizes professional relationships, examination of client strengths, and problems in the interaction among and between people and their environments. Practice content must include the following skills: defining issues, collecting and assessing data, planning and contracting, identifying alternative interventions, selecting and implementing appropriate courses of action, using appropriate research to monitor and evaluate outcomes, applying appropriate research-based knowledge and technical advances, and termination.

***Research.*** The research core area must provide an understanding and appreciation of a scientific, analytic approach to building knowledge for practice and for evaluating service delivery in all areas of practice, including ethical standards. The content of this area involves quantitative and qualitative research methodologies; analysis of data, including statistical procedures; systematic evaluation of practice; analysis and evaluation of theoretical bases, research questions, methodologies, statistical procedures, and conclusions of research reports; and relevant technological advances.

***Social Work Values and Ethics.*** This area includes specific study of social work values such as professional relationships, rights of the individual to make independent decisions, assisting client systems to obtain needed resources, changing institutions into more humane organizations, acceptance of diverse populations, and ethical conduct.

## Field and Foundation Practica

The CSWE standards require a field practicum at the master's level of 900 hours. Each educational program must establish standards for field practicum settings that define their social work services and practices, field instructor assignments and activities, and student learning expectations and responsibilities. All programs must provide the following:

1. Placements based on the objectives of the educational program and the learning needs of each student

2. Structured learning opportunities that enable students to compare their practice experiences, integrate knowledge acquired in the classroom, and expand knowledge beyond the scope of the practicum setting
3. Support for field practicum instructors

The foundation practicum allows the student to apply foundation knowledge, skills, values, and ethics to practice. It must provide opportunities to do the following:

1. Develop an awareness of self in the process of intervention
2. Gain supervised practice experience in the application of knowledge, values, and ethics; learn practice skills to enhance the well-being of people; and work toward the amelioration of environmental conditions that affect people adversely
3. Use oral and written professional communications that are consistent with the language of the practicum setting and the profession
4. Use professional supervision to enhance learning
5. Learn to critically assess, implement, and evaluate agency policy within ethical guidelines.

## *The Concentration Curriculum*

Just as the CACREP has setting-based concentrations, so does the master's of social work program. Typical concentrations are clinically oriented (individual, family, and group), institutionally oriented, or research oriented. Accredited programs must clearly explicate for each concentration the (1) conceptualization and design, (2) expected educational outcomes, and (3) content. These concentration decisions are shaped by fields of practice, problem areas, populations at risk, intervention methods or roles, and practice contexts and perspectives. Foundation content must be applied to the central issues relevant to the areas of concentration. Within the concentration, students must also complete a concentration practicum that clearly supports the student's area(s) of concentration.

## *Sample MSW Degree Programs*

Accredited social work programs contain some variability, in part because CSWE standards encourage programs to develop programs that are shaped by conditions of the community for which graduates are being prepared to serve (problem areas, populations at risk, etc.). Thus, programs with the same concentration emphasis will share the common core but will vary in their concentration curricula. For this reason, two sample curricula are provided in this chapter to give you a sense of this variability. The first of these is *Fordham University's Graduate School of Social Service* (www.fordham.edu/gss/index.html). This program offers a 66-semester credit MSW degree with two concentrations: (1) Practice with Individuals, Families, and Groups, and (2) Practice with Organizations and Communities. First-year students take 33 semester credits in the generalist or core areas. Second-year students again take 33 semester credits with emphasis on their concentrations (see Table 4.1).

Other MSW degree programs that vary somewhat from the Fordham program may be accessed on the Internet and include (1) University of South Carolina College of Social Work

**TABLE 4.1**  *Sample Curriculum for Fordham University's Graduate School of Social Service*

| Fall Semester | | Spring Semester | |
|---|---|---|---|
| **First Academic Year** | | | |
| Generalist Social Work Practice with Organizations & Communities | 3 credits | Social Welfare Policy and Services | 3 credits |
| Human Behavior and the Social Environment I | 3 credits | Human Behavior and the Social Environment II | 3 credits |
| Generalist Social Work Practice with Individuals, Families and Groups I | 3 credits | Generalist Social Work Practice with Individuals, Families and Groups II | 3 credits |
| Social Work Practice in Research I | 3 credits | Social Work Practice in Research II | 3 credits |
| Field Work I | 5 credits | Field Work I (continued) | 4 credits |
| **Total** | **17 credits** | **Total** | **16 credits** |
| **Second Academic Year** | | | |
| Advanced Practice Concentration I* | 3 credits | Advanced Practice Concentration II | 3 credits |
| Elective or Advanced Clinical Assessment and Diagnosis | 3 credits | Advanced Practice Seminars* | 3 credits |
| Social Policy Analysis, Advocacy and Practice | 3 credits | Oppression and the Struggle for Social Justice | 3 credits |
| Elective | 3 credits | Elective | 3 credits |
| Field Work II | 5 credits | Field Work II (continued) | 4 credits |
| **Total** | **17 credits** | **Total** | **16 credits** |

*Note:* Students with a clinical concentration have three electives; administration and research students have four electives.

*Source:* Compiled from information provided by Fordham University Graduate School of Social Work Internet webpage, 1998. <www.fordham.edu/gss/POS.html#2yps>

program (www.sc.edu/cosw/mswprog.html); (2) Ohio State University College of Social Work (www.csw.ohio-state.edu/msw.htm); (3) University of Minnesota MSW program (www.ssw.che.umn.edu/Admissions/ProDesMENU.html); and (4) University of Michigan School of Social Work (www.umich.edu/~socwk/msw/bulletin/curriculum39.html).

# The Master's Degree in Marriage and Family Therapy

Program accreditation for master's degree programs in marriage and family therapy is provided by two accrediting boards. Significantly more dominant of the two is the Commission on Accreditation of Marriage and Family Therapy Education (COAMFTE), an affiliate of the American Association for Marriage and Family Therapy (AAMFT). Also active in program accreditation is the Council for Accreditation of Counseling and Related Educational Programs (CACREP), which accredits a specialty area in marriage and family counseling/ therapy under its professional counseling umbrella. This section considers only the COAMFTE accreditation standards. Since marriage and family therapy (like counseling and social work) is a certification/licensure practice in many states, requirements for training make it a necessity that programs conform to accreditation standards.

### The COAMFTE Core Curriculum

The COAMFTE accreditation standards for master's level marriage and family therapy (MFT) programs encompass five core areas: (1) theoretical foundations, (2) clinical practice, (3) individual development and family relations, (4) professional identity and ethics, and (5) research. A sixth area is identified in the standards as "Additional learning" and allows students to take elective courses to augment specialized interests and background in marriage and family therapy.

***Theoretical Foundations.***    In this core area (Area I) of theoretical foundations, students learn about the historical development, theoretical foundations, and contemporary conceptual directions of the field of marriage and family therapy. The material is meant to enable students to conceptualize and distinguish the critical epistemological issues in MFT, and should be related conceptually to clinical concerns. A typical course in this area is an introduction to marriage and family therapy or foundations of marital and family therapy. Students are required to complete six semester hours or nine quarter hours in this area.

***Clinical Practice.***    Area II of the core, clinical practice, involves the theory of marriage and family therapy and mandates a comprehensive survey and substantive understanding of the major models of MFT. Included in this area are assessment (including marriage and family therapy methods of assessment) and major mental health assessment methods and instruments. In addition, the program must address a wide variety of presenting clinical problems and give students the opportunity to learn about appropriate collaboration and related disciplines. Typical courses found in the Area II curriculum include family therapy skills laboratory; divorce, single parenting and remarriage issues, family therapy interventions, family intergenerational relations, couples therapy, assessment techniques, and the *DSM IV* and diagnostic procedures. Students are required to complete 12 semester hours or 18 quarter hours directed toward these content areas.

***Individual Development and Family Relations.***    Content in the curriculum area of individual development and family relations must include material on individual development, family development, and family relationships; issues of sexuality as they relate to marriage and family therapy theory and practice (including sexual dysfunction); issues of ethnicity, race, socioeconomic status, and culture; and issues relevant to populations in the vicinity of the program. Students must take six semester credits or nine quarter hours of coursework in this curriculum area.

***Professional Identity and Ethics.***　　Students must take one three-semester credit course or four quarter hours dealing with professional identity, including professional socialization, professional organizations, licensure, certification, ethical issues related to the practice and profession of marriage and family therapy, and legal responsibilities and liabilities of clinical practice and research, family law, confidentiality issues, and the AAMFT Code of Ethics. Course content in this area should inform students about the interface between therapist responsibilities and the professional, social, and political context of treatment.

***Research.***　　The research core requirement involves at least one three-semester credit course that includes significant material on research in marriage and family therapy; research methodology, data analysis, and the evaluation of research; and content that includes quantitative and qualitative research.

### Clinical Experience Requirements

During the master's degree program, students must complete a minimum of 500 supervised, direct client contact hours (as many as 100 of the required hours may be in team practice). At least one-half (250) of the hours must occur within the program's clinical facilities in which marriage and family therapy services are offered to the public. In addition, 250 of the 500 required hours must be with couples or families physically present in the therapy room. The program must assure that students will be able to work with a wide variety of presenting problems and with clients who are diverse in terms of age, culture, ethnicity, gender, race, religion, sexual orientation, and socioeconomic status. Students must receive at least 100 hours of clinical supervision, representing at least one hour of supervision for each five hours of direct clinical contact.

### Sample COAMFTE Accredited Curriculum

A list of programs accredited by COAMFTE may be obtained at the AAMFT website (www.aamft.org). Accredited MFT programs are quite similar in curricula. The program at *Colorado State University* (see Table 4.2) provides a good example of what the master's degree in marriage and family therapy would include (www.colstate.edu/Depts/HDFS/ admiss/grad/samples.htm#therapy).

　　Subtle differences occur among COAMFTE accredited master's degree programs in marriage and family therapy. You may wish to examine these differences by looking at other program websites. Two examples of accredited programs are Brigham Young University (www.byu.edu/mft/degrees.htm#master) and Northern Illinois University (www. chhs.niu.edu/fcns/smft/smfthome.htm.#curr).

## Similarities and Differences among Accredited Specialties

Given that professional counseling, social work, and marriage and family therapy function in very similar settings and, in some cases, in shared settings, there is the need to understand the shared and unique qualities of each discipline.

**TABLE 4.2    Sample Curriculum for Colorado State University's Master's Degree in Marriage and Family Therapy**

| Fall Semester | | Spring Semester | | Summer Session | |
|---|---|---|---|---|---|
| **First Academic Year** | | | | | |
| | | | | Foundations in | |
| Selected Readings | 3 credits | Research Methods I | 3 credits | Family Therapy | 3 credits |
| | | | | Practicum— | |
| | | Skills/Techniques in | | Marriage & Family | |
| Family Theory | 3 credits | Family Therapy | 3 credits | Therapy | 3 credits |
| Marriage and Family | | Ethical and Legal | | | |
| Therapy | 3 credits | Issues | 3 credits | | |
| Practicum— | | | | | |
| Marriage & Family | | Practicum—Marriage | | | |
| Therapy | 3 credits | & Family Therapy | 3 credits | | |
| **Total** | **12 credits** | **Total** | **12 credits** | **Total** | **6 credits** |
| **Second Academic Year** | | | | | |
| | | Theories of Human | | Advanced | |
| Research Methods II | 3 credits | Development | 3 credits | Studies—Parenting | 3 credits |
| Practicum— | | Functional- | | Internship— | |
| Marriage & Family | | Dysfunctional | | Marriage & Family | |
| Therapy | 5 credits | Sexuality | 3 credits | Therapy | 3 credits |
| Group Study | | | | | |
| (Psychopathology | | | | | |
| and Systems Theory/ | | **(OR)** | | | |
| Therapy) | 1 credit | Grief and Loss | 3 credits | | |
| | | Internship—Marriage | | | |
| Thesis | 3 credits | & Family Therapy | 3 credits | | |
| Psychopathology | 3 credits | Thesis | 3 credits | | |
| **Total** | **15 credits** | **Total** | **15 credits** | **Total** | **6 credits** |

*Source:* Compiled from information provided by Colorado State University, Department of Human Development and Family Studies Internet webpage, 1998. <www.colostate.edu/Depts/HDFS/admiss/grad/samples.html#therapy>

## Similarities between Professions

Review of the training standards for these three sister professions suggests that they have much in common. These similarities are discussed next.

***Human Development.***    Although the language is somewhat different, all three disciplines call for much the same orientation in the study of human development. *Counselor education* refers to individual and family development as well as learning and personality development, in both normal and abnormal contexts, whereas *social work* refers to bio-psycho-social development and *marriage and family therapy* refers to "individual development, family development and family relationships, issues of sexuality as they relate to marriage and family therapy theory and practice (including sexual dysfunction)."

***Research Skills.***    All three disciplines want the student to be skilled in quantitative and qualitative research methods and in statistical analysis tools. Counselor education and social work also want the student to be competent in program evaluation, whereas MFT wants the student to have specific skills in research on marriage and family therapy topics.

***Clinical Practice.***    Again, all three disciplines place heavy emphasis on practical experience in professionally supervised, clinical settings. Social work requires 900 hours of combined core experience and advanced clinical experience, counselor education requires 700 hours of combined core experience and advanced clinical experience (with a minimum of 240 direct contact hours with clients), and MFT requires 500 hours of direct clinical experience, 250 hours of which must represent direct contact hours with couples or families (as opposed to individuals) present in the therapy room. Professional supervision of these experiences is prescribed, both in terms of hours (100 hours for counselor education, and 100 hours for MFT, but no minimum number of hours are specified for MSW students) and supervisor credentials.

***Diversity Skills and Knowledge.***    All three disciplines are very similar in their curriculum requirements for diversity skills and knowledge. The only obvious differences are those that reflect orientation contexts (population-at-risk content for social work and diversity issues as related to marriage and family theory and practice for MFT).

***Professional Ethics.***    Again, all three disciplines emphasize the importance of professional ethical standards in the core curricula and clinical practice. The CACREP calls for the study of the ACA ethical standards, MFT specifies the AAMFT ethical standards, and social work emphasizes its ethics code. All three sets of standards include comparable content on ethical issues.

***Appraisal and Assessment.***    Finally, appraisal and assessment standards are emphasized in all three disciplines. However, the details of this standard varies somewhat among the disciplines. For example, in both counselor education and MFT, the standard requires the study of major mental health assessment methods and instruments, whereas social work is more vague. In practice, however, preparation programs in social work require very similar assessment experiences, as do the other two disciplines. MFT also specifies that the content should address marriage and family therapy appraisal.

***Significant Differences among the Disciplines.***    A careful examination of the underlying bodies of knowledge for these three disciplines also reveals the fault lines that differentiate one discipline from the other. In some cases, these fault lines are philosophical (or population determined). And in some cases, it is difficult to understand why the differences exist, the issue of career development being a case in point.

***Career Development.***    Counselor education requires its graduates to have extensive training in career development theory and practice, including the assessment skills related to career choice. Neither social work nor MFT has a comparable requirement, although, in practice, both must encounter individual, family, or group dynamics that involve career issues.

***Group Work.***    Only counselor education identifies group work as a part of the core curriculum. MFT has no comparable requirement to counselor education's extensive curriculum standards for group work, and social work refers to it only in the context of knowledge of social systems, including families, groups, and organizations. In other words, there is no requirement in the accreditation standards for acquisition of group leader skills, group therapy models, and so on, for either social work or MFT.

***Differing Areas of Emphasis.***    Of the three disciplines, counselor education is, by far, the broadest in terms of philosophical orientation. This is evidenced by its many specialties (e.g., community counseling, career counseling, gerontological counseling, marriage and family counseling/therapy, mental health counseling, school counseling, and college counseling, and student affairs. By contrast, MFT is the most focused, by placing emphasis exclusively on the functioning of couples and families. Social work offers an interesting contrast to both, emphasizing social and economic justice and social welfare policy and services, and combating the causes and effects of institutionalized forms of oppression.

## *Summary*

Through thoughtful examination of the similarities and differences among professional counselors, social workers, and marriage and family therapists, a clearer professional identity can emerge. This is a particularly important process for each practitioner. In reality, the three professions are much more similar than different, though the differences often serve to differentiate and legitimize one discipline over the other. In their practice, the three disciplines can, at times, be almost indistinguishable.

More specifically, the clinical emphases in both clinical social work and marriage and family therapy receive greater attention throughout the preparation program. In this context, the MFT preparation tends to be quite restricted in terms of theoretical orientation to systemic approaches, whereas clinical social work programs have a somewhat broader orientation. The effect of this emphasis is that both of these specializations lead the graduate into almost exclusive clinical practice with remedial clients.

Professional counseling training is broader in terms of theoretical orientation and addressable client problems. Because counseling includes emphasis on career issues and developmental issues, the potential for preventive approaches is greater for clinicians who receive this training. It is also important to acknowledge that professional counseling embraces a variety of subspecialties, many of which do not seek to serve remedial populations.

# 5

# *Counselor Licensure*

## John M. Sutton Jr.

*John (Jack) M. Sutton Jr. is professor of counselor education at the University of Southern Maine, former chair of the Department of Human Resource Development, and coordinator of the Counselor Education program. Sutton received his B.A. in mathematics from Boston College. After an Army stint, he returned to college, earning his M.S. in counseling and his doctorate in counselor education at the University of Maine.*

*Sutton has had extensive experience in the licensure field. His efforts contributed to the passage of a licensure bill in the state of Maine, which also led to his being named to the Maine Board of Counseling Professionals Licensure. He has chaired that Board for the past six years. He also serves as the Maine representative to the American Association of State Counseling Boards and has recently been appointed chair of AASCB. In addition to his licensure duties, Sutton has served on the editorial boards of two professional journals and has a part-time private practice. His major academic interests are in clinical supervision and regulation. In the summer, you are most likely to encounter Sutton as he sails the coast of Maine, New England, and Atlantic Canada.*

## *In This Chapter...*

- What are the origins of regulation of professional practice?
- What does Sutton mean when he says licensure is a political/economic process?
- What is the difference between licensure *legislation* and licensure *rules?*
- What are the ramifications of *supervision* in most counselor licensure laws?
- What are the ramifications of the inconsistency of regulation among different state licensure laws?

*Licensure* is a statutory form of credentialing involving a legislative act of the state government (Brooks, 1986). The state legislature establishes a licensing board and gives it the power to regulate the professional title and/or scope of practice of members of that profession. Licensing boards are routinely given the responsibility of establishing academic standards, administering an examination, setting supervised practice standards, sanctioning members who violate standards of conduct, and requiring some type of continuing professional education.

The primary goal of licensing is to protect the citizens of a jurisdiction through the regulation of professions or occupations providing services to the public. The protection of consumers is accomplished through the establishment of minimal standards of practice and through a variety of activities, such as licensing, examining, auditing, and enforcement. In addition, boards routinely conduct educational and outreach programs aimed at raising the level of awareness of consumers of their rights. Key to this process is a board's commitment to behaving in a competent, efficient, and impartial manner.

## Why Regulate?

Regulation is seen as a legal function; consequently, regulatory boards are established by legislative action. Legislatures routinely invest broad powers in their boards to carry out their duties of regulation and discipline.

Although protection of the public is universally seen as the primary purpose of licensing, there is little question that it provides benefits to the profession and the practitioners of that profession. Licensing has been equated with raising the status of a profession (Hosie, 1991; Remley, 1991). In addition to increased status, other benefits may accrue to the profession, such as giving the profession legal status, providing access to third-party reimbursement, protecting the right of individual professionals to practice their profession, establishing rights of privileged communication for consumers, and regulating the use of title and/or the practice of a profession (AACD, 1980).

## History of Professional Regulation

Frederick II, a thirteenth-century Roman emperor, is thought to be the first to enact professional regulation. He set forth requirements for the practice of medicine, such as the passing of an examination, three years of the study of logic, and one year of practice under a physician after five years of study. Other provisions included disciplinary sanctions, fee regulation, and prohibitions against physicians owning an apothecary shop (Gross, 1978). It is interesting to note that conceptually, if not literally, these same standards are reflected in today's regulations.

The regulation of professions in the United States was almost nonexistent during the colonial period. It was not until after the Civil War that the regulation of the professions began to emerge (Hosie, 1991). Licensure in the twentieth century saw the demise of the old European system, which was replaced with increased university training and internships. A rapid rise in the number of professions licensed occurred as well as more stringent regulation of the professions by states (Gross, 1978).

## *History of Counselor Licensure*

The discussion of credentialing and training standards by the counseling profession began in the 1950s and 1960s. Credentialing became more focused and generated an increase of action in the 1970s, in part due to the exclusion of counselors by psychology boards, the expansion of the profession beyond school counseling, and the interest in credentialing by the profession itself (Brooks, 1986). The literature during the middle to late 70s was robust with articles about licensure, from sounding the call for licensure to debating the need for such regulation. This led to the establishment of a licensure committee by the American Counseling Association (ACA). At the same time, legislative initiatives had begun. In 1976, Virginia was the first state to pass a licensure law. In 1979, Arkansas and Alabama followed. During the 1980s, there was a steady parade of states who passed counselor licensing laws. This continued into the 90s, where, by 1999, 45 states and the District of Columbia had passed counselor licensing legislation. (California also has licensing legislation for professional counseling, but it is titled *Marriage and Family Counseling.*) Of the remaining states, it is likely that 2 of the 5 will have licensing laws in place by the time this book goes to press.

Professional counseling licensure has moved more quickly, encompassing more states in a shorter time than our sister professions of psychology and social work (Brooks & Gerstein, 1990). On the other hand, the profession suffers from a startling lack of standardization between states. This disparity is evident in every aspect of the regulatory process, from the setting of academic credentials, to testing for minimum competence, to supervising practice. One of the most troubling aspects of the lack of standardization is that the counseling profession has been unable to agree on a single title to call licensed counselors. Currently, there are at least eight different titles for licensed counselors. This lack of unity causes confusion within the profession, with other professionals, and ultimately with consumers. Unfortunately, this is our "Achilles' heel" and we remain vulnerable to fragmentation.

## *Licensure: For and Against*

When counselors, or the members of any profession, seek regulation, they are creating a means to control certain titles, skills, and behaviors. Whenever this involves the legal process, the failure to act according to the legal guidelines results in a violation or a crime. The penalties of a legal transgression are likely to be serious and cannot be taken lightly. Thus, it is imperative that professionals who seek licensure, as well as those who are licensed, be well informed as to the consequences of legal regulation, particularly in regard to what legal regulation does and does not do for the consumer, for the professional, and for the profession.

According to lawmakers, the major focus of any licensing law is to protect the public. Although licensing laws do provide some benefit to consumers, there are valid concerns about increasing costs, restrictions in services, and more benefits accruing to the professionals than the public. What is clear is that licensing has enhanced those professions who have attained it.

The strongest and clearest argument for licensing is that to be considered a true profession in our culture, a profession must attain licensure. While there is nothing inherently wrong with this motivation, counselors have an obligation to serve their clients through competent services, disclosure, and ethical conduct. Furthermore, counselors need to be aware of the more insidious threats of restriction of practice, increased cost, reduction in training reforms, and the limitations on the distribution of services (Hogan, 1983). Licensure does not come without its limitations, however, and the counseling profession has a serious responsibility to ensure that these limitations do not overtake the many important advantages licensure brings to clients, counselors, and the profession.

## Political Process

Licensing is fundamentally a political-economic process. Historically, the process begins with a professional group or organization lobbying the legislature for a bill to regulate the practice of counseling or some other profession. It is interesting to note that consumers are seldom found lobbying for such legislation; rather, it is the professionals who see themselves advocating for their clients or, more realistically, advocating for themselves.

The political process is an unfamiliar and often unfriendly one to most professional groups, who, for the most part, see the process as foreign territory. Lobbyists or a friendly legislator often have been used to introduce legislation to the committee responsible for licensing. The committee will hold hearings and/or workshops, prepare a bill, and recommend to the entire legislative body a course of action. This process can be highly political, as the committee members themselves might have an agenda and there is likely to be opposition from members of related professions. These various forces are almost certain to create changes in legislative language from what might be considered ideal by professional associations. Although the art of compromise is an essential ingredient in the political process, it can create unique differences in state laws. This has been particularly true in the counseling profession, where these differences have been substantial. The lack of standardization has been a function of a complexity of factors: the lack of strong leadership from the American Counseling Association in the early stages of the licensing process, the naivete of various state associations to the political process, the willingness to compromise, and the rapidity with which counselor licensure has moved through state legislatures. In many states, it has become more important to get a bill passed than to maintain the integrity of the profession. Those who rationalized that a less than ideal bill can be cleaned up later often learned that changing a current bill can be even more difficult than creating one in the first place.

## Statutory Authority

Each licensing board has been created by its state legislature and, in most cases, has its own enabling statute. The statute establishes the board's powers and limits (jurisdiction) and articulates its mission. The enabling legislation establishes general guidelines for the state regulation of a professional occupation. Specific topics that may be included in the statute are definitions, board composition, duties and powers, exemptions, endorsement, licensing requirements, terms of license, grandparenting, disciplinary action, and privileged communication.

The guidelines established by an enabling statute may be conceived as broad conceptual strokes that are designed to establish the board and provide it with a general direction. The statute and its provisions provide the board with initial guidance for its work. Given the nature of the enabling legislature, the statutory language is usually brief and general. In some cases, the legislature will provide clear and specific guidelines as to its intent, but more often they give only the barest details and leave it to boards to interpret their intention. Licensing boards are empowered to establish rules and regulations as the means of implementing the enabling legislation.

One of the technical but important aspects of licensing legislation is whether the statute grants title and/or practice protection. Title-protection laws restrict the use of a title such as Licensed Professional Counselor to those who are licensed. Providers who are not licensed may practice as long as their job title avoids the restricted language. Practice-protection laws, however, require anyone who practices, as defined by scope of practice, to be licensed. Practice laws are preferred because they provide better protection to the public and to the profession. The combination of both title and practice is the most restrictive form of regulation. Many of the topic headings cited earlier will be discussed in some detail later in the chapter. Three are normally contained only in the statute and will be briefly described next.

## Board Composition

Board composition, which is set by the legislature, has great variations in both numbers of members and types of boards. Most boards have both professional and public members, with the total numbers ranging from 3 to 13. Public members seem to be clearly favored by legislatures, as their number has been increasing over the years. Many legislators have included counselor educators as members, as well. A sizable minority of boards regulate counseling alone, but the majority are composite boards that regulate more than one related mental health profession. For example, counseling may be paired up with social work, marriage and family therapy, art therapy, pastoral counseling, rehabilitation, or psychology. Many jurisdictions are actively looking for ways of eliminating boards or have a moratorium on new boards, and so combining like professions into a single omnibus board becomes a functional alternative. One state, Connecticut, does not have a board and all licensing functions are handled by the state's office of financial regulation.

## Exemptions

A second feature that appears in most statutes is exemptions, referring to a group of people who may be related to the regulated profession but are clearly not part of the profession by training or purpose. A second group of exemptions are those individuals who, if included, would cause a disruption of services (e.g., workers at state institutions, interns in training, etc.). Typical categories included as exemptions are clergy, governmental employees, interns, consultants, self-help groups, human resource professionals, and other mental health professionals regulated by statute.

### *Grandparenting*

The third unique feature of most enabling statutes is the grandparenting provision. Grandparenting is designed to allow experienced practitioners to become licensed without meeting all of the academic, examination, or supervision standards that may be required by statute or rule. The rationale is that to require everyone currently practicing to meet the higher standard would be unfair, ignore the benefits of past experience, and put some practitioners out of business. These are powerful arguments for legislators and they usually insist on including some type of grandparenting clause in the statute. Grandparenting clauses invariably have an end date attached to them, after which all applicants must meet current standards for licensure.

The common theme among these three provisions relates to the pragmatism of legislatures. Although their job is to provide laws that allow government to run efficiently and effectively, they have a pragmatic side that attempts to balance the many needs of the citizens they serve. These are important points to keep in mind as you read through the remainder of the chapter and attempt to make sense of the concept of regulation.

## *Rules*

*Rules* are defined as regulations, standards, codes, and/or policies that are established by the board in the implementation of the enabling statute. For example, the statute might say that to be a licensed professional counselor, an applicant must have a master's degree in counseling of at least 48 semester credit hours. In implementing this mandate, the board might define the term *master's in counseling* in regard to graduation from an accredited institution with coursework in certain areas, including a practicum and a certain number of hours of internship. This movement from general to specific language and instructions is the challenge and responsibility of every board.

### *Rule Making*

Rule making includes all the steps a board must follow to give a rule legal effect. The typical process in rule making might include such steps as establishing the purpose for new or revised rules, drafting the new rules, holding a public hearing, and submitting rules for review, usually through the Attorney General's office.

Each state has its own idiosyncratic way of carrying out this process, but the end result is the same. Rules established by licensing boards to implement their enabling legislation are vital in the process of licensing itself. One of the reasons states are so particular about the rule-making process is that rules carry the same power as laws; and because they are much more specific than statutes, boards (through their rules) assume substantial legal power. On the other hand, they, too, must observe the law, and are not allowed to break the law, even though they, in a sense, created the law. The typical example of this is when applicants attempt to persuade the board that their very extensive experience ought to be sufficient for the board to waive certain of its curriculum provisions required as part of the master's degree. What these applicants are asking the board to do might seem logical and reasonable to them, but unless the board's rules specifically provide for the waiver of curriculum requirements, the board is being asked to break the law, which the board cannot do. When boards turn down this common request, sometimes accompanied by a letter or personal appearance from the applicant's legislator, there is the usual amount of angst and angry feelings. This example demonstrates what is often least understood about licensing board process. Professional counselors are used to operating in nonlegal settings, where negotiation and compromise are a legitimate part of the process. In the legal atmosphere of board operations, there is no room for such activities. The behavior of the board and its members is governed by the board's statute and rules, and their behavior must not only be in accordance with its own laws but any other state law that applies to the board's process.

In order to implement its enabling legislation, the board develops rules related to outlining application procedures, setting standards for licensure, providing guidelines for disciplinary procedures, and setting standards of practice. In the next few pages, these general topics will be broken down into more specific areas and discussed in detail.

## Definitions

Definitions is one of the first categories that appears in most rules. Definitions are more than a formality; they are the core of any set of rules. They clearly and concisely state the essential meaning of language that will be used throughout the document. Definitions assist applicants and licensees as they engage in applying for and/or renewing their licenses, as well as complying with the board's standards of practice. Definitions also are helpful to boards in many of their activities and may be critical in their disciplinary responsibilities. Although there is probably a point of having too many definitions, there is a need for boards to write rules that are as clear and unambiguous as possible, and definitions are a key ingredient in reaching that goal.

## Academic Requirements

All licensing boards require applicants to possess at least a master's degree in counseling or a related field. Some states do restrict the degree to counseling only but they are in the minority. Many board rules also require the graduate degree to be from an accredited institution. Some boards require specialty accreditation—for example, Council for Accreditation of Counseling and Related Educational Programs (CACREP) or Council on Rehabilitation Education (CORE)—while other boards accept institutional accreditation through the regional accrediting agencies or a national listing of accredited institutions.

Overall, counselor licensing boards are inconsistent on how they list curriculum requirements. Some boards list no curriculum requirements at all, other boards have a well-defined set of course requirements, and still other boards fall into a middle ground between the two extremes. Most boards are on the well-defined end of the continuum, with clear standards of required coursework laid out for applicants to follow. Most of these boards have taken the core curriculum standards published by CACREP and published those in their rules as the board's standards. This has had a positive effect, as the common use of this curriculum has created a level of standardization between boards, and with well over 100 counselor education programs now accredited by CACREP, there is a sense of standardization between boards and training institutions as well.

Beyond the core curriculum, most states require some form of practice requirement. This standard is noted by licensing boards by its academic titles of practicum and internship. Sutton (1997) reports that 40 percent of licensing boards mandate an hourly requirement for practicum and internship, an additional 43 percent of the boards require practicum and internship but do not list an hourly requirement, and 17 percent do not address a practice requirement within their curriculum.

The core and practice curriculum standards are an important part of the evaluation component for most licensing boards. Accordingly, applicants need to pay particular attention to how their board asks for this information to be documented. Almost all boards require an official transcript from the institution of higher education granting the master's degree. Usually, this means a transcript is sent directly from the institution to the licensing board; transcripts issued directly to students or to other third parties are not acceptable. Boards may ask for course descriptions or course syllabi as a way for them to interpret the abbreviated course titles that appear on academic transcripts. Another board request may be for verification of the practicum/internship experience. All board requests need to be taken seriously. Most board members are not from academia and are not familiar with that environment. The disparity in the way courses are described and the structure of program requirements themselves are confusing even for faculty. While not always easy, the best you can do for yourself is to comply with whatever the board requests. Arguing with a licensing board is usually a no-win situation where the end result will be a delay in being licensed. On the other hand, if you find yourself in a position where the board has made an obvious oversight or has not considered a key piece of information, you have a right to challenge or appeal the board's decision. If this can be done informally, it would be most advantageous, as a formal appeal could take several months to be heard and the delay in securing a license could be significant.

## *Examination*

Historically, examinations have been used for centuries to determine those applicants who have met a standard and deserve to be credentialed (Hosie, 1991). Since licensure boards are charged with the responsibility for determining the fitness of applicants, examinations have been among the primary means used to make this determination (Schmitt, 1995).

Almost all professions have followed this historical precedence and require some type of examination. All of the counselor licensing boards require a written examination, and there are several that also use an oral examination as part of their application process. Although this form of evaluation can provide important data in determining competence, it is fraught with legal, ethical, and technical hurdles due to the highly subjective nature of personal interviews, and it is time consuming for licensing boards. Since this form of evaluation is used infrequently, the focus of the remainder of this section will be on the written examination. For specific information on a particular state's licensing requirements, consult the National Board for Certified Counselor's webpage (www.nbcc.org/states/boards.htm) for state references.

A growing trend among counselor licensing boards has been toward participating in national testing programs. Such testing programs are often established by associations of state boards as a way of assisting member boards in evaluating applicants' qualifications

(Shimberg, 1981; Brooks & Gerstein, 1990). Although national testing programs are now favored by many professions and boards, a number of states have well staffed central testing offices to assist their boards in developing their own examinations.

Every jurisdiction that licenses counselors requires applicants to pass a written examination. Most licensing boards have chosen to use the National Counselor Examination (NCE). This examination has been developed by the National Board for Certified Counselors (NBCC). Its original purpose was to serve as the qualifying examination for certification as a national certified counselor (NCC). Because it has been the only national examination for counselors available, many boards have adopted it as their licensing examination. Other examinations in use include the Clinical Mental Health Counselors Examination (CMHCE), which is administered by NBCC. Again, this examination serves a dual purpose, for it is used as a certification examination as well as a licensing examination. Texas and Ohio use the so-called Texas Licensure Examination. California uses its own state-developed examination, as does Virginia. All other boards use one or both of the aforementioned NBCC examinations.

Licensing examination cutoff scores are an important issue for counseling boards. Although most boards have the legal authority to set their own cutoff scores, the reality is most boards do not have the financial and technical resources to accomplish this. Consequently, most boards accept the cutoff score established by the administrator of the test. This may not be entirely satisfactory to boards, but the alternative is far less satisfying.

The multiplicity of examinations used by counselor licensure boards is unique among the mental health professions. Many boards are satisfied with the content of their examinations, but many are dissatisfied. The dissatisfaction is focused on their current examination's concentration on knowledge rather than practice. Measuring mastery of subject matter does not ensure that a counselor can perform at a minimal level of competency. In addition, there is increasing concern with the use of multiple-choice formats, as they are not able to measure the complex cognitive processes often used in the practice of counseling. The counseling professions (and others) are realizing that there is a need to measure actual levels of performance if the public is to be protected and high professional standards are to be maintained (Williams, 1998). The limited usefulness of current examinations has created a movement toward instrumentation that can measure both complex behaviors and level of knowledge. This is the future direction for licensing examinations.

## *Provisional Licensure*

All counselor statutes and/or board rules require some form of supervised practice prior to full licensure. Essentially, the supervised practice is to move applicants from graduate training to practice in a way that recognizes both their training and experience as well as the safety and welfare of their clients. Most licensing boards view this time of supervised practice as an apprenticeship with a senior member of the profession. Many boards have designed this experience through the issuance of some type of provisional license. There are large discrepancies in the way boards have operationalized the process as well as what they call it. Typical language includes such titles as *provisional, temporary, conditional, associate,* and *intern.* Several states provide a lower licensing tier that does not require the same level of training or experience. Boards generally expect most applicants to have a provisional license for a period of time prior to receiving full licensure. Provisional licensure carries with it certain standards that must be met. Usually, there is a minimum time and a minimum number of hours of supervision and of supervised experience required. Beyond these minimum standards, there may be other conditions or restrictions, such as a prohibition from advertisement, a restriction from engaging in private practice, and a stipulation that both supervisor and supervisee be employed or affiliated within the same professional setting (Sutton, 1997).

Provisional licensure is unique in each jurisdiction. In addition, it is complicated by the type and amount of supervision required as well as the need to obtain a qualified supervisor. Paying close attention to board regulations, consulting with mentors and supervisors, and clarifying questions with the board clerk or administrator are important behaviors to ensure expeditious processing of application materials.

## *Supervision*

The significance of both supervision and supervised experience may be inferred by the fact that all counselor licensing boards have established standards related to both activities. The simple act of writing regulations governing supervised experiences confirms that counselor licensure boards have placed a high level of importance on the efficacy of supervision as a learning experience. Although research has not confirmed this assumption, anecdotal data have emphatically demonstrated that a good clinical supervisor has the potential of providing one of the most significant learning experiences in a counselor's professional career.

Brooks and Gerstein (1990) report that the inclusion of supervised experience requirements in licensure legislation was the result of a 1977 decision by the American Association of Counseling and Development Licensure Committee to propose such legislative language. While this might be somewhat presumptuous on their part, given the fact apprentice-type regulation has been used for many years in many other professions, there is little question that this committee's work influenced states as they developed legislation and wrote regulations. Another decision made by this committee was not to recommend specific criteria for the supervised experience requirements (Brooks & Gerstein, 1990). Consequently, the absence of specific guidance on supervised experience has, in part, opened the door for counselor licensure boards to interpret the concept in many ways. As a result, there is little standardization among board regulations.

Another difficulty relates to the supervision literature. Clinical supervision has been around as long as people have been providing counseling services. On the other hand, there has been a dearth of literature until the last 25 years and little research until the last 15 years. Consequently, it is not surprising to discover that it was not until 1987 that standards for supervision and supervisor training were published by the Association for Counselor Education and Supervision (ACES). Furthermore, it was not until 1993 that the first ethical code for supervisors was published, again by ACES. The recency of this work and the lack of clarity in the literature speaks to the difficulty faced by many counselor licensing boards as they struggle to write regulations that protect the public, and at the same time facilitate training and competent practice.

In a study that analyzed counselor licensure board regulations, Sutton (1997) found that all counseling licensing boards required the supervision of new licensees without extensive prior supervised experience. Beyond this basic requirement, there is very little similarity among boards on their regulation of supervision. A good example of the diversity is in the total hours of supervised experience required. Whereas all counselor licensing boards require supervised experience, the range is from 1,000 to 6,000 hours, with a mean of 3,000 hours (Sutton, 1997). Complicating these numbers is the fact that about half the boards allow some portion of master's work to count toward the total, while the other half accept only postmaster's experience. In addition, about one-third of licensing boards direct their licensees to complete direct service hours; the remaining two-thirds allow both direct service and other professional service to count.

Most licensing boards require 100 or more hours of supervision (Sutton, 1997). The ratio of hours of supervision (direct contact to discuss cases) to hours of supervised experience (overall work supervision) show 80 percent of the states require at least one hour of supervision for every 20 to 30 hours of supervised experience. This ratio relates favorably to the weekly supervision that appears in the literature and in the American Counseling Association's model licensure bill.

The qualifications of the supervisor is questioned by every counselor licensing board and with some differing answers. Most boards allow the supervisor to be credentialed as a licensed mental health provider (Sutton, 1997). Approximately 20 percent of the boards require the supervisor to be a licensed counselor. The movement toward limiting supervision to a member of one's profession moves in the direction of the social work and psychology professions. This movement, which appears to be gaining momentum, speaks directly to socialization and identity (Bernard & Goodyear, 1998). In states that are rural or where there are few counselors licensed, the growth of the number of licensed counselors may be truncated if supervisors are limited by profession. In addition, the benefits accrued with diverse supervisors is lost. The movement toward having counselors supervised only by other counselors may be slowed, as many boards are currently mandated by statute to allow supervision by other mental health professionals, and statutes are traditionally difficult to change.

A minority (41 percent) of counselor licensing boards require some counseling experience for their supervisors, ranging from two to five years. The majority of counselor licensure boards (59 percent) do not have any stated counseling experience requirement for supervisors (Sutton, 1997). This information is inconsistent with the standards of several independent agencies who credential supervisors (e.g., National Board for Certified Counselors, British Counseling Association, American Association for Marriage and Family Therapy), all of which require five years of counseling experience before a person is eligible for the credential. This lack of common standard may be a reflection of the newness of licensing and in particular supervision, and the lack of knowledge about supervision by licensure board members.

The area of supervisor competence has been overlooked for the most part by counselor licensure boards. Sutton (1997) reports that 71 percent of boards do not have any stated training requirements for supervisors; 18 percent require a graduate course, or its equivalent, in supervision; and 12 percent require training in supervision but do not specify the type or amount. Three boards have a specialty license available for supervisors. The standards set by these three boards for counseling experience (five years) and academic training in supervision (graduate course) are very similar to those of the independent agencies mentioned earlier. Overall, the training of supervisors has been inconsistently addressed. The result is a wide variance with current standards, which is consistent with the inconsistencies of standards within the profession (Bernard & Goodyear, 1998). In addition to the lack of knowledge on the part of boards, the lack of training available to practicing counselors could be another factor inhibiting boards from implementing higher standards for supervision. On a positive note, there have been more rule changes in supervision in the past five years than in any other area. It appears that boards are becoming more informed about supervision and translating that information into new standards for supervisors, as well as seeing supervision as a key to more efficacious services to clients.

The content of the supervisory time is of critical importance to both supervisor and supervisee. Supervisors have many modalities to choose from in conducting a supervision session. For example, they may use audio-videotapes, case note reviews, observations, co-counseling, self-reports, and case conferences. In states where the modality is not regulated in some way, the vast majority of supervision is by self-report (Borders, Cashwell, & Rotter, 1995; Borders & Usher, 1992; Fall & Sutton, 1999). The content of supervision is an area where boards are beginning to regulate more closely. Eleven counselor licensure boards place some restriction on the modality used by the supervisor during the supervision session (Sutton, 1997). These boards are using language that clearly says what is allowed (e.g., audio/videotapes, observation, and transcripts) and what is restricted (e.g., self-reports and case note reviews). The indirect modalities of self-reports and case note reviews require a high level of sophistication on the part of both supervisor and supervisee, and have been shown to have limited effectiveness except in special situations (Bernard & Goodyear, 1998).

Evaluation is considered the sine qua non of supervision. Yet, it is interesting to note that most counselor licensing boards ignore the evaluation of their provisionally licensed counselors. Generally, supervisors are required by boards to report the following types of information about the licensees they are supervising: name, address, license number, number of hours under supervision, number of hours of direct and indirect counseling experience, and the supervisor's personal identification information and signature. What is ignored, by most boards, is any reference to an evaluation statement of the competency of the supervisee to practice. The other side of this issue is the elusiveness of counselor competence, the difficulty in determining criteria for evaluation, the convoluted research results in determining the specific types of knowledge and skill necessary for effective counseling, and the dual role supervisors have of mentor and evaluator (Bernard & Goodyear, 1998). At least one state, Ohio, has decided to develop an instrument to measure counselor competence (S. Williams, personal communication, March 1998). This instrument remains under development and it is anticipated that, once completed, it will be available to all counselor licensing boards.

Another option, reported by Williams (1998), is the use of portfolio review. She describes the use of portfolio development and review as a possible method of assessing clinical competence of provisionally licensed counselors. The portfolio could serve the licensee, the supervisor, and the board in documenting counselor development as well as in designing remediation and training strategies.

The lack of consistency among counselor licensing boards in how provisionally licensed counselors are supervised raises questions for regulators. The challenge for boards is to provide thorough guidelines for supervisors, as these standards not only serve to protect the consumer but also help define supervisee competence. Supervisors and supervisees also share some of the responsibility for competent practice. Each has an important role to play in ensuring that the consumer is provided with the most effective treatment possible.

## Registration

Some counselor licensure boards have an option to register counselors in addition to licensing. Registration means anyone who is not licensed and who desires to engage in the procedures of counseling would have to register formally with or have their name listed with the licensing board. Registration typically means the individual is of a certain age, possesses good moral character, demonstrates trustworthiness and competence, completes a registration form, and adheres to the code of ethics. Registration does not imply or certify in any way that the registered counselor has met any academic, practice, or examination standards. Registration also does not carry with it the privileges of licensing, such as reimbursibility.

Registration often is a result of political pressure on legislators by individuals who do not meet licensing standards set forth in enabling legislation, but are currently practicing as counselors. Most legislators are reluctant to pass legislation that will put people out of business. Although this often creates a concern by licensed counselors that the public will not be protected from incompetent and unqualified practitioners, the reality has been somewhat different. Many individuals who register have some training and are often eligible for licensure if they chose to apply. Many of these individuals choose not to apply due to their political or moral objection to licensing. The other major group who register are those who were trained in the 1960s, 1970s, and early 1980s, and who have many years of experience with no desire to return for the additional training or to obtain the degree necessary for licensure. There has been little evidence that nontrained/nondegreed individuals are registering to practice.

Registration does place individuals under the code of ethics, and if disclosure is required, they must provide the same information as mandated for licensees. This provides the licensure board with the power to regulate and adjudicate any violations of the code of ethics by registered counselors. Interestingly, anecdotal reports show no more or less complaints against registered counselors than licensed counselors. Most counselors do not want to see this type of option available to untrained individuals, but there is the reality of compromise that cannot be overlooked when engaging with legislators in the political arena.

## Endorsement

*Endorsement,* the approval by one licensing board of another licensing board's credential, is a term in regular use by licensing boards. A related term, *comity,* defined as mutual recognition is used in the same way as *endorsement* by other boards. A third term, *reciprocity,* is an interchange of privileges and the acceptance, without review, of an individual's credentials (Emerson, 1996). Reciprocity is not currently used by counselor licensing boards, as boards have been reluctant to automatically accept licenses from other states. Although reciprocity would dramatically increase mobility within the profession, boards are concerned that such an automatic acceptance of credentials could be problematic. Statutes and rules constantly change and requirements between licensing boards could became unequal in a short period of time. Also, the time it could take one board to change the reciprocity regulation could be lengthy, resulting in the acceptance of applicants who may not be fully qualified.

Almost all licensing boards across all professions have decided to permit endorsement or comity. These two terms will be considered to have the same meaning and will be used interchangeably. In acknowledging endorsement, boards have used language such as "whose requirements are determined by the board to be substantially the same as" or "holds a license from another state acceptable to the board." Almost every counseling board that allows endorsement requires applicants to submit their academic transcripts, evidence of a valid license in good standing from another state, a passing score on an examination, and a copy of the licensing requirements from the state where the license is currently held.

The problems that endorsement applicants face are the many idiosyncratic differences between the rules promulgated by state licensing boards. When applying for endorsement, applicants are advised to follow board rules closely. It is important to present one's case in a clear and forthright manner, as there is little that can be done other than to meet whatever requirements are mandated. Arguing with a licensing board is seldom a rewarding experience. Discovering what is needed by the board, while not always an easy task, is usually less time consuming and an easier process than the angst of quarreling with the board.

Endorsement has been a particularly frustrating area for counselors who want to practice in another state. This also has been irritant for the American Association of State Counseling Boards (AASCB) as it works toward assisting state boards to write their laws and rules in a more standardized way. Each board has such an investment in its own requirements and standards that change is likely to come slowly, if at all. The result is that endorsement will continue to be problematic for licensees, boards, and the AASCB.

## *Fees*

Another universal requirement of all counselor licensure boards is that each has established a set of fees licensees must pay. In a study completed for the American Association of State Counseling Boards, Nielson (personal communication, January 1998) reported on fees charged by counselor licensing boards. He found that the fees for application and testing ranged from a low of $25 to a high of $400, with a mean of $203. The license renewal fees ranged from a low of $25 to a high of $270, with a mean of $113 and a mode of $100. It is important to keep in mind that renewal fees may be for one, two, or even three years.

Most counselor licensing boards are funded solely by the fees they charge their licensees. These fees must pay for all board expenses, from office supplies and equipment to salaries of the board clerk as well as the assistant attorney general assigned to the board. Most states assume no financial responsibility for the board. Thus, boards must manage their own revenues and expenditures. Boards may find that they have a surplus and decide to reduce fees or may find they do not have enough income and raise fees. When there are large surpluses, some states may take money for their general fund. This results in a hidden tax that generally goes unnoticed by most licensees.

## *Disclosure Statements*

Gross (1977) was one of the first to write about the use of written disclosure statements. He proposed professional disclosure be used in lieu of licensure, arguing that informed consumers have the responsibility and the resources to best protect themselves. He further stated that accurate information given to clients by counselors increases their chances of receiving what they want and need as well as providing increased protection against harm and exploitation. Witmer (1978, 1980) argues that although disclosure did not seem to be a realistic alternative to licensure, it did present the counseling profession with an opportunity to take advantage of this consumer oriented statement by making it a part of licensure.

Professional disclosure has evolved over the past 20 years and it is now required in half of all jurisdictions that currently license counselors. One of the reasons for the popularity of disclosure is that legislators see disclosure as having the potential of meeting the basic purpose of licensing (i.e., protecting the public). A second reason is that clients often are empowered as a result of receiving this information.

What, exactly, a disclosure statement should look like is best left up to individual counselors. On the other hand, most counselor licensure boards have carefully laid out guidelines for the minimal information to be given to prospective clients by licensed counselors. The following is a composite of how many boards are defining the content of disclosure statements for their licensees:

1. Name, title, business address, and business telephone number of the licensee
2. A listing by degrees, credentials, and licenses, including expiration dates
3. A statement explaining any condition on the license (e.g., if the counselor has a temporary license)
4. A description of specific qualifications or areas of competence, and a statement as to the type of clients normally seen
5. A description of the counseling theory, approach, or process used by the counselor, including a description of the initial interview or intake
6. A statement about the limits and scope of confidentiality, including such items as
   a. Harm to self or others
   b. Abuse of children, elders, or incapacitated persons
   c. Orders by the court
   d. Voluntary release by client
7. A statement that the counselor is under supervision and, when appropriate, the client's case may be discussed with the supervisor
8. Business information, such as
   a. Fees for regular sessions, intake, and crisis counseling over the telephone
   b. Third-party payments
   c. Hours of business
   d. Length of appointments
9. A statement indicating that counseling is regulated, and the name, address, and phone number of who may be contacted if there is a complaint

Counselors may want to consider including the following additional information in their disclosure statements:

1. *Additional credentials.* Boards normally require only license information; however, the licensee may want to include certifications or other special qualifications.
2. *Personal background.* This would be an individual decision based on what information is important and/or necessary for clients to know as well as the counselor's level of comfort with clients having this information.
3. *Statement about purpose.* Many licensees have found that including statements about the change process, who has control, and noting that counseling does not come with a guarantee are helpful to their client's understanding of the counseling process.
4. *Client involvement.* A statement concerning what is expected of the client in counseling can facilitate the client's progress.
5. *Release of information.* Such a statement outlines the uses and procedures for a written release of information.
6. *Cancellation of appointment.* This statement explains to clients that they will be held responsible for the fee for any session not attended and not cancelled 24 or more hours in advance. Such a statement should be included only if it is enforced.
7. *Emergency information.* Most counselors provide some type of emergency service. Typically, clients are instructed to report to the nearest hospital emergency room, call the counselor's answering service/pager, call a general hotline or crisis number, or list a colleague as emergency back-up.
8. *Client risks.* Any risks that may be associated with a counselor's particular approach or special techniques that may be used should be explained.
9. *Record keeping.* Guidelines may be provided as to what records will be maintained, what information they include, who has access, and how long the records will be maintained.
10. *Signatures.* Lawyers familiar with the mental health professions suggest that both the counselor and the client sign a disclosure statement to establish that the client has received the document.

The real purpose of professional disclosure is the protection of the consumer against harm and exploitation. Disclosure is based on the assumption that by providing clients with complete, accurate, and up-to-date information about the services being offered (usually in writing and prior to the first session), they will have the information necessary to render the most effective decisions about their own treatment. According to Farson (cited in Rogers, 1973), "The population which has the problem possesses the best resources for dealing with it" (p. 383).

The counseling profession has been a leader in promoting written disclosure to consumers. This form of disclosure has been precedent setting among the mental health professions. In addition, disclosure has made a valuable contribution toward increased effectiveness of services by allowing consumers to make more informed choices about their treatment.

## Bill of Rights

A client bill of rights can be used as part of a counselor's professional disclosure. The purpose of the bill of rights is to fully inform perspective clients of their rights. The disclosure of this information allows clients the opportunity to assume greater responsibility for their own protection as consumers of counseling services. Currently, there is at least one state, Maine, using this form of disclosure. Maine's Client Bill of Rights reads as follows:

### Clients have the right

1. to expect that a licensed or registered counselor has met the minimal qualifications as required by state law;
2. to examine public records maintained by the Board which contains the credentials of the counselor;
3. to obtain a copy of the code of ethics;
4. to report complaints to the Board;
5. to be informed of the cost of professional services before receiving services;
6. to obtain copies of his or her case records and to have the information explained clearly and directly;
7. to expect complete confidentiality except as required by law; and
8. to refuse any recommended services and to be advised by the consequences of this action. (Maine Board of Counseling Professionals Licensure, 1998, p. 37)

Other information that may be included in a client bill of rights includes the following:

1. To receive treatment in a respectful manner in an environment that is free from sexual, physical, and emotional abuse or harassment
2. To request information about all aspects of the diagnosis, treatment, and progress
3. To refuse to answer questions or provide information requested
4. To refuse or to request that sessions be recorded by audio- or videotape
5. To be informed about others, such as supervisors or consultants, with whom the counselor may discuss the case
6. To request a second opinion about treatment

A bill of rights document provides an opportunity for counselors to instruct clients about the counseling process so they may make the most informed decision possible concerning their treatment. This is a form of empowerment additive to the work of the counselor and demystifies the process itself. Furthermore, it presents counselors with an opportunity to enhance their trust relationship with clients and thereby foster more effective treatment.

## Ethics

The word *ethics* comes from two separate Greek words meaning morals and the customary way of acting (Higgins, 1958). A more common usage of *ethics* pertains to what is culturally acceptable and considered as the right way to behave (Corey, Corey, & Callahan, 1998; Cottone & Tarvydas, 1998). Ethical conduct is the result of the knowledge of what is acceptable behavior and an understanding of the foundational principles of a set of behavior (Bersoff, 1996). Thus, ethical behavior emanates from the knowledge of custom and is demonstrated with sound judgment, wisdom, and prudence. Ethics and law are similar in that they both offer guidelines, yet are different in their goals. Ethics represents a set of ideal standards set by the professions, whereas laws represent minimum standards set by the government (Corey et al., 1998).

The existence of a code of ethics is one of the commonalities among all counselor licensure boards. Many boards have developed their own codes of ethics and others have simply adopted a code developed by a professional association. One of the main reasons of adopting such a code of conduct is to protect the health and welfare of the public from unscrupulous and incompetent practitioners. Another reason is to give licensees, faced with a concern or dilemma, guidelines by which to determine the best or most appropriate course of action.

Close similarities exist among codes of ethics promulgated by licensing boards, professional associations, and certifying agencies. Logically, this makes sense as there ought to be some common understanding as to what constitutes right and wrong behavior in the same profession. What is different is the way that these groups handle violations to their codes of ethics. Professional associations/certifying agencies have the power to censure and to revoke a practitioner's membership/ certificate in that organization. On the other hand, licensure boards have broader powers of reprimand and may suspend or revoke licenses, impose remedial activities such as clinical supervision or education, as well as levy fines. The magnitude of these powers is imposing, as the revocation of a license may mean that the person could not practice his or her profession again after having made such a weighty personal commitment of time, energy, and money to enter the profession in the first place.

Codes of ethics in counseling and related mental health professions generally cover a wide range of professional behavior. The areas where most counselors face dilemmas are professional responsibility, competence, moral standards, and confidentiality.

***Supervision Ethics.***    Supervision, which is different from counseling (Bernard & Good-year, 1998), places an additional burden on practicing counselors to be aware of professional issues and responsibilities (Knapp & VanderCreek, 1997). The traditional role of ethical standards has been to provide guidelines to practitioners in monitoring and evaluating their own behaviors. As supervision takes on a more prominent role in counseling, ethical standards are being used to assist in the management of the many difficult dilemmas faced by supervisors.

The increased interest in supervision has brought out a similar increase in the concern and involvement in supervision ethics (Bernard & Goodyear, 1998). This is a relatively recent phenomenon, as the first comprehensive code of ethics specifically for clinical supervisors was published in 1993 by the Supervision Interest Network of ACES. Although most counselor licensing boards have addressed ethical behavior for supervisors, the current guidelines published by boards are inconsistent. Some boards who have adopted a thorough set of standards that would apply to almost all supervisor behavior; other boards do not provide any guidance to supervisors on what is or is not acceptable behavior (Sutton,

Nielsen, & Essex, 1998). If guidelines are not available through the licensing board, the ACES standards for clinical supervisors or the NBCC guidelines for supervisors may be consulted. Additional information on supervision ethics can be found in Chapter 7.

***Ethics Governance.***     Each jurisdiction has established standards and guidelines pertaining to the behavior of licensed counselors. These standards are taken, either directly or indirectly, from the current standards within the profession itself. Once adopted by a licensing board, the standards become binding for every practitioner licensed by that board. Furthermore, boards use these standards as a measure of appropriate and inappropriate behavior, and are charged with the responsibility of disciplining any licensee who violates the standards. Governance is a legal process and is often a foreign place for counselors. Seeking support and consultation is appropriate and often necessary when a violation has been alleged.

***Disciplinary Network.***     One of the little known assets available to licensing boards is the disciplinary network managed by the American Association of State Counseling Boards (AASCB). The purpose of this network is to provide a clearinghouse of information on individuals who have been disciplined by counselor licensing boards who belong to the network, and to distribute that information semiannually to all member boards. In addition to the counselor licensing boards, there are two certifying agencies that belong to the network: the National Board for Certified Counselors and the Commission on Rehabilitation Counselor Certification. These two agencies submit details of disciplinary action taken against their certificants and this information is included in the network's report. This information is used by member boards and agencies to protect their citizens by precluding persons who have been disciplined in other jurisdictions from receiving licenses where they have failed to honestly state previous sanctions. This is an important service provided by AASCB for its member boards and contributing agencies.

  The counseling profession is growing at a significant rate. The number of jurisdictions licensing counselors have grown dramatically over the past 20 years. This increase in voluntary governmental regulation has intensified the emphasis on codes of ethics. Consequently, there has been a substantial increase in the numbers and types of ethical violations. Ethics has been thrust into the professional spotlight like never before. Thus, it behooves all counselors, especially those who are licensed or certified, to be familiar with the code of ethics promulgated by their boards or certifying agencies; to follow it at all times; and, when faced with a question or dilemma, consult with colleagues or supervisors.

## *Continuing Professional Education*

Continuing professional education (CPE) has become a major focus for most counselor licensing boards. The licensure renewal process usually includes some type of documented participation in professional development activities (Sattem, 1998). Required CPE is the most widely used form by licensing boards to ensure the public is protected through the continued professional competence of counselors (Queeny & English, cited in Sattem, 1998).

  Sattem (1998) reports that the focus of many health care professions has shifted from technical knowledge, facts, and figures to more reflective knowledge. Reflective knowledge represents more of the art of the profession, where there are no direct answers and where the challenge is to assess a situation accurately and apply one or more basic principles to the dilemma at hand. Sattem (1997) finds that most counselor boards are in the early stages of CPE development, where the focus remains on technical knowledge with little emphasis on reflective learning. Her study further revealed that teaching methods are rooted in traditional large group lectures, which are least conducive to learning, and that evaluation is focused on the workshop/presenter rather than on what influence the training might have on clients or the counselor's practice.

Current practice among counselor licensing boards is to require licensees to complete some type of CPE. The form this takes varies widely. Most boards accept traditional types of educational experiences—such as workshops, graduate courses, institutes, seminars, and conferences—so long as they are related to maintaining the skills necessary for the safe and competent practice of counseling. Other types of learning experiences—such as formal home-study programs, professional writing, and first-time teaching/presenting—are generally acceptable but may carry a limitation on the number of hours allowed toward the total required by a board. A rather curious anomaly in current board regulations was reported by Sutton (1997), who found that only 7 of 41 boards allow supervision to be used for CPE credit, and each of those 7 has limited the number of hours that may be counted. What makes this interesting is Sattem's (1998) assertion that the counseling profession is lagging behind other health-related professions by maintaining a focus on technical knowledge rather than on reflective knowledge. Supervision, with its tutorial process and its focus on mentoring (Bernard & Goodyear, 1998), epitomizes reflective practice as described by Schon (1987).

Continuing professional education is a personal responsibility of the licensee. This professional activity can be approached in many different ways, from being a laggard to a full-time student. There ought to be some middle ground, where licensees can become the architects of their own learning. To become caught up in only what is required places individuals at a disadvantage. Probably the single-most important recommendation is to do a self-assessment, develop some professional development goals, and formulate a plan incorporating whatever the licensing board requires. Additional recommendations are as follows:

1.  Select activities that more closely follow reflective practice (e.g., supervision, small group activities, and individual education activities).
2.  Plan activities throughout the cycle rather than waiting until the end, when you are left with whatever is available and likely with less than satisfactory experiences.
3.  Look for programs that carry the approval of licensing boards, national certification organizations such as NBCC, or those learning experiences approved for credit for other related professions such as medicine, psychology, and social work.
4.  Focus on programs that are likely to have an impact on your practice and clients.
5.  Choose activities that reflect your stage of development as a counselor. Young professionals are likely to create a different plan, with different activities than the experienced counselor.

The challenge to all professional counselors is to create a coherent and integrated CPE plan within the guidelines established by the counselor licensure board. Most boards have established regulations that follow the one-size-fits-all formula, but there is usually some flexibility for licensees to use creativity and initiative in such a way that CPE influences professional practice rather than simply fulfilling an obligation (Sattem, 1997). Further, counseling as a practice-oriented profession demands that we look toward CPE that emphasizes practice-based learning, as that is the foundation of our continued development as individuals and as a profession.

## The Adjudicatory Process

One of the legal powers and responsibilities that most counselor licensing boards hold is to investigate and sanction those licensees who violate established standards of conduct, including the provision of inferior services. This is an important task for all boards, for it speaks directly to the responsibility of establishing a public trust for acting in the common good. Many legislatures and legislators alike have the understanding and belief that the public is best served and protected when practitioners are regulated. Their reasoning is that once regulated, practitioners who have violated standards of practice may be sanctioned and consumers may seek redress.

A transgression or a perceived transgression by a licensee may result in a complaint to the licensing board. The complaint is usually in written form and may be made by any member of the public, not just clients or former clients of the counselor. For example, if a counselor had a sexual relationship with a client, the complaint may be filed by the client, the counselor's supervisor, or an aggrieved third party such as the client's spouse.

Once a complaint has been filed, there usually will be an investigation by a complaint officer and an assistant attorney general. Although each state has its own procedures and rules to follow, the following explanation is offered as a composite sketch to provide a sense of the process followed in the resolution of complaints.

As soon as a complaint is received, the case is open and an investigation begins. The first step is to ensure that the person complained against is actually licensed and, if so, if the board has jurisdiction over this licensee. Assuming the complaint is valid, the next step is to notify the licensee that a complaint has been received and to provide a copy of the complaint itself. Normally, the licensee is given a period of time (generally 30 days) in which to respond in writing to the complaint.

Once all of the evidence has been gathered, the assistant attorney general assigned to the board and the board complaint officer or committee convene to organize, evaluate, and develop a presentation to the licensing board. The board essentially has two options. First, it may dismiss the case, whereupon no further action is taken. Second, it may decide that the case warrants a formal hearing. It is worth noting that it is only at the point of the board's decision to move to a formal hearing that the name of the licensee is known. Up to that point, the name is confidential to protect the licensee and to minimize, as much as possible, any bias. If a formal hearing is decided, it would be usual for the assistant attorney general to contact the licensee and his or her attorney and to offer to negotiate a settlement. This process is similar to the plea bargain used in criminal court. The purpose of the settlement is to move the case to a quick and just conclusion, saving time, money, and the stress of a formal hearing on all concerned.

At times, a formal hearing will be deemed necessary by the board or will be an option chosen by the licensee. A formal hearing has some similarities to a trial, in that evidence is presented, witnesses are examined and cross-examined, and the licensing board sits as jury. If, at the conclusion of the hearing, the licensee is determined to have violated one of the board's regulations, the board is given broad powers in disciplining the licensee. The board may issue a written warning, levy fines, direct activities such as supervision or counseling be completed during a certain time period, and, with the most serious offenses, suspend or revoke a license. Once the board has made its decision, the licensee may appeal that decision. In most states, the appeal process is handled in the regular court system.

The preceding description is meant to provide you with a generalized view of the adjudicatory process and is not intended to represent any one state. Each state has its own laws and procedures that will govern the specific conduct of a licensing board's process. In some states, the disciplinary responsibility has been taken away from the licensing board and given to a separate disciplinary board, which then acts in a similar way as just described. Several case examples may serve to assist you in understanding the process.

The first example focuses on a lack of knowledge by the licensee. A former client complains that his counselor refuses to provide him with copies of his records. The counselor concurs, saying he told the client that as soon as he paid the $100 he owed the counselor, the copies of his records would be forthcoming. When confronted with board rules, which clearly state that licensees must make copies of records available to licensees when requested, the counselor became red faced and said, "I guess I should have read the rules." This very costly omission points out the importance and responsibility incumbent on all licensees to be familiar with the regulations that govern their behavior.

In the second situation, the focus is on informed consent. A client seeks out the services of a counselor concerning marital discord. After 8 to 10 individual counseling sessions, there is a joint decision made to invite the client's spouse for couple counseling. At this time, there was no disclosure made to either party as to the change in rules as to who the client was and how this might affect future relationships with either party. Subsequently, after 8 couple sessions, the marriage dissolved, and the original client felt abandoned, accusing the counselor of not supporting him in the couple sessions. Counselors have an ethical obligation to inform clients as to the rules of counseling and to make a point of not just notifying them when the rules change but also to ensure that they understand the consequences of the changes. Some counselors will notify both parties in writing when this type of change in client status occurs.

The final case points out the importance of training and supervision. A complaint is filed by a client who has been diagnosed with dissociative identity disorder. The complaint is that records were released without permission. The facts of the case show that the client had provided a signed release to send records to a third party. The client maintained this release was not valid because it was signed by an alter rather than the main personality. This case (eventually dismissed) emphasizes the importance of extensive training and close supervision when working with clients who have serious or complicated disorders.

## *Summary*

The counseling profession has made remarkable progress in licensing over the past 22 years. As of the writing of this chapter, all but four states have established some type of licensing process for counselors. This is an improbable record in such a short period of time. In many ways, the speed with which licensure has come to this profession has overtaken the profession. The counseling profession and its members have been struggling to adjust to the consequences of regulation. Our national associations were not fully prepared, nor did they assert great influence over what happened at the state level. This resulted in states doing whatever was politically necessary to pass legislation. As a consequence, there is a great disparity in both statutes and rules/regulations among states. This disparity in how we regulate has created a divisiveness in the profession with which we have yet come to terms . In addition, further divisiveness has resulted from the licensing of certain counselors (e.g., mental health counselors) and unavailability of licensing for other members of the profession (e.g., school counselors). These serious dilemmas, which are not easily solvable, deserve our close attention.

Another area of concern is the general lack of knowledge among professional counselors about the regulatory process. Counselors, for a variety of reasons, have not developed an understanding of the purpose, function, and process of regulation. They express frustration and bewilderment at the very process they have worked diligently to create. This apparent contradiction is not to be taken lightly. The evidence is that, as a profession, we are not adapting easily or quickly to regulation. Consider the following example. The Maine counselor licensure board changed its regulations to require all applicants for licensure and relicensure to submit a copy of their professional disclosure statements. Shortly after the change went into effect, the board began to receive daily phone calls and letters from licensees stating, "What are you doing to us? Why are you instituting new regulations?" This was rather puzzling, since the requirement for disclosure was in the enabling statute as well as in the original rules promulgated four years prior to the change requiring the submission of disclosure statements. What was clear was that there were hundreds of licensed counselors who had not read the rules governing their behavior and who were not in compliance with those regulations. The attitude was *Do not bother us with your rules; just let us practice*.

Counselors have been slow to understand the nature of licensing and its implications. The ground swell of activity that often accompanies the political action necessary to have legislation passed seems to evaporate when regulations are written that place restrictions or requirements on counselors. They feel controlled by the actions of the licensing board. They express frustration and irritation at the board for making their professional lives more difficult. At times, there is a sense of fear that is experienced by counselors when they realize that any person may file a complaint against them and boards have broad powers to sanction their licensees and thus their livelihoods.

The threat of sanctions and the uncomfortableness of having a small group exert power over professional behavior still has not motivated many licensed counselors to be fully aware of the law and regulations that govern their behavior. Whether laws and regulations are too lengthy, complicated, irrelevant, or unimportant, many counselors are ignoring the reality of what it means to be a licensed counselor.

In the movement toward licensure, the counseling profession has been profoundly influenced. With licensure a reality in 45 states and the District of Columbia (as of 1999), we now practice in a profession that has been legalized. The legalization of counseling has resulted in the establishment of standards and examinations as well as guidelines on the appropriateness of counselor roles and activities. All of this has been done in the name of protecting the public from unqualified professionals. Although other benefits have accrued—such as the right to practice, third-party reimbursement, and recognition of the counseling profession—it has been consumer protection and accountability that have been the primary focus of this movement.

Licensing is here to stay. Counselors will have to continue to adapt to and accommodate the consequences of licensing. They will have to become acclimated to the powers invested in boards by legislatures as well as the prominent role accountability plays in the licensing process. We appear to be in a maturation process that the profession needs to proceed through before the acceptance of regulation takes hold. In the meantime, counseling professionals have the responsibility to reflect on their own behavior as it concerns licensing matters, to ensure they do everything in their power to be aware of what is required and expected of them as licensed counselors, and to protect the clients who are entrusted to their care.

# 6

# *Becoming a Private Practitioner*

## Lynn E. Brueske and Robert S. Walton

*Lynn E. Brueske and Robert (Scotty) S. Walton are principals in the Walton-Brueske Counseling Group, P.A. in Jacksonville. Both are licensed mental health counselors. Brueske, who has been involved in community mental health since 1984, serves as an adjunct professor with the University of North Florida. She has also served on the Board of Directors of the National Academy of Certified Clinical Mental Health Counselors and presently serves on the National Board for Certified Counselors (NBCC). She holds the specialist in education from the University of Florida. Brueske has competed in the New York City marathon, the Jacksonville marathon, and the Boston marathon, and loves fly-fishing and scuba diving. Walton received his B.A. and M.A. from Old Dominion University and his doctorate from the University of Southern Mississippi. Following his studies, he completed a clinical internship with the Eastern Virginia Graduate School of Medicine, and later served on the faculty of the Eastern Virginia Medical School as an instructor in the department of psychiatry and the behavioral sciences. He has also been an adjunct professor at the University of North Florida. Walton is a founder and past president of the Northeast Florida Mental Health Counselors Association, a founder and charter member of the Licensed Professional Counselors of Hampton Roads, and past president of the Florida Mental Health Counselors Association. In his spare time, he enjoys fly-fishing, golf, and gardening.*

## In This Chapter...

- What areas of concern stand out most vividly for you if you were to consider private practice?
- What problems (and solutions) present themselves when a counselor wishes to move to another state?
- What are the pros and cons of full-time versus part-time private practice?
- What are the greatest challenges to starting a private practice?
- How is paperwork important for the private practitioner?

Fall down seven times…Get up eight. (ancient Japanese proverb)

Private practice is a major undertaking. At issue is the choice of whether to work for others or to work for ourselves. If you choose to become a private practitioner, you are choosing to become an entrepreneur. If all goes well, you may take a bow. If it does not, you have no one else to blame except the face in the mirror. The risks of private practice are real. So, what are the arguments for taking such risks?

Many of us longed to work for ourselves. It is rather like the difference between owning your home or renting it. In the former case, you are building equity for yourself and family. In the latter, you are building equity for the landlord's estate and family. In either case, much of the costs are tax deductible. This may be the basic argument for free enterprise. To the entrepreneur, it does not make any sense to feather someone else's bed when you can feather your own. In today's market, you can work for yourself even if you work in a group practice setting by contracting with the practice owner to be a private contractor. There are many ways to become self-employed, if that is the goal. You may buy into a practice, share office space with other professionals, or, if you have the referral base and true grit, you may decide on solo practice. It is a world filled with promise and headaches. Blended into these risks and rewards are a number of issues about which you should be fully informed.

## Ethical Issues

Capitalism and free enterprise are what make our country prosperous. On the other hand, unbridled capitalism may be as great a blight on the world's society as was totalitarianism. In either case, the rights of the many are controlled by the whims of the few. Who was it that said "Power corrupts, absolute power corrupts absolutely"? We take this global principle and apply it directly to private practice in the mental health field. We are talking about operating in the field within your moral-ethical framework. As a professional, you are also accepting the responsibility to operate within the ethical guidelines of your profession. It does not take a rocket scientist to know it is wrong to have sex with a client or a supervisee. Your basic tenet should be *to do no harm*. Write that on a poster and hang it on your wall. Write it in your brain. Live by it. Try to help your clients, but do no harm. This chapter will give you some simple guidelines for operating ethically in private practice to help you think through some of the ethical dilemmas you will surely face some day.

## Clinical Competencies versus Limitations

No one can do everything well. As you begin practicing, you have certain clinical strengths that you may have garnered as a student and an intern. As a licensed professional, or the equivalent, you have mastered the basic skills of your profession and are considered competent to provide psychotherapy services. Your scope of practice may be broad, whereas your competency base is more limited. However, enhancing your knowledge base is not difficult. In many cases, all that is required is taking coursework or workshops and seeking some additional supervision to help you become grounded in the new technical skill(s).

Your ethics and licensing law requires you to stay within your knowledge base. This is not to say that practitioners cannot try new things in the context of therapeutic interactions with clients. It is our belief that clients are truly counselors' greatest teachers. We are referring to more comprehensive skills, such as becoming a marriage and family therapist, a hypno-therapist, or a sex therapist. These are technical skills that have their own theory and basic assumptions. These skills are in addition to basic skills required for an advanced degree and licensure in the profession. So, moderate yourself while you are growing into a new set of clinical shoes. As you accomplish new skills, add them to your toolkit and use them with your clients, for your edification and their benefit.

## Scope of Practice

Licensure requirements in some states require that counselors develop basic competencies in a variety of areas, leading to the ability to perform psychotherapy. The scope of practice in these states may be limited to specific areas. Most states view the licensed professional counselor (LPC) and licensed mental health counselor (LMHC) licenses as the minimum requirements necessary to achieve competency and practice psychotherapy. Licensure in some states, such as Florida, give the LMHC the capacity to assess, diagnose, and treat mental and emotional disorders. This is a very broad scope of practice for mental health counselors, matched in few other states. This definition refers to advanced skills that may require years of experience and additional training to achieve. *Assessment,* for instance, refers to the ability to give and interpret intellectual and personality assessment tests, as well as other assessment techniques that help one achieve an adequate level of knowledge about a client in order to reach a diagnosis. The only requirement is that the counselor be trained and competent to administer, score, and interpret the instruments and techniques being used. Your ethical and legal responsibility (see your licensing law) is to guard against offering services for which you have not been trained and are not competent to perform. The only exception is when you are in training, *under supervision* and in the process of learning the new skill. In such an instance, you would be following an ethical course and continuing your own education, as well. In summary, you would do well to know your state law backward and forward. Understand the scope of practice that sets both the limits of practice and the breadth of services you may offer.

## Licensure Definitions

At this writing, 45 states and the District of Columbia have licensure laws establishing the LPC, LMHC, or similar license. Your state's licensure law and the definitions of profes-sional services regulated by state law define the scope of practice for mental health coun-selors in your state. For example, consider this more comprehensive quote from Florida's Chapter 491, which licenses mental health counselors: "The practice of mental health counseling includes methods of a psychological nature used to assess, diagnose, and treat emotional and mental disorders (whether cognitive, affective, or behavioral), behavioral disorders, interpersonal relationships, sexual dysfunction, alcoholism, and substance abuse. The practice of mental health counseling includes, but is not limited to, psychotherapy, hypnotherapy, and sex therapy" (Florida Law, Chapter 491.003, Definitions, (9)). As you can see, just this portion of the law establishes a very comprehensive scope of practice for LMHCs in Florida. Definitions in Florida's Chapter 491, covering the LMHC license, among others, defines LMHCs as psychotherapists and protects the title of psychotherapist from use by unlicensed people. Therefore, Florida law is both a practice act and a title act, capturing and defining both the titles and the practice of certain professional services. Your job is to discover what your state law governs and then operate within those boundaries.

## Certifications

A small number of states have laws that certify rather than license LPCs and LMHCs. Certification by state law, although not a license, will still define a limited scope of practice for the professional services regulated by the certifying process. If you practice in a state with no licensing or certification laws, we recommend that you look into national certification. The National Board for Certified Counselors (NBCC) is the body that certifies counselors nationally. The general certification is that of national certified counselor (NCC). Within NBCC, there are five specialty certifications, including the master addictions counselor (MAC) and the certified clinical mental health counselor (CCMHC). The CCMHC credential has been accepted by Tricare (formerly Champus) insurance, for billing purposes in states with no licensure laws. Tricare is the federal insurance provided for active duty and retired military and dependents in all branches of military service. We hold NCC and CCMHC certifications from NBCC, and recommend them to you as an additional credential, similar to specialty certifications offered to other professionals.

## Education and Experience

State licensure law defines both the educational and the supervised experiential requirements for licensure. Both sets of requirements may vary from state to state. Since the LPC and LMHC licenses are seen by many states as a minimum competency level, the coursework and number of graduate hours of education may differ.

After completing your master's degree program, including graduate coursework and one or more supervised practicum/internship experiences, you have achieved the first major milestone in the path toward private practice. In your first employment, at a postmaster's level, you will surely be supervised by a more senior clinician. Most graduate programs are designed to train the student in basic technical skills of the profession, but no one expects that the graduate is now ready to become a freestanding practitioner. Rather, a new level of training begins, so that you may hone basic skills into a well-grounded theoretical and experiential knowledge base that marks the initiation of the second phase of training. During this second phase, you may also be completing clinical supervision requirements leading toward licensure in your state. Supervised clinical experience requirements are clearly stated in the licensing laws in most states and for most certifications.

Once you have achieved licensure, you have completed the second phase of professional training and are now considered a freestanding practitioner. Yet, in this seemingly lofty position, you may still not have mastered some technical skills that, by their nature, require more face-to-face clinical experience and supervision. The point we wish to make is that there is a third phase of professional practice, supervision from a mentor or other form of collegial consultation, that becomes an educational tool helping you refine your technique and enhance your knowledge base.

The fourth and last stage of this process is when you begin to serve as the mentor and clinical supervisor for upcoming clinicians. At this level, you have achieved a senior clinician status and your responsibilities increase yet again. Clinical supervision of and mentoring of young professionals is both a rewarding and a daunting experience and is not for the fainthearted. Clinical supervision carries with it the legal and ethical responsibility to help the intern achieve competency, while monitoring and protecting the intern's clients from harm. Clinical supervision may be one of the most challenging and rewarding stages in the growth and development of the counseling professional.

## Consultation

Consulting with businesses, other professionals and professional groups, and agencies of government is a way of expanding your practice. Consultation requires advanced skills and area(s) of expertise, giving you another salable skill. The old saying "Variety is the spice of life" is true in private practice. Variety wards off burn-out. It also offers other areas of income. We liken successful solo private practice today to a series of part-time jobs. One possibility is consultation, where you are creating a client base that may be at a governmental or corporate level and is certainly more affluent than your average private for-pay client.

## Professional Identity

The need for counseling professionals to join and support their local, state, and national professional associations cannot be stressed enough. The healthy growth and development of this profession has already been deeply affected by several state and national professional associations. There are many ways professional associations can help you, such as through legislative efforts, public advocacy, clinical supervision sources, and continuing education.

Trends in the counseling profession remain quite volatile today, whether they are trends in marketing, changes in service delivery models, or trends that affect the qualifications of the licensed professional. National, state, and local associations represent existing conduits through which information flows. Typically, you will find commentary about ongoing trends in your association's newsletters.

*Networking* means different things to different people. Often, it refers to the ability of local professionals to meet and exchange ideas. Networking is also an opportunity to market yourself and to talk with other professionals about your services, specialties, and interests. Networking also may help you create a collegial consultation network for continuing your education. Association members may organize educational groups, such as journal clubs, study groups, and the like. Professional support groups offer the opportunity for support and personal growth to the practicing professional.

# Getting Started

## Credentials for Private Practice

Begin your planning for private practice by checking your state requirements for practice. Obtain a copy of your state licensure/certification law and read it carefully. It will specify what graduate degree is required for practitioners. The master's degree in counseling or a related field is considered the terminal degree for practice in the United States, except for psychologists. State licensure laws will specify the requirements necessary from a master's-level training program: specific coursework, number of graduate hours, practicum and internship experience, supervisory experience, and so on. The state licensure law will also delineate under what circumstances a professional can practice without being licensed or under the supervision of a qualified supervisor as well as the requirements for license eligibility. If you hold an educational specialist degree (Ed.S.) or a master's degree in education (M.Ed.) you will likely be considered under the same criteria as a master's degree (M.A.). If you hold a doctorate in education (Ed.D.) or a doctorate in psychology (Psy.D.), you will likely be considered under the same criteria as a doctorate of philosophy (Ph.D.). States differ in their requirements for practice, so attend to your state laws carefully.

If you intend to practice in a state that does not have a licensure law, contact the state's Department of Business and Professional Regulation, the Department of Health, or their equivalents, to find out what guidelines and/or restrictions exist for the practice of counseling. Also, talk to other practicing professionals in the area and ask about practice stipulations.

*A Word of Caution.*    Lincensure/certification laws and regulations may seem unnecessary or a hassle to you. You may think about opening your practice without adhering to the requirements. After all, you just want to help people and you have been trained to do so. *Do not do this!* The laws have been developed over many years by state legislators and members of the counseling profession. The laws protect the consumer of services (the client) and they also protect you (the practicing professional). If you try to practice outside of these rules, you will be practicing unethically and illegally, and ultimately you will be reported by your professional peers, thereby jeopardizing your future ability to practice.

Also check with your city or county Tax Assessor's Office. Many municipalities require an occupational or trade license, which involves an annual fee for operation of a business. In most cases, you will be listed as a "consultant" for these purposes. Again, local professionals can advise you about the local requirements.

Licensure requirements vary from state to state. If you are licensed in one state and then move to another licensing state, there very well may be some consideration of your existing credentials in your application for licensure in the new state. Oftentimes, your graduate education and training and supervision experience will be accepted. You may still need to take a course to meet specific state rules. Florida, for example, requires a course or continuing education on AIDS and HIV. You might have to take the state licensing exam if it is different from the one you took previously. No two states have absolute reciprocity, but most states will give you partial credit for your credentials to date.

Licensure and certification may be granted for limited periods of time, usually two to five years. At the end of those time periods, the credential(s) must be renewed. Renewal generally consists of continuing education in the form of workshops or graduate coursework that is approved by the state for licensure purposes, or the certifying organization, in the case of certification. Your licensure laws and rules will delineate the specific number of hours and type of continuing education you will need for each license cycle. Your certification organization will provide the same information for you regarding your certification renewal requirements.

## Full-Time or Part-Time Private Practice

The number of hours you invest in your practice each week will vary. How you spend those hours may vary even more. Full-time private practice used to be based on the number of clinical hours you completed each week, the average being usually somewhere between 20 and 25. The remainder of your week was spent in paperwork, phone calls, other administrative work, and perhaps some networking with other professionals. Today, full-time private practice is better defined as how you spend the majority of your work week and your main source of income. Some weeks you see a full caseload and have lots of clinical hours. Other weeks you see only a few clients and spend the rest of your time doing clinically related projects, readings, research, meetings, continuing education workshops, and more. Part-time private practice generally means that you have another job, full or part time, or you spend the majority of your work week in some other way. You might work at an agency during the day and spend two to three evenings a week in your practice, you might be raising children and have four hours a week available for clients, or you might teach full time and see a few clients in an evening or on a Saturday.

Private practice today is a result of how large a client base or potential client base you have. A client base takes several years to develop and will be mediated by whether you choose to become involved with managed care companies, insurance issues, private pay, specialties you develop, populations you prefer to see or those you prefer not to see, whether you work evenings or weekends, and the list goes on. Private practice is no longer one easily definable modality; rather, it is a constantly changing entity with its own rules and implications.

Many professionals want hospital privileges as part of their practice. If you need to hospitalize a client and want to work with that client during their hospital stay, you will need "privileges" in order to do inpatient treatment. Hospital privileges may be limited to certain types of mental health professionals (e.g., clinical psychologists and clinical social workers, but not mental health counselors or marriage and family therapists). Hospital privileges may be inclusive of all licensed professionals, or they may be limited to mental health professionals who work for or under the direct supervision of a physician or psychiatrist who is a member of that hospital's medical staff. The regulations are wide and varied. Check with your local hospitals that have psychiatric treatment facilities to find out the specific requirements for privileges. If you do not have privileges, your inpatient clients will be treated by hospital staff.

The amount of paperwork and administrative duties you will complete each week is related to the number of clients you see each week. Each client contact minimally requires a progress note, a notation of date seen, the type of therapy (evaluation, individual, family, group, etc.), charges, payments, adjustments, and an account balance. Additionally, each client contact may require a report to be written, previous treatment records requested, telephone calls to be made to other professionals involved with the case to coordinate treatment, contact with the psychiatrist or physician who is prescribing medications, and so on. If you are contracting with a state or city agency to provide services to children and families, you may have these additional duties every week or two for every client you see. If your clients are members of managed care companies, you will have reports to file or telephone calls to make for authorization of sessions every three to six sessions. Each one of these notes, reports, telephone calls, and so on, takes time. You will also need some time each week to take care of the business end of your practice. Bills must be paid, the office must be cleaned, and office supplies must be replenished.

Rounding out your week will be the time you invest in marketing yourself to potential referral sources, including other professionals in the area, physicians, psychiatrists, hospitals, employee assistance programs (EAPs), corporate businesses, and anyone else you can think of to approach. Part of marketing involves a wide variety of nonclinical activities, including returning telephone calls to potential clients who will want to know who you are, what licenses or degrees you have earned, what the difference is between you and a social worker or a psychologist, what kind of therapy you do, how much experience you have with their particular type of problem, what your hours and charges are, if you have a sliding fee scale, if you accept insurance, what insurance you accept, how much insurance will pay toward your fees, if they are responsible for the difference between the insurance payment and the balance of your fees, if you give discounts, if you charge more to see two or more people together in a session, if you prescribe medication, if you are a Christian, if you are gay, if you are married, if you have children, and if you will see them on a Saturday or Sunday and if not, why not?

Somewhere in the midst of all of this, you need to attend to some of your own professional needs. Networking with other professionals can be a valuable time for you. It will give you the reality check you are looking for in comparing what others are doing in the community. Networking gives you the chance to compare notes on slow client times versus busy client times, new treatment facilities in the area, referral sources, upcoming workshops, and new therapy trends. Most of all, networking with colleagues gives you the opportunity to air out your worries or concerns about whether all of this is really worth it.

### *Solo, Joint, or Group Practice*

So, do you go it alone or pool your potential resources with others? There are pluses and minuses to each. Independent practice allows you freedom; you are your own boss, with all of the rights and accouterments attached to independence. Solo practice is more expensive, since you will be responsible for all of the costs of doing business (discussed later). Solo practice is also lonely. If you decide to go this route, we strongly suggest that you have experienced colleagues and/or a clinical supervisor with whom to consult about cases, procedures, and independent private practice issues that will arise.

Joint practice with another therapist offers a sharing of expenses, someone with whom to discuss cases, as well as someone with whom to have a conversation throughout the day. Often, it is pleasant just to hear someone else rumbling around in the office. It is also very comforting to have another professional around if a potentially violent or explosive client comes in for a session. In joint practice, you must consider someone else's needs and schedule, especially if you share a secretary, group room, bathroom, or office equipment.

Group practice has the same advantages and disadvantages as joint practice, only multiplied by however many people share the practice. It is comparable to the difference between being a couple and being a family. Each individual has his or her distinct needs and ways of accomplishing those needs. The larger the group, the more negotiation and compromise skills each must have.

Whichever kind of practice you intend to have, you must have a system for dealing with emergency and on-call coverage. Your clients must have access to you, or your representative, 24 hours a day, seven days a week, weekends and holidays. If you are in a solo practice, you are *it!* You might consider trading emergency coverage with another professional who is in a similar position. If you are in a joint practice, you and your colleague can decide whether to trade on-call duty with each other, or each counselor cover his or her own clients and emergencies. In a group practice, you are far more likely to be on call the number of days in a month divided by the number of professionals in your practice. This is mitigated by who is able to practice independently according to your state laws. Those who cannot practice independently cannot legally and ethically be on call.

Remember, your clients really do not want to talk with a different therapist after they have begun working with you. They will if they have to, but that is not their preference. We suggest that you notify your clients, in advance, when you will not be available and who will be, so that they are not surprised if they call during an emergency.

> *Example:* We tell our clients when we are going out of town. We explain that we will be checking our telephone messages every evening between 7:00 and 8:00 P.M. and to leave us a message and we will call them that night to deal with whatever the problem is. If they cannot wait for our return call, they should go to the Emergency Room at the nearest hospital. We have returned calls while in Europe, fishing in Yellowstone, and diving in the Florida Keys. Our clients call only when they really need some help and they truly appreciate the fact that we will spend some time with them, regardless of where we are or what we are doing.

### Specialist or Generalist

In this day of competition for mental health dollars, most new graduates think that specialization is the way to go. Many have worked with a particular population during practicum or internship, and feel comfortable and knowledgeable about helping with that kind of client or diagnostic issue. We caution you against too specific or too narrow a practice, simply because it is not economically feasible to do so. We strongly believe that you need to have a general practice and be able to treat most problems that are presented to you. Of course, you will gain experience the longer you work in the field. As you amass experience, one or two areas may pique your interest, or you may develop an affinity with that population, or you may want to pursue additional training in a particular area. That is when you need to consider adding a specialization to your general practice. A specialization can become a great way of getting referrals from other counselors, physicians, attorneys, and others. It is highly unlikely, however, that you will be able to practice exclusively based on your specialty or specialties.

> *Example:* In our practice, we do clinical counseling, working with all sorts of people, problems, and diagnoses. We also specialize in personality disorders, eating disorders, and attention deficit hyperactivity disorders.

## Building a Referral Base

Begin building a referral base even before you plan to open your doors. Getting the word out about who you are and what kind of problems or populations you treat is very important. Send a letter or brochure about yourself and your services to local physicians in your community. If you plan to work with children, contact local pediatricians. If you work with couples and families, contact local family practice attorneys. Offer to conduct some inservice workshops to businesses or business/social groups in your area. Popular topics are communication issues, violence in the workplace, and anything dealing with stress management. Make sure that you are knowledgeable about your subject and able to do public speaking. Write an article about a specific mental health issue and treatment for your neighborhood newspaper. Attend your local professional association meetings, introduce yourself, and give a brief description of your practice treatment focus. Other professionals will make referrals if clients are beyond their training or scope of practice. Once you start working with clients, they will become your best source of future referrals—word of mouth. Building a referral base takes time and nurturing. Avail yourself of as many opportunities to advertise yourself as you possibly can.

## Competing with Other Professionals in the Community

Wherever you decide to practice, there will be other mental health providers practicing there, too. Unless you are in a very small community, there will always be plenty of clients to go around. Human beings always have problems and the need to resolve them. When you establish your niche, you will find that other professionals will accept you and will refer clients to you. With experience and a good clinical reputation, you will eventually be able to hold your own amidst whatever the competition.

## Establishing Your Fees

In a community with a large number of providers, fees may vary considerably, depending on degrees, experience, and specialties. Fee variance affects the client's choice of provider.

Some clients really do "shop around" to find the cheapest cost of therapy, and some clients recognize that they will get what they pay for.

In most communities, fees are still established based on the medical model: psychiatrists charge the most (even for 15-minute medication management appointments), clinical psychologists have the next highest fees, and mental health counselors, marriage and family therapists, and clinical social workers have the lowest fees. All of these are referenced by education and years of experience. A new clinician is going to have a lower fee than a clinician with 20 years of experience. Someone with a Ph.D. will be able to charge more than someone with an M.A.

Talk with other professionals in your area and find out who charges what and for how long. Charging the same fee for a 60-minute hour as a 50-minute hour may make a difference in your community or it may not. Will you offer a 30-minute session* for a different fee (usually one-half the standard fee plus $5 to $10)? Call therapists' offices and ask about their fees, education, and experience. Generally speaking, new therapists charge a fee one-half to two-thirds of that of a senior same degreed/licensed/certified/titled therapist: psychologist to psychologist, counselor to counselor/social worker/marriage and family therapist.

When deciding on your fees for service, you must also decide if you will establish a fixed fee or offer a sliding fee scale, adjustments,† and pro bono work. A *fixed fee* means that every client is charged a standard rate for every session. A *sliding fee scale* is a reduced fee based on clients' income (get comparison fee scales from agencies and nonprofits). An *adjustment* is when you charge the standard fee and give a reduction based on clients' financial needs, or when you give a discount to another professional. *Pro bono* is either a no-charge session or a very minimal charge (up to $10 to $15) as a way of contributing your services back to the community.

After you set your fee schedule, make a decision about private pay and insurance. Private pay means that the client pays your fee completely (no insurance is involved). You will need to discuss when you expect payment for services with each client. If you become involved with insurance, understand that you have a few options. If your client pays you and you bill insurance for them (they receive the insurance payment), this is a private pay scenario. If you bill insurance and you get the payment, understand that it will generally be

---

*A 30-minute session has unique properties. It is useful when doing a maintenance session for a quick check-up on how the client is doing. It is less expensive than a regular session. It gives you a little break from a back-to-back session day. A 30-minute session rarely works in the initial phases of therapy, because there is just not enough time to get the background information or begin the necessary interventions for competent treatment. Once clients are used to a full session, however, they will have difficulty working in half the time, and expect you to be as wise and work as much as you would in a full session. There is more demand on you to be a timekeeper in a shorter session. If you let them, clients will keep talking long after you tell them their time is up.

†Adjustments are just that, an adjustment to the standard fee. If you plan to bill insurance, you must charge the same fee to everyone; otherwise, an insurance company can come back to you and demand a refund because you charged other clients lower fees (the insurance company does not have to pay the higher charge). Charge the same fee to everyone, then use an adjustment to consider special needs. That way, if your fees are ever audited or reviewed, your records will show the same fee for each and every client, with an adjustment on an as needed basis. If you plan to offer reduced fees often, we suggest a sliding fee scale rather than adjustments, because a sliding fee scale is consistent among income categories.

four to six weeks before you receive your money, unless there are problems. You still must settle the matter of the copayment with the client. Some therapists collect the copayment at each session, some collect a part of it once a month, some collect it after the insurance payment has been received.

Standard practice these days is to have a statement of financial responsibility added to your statement of informed consent (see The Cost of Doing Business). Having the client sign and date these agreements is considered a legal document, which will often make collection of fees easier.

## Managed Care and Third-Party Reimbursement

### Some History

To become knowledgeable in this field, you will need some general information about insurance plans, acronyms, and more. Here is a quick overview. All forms of insurance benefits, including managed care policies (HMOs, PPOs, PPCs, POSs) and indemnity plans, encompass what is called third-party reimbursement. *Third-party reimbursement,* simply put, is when an insurer, or its intermediary, makes a payment on a health care claim. Health maintenance organizations (HMOs) place greater emphasis on prevention and maintaining wellness and less on tertiary care. HMOs traditionally offer little coverage for mental health services. Preferred provider organizations (PPOs) and preferred provider care (PPCs) essentially offer more comprehensive care, but control costs by contracting with preferred providers, those licensed professionals willing to provide services for the payment level agreed to in the contract with the PPO/PPC. Newly on the scene is a point of service, meaning that the point of service (the provider of services) is the choice of the consumer, giving freedom of choice to the consumer, and can be a freestanding plan or a rider on any managed care plan. *Managed care,* simply put, is when the health care policy (e.g., PPO, PPC, HMO) or category of coverage (e.g., mental health claims) is controlled by a managed care intermediary, for a self-insured corporation, or is a subset of an insurance corporation. All large insurers (e.g., Blue Cross, Prudential, and Aetna) have established their own HMOs and PPOs and sometimes serve as the intermediary for self-insured corporations.

In the 1960s, nearly all health care insurance policies sold in the United States were indemnity plans. As a result, nearly all state law was originally passed to regulate indemnity insurance. When health care costs began to rise rapidly in the 1970s, HMOs were born to control both costs and the utilization of services. The shift from indemnity to managed care continued, and today, more than 90 percent of health care policies in many states are some form of managed care. Laws were eventually written to regulate HMOs. By now, with insurance utilization and costs rising, there was a shift away from control by providers and consumers, toward more control from the insurance industry. Today, the insurance industry spends millions of dollars each year lobbying state and federal legislatures for continued control. The public knows that HMOs, PPOs, PPCs, and so on are not the panacea they were thought to be, and in fact may deliver inferior health care. However, control still remains with the insurance industry.

The employee benefits of a *self-insured corporation* fall under federal control. Federal benefits standards, known as ERISA standards, were created by Congress to control all benefits offered to employees by self-insured companies, including health care, when it is seen as a benefit of employment. ERISA stands for the Employee Retirement Income Security Act of 1974. Ironically, these federal standards, which were written to protect the rights of employees of the larger, mainly self-insured corporations, gave control of the policy design to the self-insured corporation. Health care insurance was seen as a company benefit. Policies written for the employees of a self-insured company can include or exclude any type of health care service or any category of provider they wish. As a result, licensed mental health counselors have trouble being included on the provider panels of self-insured corporations' health care policies.

There may be an exception to ERISA that has not been fully litigated. In July 1992, the Fourth Federal Circuit Court (Richmond, VA) handed down a decision in the matter of *Stuart Circle Hospital* v. *Aetna Health Management,* File No. 91-736. This was a fairly complicated decision, but in the main, it provides that a state's PPO statute regulates the business of insurance, finding that it *prohibits the unreasonable restriction of the insured's choice of physician and hospital.* Virginia has very strong "any willing provider" and "freedom of choice" statutes (the consumer, by state law, has the right to see the provider of his or her choice). This issue may still be under litigation. The decision may mean that if there are strong state statutes providing freedom of choice to consumers, ERISA standards *may not* preempt them. State law is preempted by federal law, specifically ERISA, with the possible exception of statutes that govern the business of law.

## To Be or Not to Be a Managed Care Provider

Each counselor who is offered an opportunity to contract to provide services as a participating or preferred provider in a managed care plan must make some decisions about the provisions of the provider contract. There are pros and cons of any business decision, yet if you are in business for yourself, you must act and do what you think is best. Deciding whether to participate in managed care contracts is such a decision. You will find yourself making decisions about the contracted fees known as *UCRs (usual and customary remittance), the number of sessions allowed,* and *the frequency and length of sessions.* The number and length of sessions allowed may or may not consider what is best for the consumer's welfare. You will make these decisions based on the best information you can gather about the current mental health service delivery market. Whether you like it or not, you must market yourself and your services (products), just as any other entity that sells a product. Here are some considerations about managed care contracts and payments that may help you decide what to do.

***Pros.*** Your name will be listed in preferred provider publications by the insurer. The Blue Cross Corporations in each state, for example, regularly print and update provider lists for their members. This means you are on the list of providers that the client sees and from which he or she chooses a provider. It is one way of placing your name before the consumer. You may receive referrals directly from the insurer or managed care entity, especially if serving as an intermediary who manages mental health care in your area for a self-insured corporation. You may find it easier to begin practice by having some regular referral sources on which to count. Participating in a managed care panel should provide you with such referrals.

The alternative is to market yourself and generate all referral sources yourself via face-to-face meetings with referring sources such as other health care professionals, corporate departments of human resources, employee assistance programs, and the like. You will be working for a low fee and may have the chance to see more clients. As a result, you will gain in expertise proportionately to the numbers of client hours you experience.

***Cons.***     What would happen if every licensed mental health counselor was placed on managed care provider panels? In most cases, we would have successfully obtained employment for our professionals at near subsistence income levels. In other words, *minimum wage!* It is very hard to raise a family and offer your children the educational tools needed to survive in the twenty-first century on these wages. Managed care contracts can be restrictive as to treatment methods and number of sessions allowed. External controls on the professional can feel very intrusive. Sometimes, restrictions of client services may feel like they go against ethical and professional guidelines. No contract can force you to act against your better judgment. You may simply speak to the client about the perceived dilemma and point out the restrictions in his or her insurance. The client is getting what he or she pays for. Buy a cheap policy, get minimal coverage and provider access. Since the fees you contract to work for will be low, you will work more hours.

> *Example:* We have a friend working for several managed care companies in southern Florida. He sees up to 20 clients per day, three days per week. We wonder how he can see up to 60 clients in three days and we also wonder what the quality of care is after the first 10 clients each day. This is a very hard way to make a living.

It is a commonly held belief that there has been a concerted effort in our nation to limit the income of licensed mental health counselors to about that of a public school teacher. In our practice in Florida, Blue Cross's PPC and HMO offers us 25 percent of our normal fee, which is already two-thirds of the fees of Ph.D.s in Florida.

As you can see, there remain many road blocks that control and limit access to insurance benefits, even in the most progressive states. Yet, in today's market, counselors can compete if they are willing to work for the payment offered by the managed care company. Times are not what they were 20 years ago. In those days, if you provided good services, clients would come. The word got around in the medical community and a referral base developed. In today's market, a physician may not be able to refer to you unless you are on the client's panel, despite your qualifications. Today's licensed professionals must spend at least one-third of their weekly time marketing their practice. You must work to gain inclusion on managed care panels if you choose to go that route. The choice of not participating in managed care panels at this writing may be an even more difficult choice, as you are immediately limiting your practice to clients with policies such as point of service plans that will allow them to see the provider of their choice. Another alternative is to offer a lower fee for service for those clients whose insurance has no mental health coverage or will not accept you as a provider. We find many colleagues in private practice who work around managed care this way. Some of them work in a series of part-time jobs—such as their practice, consulting, teaching, and the like—to exist as freestanding practitioners.

Despite these difficult business decisions, it is likely that we would choose counseling as a profession if we had to make that decision again today. Private practice is not for the timid!

## Joining Managed Care

Taking the philosophical leap to managed care was, for us, the hardest step. We, who have been working in the field for 20 or more years, find the restrictions and controls of managed care to be very intrusive. It should be much easier for the beginning practitioner. The bottom line is that you must have a referral base to survive. In order to gain the experience needed to become a seasoned professional, gain recognition in your community, and develop a reputation for quality work, you may well need to pursue third-party reimbursement from managed care payers. Otherwise, your client population are those clients who can afford to pay your fee out of pocket. We also recommend that beginning counselors see clients who have no insurance on a reduced fee basis. We recommend that all licensed counselors do some pro bono work for the good of the community. It is also free advertising and a way of becoming known in your community, but it will not pay the bills. To bill for insurance coverage, you must choose to be either a participating or a nonparticipating provider. Many managed care policies do not accept any form of nonparticipating providers. So, as a beginning practitioner, it is wise to apply to be accepted on provider panels of managed care plans.

**Getting on Panels.**    It would seem that insurers would accept anyone willing to work for a reduced fee, but this is not the case. Insurers limit their panels as a way of limiting access to services and limiting utilization. Further, insurers who contract with providers become liable for the services of the provider; therefore, insurers want control over who works for them. In addition, many insurers still do not know what licensed counselor's credentials and scope of practice are. Educating insurers becomes a major aspect of marketing the profession and needs to be an important goal for marketing counselors, by professional associations and practices, alike.

We suggest that you approach your local, state, and national professional associations to obtain a list of insurers and managed care companies that sell and manage all health care insurance, including mental health benefits in your area. Apply to all of them. Many panels will be filled and thus closed to new applicants. Be persistent. Sometimes the squeaky wheel does get the oil.

**Applying for Independent Provider Numbers.**    Your first applications for provider status should be sent to basic health care insurers in your area, such as Blue Cross, and if you are in an area with military installations, Tricare (formerly Champus) is a must. Sometimes insurance companies will dominate a large portion of the market in a community or state, such as Kaiser Permanente in California. Apply! Apply! Apply! These insurers will assign you a provider number after you complete their applications and meet their educational, licensing, and liability insurance guidelines. Provider numbers are often your corporate employer identification number (EIN), your social security number, or a number assigned by the insurer. Now, your foot is in the door. Your provider number will eventually be published in documents shared among insurers. Insurers will begin to know who you are.

***Contracts.***    It is important for you to understand that if you become a panel provider for a managed care company, you will sign a contract with the insurer that spells out the terms of the contract. Those terms will include, but are not limited to, the following: the fee you may charge for specific services; the amount paid by the consumer and by the insurer; limits in service or the number of sessions authorized; and the methods for requesting additional sessions, recordkeeping, outpatient treatment reports, and other reports that must be routinely sent to the insurer. These are detailed legal contracts between you and the insurer, covering virtually every contingency of the provider-insurer relationship. The contract is binding until the contract is terminated by provisions cited within the contract. We recommend that you seek the assistance of a seasoned professional in your professional community who has dealt with many such contracts to help you with your first few contracts. Help also may be found in your local or state professional association. If no mentor is available, seek the assistance of a competent contract attorney. That attorney may well assist you for little or no fee on the chance of receiving referrals or further work from you in the future. Do not be afraid to ask about a discount.

***Limits to Practice.***    Indemnity policies were among the first written for health care services. They control access and utilization, and the overall costs of treatment was a matter between the professional and the patient. The utilization and cost of health care has risen rapidly since the 1960s. Managed care companies were created as an alternative to indemnity policies. The job of managed care is to do just that—manage and control as many aspects of health care delivery as possible, so as to control costs.

Treatment methodologies are going to be affected by limits in frequency or the number of sessions. There is not much sense in attempting to use a dynamic or psychoanalytical model when you are limited to six sessions. Managed care is one reason our profession has moved toward cognitive-behavioral, directive, and brief psychotherapy treatment models in the last two decades. In a managed care model, clients must be evaluated and diagnosed quickly. Insights must be shared, and treatment plans with behaviorally stated goals and objectives created. The number of sessions remaining of the total number of sessions authorized by a managed care company is what is available for treatment. On average, the total number of sessions authorized by many HMO plans is six sessions. As you can imagine, you will be busy trying to sort out and treat patient issues very quickly. PPOs and PPCs allow for a broader range of services, but often set annual limits (e.g., $1,000 per calendar year for outpatient mental health services). POS policies allow the consumer to go to the provider of his or her choice, but service limits and UCRs do not vary, whether you are a participating provider or not.

## Third-Party Reimbursements: Your Fee versus the Managed Care Fee

Participating providers for HMOs, PPOs, PPCs, and POSs are paid a flat rate by both the insurer and the client. HMO policies generally pay less and the client's portion, known as the *copayment,* is generally limited to a dollar amount (e.g., $10 per session). PPOs and PPCs often agree to pay a percentage of the UCR (usual and customary remittance) or rate of payment set by the PPO/PPC for a specific service. Imagine this hypothetical scenario:

Your fee, for instance, might be $100 per hour. The PPO may establish a UCR for an hour of psychotherapy at $50 per hour. The PPO agrees to pay 80 percent of $50, or $40, and the patient pays 20 percent, or $10. You must write off 50 percent of your hourly fee.

Health care for self-insured corporations are often managed by a larger insurance company. Nervous and mental claims are often split out and managed by a freestanding managed care corporation, serving as the independent contractor for the insurer or the self-insured corporation.

Many indemnity, PPO, and PPC policies set a deductible that is the responsibility of the subscriber. Deductibles are generally annual. When the consumer begins to use his or her health care policy at the beginning of the policy year, the deductible amount, which is a term of the policy, is deducted from claims made on the policy, until the deductible amount has been reached. The insurer begins to pay his or her contracted portion of the difference for claims in excess of the deductible over the calendar year. Copayments, as previously stated, are the portions of the claims that are the patient's responsibility. This is the contracted amount, and not necessarily the actual balance.

*Adjustments* are exceptions to your normal fees that must be documented. For example, using a base fee of $100 per hour, let's say you are a participating or contracted provider for some insurers, at a rate of $50 per hour, while other insurers contract with you at $75 per hour. If you do not document the contracted difference on each client's billing record, then the insurer paying $75 per hour has the legal right to sue you for the difference between their contracted fee and the lowest fee you charge. Therefore, in each client's billing record, you must document the contractual agreement and note the adjustment from your normal fee and the contracted fee (e.g., $100/hour billed; PPO pays $40; client pays $10; contractual adjustment $50; balance $0). Suffice it to say that all contractual adjustments must be documented, or you open yourself to liability.

When you achieve the lofty position of a senior professional in your community, you reach a point where you may decide to become a *nonparticipating provider*. If you withdraw from managed care panels and become nonparticipating, you will lose any referrals you were receiving from them. They will remain with the contracted providers who accept a lower fee. You must pursue referrals on your own, from other professionals, the phone book, and word-of-mouth referrals from previous clients. You may set up reduced rates for uninsured clients, installment payments, and other creative ideas that will help you remain in private practice. If you have become listed as an independent provider with several insurers, you will have established provider numbers and be incorporated into a national register of providers. Even if you have not applied to a specific insurer, the company will be able to locate you in your community and could decide to recognize you as a nonparticipating provider. Under those circumstances, the insurer will pay you the agreed UCR for nonparticipating providers. You may then choose to bill the client for all or part of the balance. Please remember, even in this instance, any adjustment you make in a fee must be fully documented, or you risk the liability of having to repay an insurer for part of their UCR. Billing practices should be made available to each client or posted in the waiting room. Our notice simply states that the consumer will be responsible for the difference between our fee and the payment made by the insurer, if any. We operate in a fee-for-service environment. Clients coming to us for treatment know that there is a fee. The majority also know whether their insurance covers mental health care, or can find out by contacting the insurer. There are times in our practice when clients have no insurance or do not wish us to bill their insurance due to their fear that their employer can somehow access those records. This may be real in a self-insured company. We have a billing policy that governs all circumstances, from contracted fees to our professional decisions. We do some contractual work, sometimes have "starving student" rates, do pro bono work, or issue discounts to other professionals and people to whom we wish to give a break. In all instances, we document those decisions in a billing record. All potential clients seeking information about our practice hear the basic fee and billing policy. Exceptions are a private matter.

## The Cost of Doing Business

### Overhead Expenses

Office space is your greatest ongoing operational expense. You can rent your own office, share an office, or rent a room in someone else's office. This choice will depend on whether you are in solo, joint, or group practice. You might also use a home office, depending on the zoning in your area and whether you want privacy in your personal life. Remember, the fewer the people to share expenses, the greater the cost to each person. Some people choose to own their own building and sublet space. Unless you are in the financial position to do this, we recommend renting space.

Along with an office comes monthly utility bills (electric, water, and sewer), telephone bills, pagers, an answering service, and more. Utilities are often included, all or partially, in your rent. Telephone service includes buying or renting your equipment, monthly charges for your basic services (business line(s), emergency 911 coverage, Federal Communications Commission charges for interstate toll access, a surcharge for the telecommunications access system), optional services (additional listings, call forwarding, message waiting, directory advertising, memory call/mailbox), local usage charges, and then, of course, any long distance calls—plus tax.

A few words are in order about directory advertising. The advertisement that you place in the yellow pages of your local telephone directory is a very important source of information about you and your services. You will be astonished at how many potential clients will call for information about you based on this ad. It is a great resource for new clients. This comes with a hefty price tag, however. For a three-line listing in the yellow pages, you might pay from $150 to $250 *every month!* Plan this ad carefully and do not let the yellow pages advertising customer service representative talk you into anything more than you can realistically afford. Whatever you agree to, you will be paying for it for the life of that directory in which the ad appears. If you list yourself in multiple categories (e.g., Individual, Marriage, and Family Counselors, Counselors—Human Relations, etc.), the price of your monthly advertising goes up.

Another decision to consider is whether to carry a pager or a cell phone. You have to be reachable in case of emergencies. Perhaps you will use an answering service during the day that will also pick up your calls after office hours and forward them to you. If you decide to use a voice-mail system for your calls, you still must have some other system in place for emergencies.

Now comes the question about having a secretary. Secretaries are wonderful to have. They are your front line for telephone inquiries, they are your greeters for clients coming to a session, and they produce an enormous amount of typing, report writing, letters, and perhaps billing and insurance, if you do not have a billing clerk. The question is: Can you afford a secretary? He or she requires a salary, insurance coverage, vacation pay, sick leave, and a retirement plan, depending on whether you incorporate. We suggest that you begin without a secretary. See what you can accomplish yourself, first. You will still be the one who writes the letters and reports. A secretary just takes your work and puts it into a more presentable form. You can easily learn to do just that with a good word processor on your computer. You will know what is going on in your practice if you learn how to do your own billing and insurance. There are lots of good computer billing programs to set up the format for you. All you will have to do is put in your statistics (date, type of sessions, and payments received). The insurance billing programs operate similarly. In the very near future, most insurers will expect billing to be done electronically.

Establish a bank account strictly for the practice. It will be much easier for you to track your income and expenses with a dedicated account. All expenses that relate to your practice should be paid by the practice. This checking account will create a paper trail for you that will make your professional life a little easier. (Financial reporting will be discussed later.)

Your license(s) and certification(s) are generally renewed annually or biannually. You will receive information about those charges whenever you initially apply for the credential(s). You may also be required by city ordinance to register for an Occupational or Trade License (refer to Getting Started), which is generally an annual renewal.

Additional overhead expenses include any expenditure that is business related. If you attend a professional meeting or conference, the cost of the conference, your hotel room, meals, gas or fare, coffee, juice, water—are all business expenses. If you have a meal with someone and discuss your practice, if you travel (car, plane, train, or ship) to conduct the business of mental health, if you take someone to play golf or tennis and discuss business, all of these are business-related expenses and should be paid by your practice. Keep receipts of *everything,* even that cup of coffee. A good accountant can help you set up your system for accounts receivable and accounts payable, advise you on what you can claim as legal expenses, and explain how to maintain records in case of an audit by the Internal Revenue Service.

We advise that you have a billing clerk, a certified public accountant (CPA), and an attorney available to you when you need them. Each can be hired as contracted services on an as-needed basis. A billing clerk will bill your client accounts and insurance claims, if you decide not to do these yourself. A CPA will be absolutely necessary and invaluable in helping you set up your financial accounts and reporting system (refer to Financial Reports). An attorney will be very helpful if you encounter being subpoenaed or deposed, the threat of a suit, collection of past due accounts, and/or bad checks received.

## Business Forms

Several standard forms will be needed in order to see clients. These are simple to design. They consist of an Application for Services, a Statement of Informed Consent, Progress Notes, letterhead, business cards, appointment cards, and receipts.

Chapter 6

*Application for Services.*   The application should request the following information: name of client, address, telephone number, birth date, age, marital status, place of employment, telephone number at employment, social security number, spouse/next of kin (and address, if different), who to notify in case of an emergency (include name, address, and telephone number), previous professional treatment, psychiatric hospitalization(s), current medications (including dosage), health insurance information, a brief description of the problem for which the client is seeking services, and the referral source. Have a line for the client's signature and date, and a second line for the signature of the parent or guardian, if necessary, and date. These signatures give you legal permission to provide treatment. Also include on the application a statement about confidentiality, such as, *The information contained herein is confidential.* Ask colleagues for a copy of their applications and compare. Over the next few years, you will discover what information you really need on your application. Your application should be a formal document, so include your name, address, and telephone number printed on it.

*Informed Consent.*   This is a statement of who you are—your degree(s), license(s), certification(s), treatment methods, and fees. There should be a statement about confidentiality, including when confidentiality must be breached. Include a place for the client to sign and date the form, signifying their understanding of the covered information. Also on this page you can have a statement of client acknowledgment regarding the client's responsibility for payment of his or her account. This can be simply stated as *I acknowledge that I am financially responsible for the balance of my account.* This could be placed on the application, if you prefer. This simple statement will be very helpful if you have to pursue payment legally.

*Progress Notes.*   Progress Notes are basically sheets of paper with horizontal lines on which to write your contact notes (session content, telephone calls, documentation of written correspondence from you, etc.). Progress Notes should have a place for the client's name (at the top or bottom), client case number (optional), a place for the date/time of the contact, and perhaps the CPT (Physicians' Current Procedural Terminology) code for individual, family, group session, and so on. You may choose to include your name and address printed on Progress Notes if you wish.

*Letterhead.*   Your letterhead is a visible representation of you, so choose the paper, ink, and printing style carefully. Think about how you want to be seen, professionally. The letterhead should include your name, degree(s), license(s), certification(s), title(s), address, telephone number, fax number, and e-mail address. You will use letterhead for all official correspondence that goes out of your office. E-mail and faxes will not replace the need for letterhead. We suggest that your matching envelopes have only your return address. Not listing your name as part of the return address is one more way of trying to provide confidentiality once paperwork leaves your office. It is subtle yet appreciated by many clients.

***Business Cards.*** You will need business cards to give to clients as well as potential clients, other professionals, and referral sources. Business cards should have the same information as on your letterhead.

***Appointment Cards.*** Appointment cards can be a separate entity or can be printed on the reverse side of your business card. Some clients want a written record of their next appointment, some do not. Also state your policy about cancellations or missed appointments and charges on this card. For example: *24-hour notice of cancellation is required to avoid being charged*. You will have fewer missed appointments or calls to check on appointment times if you give an appointment card.

***Receipts.*** After every session or charge to the client, you should give a receipt that includes the date of service, the kind of service, the charge for the service, the amount of payment ($0.00, if no payment), and the current balance of the account. When a payment is received, a receipt should be written. Receipts should include the same information about you as on your business card. They should also include your policy about cancellations or missed appointments.

## Marketing Yourself

In order to build your practice and keep it healthy and viable, you will need to invest some ongoing time and energy in marketing. There are two ways to market yourself: formally and informally.

*Formal* marketing includes advertisements in your local telephone white and yellow pages. Earlier we gave you some idea of the cost of this particular service and its benefits. A name, address, and telephone number listing in the business section of the white pages, as well as the residential section, is an easy reference for your current clients or potential clients who have already learned of your name.

Other forms of advertising include ads in local and neighborhood newspapers, local magazines, and brochures to distribute to possible referral sources. Put a small ad (business-card size) in the newsletter of a business or social group, see what response you get from it, and then decide whether to advertise that way again. Not everything you try will work, but you will learn from it all.

Place an announcement of the opening of your practice in the Metro, Community, or Arts and Entertainment section of the Sunday newspaper. Newspaper space is also expensive, so be careful. Design a small professional ad that gives the same information as on your letterhead, including the opening date of your office. If you have specialties, list them, but not at great additional space or expense. In this case, understated is better.

Another tool to consider is a brochure. This is a way to list all of your pertinent information in a descriptive style for distribution. Brochures can accompany any other correspondence that you send out as well as distributed at speaking engagements, business and social groups, and anywhere you may meet potential referrals or referral sources.

*Informal* advertising is using the same strategies that we discussed earlier in Building a Referral Base. Just because you spoke to those people once does not mean that your work is finished. You will need to do periodic maintenance to continue your relationship with your referral sources.

## *Whether to Incorporate*

Incorporation is not necessary when you first begin your practice, but you should consider it after your first year or so. Incorporation brings with it many benefits. The primary benefit of incorporation is the protection of your personal assets. Incorporation allows your practice to pay for all your professional expenses from your gross income rather than your net income. It sets you up as a small business rather than as an individual delivering services. Incorporation also increases your accountability and financial paperwork. When considering incorporating, talk to a CPA and an attorney. Both can advise you on the process involved, the financial reporting required, and the legal protection offered by incorporation in your state. You will most likely become an S corporation, but you should become educated about which type of corporation will best suit your needs.

## *Financial Reports*

If you are not incorporated, you will still have to file financial reports, primarily through your annual income tax. If you have kept good records in your practice bank account, this will be an easy process, since you will have records of all deposits and expenses relating to your practice.

If you have incorporated, the amount of financial reporting increases dramatically. Again, a CPA can get you started or can be hired to do the numbers work for you. Most of these documents are easy to do once you understand the formulas involved. You will be dealing with the federal government, the Internal Revenue Service, and your state and municipal governmental agencies. Each has its own forms, which will be sent to you via the mail. Some are an annual process, most are quarterly. Here are a few examples of the documentation:

- *Federal forms.* In addition to your personal income tax, you will need to file an annual corporate tax return, which is due by March 15th each year. Also, you will need to file a Federal Annual Unemployment (FUTA-940) Return every year. On a quarterly basis, you will file an Employer's Quarterly Federal Tax Return (941). All of these come from and are returned to the Internal Revenue Service.
- *State forms.* Once you incorporate, you will be sent a Corporation Annual Report from your state's Department of State. This documents that your corporation is still in existence and that your Officers and Directors are current. Also, you will need to file an annual Intangible Personal Property Tax Return with your state's Department of Revenue. On a quarterly basis, you will also file an Unemployment Compensation Employer's Quarterly Report with the state's Division of Unemployment Compensation.
- *Municipal forms.* Annually, the Property Appraiser will send you forms for filing your Tangible Personal Property Tax Return.

### *Practice Cycles: A Final Caution*

Interestingly, there are cycles influencing when and why consumers choose to seek psychotherapy. Our observations about the cycles are not scientific, but we wish to share them anyway. Since we have been in practice, we have seen emotional cycles that affect consumers and motivate them to seek help. In the fall and early winter, at the beginning of the holiday season, we have long observed that many people experience a nonenergetic depression. Such depression can be related to aging, loss of family relationships (via loss of spouse due to death or divorce), or loss of children due to maturation (the empty-nest syndrome). We have also observed that some marital relationships enter crises after the Christmas/holiday season. Another cycle seen is a more energetic depression that seems associated with the onset of spring, and the need to grow, renew oneself, and self-doubts almost indigenous in many people. We have also observed that more parents seek therapy about the time that school lets out, and that students seem to need professional attention most often about the time that school begins again in the fall. Our business often decreases just before major holidays and during high summer, but always seems to gear up again after each fall. You will also notice cycles that affect your treatment populations, that may seem stable enough that you will be able to take a vacation. These observations are not scientific, but they do help us conceptualize the potential needs of our clients. Be watchful and see if you notice similar patterns

We leave you with one final thought: We hope you will perform so as to gain *your own approval* that you did your best. We would also suggest that you place a *Do No Harm* placard in your office which, though meant for you, may also be taken as advice by your clients.

# 7

# Ethics and Counseling Practice

## Robert H. Pate Jr.

*Robert (Bob) Pate Jr. began his professional career as a professor at St. Andrews Presbyterian College in North Carolina. From there, he spent a year as a visiting professor at Oxford and Cambridge Universities in England under the auspices of George Peabody College. He has been a professor of counselor education at the University of Virginia since 1968, serving as chair of the Department of Human Services and Interim Dean of the Curry School of Education. Pate received his B.A. in psychology from Davidson College, and his M.A. and Ph.D. from the University of North Carolina at Chapel Hill. His professional services are extensive, including six years (one as chair) on the board of directors of the National Board for Certified Counselors (NBCC), member of the American Association of State Counseling Boards Test Committee, member of the Virginia Counselors Association Board of Directors, and member of the Virginia Department of Education School Counselor Advisory Committee. In addition to his long-time interest in professional ethics, Pate is interested in the relationship of spirituality to counseling and to legal aspects of counseling. In his private life, he is an active church member, an avid reader of novels, and a committed grandfather of four.*

## In This Chapter...

- Why does counseling have ethical standards when other careers that require similar amounts of education either have no codes of ethics or certainly do not emphasize ethics?

- Where do the ethical codes come from? Who determines what is ethical, and on what basis are decisions about what is ethical behavior for professional counselors made?

- Why are the codes so similar? If codes of ethics for counselors can be similar, why do we need so many?

*Note:* Various quotations in this chapter are reprinted from American Counseling Association, *Code of Ethics and Standards of Practice: As Approved by Governing Council, April 1997 (Effective July 1, 1997).* © ACA. Reprinted with permission. No further reproduction authorized without written permission of the American Counseling Association.

By this stage in your journey as a counselor, you have been introduced to the idea of ethical standards that govern the practice of professional counseling. I trust you have read the Ethical Code and Standards of Practice of the American Counseling Association (ACA) and the Ethical Code and Standards for WebCounseling Practice published by the National Board for Certified Counselors (NBCC). You may have read even ethical codes for the specialized area of counseling of your choice. If you have not read these codes recently, stop here and read the ACA ethical standards (Appendix A) and the NBCC ethical standards (Appendix B).

After reading the referenced ethical standards and other statements about counseling ethics, you will likely have some questions. Among them might be the following:

- Some of the sections of the ethics statements are very specific while others are very general. Why are the sections so different?
- I thought state licensure laws governed the practice of counseling. Why do we need professional ethical standards in addition to laws to regulate counseling?
- Despite all the laws and ethical standards, we have discussed situations that do not seem to be covered by either. How is that possible?
- Good people—and those who want to enter counseling are good people—do not need ethical codes and bad people will not follow them. Why bother?

The purpose of this chapter is to provide a structure and information to allow you to explore questions about ethics in the profession of counseling. The ethical codes you will review do not provide guidance for every dilemma you will encounter in your career as a counselor but you will learn how to use ethics in your decision-making process. The chapter is not designed to teach the ethical response for various situations addressed by the ethical codes that should govern the behavior of members of the psychologically based helping professions.

The American School Counselor Association has an ethics section in its Internet site. That section is prefaced by a discussion of Immanuel Kant's Categorical Imperative as a basis for making ethical decisions. Likewise, the National Association of Social Workers Code of Ethics (1996) has a preface, purpose, and principles section that precedes the actual ethical standards. The NASW Code of Ethics addresses its own limitations by including the following statement:

> A code of ethics cannot guarantee ethical behavior. Moreover, a code of ethics cannot resolve all ethical issues or disputes, or capture the richness and complexity involved in striving to make responsible choices within a moral community. Rather a code of ethics sets forth values, ethical principles and ethical standards to which professionals aspire and by which their actions can be judged. (NASW, 1996)

## Why Do Some Occupational Groups Require Ethical Behavior of Members?

What exactly do we mean by professional ethics? We mean the codes of responsible professional behavior for certain occupations. The occupations are those which society has accorded special status and therefore provided the opportunity for abuse, absent some limitation on the practitioners' behavior. Individuals who are paid for certain activities are often labeled *professional*. Athletes and actors are referred to as professionals, the modifier separating the professional from those who engage in the same activity without pay. Occupations are also labeled as professions based on the level of skill of the practitioner. For example, *professional* secretaries have been accorded a special week, which has received wide recognition due in significant part to the advocacy of the floral industry. Our society often confuses a high level of skill with a profession. An individual may possess a high level of expertise and deserve to be called a professional in the sense that professional denotes a high level of skill. Certainly, those who truly earn the modifier *professional* have a high level of skill for which society is willing to award status and economic rewards. But in the sense that we will consider professions, the presence of pay and skill may entitle one to be called a *professional* but that does not make one's occupation a profession.

Members of an occupational group that are *true* professions have codes of behavior that are administered by those who are members of the occupational group. For the purposes of this chapter, I have followed the definition of a profession used by sociologists (e.g., Freidson, 1994). That definition requires members of a profession to accept responsibility for self-regulation in return for the privileges granted to its members. Lewis and Maude (1952) suggest that "a moral code is the basis of professionalism, though it may not always prove easy to stretch even this to such professions as journalism or the arts" (p. 64). The general theme the sociologists suggest is that a profession has responsibilities to the public and that typically codes of behavior are developed to guide members to accept those responsibilities. Ritchie (1990), who studied counseling, concludes that one hallmark of the evolution of counseling into professional status was the presence of ethical codes.

The members of the counseling professions ask society to grant them certain privileges. Note that I have deliberately used the singular to state *counseling profession*. Counselors are divided as to whether professional counseling is one profession with specialized areas of practice or a number of separate but closely related professions (Myers, 1995). Although I am among the group that thinks of counseling as one profession with areas of specialized practice and interest, for purposes of this chapter, I acknowledge the reality of separate professional identities and organizations that has produced numerous separate ethical codes. The desirability of separate ethical codes will be a later topic.

Among the privileges professional counselors expect to be accorded is the ability to hold positions in public schools that are denied to those who do not have prescribed education and experience. Likewise, counselors ask that those who meet certain standards be allowed to practice independently for a fee and to be reimbursed by third-party payers on the same basis as other qualified providers of mental health care. Other counselors who work in environments that do not demand a specified set of credentials want to be accepted as professionals by virtue of their qualifications and the characteristics of their profession. The public that grants status and privileges to professions has legitimate expectations of the members of the profession. In general, the expectations include competence of the counselor and the ability of the person receiving service to *trust* the provider of the service. The concept of trust or having faith in the provider of services is critical for counselors because the relationship between the helper and the helpee is essential to the success of the endeavor.

The members' acceptance of social responsibility is one step in the process of an occupation becoming a profession, and that responsibility leads to ethical codes that are administered by members. The violation of ethical codes can lead to revocation of professional privileges. Members of the professions that are granted privileges by society have the potential to use those privileges to harm members of the public. Associations of the members of the profession as well as governmental agencies enforce codes of behavior often called *ethical codes*. A licensed professional counselor (LPC) who violates ethical codes might be sanctioned by the revocation of counseling privileges by the state that issued the license, by forced removal from professional associations, and by revocation of the privilege of using credentials awarded by professional organizations. The person sanctioned by revocation would still possess a graduate degree in counseling but would no longer be a professional counselor because he or she could not legitimately practice.

This chapter is organized in the following major sections in which answers to the earlier questions are provided. The bases of ethical codes, the content of the codes, the enforcement of ethical codes, challenges in counseling ethics, and making ethical decisions will be addressed in major sections of the chapter.

# The Bases of Professional Ethical Codes

Ethical codes are one source of guidance for counselors but there are other sources of direction for decisions concerning behavior. Each person has a unique set of experiences that have influenced their concepts of proper behavior. Many of these experiences are the result of early teaching by parents and others important to the development of the individual. Early learning creates our value systems, and from those value systems and the influence of social institutions, we have general sets of personal guidelines that govern our behavior. Because early learning and experience are so important in the formation of values (a basic foundation of ethical systems), we need to be aware that the ethical codes of counseling are culturally based. The ethical codes you will study and that guide our professional behavior are based on a western cultural orientation and value system. Pederson (1997) has demonstrated the problems in basing our ethical standards on a limited worldview.

## How Do Good People Make Choices about Ethical Dilemmas?

In nearly all religious traditions, there is something akin to the Golden Rule. The principle of treating other people as we would like to be treated is certainly important, but as we mature in our ability to extend empathy to others, we try to treat others as *they* want to be treated. As our learning continues, we are exposed to other rules and systems for making decisions. For example, Rotary International, a civic organization, has a test of behavior that is often cited as a test for any anticipated behavior. The Rotary Four-Way Test is as follows:

1. Is it the TRUTH?
2. Is it FAIR to all concerned?
3. Will it BUILD GOODWILL and BETTER FRIENDSHIPS?
4. Will it be BENEFICIAL to all concerned?

Using the Rotary Test might help us in some life situations, but certainly each counselor can think of many situations for which the answers to the four Rotary questions would provide little direction.

In his 1995 book, *How Good People Make Tough Choices: Resolving the Dilemmas of Ethical Living,* Rushworth Kidder offers some suggestions to help with our thinking about resolving dilemmas. Because counselors are good people and the ethical dilemmas that they face are difficult, Kidder's concepts are one useful way to look at how we might make ethical choices.

Kidder suggests that *ethical dilemmas,* the decisions that are most difficult, typically involve right versus wrong choices. I would expand Kidder's concept to choosing the "least bad" or "most good" alternative. Kidder labels right versus wrong choices as *moral temptations.* A professional counselor's choice about an exploitative dual relationship would therefore not be a dilemma but a moral temptation to be resisted. Kidder suggests that the dilemmas we face typically require choices between truth and loyalty, individual and community, short term and long term, or justice and mercy. Counselors often face a truth versus loyalty decision when confronted with direct and specific client questions about which they have definite opinions. Individual versus community decisions can occur when counselors must decide who will receive scarce services. Choices between the short term and the long term often occur when counselors are forced to choose among preventive, developmental, and remedial services. Fortunately, most counselors are not placed in the role of administering consequences but some counselors face the justice versus mercy dilemma of how hard they should work to help counselees avoid the consequences of their behavior.

Kidder (1995) suggests that we make decisions based on ways of thinking that we believe appropriate to the circumstances. The ways of thinking are ends based, rule based, and care based. If counselors made decisions by *ends-based thinking,* they would attempt to determine the consequences of the alternative choices and make the choice that would produce the best outcome. If counselors were prophets and could forecast outcomes accurately, this would be the way we would make most decisions. However, since we cannot accurately forecast outcomes, we often rely on *rule-based thinking* because the rules are, or should have been, developed on the basis of collective experience and wisdom. Our ethical codes and standards of behavior contain the rules of behavior for counselors, but, as the National Association of Social Workers Code of Ethics (NASW, 1996) preface indicates, codes cannot address every dilemma. Even when there is a rule, rule-based thinking has its limitations because the rules just do not seem to fit all situations. What about *care-based thinking?* Counselors are often faced with questions about who to care for. Counseling journals during the past decade have contained numerous articles about the dilemma of attempting to build a helping relationship with a client or warning those who might be harmed by the client (e.g., Cohen, 1990; Erikson, 1993).

Scott (1998) suggests six major approaches to making ethical choices:

1. Looking to moral principles and drawing on traditional morality—deciding what is right and wrong
2. Applying moral strategies, using a pragmatic or utilitarian approach—deciding what is good or bad based on the outcome
3. Evaluating the situation, following appropriate rules—deciding what fits or does not fit the rules

4. Following one's intuition—acting based on intuition of what is proper
5. Following the pleasure or power principle—acting to gain the most personal benefit
6. Seeking the greater good—acting for what is best for most people in the long-term

The ethical dilemmas counselors face are not the result of any shortage of "good systems" by which ethical decisions can be made. The dilemmas are knowing which system to apply to a given question and, even harder, which element of the system should assume priority. Some guidance is available.

## How Do Counselors Make Decisions about Ethical Dilemmas?

Through various publications and programs sponsored by the American Counseling Association (ACA), counselors have learned that there are five general principles that guide the ethical conduct of counselors in relationships with those whom they serve:

1. *Autonomy* refers to independence and self-determination. Under this principle, counselors respect the freedom of clients to choose their own directions, make their own choices, and control their own lives. We have an ethical obligation to decrease client dependency and foster independent decision making. We refrain from imposing goals, avoid being judgmental, and are accepting of different values.
2. *Nonmaleficence* means to do no harm. As counselors, we must take care that our actions do not risk hurting clients, even inadvertently. We have a responsibility to avoid engaging in practices that cause harm or have the potential to result in harm.
3. *Beneficence* means to promote good or mental health and wellness. This principle mandates that counselors actively promote the growth and welfare of those they serve.
4. *Justice* is the foundation of our commitment of fairness in our professional relationships. Justice includes consideration of such factors as quality of services, allocation of time and resources, establishment of fees, and access to counseling services. This principle also refers to the fair treatment of an individual when his or her interests need to be considered in the context of the rights and interests of others.
5. *Fidelity* means counselors make honest promises and honor our commitments to clients, students, and supervisees. This principle involves creating a trusting and therapeutic climate in which people can search for their own solutions, and taking care not to deceive or exploit clients. (Herlihy & Corey, 1996, pp. 4–5)

Counseling is a helping profession with dilemmas similar to other professions with similar goals. The five principles, which are the basis of ACA ethical training on the topic of resolving ethical dilemmas, were the basis of a discussion of ethics in counseling psychology by Kitchner (1984). The bases suggested for making moral counseling decisions when faced with a dilemma are remarkably similar to those suggested for the medical profession in the current and earlier editions of a widely used text on biomedical ethics by Beauchamp and Childress (1995). Their four principles on which they base biomedical ethics are autonomy, nonmaleficence, beneficence, and justice. Beauchamp and Childress list the general ACA principle of fidelity among four principles relevant for professional/patient relationships. The other three principles they list as relevant for professional/patient relationships are veracity, privacy, and confidentiality. Those principles should also provide guidance for counselors as we attempt to make decisions about the proper action when we are faced with ethical dilemmas. Before applying the principles, counselors must know what their profession suggests as proper behavior. We must know the basic content of ethical codes for counselors.

## *Content of Ethical Codes for Counselors*

Codes of ethics for counselors are based on values, moral principles, and commonly accepted rules of proper behavior applied to situations counselors might face. An examination of the ethical statements of counselor organizations will lead the reviewer to conclude that there are similarities among ethical statements. If our analysis of guidelines of proper counselor behavior includes state regulations, we will discover that these statements overlap the practice standards that are part of many state licensure statutes or regulations that govern the practice of counseling in the jurisdiction. From reading the ACA and NBCC ethical statements, you should gain a perspective of the content typical of ethical statements affecting counselors.

In a text entitled *Psychology and the Law for the Helping Professions,* Swenson (1997) reports on his examination of 17 ethical statements. As a result of that examination, he organized the content of ethical statements into seven general areas and five areas that are related to specialized areas of counseling practice. The seven general areas are as follows:

1. Rules related to professional responsibility
2. Rules related to competence
3. Rules related to moral and ethical standards
4. Rules related to advertising (public statements)
5. Rules related to confidentiality
6. Rules related to the welfare of the consumer
7. Rules related to professional relationships

The five special situations or problems Swenson suggests are as follows:

1. Multiclient situations
2. Information and technology
3. Assessment
4. Research with human subjects
5. Care and use of animals

With the exception of the special situation or problem of dealing with animals, the 1995 ACA Ethical Standards are structured in a fashion consistent with Swenson's general outline. The sections in the ACA standards are as follows:

1. The counseling relationship
2. Confidentiality
3. Professional responsibility
4. Relationships with other professionals
5. Evaluation, assessment, and interpretation

6. Teaching, training, and supervision
7. Research and publication
8. Resolving ethical issues

The last item, which addresses resolving ethical issues, was considered "Collegial Enforcement of Ethical Codes" in Swenson's (1997, p. 85) analysis. Although the National Board for Certified Counselors is a certification board and not a membership organization, the structure of the NBCC code is consistent with the Swenson and ACA schemes. The NBCC Code sections are as follows:

1. General
2. Counseling relationship
3. Measurement and evaluation
4. Research and publication
5. Consulting
6. Private practice

The NBCC code contains material related to each of the Swenson sections with the exception of dealing with animals. The separate sections on consulting and private practice seem appropriate for an organization that deals with practitioners who tend to stress independent practice and who may use their credentials to promote their practices.

No matter what the formal structure of ethical codes, most reviewers agree that the content of codes is far from internally homogeneous. Some statements are very specific and give explicit guidance, other statements suggest principles on which counselors should make decisions, and still others talk about the kind of person a counselor should be. Codes are often divided into the elements that are aspirational—that is, what the counselor should aspire to be but that cannot easily or fairly be enforced—and mandatory. Mandatory elements are those that are specific enough to enforce through the disciplinary aspects of the codes. Despite the number of codes and the varied formats, I believe there are some consistent elements of the codes. An example of some of the elements I believe are common and essential to a complete ethical code for counselors will demonstrate instances of overlap and duplication in some areas and unique contribution in others. The examples will also illustrate the aspirational nature of some standards and the mandatory nature of others.

## Examples from ACA and NBCC Codes of Ethics

***Social Responsibility.*** The ACA code preamble states, "Association members recognize diversity in our society and embrace a cross cultural approach in support of the worth, dignity, potential and uniqueness of each individual." The NBCC code addresses the same topic in Section A: General, 12: "Through an awareness of stereotyping and unwarranted discrimination (e.g., biases based on age, disability, ethnicity, gender, race, religion, or sexual orientation), certified counselors guard the individual rights and personal dignity of the client in the counseling relationship." Other sections of the ACA code make statements that reinforce the social responsibility of the professional counselor. For examples, see C.2.a, C.5.a, and D.1.i of the ACA code.

*Professional Competence.*    Section A.6 of the NBCC code states, "Certified counselors offer only professional services for which they are trained or have supervised experience. No diagnosis, assessment, or treatment should be performed without prior training or supervision. Certified counselors are responsible for correcting any misrepresentations of their qualifications by others." Section C, Standard C.2.a. Boundaries of Competence of the ACA Code, states, "Counselors practice only within the boundaries of their competence, based on their education, training, supervised experience, state and national professional credentials, and appropriate professional expanse. Counselors will demonstrate a commitment to gain knowledge, personal awareness, sensitivity and skills pertinent to working with a diverse client population."

*Duty to Clients.*    The NBCC Code in Section B.1 Counseling Relationship, addresses duty to clients by stating, "The primary obligation of certified counselors is to respect the integrity and promote the welfare of clients, whether they are assisted individually, in family units, or in group counseling." Section A.1.a The Counseling Relationship of the ACA code is similar. It states, "The primary responsibility of counselors is to respect the dignity and to promote the welfare of clients."

*Dual Relationships.*    Dual relationships are troublesome dilemmas to many professional counselors. Examples of the conflict between serving clients in locations without alternatives to counselors forming counseling relationship with potential clients with whom they have some other relationship are often cited. The NBCC Code, Section A.8 and 9 states, "8. Certified counselors are aware of the intimacy in the counseling relationship and maintain respect for the client. Counselors must not engage in activities that seek to meet their personal or professional needs at the expense of the client. 9. Certified counselors must insure that they do not engage in personal, social, organizational, financial, or political activities which might lead to a misuse of their influence." The ACA Code includes the following statement about dual relationships.

> a. Avoid When Possible
> Counselors are aware of their influential positions with respect to clients, and they avoid exploiting the trust and dependency of clients. Counselors make every effort to avoid dual relationships with clients that could impair professional judgement or increase the risk of harm to clients. (Examples of such relationship include, but are not limited to, familial, social, business, or close personal relationships with clients.) When a dual relationship cannot be avoided, counselors take appropriate professional precautions such as informed consent, consultation, supervision, and documentation to ensure that judgement is not impaired and no exploitation occurs. (A.6. Dual Relationships)

Sexual dual relationships can be both a legal and an ethical issue. Sexual relationships with clients violate the practice standards that are incorporated in the statutes or regulations governing professional counseling in many states. In addition, sexual relationships with clients have been held by courts to be malpractice (e.g., *Simmons* v. *The United States,* 1986). This issue is of such concern that it merits separate statements in sections of codes related to relationships with clients. Despite the clear legal and ethical statements on the subject, sexual misconduct continues to be the most frequently reported ethical violation.

The statements of the codes used for this analysis illustrate the similarity of the codes on the subject of sexual misconduct. The NBCC Code A.10 states, "Sexual intimacy with clients is unethical. Certified counselors will not be sexually, physically, or romantically intimate with clients, and they will not engage in sexual, physical, or romantic intimacy with clients within a minimum of two years after terminating the counseling relationship." The ACA Code has a section (A.7) that addresses "Sexual Intimacies with Clients." That section states:

> a. Current Clients
> Counselors do not have any type of sexual intimacies with clients and do not counsel persons with whom they have had a sexual relationship.
> b. Former Clients
> Counselors do not engage in sexual intimacies with former clients within a minimum of two years after terminating the counseling relationship. Counselors who engage in such relationships after two years following termination have the responsibility to thoroughly examine and document that such relations did not have an exploitative nature, based on factors such as duration of counseling, amount of time since counseling, termination circumstances, client's personal history and mental status, adverse impact on the client, and actions by the counselor suggesting a plan to initiate a sexual relationship with the client after termination.

The two-year statement common in ethical codes is an example of common misconceptions. Many counselors have been led to believe that sexual relationships with former clients are always permissible after two years. A careful reading of the ACA code provides the proper perspective. It is only after two years that a counselor has an opportunity to establish that the sexual relationship is permissible.

***Confidentiality and Duty to Third Parties.*** Confidentiality is a hallmark of the profession of counseling, but how is an ethical requirement to maintain confidences of the client to be balanced with preventing harm to the client or others? The ACA Code B.1.a is clear: "Counselors respect their clients rights to privacy and avoid illegal and unwarranted disclosures of confidential information." The NBCC Code is equally clear in B.16: "The counseling relationship and information resulting from it remains confidential and, consistent with the legal and ethical obligations of certified counselors." The code balances the responsibility of the counselor to maintain confidence with the protection of clients and third parties. Although ethical codes recognized this dilemma before the California Court ruling (*Tarasoff* v. *Regents of the University of California at Berkeley,* 1976) that is now associated with the duty of counselors to third parties, ethical codes are now explicit in addressing the duty. The ACA Code in B.1.c provides a basis for allowing disclosure by stating, "Exceptions. The general requirement that counselors keep information confidential does not apply when disclosure is required to prevent imminent harm to the client or others or when legal requirements demand that confidential information be revealed. Counselors consult with other mental health professionals when in doubt as to the validity of an exception." The NBCC Code addresses the issue of protection of third parties by Section B.4:

> When a client's condition indicates that there is a clear and imminent danger to the client or others, the certified counselor must take reasonable action to inform potential victims and/

or inform responsible authorities. Consultation with other professionals must be used when possible. The assumption of responsibility for the client's behavior must be taken only after careful deliberation, and the client must be involved in the resumption of responsibility as quickly as possible.

Duty to third parties is addressed by state statutes in addition to ethics codes and case law. The general admonition that counselors become familiar with the statutes in regulations in the jurisdiction in which they practice is certainly appropriate when considering questions about disclosures to protect third parties or the client. For example, a Virginia statute requires disclosure to protect persons but not property (Code of Virginia, 1994).

***Professional Behavior.***     The NBCC Code addresses the duty of a counselor as a member of a profession in Section A.13, which states, "Certified counselors are accountable at all times for their behavior. They must be aware that all actions and behaviors of the counselor reflect on professional integrity and, when inappropriate can damage the public trust in the counseling profession. To protect public confidence in the counseling profession, certified counselors avoid behavior that is clearly in violation of accepted moral and legal standards." Section C of the ACA Code is entitled Professional Responsibility. Section C.3.c states, "Counselors make reasonable efforts to ensure that statements made by others about them or the profession of counseling are accurate." Ethical codes recognize the obligation of professional counselors to other members of their profession.

***Duty as a Behavioral Scientist.***     The NBCC Code (Section D.12) states, "Certified counselors should communicate to other counselors the results of any research judged to be of professional value. Results that reflect unfavorably on institutions, programs, services or vested interests are not withheld." Similarly, the ACA Code states, "Counselors communicate to other counselors the results of any research judged to be of professional value. Results that reflect unfavorably on institutions, programs, services, prevailing opinions, or vested interests are not withheld." The similarity of the statements is an example of the overlap and similarity among ethical codes for counselors.

## Enforcement of Ethical Codes

As the status and stature of professional counselors have grown so has the need for professional disciplinary processes that are fair to counselors and that protect those served by professional counselors. During my early professional education, the only ethics code of real concern was that of the American Personnel and Guidance Association, the antecedent organization of ACA. The code of the American Psychological Association was occasionally mentioned, due to its sections on research and assessment. The early, limited focus of ethics education and discussion in counselor education was based on the assumption of "guidance counselors" working for salaries. The definition of *professional counseling* has changed so that counselors are recognized as psychologically based helping professionals who deal with a wide range of client concerns in diverse settings. As a result, counselors now have state licensure boards and professional credentialing boards in addition to professional membership organizations. Each of the groups or organizations has a legitimate interest in ensuring the professional behavior of its licensees, certificants, or members. The interest may be different and the disciplinary processes will vary based on the purpose of the organization.

The codes and procedures of state governments fall under constitutional requirements for due process within the Fourteenth Amendment to the U.S. Constitution. That amendment prohibits depriving citizens of life, liberty, or property without due process. A professional counselor who wants to practice privately in a jurisdiction that has a practice act, a licensure act that regulates counseling activities, and not the title *licensed professional counselor,* has no choice about seeking licensure in the jurisdiction. Because counseling licensure boards are creatures of state governments and licensure can be required for practice, a professional license is a property right protected by the constitutional requirement for due process. In addition, because many state licensure boards have standards of conduct incorporated into their codes, violations of what many professionals would call ethical standards are being addressed in proceedings that are judicial in nature if not in fact.

Membership organizations and certification boards are different because their relationship with members and those certified is contractual. However, the absence of a legal requirement for due process does not mean that a certification or membership organization should ignore fundamental fairness. Because they are free from some constraints, they have the opportunity to devise creative means to be fair to counselors while protecting the public.

A person who voluntarily associates with any group that has disciplinary procedures should become familiar with the procedures to which they have agreed; the agreement is a contract. Nongovernmental agencies are typically required only to comply with their contracts. For example, a requirement that an accused counselor cooperate with the disciplinary procedures or face sanctions for the failure to cooperate is common. Counselors may have a choice about becoming subject to a private organization's disciplinary procedures. Membership and certification are voluntary, but some may say that the competitive and professional advantages of certain credentials and memberships make their desirability less than truly voluntary. The number of professional counselors who do not hold professional memberships or nongovernmental credentials suggest that that belief is, much to the regret of the organizations, not universal.

Organizations that have latitude in development of ethical enforcement procedures face difficult questions that must be answered. The questions are difficult because the protection of the public must be balanced against the protection of the counselor. Unlike the governmental agencies whose procedures are governed by constitutional guarantees of due process, the organizations that can have procedures based on contracts have both the opportunity and the obligation to consider conflicts between rights.

An enforcement procedure for professional ethics must protect the public that has trusted the profession with self-regulation while balancing that protection with protecting the rights of the regulated members. In criminal law, one is presumed innocent until proven guilty, and evidence must establish guilt beyond a reasonable doubt, whereas in civil proceedings, the standard is a fair preponderance of evidence (Swenson, 1997). The different standards result from the concept that the more severe the possible punishment, the higher the standard of proof required. In professional regulation, should the counselor be assumed innocent unless the same high criminal standard of proof is met? If that standard is established, is the public or the profession protected? For example, would the public comprehend that a counselor accused of a serious ethical violation continued to practice with the endorsement of the profession because appeals were not exhausted or because a reasonable doubt of guilt existed? Conversely, would punishment before the process is completed or when there was reasonable doubt of guilt be fair to the professional?

The ethics enforcement procedures of counselors should also be consistent with the philosophy of the profession. Counseling is a profession based on the assumption that people can change and develop in response to assistance. Should the goal of ethical enforcement procedures be rehabilitation or should it be punishment? Punishment may protect the public, but it could be inconsistent with the philosophy of those responsible for the process. Professional organizations have the ability to establish procedures based on education and rehabilitation. But freedom from legal requirements does not remove fundamental questions involving competing rights of public protection and rights of the accused.

When any professional organization establishes disciplinary procedures, one consideration is efficiency. Efficiency can include speed and costs. Procedures that model the governmental procedures can be slow and costly. A state licensure board is acting on behalf of the citizens of a state whose codes or regulations were violated, and therefore the board ultimately has access to the resources of the state. Legal procedures can consume major amounts of the donated time of the leaders of a professional organization and significant amounts of its budget. To make procedures too efficient can lead to the appearance of unfairness or even outright injustice.

The discussion of enforcement should not lead you to believe you are entering a profession populated by unethical practitioners who must be forced to behave ethically. A review of the actual numbers of ethics cases handled reported by the ACA and the Virginia Board of Professional Counselors and Marriage and Family Therapists is enlightening. The ACA Ethics Committee reported that in 1996–97, 17 ethics complaints were processed (Forester-Miller & Shumate, 1998). A skeptic might wonder if bodies other than the ACA Ethics Committee handled the ethics violations. I have no data to address that issue directly but data from a state board that has a toll-free ethics line and uses state paid investigators are similar. The Virginia Board held 15 formal and informal hearings over a two-year period (Brown, 1997). The 15 hearings came from a population of nearly 2,400 licensees. The number of violations compared to the number of practicing professional counselors is small, but we should aspire to have even fewer violations.

## Challenges

Major challenges arise in the counseling professions as they attempt to ensure that counselors practice ethically. First, not all counselors are affiliated with professional counseling organizations that have ethical codes. Only counselors who are governed by practice acts—acts that prohibit the practice of counseling in other than act exempt settings—have mandatory standards of practice. Most counselors who are governed by ethical codes and standards of practice have voluntarily become subject to those standards. That certainly shows a professional commitment on the part of those counselors, but those who are intended to benefit from the standards should not be expected to conduct the research necessary to understand what codes and standards, if any, cover their counselor. Second, in addition to the absence of universal coverage of counselors by ethical standards, there are two additional challenges worthy of special consideration. They are the numbers of overlapping ethical codes and standards and the challenges of counseling services offered via the Internet and other media that do not require face-to-face contact.

## Competing Codes

A major challenge to the counseling professions as they attempt to ensure ethical counseling services is the number of overlapping and competing ethical codes. Most counselors do not fully appreciate the various organizational complexities that have led to ethical codes and standards of practice. It is not far-fetched to think that one counselor would be a licensed professional counselor, certified by the National Board for Certified Counselors, a member of the American Counseling Association (ACA), and a member of current or former divisions of ACA. One counselor can be subject to many ethical codes. For example, the National Career Development Association (NCDA; 1991) has an ethics code patterned after the NBCC code and has many sections that address counseling, not limited to only career counseling. In addition, many counselors practice in areas that have ethical codes or guidelines. For example, the Association for Specialists in Group Work (ASGW) has a promulgated Best Practice Guidelines for Group Workers. The statement is intended to "clarify the application of the American Counseling Association (ACA) Code of Ethics and Standards of Practice to the field of group work" (p. 1). Although the ASGW Best Practice Guidelines recognize the preeminence of the ACA standards, the guidelines are structured like an ethical statement. Specialized areas of counseling have developed separate ethical codes that address the complexities of the area of practice. For example, the Commission on Rehabilitation Counselor Certification (1995) has an ethical code that addresses specialized practice in rehabilitation. Herlihy and Remley (1995) present unified ethical standards for the counseling profession as a challenge to the profession. That challenge has not yet been accepted.

The problems resulting from the multiple codes are many. Currently, there is no good system for communication among the various bodies that have codes and standards. The possibility exists that one group could sanction a counselor for an ethical violation while other bodies with whom the counselor is affiliated would have no knowledge of the ethical charge or finding. Conversely, one ethical charge could force a counselor to have to prepare multiple defenses. Because the bodies that have ethical codes and practice statements do not have uniform enforcement processes, a counselor could be forced to prepare multiple defenses for the same allegation. The current overlapping system of ethical codes and enforcement procedures best protects neither counselors nor the public. One suggestion has been offered that counselors have a single code with special supplements for areas of specialized concern or practice. That approach would be similar to medicine, which has special annotations for psychiatry. The Group Specialists statement may be a step in that direction. If a single code is impossible, at the very least a coordinated system would prevent multiple charges, which would protect the counselor and would ensure that all groups with whom the counselor is associated knew of violations. Even if the problem of multiple codes is solved, the problem of those who offer counseling services but who are not governed by any regulatory body or ethical code will exist. No better example exists than counseling services offered electronically through the Internet.

## *Internet Counseling and Technology*

One issue that vexes those who deal with counseling ethics is how to work with counseling services offered via electronic means. The issue is not new, for many counselors have been uncomfortable with radio counselors, newspaper advice columns, and telephone counseling. The explosion of the Internet has made offering counseling via the Internet not only a vague possibility but also a reality. The Internet can be used as an advertising medium, including a means to have potential clients contact counselors, and a means to make information available to those who need counseling in an organized and indexed fashion. Those are not really new uses of technology, and previous ethical standards have addressed changes technology has made possible. However, ethical standards have not addressed the possibility counseling offered in real time or by e-mail through the Internet. How are ethical codes to address the ethical problems associated with counseling services that do not involve the traditional face-to-face interaction between the counselor and client? The dilemma is akin to the dilemma of parents of adolescents who wonder how to talk with their children about alcohol, drugs, and sexual activity without endorsing and encouraging the behavior. The prevalence of counseling that is not traditional cannot be responsibly ignored. The problem is compounded because the ability of counseling regulatory agencies to impose legal regulations on the practice of counseling that is offered across state and international boundaries by the Internet is far from certain.

My browsing of Internet sites revealed a great variety; I found sites that

1. simply promoted a counselor's home or office practice
2. provided information about counseling and counselors
3. offered self-help material like that typically available in printed fashion
4. offered therapeutic interventions either as an adjunct to face-to-face counseling or as a stand-alone service

Some sites were poorly constructed, poorly edited, and poorly presented. Anonymous individuals as well as individuals with no credentials or fraudulent credentials operated other sites. Individuals with appropriate credentials and years of professional experience were associated with others. However, these latter seemingly legitimate credentials were all based on education and experience gained in face-to-face counseling; the relevance of these credentials to the practice of offering counseling through the Internet is unknown. I encourage you to search the Internet to see the continuing evolution of Internet counseling sites.

At the time this is being written, the National Board for Certified Counselors (NBCC) has taken a leading role in initiating discussion and proposing standards for Internet counseling services. The NBCC board, realizing that the issue could not be responsibly ignored, began to search for a means to recognize the existence of counseling that did not involve a face-to-face interaction without necessarily endorsing such practices. Like many parents, the NBCC directors determined that although many would prefer that "distance counseling" not exist except in the most extraordinary circumstances, there were some forms and practices that were not as troubling as others. NBCC elected to recognize rather than ignore the existing practice, knowing that by doing so, it also risked appearing to endorse such practices subsumed under web counseling. As the reaction of those in the field proved, the board's decision was not universally accepted as appropriate. As the Counselor Educators and Supervisors Network (CESNET) comments and others reported in *Counseling Today* demonstrate, the decision was not understood as recognition as opposed to endorsement.

The NCDA (1997) published a statement on the practice of career counseling using the Internet, but that statement did not provoke the discussion that the NBCC standards precipitated. Perhaps due to its title, which did not include the term *counseling,* the NCDA statement was viewed erroneously as not addressing the field of counseling. The revision to the NBCC code did not contain standards for the practice of web counseling. While the NBCC Code of Ethics was being revised, the NBCC appointed a special task force to examine the practice of on-line counseling and develop standards for the practice of web counseling. The revised NBCC Code of Ethics required that those certified by NBCC who *elected* to engage in distance counseling be guided by the standards for web counseling that were referenced in Section B.12 of the NBCC Code of Ethics. The reference to a second set of guidelines was based on the belief that the web counseling standards would change faster than the ethical code. The NBCC WebCounseling standards were approved before the ethical code revision was formally adopted.

Many unknowns exist about Internet counseling. We need to know if the lack of visual input makes a difference in the outcome of the counseling process. Numerous questions are unanswered about the legality of counseling across state or national boundaries or how malpractice liability will be established. Answers are necessary in order to develop adequate ethical codes.

Other professions face similar issues regarding the appropriateness, if not ethics, of Internet services. Examples range from the availability of Viagra, a drug prescribed for male impotence (and popularized by the media as well as late-night TV talk show jokes), to organizations that have posted fill-in-the-blanks legal documents on the Internet that may violate the legal codes of some states. However, an equal number of popular press articles show how the Internet has made current medical information research available to practitioners without previous access. Some stories feature the sharing of information by those who are victims of low-incidence diseases. In the meantime, other professions are being transformed because of electronic communications. Developments such as the enactment of the California Telemedicine Development Act of 1996 (amended in 1997) mean that professional services formerly limited to face-to-face interactions will be considered appropriate for other delivery systems.

Many professional counselors do not like or even accept the concept of on-line counseling, but it seems apparent that it was not possible to stop individuals from opening practices and soliciting clients without regard to jurisdictional boundaries. Many counselors acknowledge that the Internet offers many potential benefits in addition to potential problems (Sampson, Kolodinsky, & Greeno, 1997). Although legislative bodies will certainly act to protect the public, the counseling profession should not remain silent.

## *Making Ethical Decisions*

This chapter began with the concept that ethical codes alone do not provide answers to all counselor questions about proper behavior. A starting point for counselors faced with decisions about proper behavior is a review of the applicable statues and regulations. In some instances, counselors believe there is a conflict between legal and ethical requirements (MacNair, 1992), but decisions should never be made in ignorance of the law. Some critics suggest that any act that is not consistent with applicable legal standards should be undertaken only if the counselor is willing to accept the consequences. I add to that admonition a suggestion that the counselor carefully consider imposing his or her view over the view that has been developed by legal considerations. Reporting child abuse is an often-cited example of the counselor knowingly violating a legal requirement for the "good of the client." I suggest any counselor faced with a dilemma of "competing bads" consider the reasons that people who are genuinely concerned about the welfare of children have instituted mandatory reporting. A decision not to report would surely require circumstances that the framers of child abuse legislation did not consider.

The ACA system of making ethical decision (Forester-Miller & Davis, 1995) is actually not an ACA system but a synthesis of the work of many who have considered how to deal with ethical dilemmas. That this system is based on the thinking and work of many counselors concerned about making ethical decisions adds to its importance.

The ACA system suggests the following steps:

1. Identify the problem. This step includes gathering information about all applicable legal requirements. The policies and procedure of the employer are also gathered at this stage.
2. Apply the ACA Code of Ethics.
3. Determine the nature and dimensions of the dilemma.
   a. Consider ACA ethical decision-making principles. (I would add here to consider other ethical decision-making systems and considerations such as those presented early in this chapter.)
   b. Review professional literature.
   c. Consult with professional colleagues.
   d. Contact professional organizations for guidance.
4. Generate potential courses of action.
5. Consider the potential consequences of all options and determine a course of action.
6. Evaluate the selected course of action.
7. Implement the course of action.

The ethical challenges and dilemmas that face professional counselors will change as the development of the profession of counseling continues. The general principles that should guide the behavior of counselors will not change as rapidly and will likely continue, even if given clarification and new terminology. The relationship rests on the fundamental concept of a person seeking help being able to know that his or her helper can be trusted to act in the best interests of the person asking for help. The counselor can do no better than to start the questioning of any potential behavior than by asking the questions suggested by the ACA general principles for ethical decision making: Am I acting to promote client autonomy, to avoid potential harm to my client, to promote client welfare, to ensure fairness to all involved in the relationship, and to create a relationship of trust?

# 8

# Legal Issues in Counseling Practice

## Carolyn B. Woodworth

*Carolyn B. Woodworth is an attorney and a clinical counselor in private practice at Cape Elizabeth, Maine. She has a B.A. in English from Carleton College, a doctorate of jurisprudence from Harvard Law School, and an M.S. in clinical counseling from the University of Southern Maine. She has worked with the Portland, Maine, law firm of Drummond, Woodsum & MacMahon and is a visiting associate professor of law with the University of Maine Law School. Woodworth's interests include play therapy, trauma work, geriatric issues, and depth-oriented therapy and promotion of wellness. Her pastimes include black-and-white photography, modern languages, and the Maine beaches.*

## In This Chapter...

- What distinguishes "black-letter" law from case law? What is the impact of their differences?
- What does the principle of informed consent mean in terms of counseling practice?
- When and why does the counselor obtain informed consent?
- What is the legal difference between *confidentiality* and *privilege?* How will this affect the practice of counseling?
- What special conditions for consent and confidentiality exist when working with minors?
- What are the conditions that determine negligence in counseling liability cases?
- What is *third-party liability* and how does it affect the practicing counselor?
- What are the preventive steps involved in risk management?

> Law, simply stated, is a body of rules of action or conduct duly prescribed by controlling authority, and having binding legal force. (*United States Fidelity & Guaranty Co.* v. *Guenther,* 1930, p. 37)

Professional mental health practice and law influence one another. Legal rules of action or conduct affect counselors, as individuals and in the practice of their profession. Issues confronted in counseling practice—and the ways in which individual counselors, scholars, and professional associations address those issues—play a role in shaping the law.

Fewer legal actions are brought against counselors and other mental health practitioners than against practitioners in most medical specialties (Smith, 1996), but the threat of lawsuits and legal liability has an impact on counselors and clients. Concerns about liability have had both positive and negative effects on mental health practice. Positive effects include more careful treatment of clients by practitioners (Swenson, 1997) and increased efforts by practitioners to involve clients in decisions about their care (Weiner & Wettstein, 1993). Negative effects of liability concerns include unnecessary defensiveness (Weiner & Wettstein) and reduced innovation (Swenson) on the part of the practitioner, as well as increased practitioner stress, increased liability insurance costs and fees charged to clients, and decreased trust between client and practitioner (Swenson).

## *Legal Terminology*

Law that affects the practice of professional counseling comes from many sources, including the codified or "black-letter" law of the federal and state constitutions, statutes, and regulations, and common law or case law, which is established in the process of judicial decision making. Black-letter law changes over time as legislatures and regulatory bodies are presented with new issues and initiatives or seek to clarify or amend rules that are already in place. Case law, too, changes over time as judges apply existing rules to new facts or create new rules as well as write opinions that become part of the body of law.

Action or conduct that violates a criminal statute may result in criminal charges and prosecution. Action or conduct that is legally wrongful, whether or not it also violates criminal statutes, may result in civil liability, which must be established in a legal action brought in court by a private party or parties. Litigation is a process that seeks to establish the true facts of events that may have occurred long before a legal action is brought (Committee on Psychiatry and Law, 1991). The process is adversarial and it reflects a fundamental belief that the truth is best discovered when evidence "is tested by those who have an interest in the outcome" (Committee on Psychiatry and Law, p. 13).

Sound professional practice takes the law into account. Legal issues related to informed consent, confidentiality, and duties of care to clients and others need to be addressed in every counseling relationship, and will, for some clients and in some counseling situations, require extensive exploration by the counselor before an appropriate course of action can be chosen. The goal of this chapter is to provide some of the history and current flavor of these concepts and to stimulate thinking by counselors and student counselors about legal risk management.

This chapter does not constitute legal advice or legal counsel to any counselor or counseling student. To obtain legal advice, students and counselors should consult an attorney in their state who is knowledgeable about mental health care law and practice.

## *Informed Consent*

The doctrine of informed consent has its roots in early twentieth century medical case law, which recognized that "[e]very human being of adult years and sound mind has a right to determine what shall be done with his own body; and a surgeon who performs an operation without his patient's consent commits an assault, for which he is liable in damages" (*Schloendorff* v. *Society of New York Hospital,* 1914, p. 93). More recent legal history has seen an expansion of both the definition of consent and the number of health care situations in which it will be applied.

In its early form, the patient consent requirement was cursory. A doctor who wished to perform a medical procedure on a patient needed only the patient's permission to proceed; he or she was not required to explain the procedure in detail or to explore with the patient its risks and possible alternatives (Janofsky, 1996; Reisner & Slobogin, 1990). Lack of patient consent to the procedure performed could trigger a successful lawsuit for assault and battery, if, for example, the patient consented to an operation on one body part but the surgery was actually performed on another or the patient agreed to undergo one procedure but another operation was in fact performed.

The principle that medical consent should be *informed* has its origins in the prosecution of Nazi doctors in the war-crime trials at the end of World War II, and was applied first to research with human subjects and later to patient care (Janofsky, 1996). In its modern form, informed consent for treatment requires a consent that is competent, knowing, and voluntary (Crawford, 1994; Janofsky). *Voluntariness* means that an individual's choice to undertake treatment has been made freely, without improper influence or pressure from his or her doctor or counselor, family members, or others. *Competence,* for this purpose, can be described as the capacity to understand and make an informed decision about a proposed treatment or plan of care, including the nature of the treatment and its risks and likely benefits. Janofsky notes that judgments about competence take into account both the client's mental capabilities and the nature of the decision to be made. Thus, an individual may have the capacity to consent to a simple, minor treatment but not to a treatment that is risky and complex (Janofsky, 1996).

In general terms, the knowledge required for informed consent includes specific information about the nature of the treatment proposed, the likely benefits and foreseeable risks of the treatment, and the alternatives to the treatment, including, in some circumstances, the alternative of undertaking no treatment. The legal standard for measuring what information must be communicated, however, will vary from jurisdiction to jurisdiction. Some states follow a "professional's standard" (Sexton et al.,1993, p. 270) rule, under which required disclosures are determined by reference to the practice of others in the profession. In a court proceeding in which this standard governs, disclosures made to a client would be measured against what a reasonable practitioner would disclose prior to treatment in similar circumstances (Janofsky, 1996; Reisner & Slobogin, 1990). Other states follow a newer, client-focused rule that stems from a conviction that a "patient's right of self-decision shapes the boundaries of the duty to reveal" (*Canterbury* v. *Spence,* 1972, p. 786) and requires disclosure of the information a hypothetical "average" or "reasonable" client would need in order to make an informed decision about treatment. Two common exceptions to the requirement of informed consent are an exception for a "genuine emergency" (*Canterbury* v. *Spence,* 1972, p. 788) in which consent cannot be obtained, and an exception known as *therapeutic privilege,* which allows a health care provider, in very limited circumstances, to withhold information he or she reasonably believes would be harmful to the client.

To date, most successful informed consent claims in mental health litigation have involved the administration of psychotropic medications or treatments such as electroconvulsive therapy (Reisner & Slobogin, 1990; Weiner & Wettstein, 1993). Plaintiffs add claims based on lack of informed consent to claims based on professional negligence in many lawsuits (Weiner & Wettstein, 1993), however, and the doctrine of informed consent is still evolving. The requirement of informed consent is also shaping definitions of good professional practice in the form of ethical codes and practice guidelines. It benefits both practitioners and clients by "alerting therapists to the need to communicate with their patients and involve them actively in treatment decisions" (Weiner & Wettstein, 1993, p. 170).

In counseling, the process of obtaining informed consent is ongoing. It should begin at the time of an initial or intake meeting with a client and be updated as the counseling progresses and as new issues or changes in the client's condition become apparent. Ethical guidelines identify the broad contours of informed consent for the counseling process and can be reference points in preparing for individual client discussions. Some of the information necessary for informed consent (e.g., counselor qualifications, fees and billing procedures, etc.) can be included in a standard disclosure statement provided to clients at a first meeting. Information specific to an individual client's treatment and decisions about treatment, however, should be discussed with the client in person and noted in the client's file. Detailed written disclosures signed by the client can be very useful in documenting the informed consent process for legal purposes and are recommended even when they are not required (Crawford, 1994). Such written disclosures, however, should be a part of an overall, thorough discussion and consent process between counselor and client and not a substitute for the process itself.

Informed consent should include a discussion of the limits of counselor/client confidentiality and privilege (Arthur & Swanson, 1993), both at the beginning of the counseling relationship and, as appropriate, as the counseling proceeds.

## *Privacy, Confidentiality, and Privilege*

Clients enter into a counseling relationship with the expectation that thoughts, feelings, and information shared with the counselor will not be disclosed to others (Smith-Bell & Winslade, 1996), and assurances of nondisclosure can be central to the counseling process. The Supreme Court stated the following in the 1996 *Jaffee* v. *Redmond* decision:

> Treatment by a physician for physical ailments can often proceed successfully on the basis of a physical examination, objective information supplied by the patient, and the results of

diagnostic tests. Effective psychotherapy, by contrast, depends upon an atmosphere of confidence and trust in which the patient is willing to make a frank and complete disclosure of facts, emotions, memories, and fears. Because of the sensitive nature of the problems for which individuals consult psychotherapists, disclosure of confidential communications made during counseling sessions may cause embarrassment or disgrace. For this reason, the mere possibility of disclosure may impede development of the confidential relationship necessary for successful treatment. (p. 10)

Nondisclosure can be discussed in terms of the three related, but distinguishable, concepts of privacy, confidentiality, and privilege—all of which have significance for counseling clients and counselors. The word *privacy,* in common usage, means the condition of being secluded from the view of others (Berube et al., 1982) and, in a counseling context, has been defined by Corey, Williams, and Moline (1995) as the "freedom or right of clients to choose the time, circumstances, and information others may know about them" (p. 168). *Confidentiality,* which, like privacy, relates to a notion of "limited access and the exclusion of others" (Smith-Bell & Winslade, 1996, p. 64), is an ethical responsibility and affirmative legal duty on the part of the counselor not to disclose client information without the client's prior consent. *Privilege* is a common law and statutory concept that protects confidential communications made within certain special relationships from disclosure in legal proceedings. Rules of privilege vary from jurisdiction to jurisdiction. Unless common law or statutory privilege is available, communications to a counselor that would be protected by confidentiality from disclosure in a nonjudicial setting may have to be disclosed in court.

## *Confidentiality*

Codification of a professional duty of confidentiality dates back to between the first and sixth centuries B.C., with a provision of the Hippocratic Oath for physicians that requires "whatever, in connection with my professional practice, or not in connection with it, I see or hear, in the life of men, which ought not to be spoken of abroad, I will not divulge as reckoning that all such should be kept secret" (Cayne et al., 1987, p. 218). Modern principles of confidentiality can be found in professional ethics codes, case decisions, state laws and regulations, and, in some instances, federal legislation (e.g., confidentiality of records of individuals participating in certain federally funded treatment programs) (Reisner & Slobogin, 1990). A counselor's general duty of confidentiality protects all information related to the counseling relationship, including words spoken in the counseling sessions; observations by the counselor; notes, records, and assessment results; and the identity of the client (Weiner & Wettstein, 1993; Welfel, 1998). The client's right of privacy with respect to this information, however, is not absolute.

Exceptions to confidentiality protection for mental health clients are not uniform among the 50 states; therefore, counselors and those with whom they consult need to be familiar with the precise parameters of the rules of the state in which they practice. Situations in which disclosure of client information is commonly permitted or required include emergencies in which the client or others are in imminent danger of serious harm, civil commitment proceedings preliminary to involuntary hospitalization of a client, circumstances in which a duty to warn others of danger from a client exists under *Tarasoff* principles (to be discussed), discussions with supervisors and consultants, and mandatory reporting to state authorities of abuse and neglect (to be discussed) (Wiener & Wettstein, 1993).

A client may choose to authorize his or her counselor to disclose confidential information to a third party (e.g., a medical insurer). Any authorization for disclosure should be in writing, signed by the client, and recorded in the client's file. Even though the client has given written consent to a release of information, however, caution and care will be necessary in responding to information requests. If the client signs a release for the disclosure of counseling records, but does not know what information is in the records, it may be necessary to review the records with the client before they are provided to a third party as requested (Weiner & Wettstein, 1993). It is also possible that although a client has signed a broad, "blanket" release or waiver of confidentiality, a release of some but not all of the client's record will satisfy a request for information.

## *Privilege*

Confidentiality is a broad, comprehensive professional duty to guard the privacy of client information. Privilege, by contrast, is narrow and limited in scope. *Privilege,* or *testimonial privilege,* as it is sometimes called, is the right of a client to prevent disclosure of confidential communications to his or her mental health practitioner in a courtroom or in proceedings related to trial.

Privilege is an exception to a fundamental legal principle that the public has a right to every person's evidence in court and that all relevant information should be available in the judicial process for seeking the truth. It is defined by law and differs from jurisdiction to jurisdiction. Information that is protected by an ethical or legal obligation of confidentiality may or may not be protected by privilege from disclosure in court. Whether privilege is available to protect client communications to professional counselors will depend on governing law.

***Practitioner/Client Privilege under State Law.***      The availability of privilege for confidential communications between a mental health practitioner and a client depends on the profession of the practitioner and the law of the jurisdiction involved (Reisner & Slobogin, 1990). Privilege rules vary from state to state, creating a patchwork quilt in which clients of practitioners in certain professional groups may successfully assert privilege in some states but not others (Remley, Herlihy, & Herlihy, 1997, p. 214). Most states protect communications to psychiatrists under either general physician/patient privilege laws or privilege statutes specific to psychiatrists and their clients, and grant privilege to psychologist/client communications under professional licensing laws (Reisner & Slobogin, 1990). Clients of other professionals, such as professional counselors and clinical social workers, will have the protection of privilege in certain states but not in others. As of 1995, 34 states had extended some form of privilege to communications between counselors and their clients (Brief of Amicus Curiae American Counseling Association in *Jaffee,* 1996), but each state's specific rules must be consulted to determine whether the privilege is available to clients of counselors who have particular professional credentials, and, if privilege is available, to determine what information is protected and in what situations the privilege will apply.

The scope of protection offered by any client/practitioner privilege and the number and type of exceptions to a general grant of privilege will vary from state to state (Reisner

& Slobogin, 1990; Remley et al., 1997). Testimonial privilege rules in some states, for example, protect only communications to the practitioner and do not protect the practitioner's observations, diagnosis, or plan for treatment (Weiner & Wettstein, 1993). Situations commonly excluded from grants of privilege for client communications include court-ordered mental health examinations and civil commitment proceedings (Weiner & Wettstein, 1993). There are also likely to be limitations on the assertion of privilege in court actions in which a client raises the issue of his or her mental health and in malpractice actions brought by clients against practitioners (Weiner & Wettstein, 1993).

Counselors should be aware that privilege may not apply where a third party is present during a communication (Arthur & Swanson, 1993; Reisner & Slobogin, 1990). For that reason, any privilege available for individual counseling may not extend to client communications during group counseling or couples and family therapy (Corey et al., 1995; Reisner & Slobogin, 1990). Informed consent disclosures to clients should address these and any other limitations on privilege under the applicable law.

Court proceedings in which clients are involved can bring issues of confidentiality, privilege, and informed consent immediately to the fore, and the first notice to a counselor that such proceedings are underway may be in the form of a subpoena. A *subpoena* is a document that commands an individual to appear and give testimony in a legal proceeding. A subpoena *duces tecum* requires the production of documents or papers. Subpoenas require action; they cannot be ignored. A counselor who is served with a subpoena that requires testimony or the production of records relating to a client or former client should immediately contact the client and, if the client is represented by an attorney, the client's attorney for guidance on how to proceed. If the client does not give informed written consent to the counselor's testimony and/or disclosure of the records described in the subpoena, or if it is unclear to the counselor how he or she should respond to the subpoena, the counselor should seek advice from his or her own attorney.

### *Federal Privilege: Recent Guidance.*

Most legal actions in the United States are handled in state courts, where state privilege rules will govern, but certain cases are heard in federal courts, where federal rules may control. The 1996 U.S. Supreme Court decision in *Jaffee* v. *Redmond* recognized a federal "psychotherapist" privilege in a case that contained a claim based on federal law and a claim based on the law of Illinois. *Jaffee* v. *Redmond* involved the fatal shooting of a man by a police officer who, after the shooting, received counseling from a licensed clinical social worker. The family of the man who died filed a lawsuit in federal court and sought access to the social worker's counseling notes. The Court noted that if the lawsuit had been brought in state court, Illinois law would have protected conversations between the officer and her social worker, at least with respect to the state law claim.

The Supreme Court concluded that psychotherapist privilege should be recognized under Rule 501 of the Federal Rules of Evidence and that this privilege should extend to "confidential communications made to licensed social workers in the course of psychotherapy" (*Jaffee* v. *Redmond,* 1996, p. 15). The Court, however, found it neither "necessary nor feasible" to delineate the "full contours" (p. 18) of the new federal privilege, leaving to future cases questions not answered in the Court's opinion. Issues left for consideration in future cases include determining which categories of mental health professionals not described in the opinion (e.g., professional counselors) will be treated as "psychotherapists" for purposes of the privilege (Remley et al., 1997) and determining how Rule 501 should be applied where the federal privilege rule and a state privilege rule differ and the lawsuit in question contains both federal law and state law claims (Bryson, 1997; *Jaffee* v. *Redmond,* 1996). The reasoning and holding of the *Jaffee* opinion, however, should be very helpful to clients of licensed professional counselors who assert privilege in future federal court actions that involve questions of federal law.

## Consent and Confidentiality with Minor Clients

Children's legal rights in the United States have evolved over the course of the nation's history. Current issues of consent and confidentiality for minors reflect that evolution. Nurcombe and Partlett (1994) identify four periods in the history of law regarding children: From 1600 to 1800, under principles derived from English common law that fit with the way families worked in an agrarian society, children were regarded as property of their parents. From 1800 to 1900, in which the rise of industry and the increase in urban poverty sparked new legislation protecting children, family courts were created and the standard of the "best interest of the child" was first applied in case law. From 1900 to 1967, the legal system relied heavily on judicial discretion in dealing with abused, abandoned, and delinquent children. In the present era, in the law regarding children, "rights rather than protections have become the legal touchstone" (p. 43). As described by Quinn and Weiner (1993), in this present era, "issues regarding minors often include a balancing of the rights of children and the rights and duties of their parents and the state. In day-to-day clinical practice, it must be determined who has the authority to speak for the child: the parents, the state, or the child himself" (p. 310).

As a general rule, minors are legally incapable of giving consent to health care treatment (Quinn & Weiner, 1993; Reisner & Slobogin, 1990), and parents or another substitute decision maker (e.g., a guardian) will need to give consent on the minor's behalf. If parents are separated or divorced, it will ordinarily be the custodial parent who has authority to give consent to treatment (Arambula, DeKraai, & Sales, 1993), but a counselor should ask to see a court order or other legal evidence if a parent's authority to consent is unclear. In certain circumstances, the refusal of a parent or other substitute decision maker to consent to treatment for a minor can lead to intervention by the state on behalf of the child, and a court order may be required before treatment can proceed.

Exceptions to the general rule that minors cannot legally consent to treatment vary from state to state. Rae, Worchel, and Brunnquell (1995) find that these exceptions can usually be placed in one of two categories: exceptions related to the nature of the problem for which treatment is needed and exceptions related to the status of the minor under state law. Exceptions related to the nature of the problem might, for example, permit certain minors to seek pregnancy testing, or to obtain treatment for alcohol or drug dependency or physical or sexual abuse, without a parent's consent (Rae et al., 1995; Reisner & Slobogin, 1990). Specific state and federal statutes and regulations will need to be consulted to determine when and how minors are permitted to consent to particular treatments and services in a given jurisdiction. *Status of the minor* exceptions, usually referred to as *emancipated minor* or *mature minor* rules, relate to a minor's age and maturity, and/or to life circumstances that indicate that the minor is capable of making certain decisions on his or her own.

Under the legal doctrine of *emancipation,* a minor who is no longer subject to parental guidance, financial support, or control can give "independent consent" (Reisner & Slobogin, 1990, p. 218) to health care treatment. The burden of proving that a child is emancipated is on the party who wishes to show that emancipation has occurred (Nurcombe & Partlett, 1994). Emancipation of a minor, under the traditional rules, can be partial or complete. A court that is asked to rule on whether a child is emancipated will determine whether the child has the skill and capacity to manage his or her own affairs, and is likely to consider such factors as whether the child is living independently, is self-supporting and taking responsibility for payment of debts, owns property, or is married or serving in the military (Nurcombe & Partlett, 1994; Quinn & Weiner, 1993). Laws regarding emancipation vary considerably from jurisdiction to jurisdiction, and, unless there is a court order declaring a minor to be emancipated, counselors will need to consult legal counsel and/or the statutes and case precedent of the state in which they practice when emancipation issues arise (Salo & Shumate, 1993).

In states that recognize some form of *mature minor* status, certain minors, usually adolescents over the age of 14 or 16, may be allowed to consent to certain services or treatment without the requirement of parental consent. Mature minor rules are part of an effort to recognize that children who are older and developmentally more capable should be able to make or participate in more decisions than younger children. Unlike emancipated minors, mature minors are not required to be financially self-supporting or living on their own. The rationale for giving them increased power to make health care decisions is their maturity and level of development (Quinn & Weiner, 1993). There may be no clear answer under state law as to whether an apparently mature minor can consent to mental health treatment (Nurcombe & Partlett, 1994), and in this area, as with emancipation, legal guidance may be needed.

Some states require consent for treatment from both parent and child where the child is over a certain age (Arambula et al., 1993). In practice, even a minor who is not legally capable of consenting to mental health treatment can participate in treatment decisions and in the process of informed consent. Nurcombe and Partlett (1994) advise that formal informed consent to treatment should be obtained from all clients over the age of 13. Other commentators recommend that minors' permission for treatment be obtained under the concept of *assent,* which Rae and colleagues (1995) describe as follows:

> [Assent] recognizes that minors may not be cognitively or developmentally able to consent to some procedures, yet acknowledges the importance of providing them with some semblance of control over decision making. Assent is essentially veto power (Koocher & Keith-Spiegel, 1990). Parents retain the ability to consent to treatment, while concomitant assent allows the child to express a preference. The dilemma this presents is that it does give the child a relatively large degree of power, if adults are indeed serious about assent. (p. 25)

Different children will have different needs in the process of informed consent. Assent for minor clients allows a practitioner to adapt the level and type of client participation in the informed consent process to suit the developmental stage and capabilities of each child (Rae et al., 1995).

Issues of confidentiality and access to records are intertwined with issues about legal power to consent. Arambula and associates (1993) conclude that where the law permits a child to consent to his or her own treatment, a release of treatment information to parents without the child's consent is a breach of confidence. Quinn and Weiner (1993), however, emphasize that although many states that allow minors to consent to treatment prohibit the release of treatment records without the minor's consent, laws regarding confidentiality for minors have not, in general, "kept apace" (p. 324) of the laws regarding their treatment rights. Parents who have the legal authority to consent to mental health treatment for their children are likely to have rights to obtain information that comes from that treatment (Arambula et al., 1993; Knapp, 1997), unless state law or a judicial determination recognizes an interest in nondisclosure that overcomes the parents' rights (Arambula et al., 1993). If a child lacks legal power to consent to treatment, moreover, his or her parent or other substitute decision maker will ordinarily have the ability to claim or waive any privilege available for the child's treatment information, unless the relevant law provides, an age for the assertion of privilege that differs from the age required for consent (Arambula et al., 1993).

Counselors who work in schools will need to become familiar with the requirements of the Family Educational Rights and Privacy Act of 1974 (FERPA), often referred to as the Buckley Amendment, which governs access to student records. FERPA, together with state laws and school policies, will shape counselor decisions regarding confidentiality and appropriate recordkeeping procedures for students in their schools (Jacob-Timm & Hartshorne, 1998).

In practice, it is often possible to arrive at an understanding between the counseling professional, parent, and child that preserves the child's confidentiality even where that would not be legally required. Goldberg (1997), for example, writes that she believes it is usually best "to discuss the issue of confidentiality at the first session with the child and parents together, and to encourage the parents to respect their child's need for privacy" (p. 104), and she assures parents that they will be informed if there is an imminent risk of harm to the child or to someone else. Other ways of handling requests by parents for information about their child's counseling include discussing a request with the minor client and learning whether he or she is willing to have the counselor share certain information with the parent (Remley, ERIC/CAPS Workshop, as cited in Salo & Shumate, 1993), or, when the counselor believes sharing certain information is in the best interest of an adolescent client, scheduling a joint session with the client and his or her parent in which the counselor can help the client communicate the information directly to the parent (Quinn & Weiner, 1993). Ethical principles and a concern for the therapeutic relationship require that counselors take steps to protect the confidentiality of minor clients. The concept of assent would also require that the counselor discuss the nature and limits of confidentiality with minor clients, in terms the clients can understand.

## *Liability Issues for Counselors*

Although malpractice actions against mental health professionals are still fairly uncommon (Reisner & Slobogin, 1990) and only a small number of claims actually filed against such professionals are successful (Smith, 1996), there appears to be increasing concern among practitioners about professional malpractice. Legal actions claims *are* brought against mental health practitioners, and the threat of these actions affects the way they view themselves and conduct their practices.

## Claims by Counseling Clients

For a number of reasons—including difficulties in proving emotional injury, the reluctance of clients to bring their mental health issues into the public forum of a courtroom, and the bonds that develop between client and practitioner in the course of the therapeutic relationship—clients are less likely to sue a mental health practitioner than practitioners in most medical specialties (Reisner & Slobogin, 1990; Smith, 1996; Wettstein, 1994). Most malpractice claims asserted against mental health practitioners are based on a theory of negligence (Reisner & Slobogin, 1990). Other possible causes of action, less frequently asserted, include federal civil rights claims (e.g., a claim arising out of proceedings for involuntary commitment to a publicly funded institution), breach of a contract to provide a certain result, and breach of client confidentiality or breach of the obligation to obtain informed consent (Reisner & Slobogin, 1990; Smith, 1996; Wettstein, 1994). Claims for assault and battery, libel, and malicious infliction of emotional distress have also been asserted (Crawford, 1994).

Nurcombe and Partlett (1994) describe the adversarial process of litigating disputes in the courtroom as a modern variant of the ordeal of trial by battle, and it is understandable that most professionals who are the target of a legal action by a client approach the litigation system with dread. Mental health practitioners, however, are not "the insurers of the patient's outcome" (Wettstein, 1994, p. 114). Under negligence rules, practitioners are responsible only for client injury caused by treatment that falls outside of a reasonable standard of care (Crawford, 1994; Wettstein, 1994).

To show negligence, a claimant needs to establish that the party against whom he or she has filed suit owed the claimant a duty or obligation that was recognized by law and that this duty or obligation was breached, causing loss or damage to the claimant (Reisner & Slobogin, 1990; Smith, 1996). Professional malpractice suits are based on the tenet that a member of a profession who renders services to a client has a duty to perform those services with the same skill and proficiency that would be exercised by other professionals in the field (Reisner & Slobogin, 1990). A few jurisdictions, following an older legal rule, measure levels of care and treatment against local standards of practice (Reisner & Slobogin, 1990), but standards of care are usually determined by looking at evidence of national practice (Crawford, 1994; Reisner & Slobogin, 1990). Bertram and Wheeler (1995) define the critical issue in a counselor malpractice action as whether the counselor provided a "level of care and treatment that is consistent with the degree of learning, skill and ethics ordinarily possessed and expected by reputable counselors practicing under similar circumstances" (p. 6).

Belger (1997) concludes that the filing of lawsuits by clients against mental health practitioners stems from the "malignant synergy of a bad outcome coupled with bad feelings; that is, only when elements of hostility, antagonism, frustration, anger, dissatisfaction, and feelings of betrayal and abandonment are present does the bad outcome actually provoke litigation (Goisman & Gutheil, 1992)" (p. 45). As this chapter's section on risk management will discuss, the way a counselor pursues his or her day-to-day practice of counseling and the way he or she responds to and communicates with clients can affect the way in which problems that arise in the course of counseling will be resolved. Problem areas that carry a heightened risk of legal action by clients can also be identified, however, and special caution and attention to issues in these areas can be useful in minimizing legal risks.

An increasingly common source of litigation against mental health professionals is sexual contact between a practitioner and a client (Belger, 1997) or former client, and the number of lawsuits based on sexual activity between practitioners and spouses or other relatives of clients is also increasing (Weiner & Wettstein, 1993). Improper sexual activity can also result in censure or reprimand, the loss of a professional license, and, in many states, criminal penalties. Practitioners should be aware that many professional liability policies limit or exclude coverage for suits based on sexual misconduct. Another area of heightened liability concern is that of suicide or self-harm by clients (Belger, 1997; Smith, 1996). Thorough risk management practices specific to client suicide and self-harm are essential; Bongar and colleagues (1998) is an excellent source of guidance on that topic.

Other areas identified by commentators as particularly problematic for liability purposes include alternative therapies that constitute a "radical departure" from customary practice (Belger, 1997); inadequate or improper diagnosis (Belger, 1997; Smith, 1996; Weiner & Wettstein, 1993); negligent psychological assessment (Weiner & Wettstein, 1993); breach of confidentiality that results in harm to the client (Smith, 1996; Weiner & Wettstein, 1993); recovered memory work exploring the possibility of childhood abuse, particularly that involving age-regression therapy; hypnosis and/or sodium amytal interviews (Knapp, 1997); failure to refer or provide for continuity of client care (Weiner & Wettstein, 1993); and the use of paradoxical techniques (Knapp, 1997; Sexton et al., 1993).

## Liability to Third Parties

***Duty to Protect.***   Liability to parties who are not clients is a relatively recent development in the law of mental health practice (Reisner & Slobogin, 1990; Wettstein, 1994). Some cases that impose liability for injury to third parties do not involve issues of client confidentiality. Such a case might be based, for example, on the failure of a psychiatrist who prescribes a sleep-inducing medication to warn the client not to drive a car after taking the drug. Much more troubling to most practitioners are liability issues stemming from the 1976 California Supreme Court decision in *Tarasoff* v. *Regents of the University of California,* which defined a duty of care to nonclients that may require the breach of client confidentiality in order to protect third parties from harm.

The court in *Tarasoff* summarized the facts out of which the case arose as follows:

> On October 27, 1969, Prosenjit Poddar killed Tatiana Tarasoff. Plaintiffs, Tatiana's parents, allege that two months earlier Poddar confided his intention to kill Tatiana to Dr. Lawrence Moore, a psychologist employed by the Cowell Memorial Hospital at the University of California at Berkeley. They allege that on Moore's request, the campus police briefly detained Poddar, but released him when he appeared rational. They further claim that Dr. Harvey Powelson, Moore's superior, then directed that no further action be taken to detain Poddar. No one warned plaintiffs of Tatiana's peril. (1976, p. 339)

Tatiana's parents filed suit against Dr. Moore, Dr. Powelson, and others, and the case made its way through the California courts. An issue in the case was whether Drs. Moore and Powelson owed a legal duty to Tatiana, who was not their client. The court found the following:

[O]nce a therapist does in fact determine, or under applicable professional standards reasonably should have determined, that a patient poses a serious danger of violence to others, he bears a duty to exercise reasonable care to protect the foreseeable victim of that danger. While the discharge of this duty of due care will necessarily vary with the facts of each case, in each instance the adequacy of the therapist's conduct must be measured against the traditional negligence standard of the rendition of reasonable care under the circumstances. (p. 345)

Under *Tarasoff,* a therapist may be required to "warn the intended victim or others likely to apprise the victim of the danger, to notify the police, or to take whatever other steps are reasonably necessary under the circumstances" (p. 340) in order to discharge his or her duty to use reasonable care to protect third parties.

*Tarasoff* triggered much debate among scholars and practitioners, and its reasoning has been followed, expanded, or adapted by the courts of many states. The issues in many post-*Tarasoff* cases have been whether the practitioner determined or should have determined that a client was a danger to others, whether that danger was to an identifiable victim or class of victims, and whether the practitioner took or should have taken reasonable action to prevent injury to the victim (Weiner & Wettstein, 1993). Although a number of cases have declined to follow *Tarasoff* (Perlin, 1997), the trend in the case law has been to impose a duty on practitioners to prevent foreseeable harm to third parties (Weiner & Wettstein, 1993). The controversy *Tarasoff* engendered has been the impetus for enactment in many states of *duty-to-warn statutes*. These statutes attempt to define or limit the scope of a practitioner's duty to warn or protect third parties and often prescribe the ways in which the duty can be discharged (Nurcombe & Partlett, 1994).

Cases and statutes regarding the duty to warn or protect vary from state to state, making it essential that counselors become and remain familiar with legislation and case decisions in their states of practice. State law should also be consulted when examining ways in which a duty to warn or protect can be discharged in a given situation. Weiner and Wettstein (1994) list options for consideration by a professional treating a dangerous client that include changing the client's treatment program, recommending that the client undertake voluntary hospitalization or initiating involuntary commitment procedures, contacting police, warning the victim, and/or warning others who are able to notify the victim. Knapp (1997) and Weiner and Wettstein (1994) also urge practitioners to consider, in appropriate circumstances, involving clients in the process of warning potential third-party victims— for example, giving necessary warnings in the presence of the client and with the client's consent.

Balancing "confidentiality against the protection of the public is a heavy burden, at a time of subtle and fluctuating legal doctrine" (Nurcombe & Partlett, 1994, p. 240), and there will often be no easy answers about appropriate responses to the threat of violence by clients. Weiner and Wettstein (1993) and Knapp (1997) emphasize acting in conformity with professional standards, consultation with colleagues and/or psychiatrists or others who have special expertise, carefully documenting the decision-making process and actions taken, and seeking legal advice as appropriate. With these issues, as with many other legal and ethical problems confronted by counselors, informed, thoughtful, and careful responses to individual client situations will be needed.

## Special Issues Related to HIV and AIDS

The ethical and legal issues related to treatment of clients infected by human immunodeficiency virus (HIV), the virus that causes acquired immune deficiency syndrome (AIDS), have been and continue to be the subject of much discussion and concern among counselors and other mental health professionals. The information that a client has tested positive for HIV is highly sensitive, and improper disclosure of that information could result in stigma and harm to the client. A situation, however, in which a client, without disclosing his or her status as HIV positive, is engaging in high-risk behavior (e.g., having unprotected sex or sharing needles) carries with it a grave risk of harm to others and may come within the *Tarasoff* doctrine of duty to protect or warn (Harding, Gray, & Neal, 1993; Stanard & Hazler, 1995).

Harding and colleagues (1993) and others urged the American Counseling Association to work toward specifying practical guidelines on confidentiality and AIDS. As a result, the ACA Code of Ethics (1995) now contains a subsection that addresses disclosure to endangered third parties of confidential information in the context of "contagious fatal diseases" (Section B.1.d). Counselors must be aware, however, that the legal arena within which HIV/AIDS-related issues must be confronted is complex, and that confidentiality and disclosure decisions regarding AIDS and HIV cannot be made without taking all relevant legal requirements into account. Many states have enacted specific statutes and regulations governing the confidentiality of HIV or AIDS status (Furrow et al., 1995; Hughes & Friedman, 1994). Violations of these laws and regulations may lead to civil liability and, in some states, criminal charges (Hughes & Friedman).

The interplay between general confidentiality requirements, duty to protect law, and statutes and regulations specific to HIV and AIDS status is intricate, and the law regarding HIV and AIDS is still developing. Counselors who confront legal questions about HIV or AIDS in their practice with clients should seek the advice of an attorney who is knowledgeable in this area.

## Failure to Report Abuse

All 50 states have adopted some form of mandatory reporting for suspected child abuse or neglect, and most states have criminal penalties for failure to report in accordance with the terms of their statutes (Weiner & Wettstein, 1993). The statutory language that describes the circumstances in which reports must be made, and the list of professionals required to make reports, vary from state to state; thus, counselors should become familiar with the requirements of their state's statute. Some states also require reporting of abuse of dependent elders, abuse of individuals in nursing homes or institutions, and abuse of individuals who have mental illness or are developmentally disabled (Weiner & Wettstein, 1993). Counselors practicing in states that have such rules will need to become familiar with the specific language of these reporting requirements, as well.

Research suggests that there is considerable concern and reluctance by mental health practitioners regarding the reporting of possible child abuse revealed by clients in counseling (Crenshaw, Lichtenberg, & Bartell, 1993), and that clinical considerations and legal obligations in this context may be difficult for practitioners to reconcile. A counselor who fails to comply with statutory reporting requirements for abuse, however, may be subject not only to penalties as set forth in the governing statute or regulations but also to liability in a civil suit if a child is hurt or an injury is aggravated by the failure to report (Belger, 1997). Here, as in other parts of professional practice, careful attention to both legal and ethical requirements is essential.

## Risk Management

Some risk of liability is inherent in the practice of every profession (Knapp, 1997), and bases for legal actions against mental health practitioners are expanding (Weiner & Wettstein, 1993). There is a danger that fears about liability will lead to narrow, rote responses by counselors to difficult client situations, but a healthy level of concern about risk reduction and risk management can contribute to sound professional practice and good client care. Liability concerns can be an impetus for examining and adopting practices that more fully involve clients in the counseling process. They can also stimulate the formation of alliances with colleagues and consultants that will enrich the counselor's decision-making process as difficult client issues arise.

Knapp (1997) defines *risk management* as actions practitioners can take that will reduce the risk of liability in the form of a lawsuit for malpractice, a disciplinary action before the review board of an institution, or an ethics charge before a state licensing body or professional association. Many of the counselor actions that can be helpful in minimizing those liability risks can be grouped according to the following themes:

**1.** *Competence.* A first principle for risk reduction is that counselors be aware of the limits of their skill and training and not practice outside the boundaries of their competence (Corey et al., 1995). Counselors need to keep their strengths and limitations in mind in deciding whether to accept new clients and whether and how to continue working with a client as new issues and treatment decisions come into play in the counseling process. Competence is an ethical as well as a risk management requirement, and guidance for sound decision making in this area can be found in ethical codes and standards of practice.

Practicing within one's competence involves knowing when to seek supervision, consultation, and additional training and supervised experience, and deciding, perhaps after discussing the matter with a supervisor and/or consultant, when it is appropriate to refer a client to another professional who is better able to assist him or her (Corey, Corey, & Callahan, 1998). Taking on or continuing to work with a client whose needs are beyond the skills of the counselor is unwise and unethical. Referral to another professional who has the appropriate skills, training, and experience can prevent problems for the counselor while serving the client's best interests.

**2.** *Communication and attention to the therapeutic relationship.* Legal and ethical issues cannot be divorced from their clinical context; they arise in the course of a relationship between counselor and client. Attention to that relationship and to the lines of communication between counselor and client is essential not only to providing proper care to the client but to minimizing the risk that mistakes or misunderstandings in the treatment process will lead to client claims.

A counselor's ongoing obligation to obtain informed consent provides a structure for communicating with the client about the counseling process, about matters such as payment schedules and missed appointments, and about the client's experience in counseling as work with the counselor progresses. The counselor should be attentive to signals from the client that further or new discussion regarding any of these items may be needed, and, as appropriate, should invite the client to share concerns and offer feedback to the counselor.

An actual or threatened client claim may indicate that communication between counselor and client has not been adequate, or that, in some other way, the interaction between counselor and client has failed to address the client's needs (Weiner & Wettstein, 1993). Buffone (1991) identifies certain clients as "high risk" for liability purposes, and, for such clients, recommends heightened attention to communication and problem solving. Individuals for whom heightened attention may be appropriate include clients who verbally or nonverbally express dissatisfaction with the counselor or treatment, clients who seem to have unrealistic expectations for the counseling process or are critical of previous providers, and clients who are late in payment or show excessive concern about fees.

Problems with unpaid fees should be addressed promptly, and unpaid balances should not be allowed to accumulate and become a subject of dispute (Swenson, 1997; Weiner & Wettstein, 1993). Clients should be treated with empathy and respect, and their concerns about the counselor or the counseling process should be addressed promptly and directly (Swenson, 1997). Where a counselor's best efforts at communication and problem solving have not been successful, however, he or she should consider referring the client to another competent professional (Buffone, 1991; Swenson, 1997).

**3.** *Supervision and consultation.* Risk management requires the thoughtful and timely use of supervision and consultation. Feedback from supervisors, colleagues, and other consultants can be very helpful in gaining perspective on a clinical problem or legal and ethical concern, and the supervision or consultation process can be invaluable in helping the counselor generate possible responses to problems. Participation in supervision is integral to effective mental health care practice (Welfel, 1998) and may be a condition of licensure. Failure by a counselor to seek supervision when he or she is aware or should be aware that trouble is brewing, moreover, may provide an additional basis for a liability claim (Belger, 1997). A process should be in place in which the counselor can obtain both ongoing supervision, and, as needed, supervision to address specific problems and concerns as they arise.

Consultation regarding legal and ethical matters can and in some cases should be with more than one individual, and there are circumstances in which it may be particularly useful for a counselor to consult with a professional in another mental health field. It may be appropriate, for example, for a counselor to consult with a psychiatrist who has expertise with violent clients to evaluate the threat of harm by a client to others. Weiner and Wettstein (1993) note the value of establishing relationships with other mental health professionals before the need to seek consultation or advice arises. Establishing a relationship with an attorney knowledgeable about mental health care issues can also be helpful. A network of positive and collaborative professional relationships that is already in place will contribute to efficient, effective problem solving when difficult practice issues are confronted. Supervision and consultation should be documented, both by the counselor and by the supervisor or consultant.

**4.** *Recordkeeping.* It is an axiom of practitioner risk management that what is not documented did not occur (Knapp, 1997). In an action against a mental health practitioner, accurate, contemporaneous records enhance the credibility of the practitioner's testimony in a deposition or at trial (Weiner & Wettstein, 1993) and document the care provided. Weiner and Wettstein (1993) counsel that, in this context, records will be most useful when they show the practitioner's "thinking and decisionmaking about the [client's] care, rather than simply documenting that an event occurred" (p. 179).

Mitchell (1991) identifies attorneys as "among the most dreaded" users of records kept by counselors, and warns that, to such users, "[w]hiteout on the record suggests changes; out-of sequence notes suggest alteration. Any missing, incomplete, changed, or wrong dates create doubt. Meaningless notes suggest incompetence" (p. 9). Weiner and Wettstein (1993) divide common recordkeeping pitfalls into errors of *overdocumentation,* such as the inclusion of irrelevant or sensitive material or observations disparaging to clients or other care providers, and errors of *underdocumentation,* which include failure to document telephone calls, significant events or decisions, or disclosures for informed consent, and failure to obtain and review prior records. Good risk management involves avoiding these and other pitfalls while maintaining a legible, objective, and accurate record of the counseling process and client care.

**5.** *Insurance.* Counselors should purchase and maintain professional liability insurance and be familiar with the terms of the policies. Counselors who practice in agencies, schools, or other organizations should review the terms of insurance policies that cover the organization and seek advice about the purchase of individual coverage. An insurance agent with expertise in the professional malpractice area can provide information about specific companies, policies, and coverage options.

In reviewing professional liability policies, counselors should pay particular attention to exclusions from coverage and requirements for reporting claims or circumstances that might give rise to a claim. Retiring counselors and counselors switching from one liability policy or carrier to another should seek insurance advice specific to those transitions.

**6.** *Knowledge of ethics and relevant law.* Inherent in all the risk management and risk reduction commentary is a conviction that familiarity with ethical and legal guidelines and imperatives, as well as sensitivity to ethical and legal issues that arise in counseling practice, will be useful in avoiding liability claims and problems. Keeping informed, being proactive in identifying possible problems, and seeking consultation and legal advice when issues arise are all essential to minimizing liability risks and maintaining a sense of balance in the face of possible claims. Continuing education, newsletters of professional associations, and books and periodicals available at libraries are sources of information about ethical and legal problems and decision making. Risk management seminars and other resources made available to counselors by their liability insurers can also be helpful. The ACA Insurance Trust, Inc., for example, provides a toll-free risk management hotline through which counselors insured under its program can seek guidance on liability issues.

**7.** *Practitioner self-care.* The ability to approach practice issues and potential problems thoughtfully and carefully may hinge not only on advance attention to risk management procedures but also on the counselor's frame of mind and confidence in his or her ability to meet challenges. Liability issues are a source of concern and a potential drain on a counselor's energy. Self-care is an essential component in practice management (Belger, 1997). With the stress and tension generated by situations that present a potential for counselor liability, attention to the counselor's own health and emotional well-being can be a key to maintaining a sense of perspective and balance. Counselors should also be alert to signs of reduced effectiveness or burn-out and, as appropriate, seek prompt assistance in addressing those problems.

The theme of self-care is interwoven with other risk management practices and relates to managing stress, being thoughtful and careful in responding to problems, and seeking support and guidance as necessary. "Key factors in averting malpractice claims include taking time to be self-reflective, taking time to properly keep records, taking time to find the right consultants, and making time to continually work with the client to explore how the relationship is working for the client" (Belger, 1997, p. 45). A careful and introspective approach to the daily challenges of practice is good for the counselor and will benefit his or her clients, as well.

## Parting Thoughts

Legal issues need attention in counseling practice. Clients have rights that must be protected, and counselors have duties of care to their clients and, in some circumstances, to others who could be harmed by clients. Sensitivity to legal issues can help a counselor build and maintain a sound professional practice and minimize the potential for liability.

Managing legal issues in counseling is largely a matter of being vigilant, open, and curious, and staying informed. A counselor who learns and stays abreast of legal requirements can implement procedures, such as informed consent or recordkeeping protocols, that will reduce the potential for errors in practice while meeting client needs. One can also develop a legal "antenna" that provides an early warning when a possible legal problem is brewing. Spotting issues early gives the counselor time to seek guidance from supervisors, consultants, and legal advisors, and, as appropriate, to work with the client to address the issues before they escalate into serious legal problems.

Legal problem solving is enhanced by thoughtful, thorough work in defining the problem and considering possible solutions. Legal and ethical requirements will provide the framework in which solutions are generated, but creativity, attention to client needs, and a willingness to seek support, information, and input are invaluable parts of the process. Clear answers to legal issues that arise in the practice of counseling will not always exist, but, with careful attention to themes of risk management highlighted in this chapter, appropriate, reasonable responses to problems can almost always be found.

# 9

# Clinical Supervision

## An Overview of Essentials

### Janine M. Bernard

*Janine M. Bernard's undergraduate major at Stonehill College in Massachusetts was English literature and people. Choosing the second of these, she completed her M.A. in counseling (with an emphasis in college student personnel) at the University of Connecticut. After a brief exposure to resident life at Boston University, she enrolled at Purdue University, where she completed her doctoral study in counselor education. Since then, she has taught at Purdue, Ball State University's Germany program, and, for the past 14 years, at Fairfield University, where she is chair of the Counselor Education Department. Bernard has written extensively on clinical supervision, including the text,* Fundamentals of Clinical Supervision *(Allyn and Bacon). She is past president of North Atlantic Association for Counselor Education and Supervision and past chair of the National Board for Certified Counselors. Her interests and passions include good literature and the performing arts. Bernard enjoys time with friends, the seashore, walking the dog, and having a cat in her lap.*

## In This Chapter...

- What are the objectives of clinical supervision?
- What should be considered in selecting a postdegree supervisor?
- What is meant by *institutional constraints* to clinical supervision?
- How do supervisor roles complement or confront the counselor?
- What is *impression management* and how does it sabotage good clinical supervision?

Throughout one's professional education, others primarily determine the process of clinical supervision. That is, the *who,* the *when,* and the *how* of supervision are decided by clinical faculty and site supervisors. The *why* of clinical supervision is rarely even voiced. It is a given that supervision is as necessary to training as textbooks are to counseling theory. With the growth of state licensure in the last two decades, postdegree supervision has become normative for an increasing number of professional counselors. Again, many of the conditions of supervision are dictated by these licensure laws. Yet, within these parameters, professional counselors make choices, although they often do so without having considered the foundation that constitutes good supervision. Even if the *by whom* of supervision is not a choice, understanding some of the elements of supervision will help make the experience more meaningful and productive.

This chapter is written primarily for counselors at the end of their training programs or early in their careers. For the most part, the assumption will be made that you are more likely to be a consumer than a provider of supervision. At the same time, relative newcomers to the profession are sometimes asked to provide supervision, or at least to be involved as a supervisor at some level. Therefore, this chapter serves as an outline of some of the critical areas that the new supervisor should investigate.

## *The Role of Supervision within the Profession*

Although supervision is valuable throughout one's career, it is far more likely that you will seek supervision prior to certification or licensure. Before proceeding, however, I would like to address the question often ignored during training: Why is supervision necessary?

The most obvious answer to this question is that supervision is required (for internship, for certification, for licensure, as part of one's job, etc.). This is probably also the weakest answer, because it includes no criteria to evaluate the experience. When you accept supervision only in a pro forma manner, you are positioned to neutralize its effects. In fact, supervision is necessary for ethical, legal, and developmental reasons. All three of these protect and enhance you, the professional counselor.

Ethically, supervisors serve as gatekeepers for the profession. When they evaluate you, grade you, endorse you, or renew your contract, they are saying that you can do the job at least at a minimally acceptable level of competence. This is essential for the profession and therefore for you. When professional counselors claim that they can do certain things, it is your clinical supervisor who affirms that *you* can justifiably be represented in that group of professionals. This is a big responsibility and one that supervisors assume cautiously and seriously. An additional responsibility of the supervisor, that of assuring that the client is protected, has legal as well as ethical implications. Ethically, clinical supervisors are mandated to assure that their supervisees do no harm; legally, they may be held liable if this is not accomplished adequately. As you can see, then, your clinical supervisor serves as a buffer between you and the full responsibility of your role as professional counselor. *Without supervision, you may be held accountable for more than you could be expected to know in light of your limited experience.* It is important to understand, however, that ignorance is not a legal defense for incompetence if you claim membership in a mental health profession (Meyer, Landis, & Hays, 1988). Therefore, even when supervision is not mandated for the new professional, it is strongly recommended.

Finally, clinical supervision is designed to make you a better counselor. Counseling is part art and part science. Degree programs can teach the technical and knowledge aspects (science) of counseling in relatively uniform ways. The art of counseling, however, is unique to each counselor. To become more expert in the practice of counseling, you need both experience and oversight. If you rely on experience alone, you will be insensitive to your own blind spots. A clinical supervisor can help you move further along your personal developmental path. Without supervision, you are vulnerable to repeating the same mistakes over and over. In fact, without supervision, those mistakes might not even be identified as mistakes. Even when the counselor is reasonably competent, good supervision can offer a unique perspective on the counselor's work. Not only does this help reduce burnout (a chronic problem among the mental health professions [Murphy & Pardeck, 1986]) but it reinfuses the excitement about your work that can only be present when you are learning something new.

## Supervision as Distinct from Consultation

Occasionally, the terms *supervision* and *consultation* are used interchangeably, which can be very confusing for the new professional. Unlike consultation, supervision is usually conducted by a senior member of the same profession. Furthermore, supervision is evaluative, extends over enough time to allow the supervisor to make an adequate assessment of the counselor's skills for the purpose of some sort of endorsement, and meets the objectives of supervision already mentioned (Bernard & Goodyear, 1998).

Consultation, on the other, may be either a short-term or long-term relationship, often employs persons from other professions, and is not evaluative in nature. A common example of consultation is the relationship set up by a counseling service with a psychiatrist. The psychiatrist is asked to evaluate all clients who may have a biological condition that is complicating their behavioral or emotional problems and who may benefit from medication. The psychiatrist would assess, diagnose, and prescribe medication for appropriate clients and monitor the effect of those medications. When in a consultant role, it is important that the psychiatrist respect the counseling center staff as mental health professionals and be willing and able to work with them. The supervision in this situation would be limited to the medical condition of the client, not overall treatment planning (though certainly some treatment options will be determined by the psychiatric diagnosis). The psychiatrist would have no role in evaluating the counseling competence of center staff. This collaborative relationship is much more descriptive of consultation than supervision.

## Clinical Supervision as Distinct from Administrative Supervision

A final distinction should be made because *supervisor* can mean different things in the day-to-day life of the professional counselor. Your supervisor may be the person who runs the agency, who is there as a back-up professional, who serves as a mentor, your employer, a troubleshooter, or who gives you an annual evaluation of your performance. All of these functions would make this person an administrative supervisor. Although administrative supervisors often contribute to your professional and clinical development, they cannot be considered clinical supervisors unless they are also actively involved with you in the systematic discussion of your client cases. More than anything else, this is often a matter of boundaries; that is, in order for clinical supervision to occur, time and attention must be given to clinical issues and to the clinical development of the counselor. Clinical supervisors also must have knowledge and skills that are different from administrative supervisors, an outline of which will follow.

## Selecting a Supervisor

As stated at the opening of this chapter, most novice counselors are accustomed to being assigned a supervisor, not choosing one. In a way, everything in this chapter can be used to enlarge your vision when making this important choice. Some things, however, are the cornerstones to the selection process. Stated briefly, there are two questions that you must address as fully as possible: Why am I seeking supervision? and What kind of supervisor will meet my professional goals?

### Why Am I Seeking Supervision?

Usually, there are two levels to the answer for why someone is seeking supervision. Certification or licensure might be the uppermost level. Beyond that, however, it is important for you to realize that not every supervisor who meets licensure or certification requirements will meet your needs. To help you identify your needs, consider the following:

• *Specialty of the supervisor.* Perhaps you would like to use the supervision experience to learn more about substance abuse or depression or any number of mental health themes.

• *Supervision method.* Perhaps you have heard that a particular supervisor uses a lot of live supervision and you would like an opportunity to experience that particular supervision method.

• *Individual characteristic.* Perhaps, having only had male supervisors in the past, you want to work with a female supervisor or someone different from you in a way that is significant to you. (It should be noted that individual differences will be most beneficial if they are addressed openly in supervision [Cook, 1994]. For example, choosing a supervisor of a different race will not automatically make you more sensitive to racial issues in counseling unless you and your supervisor are both open to addressing this theme in supervision sessions.)

• *Supervision style or skill.* You may have learned that a particular supervisor is very challenging (something you think you have not experienced in supervision), or very organized, or very good at documenting treatment plans. In each case, it is important that you understand the implications of choosing someone because of a particular trait, especially if the trait is complementary to your own traits. Some things can be learned easily from others; other things, because they challenge your personal style, are much more difficult. Again, a discussion looking at the costs and benefits of your choice should be one of the first discussions you have with a prospective supervisor.

Once you start considering your needs (or wants), the list could be extensive; in fact, you may need to realize that no supervisor will meet all your criteria. But going through an exercise such as this will make you more cognizant of the multiple aspects of supervision and the various gains that can be accomplished through supervision.

## What Kind of Supervisor Will Meet My Professional Goals?

As you have probably surmised, there is no clear boundary between this question and the former question. What you want from supervision in part defines the kind of supervisor you are seeking. A necessary place to begin has to do with credentials of the supervisor. If you are attempting to become certified or licensed, there may be particular criteria that the supervisor must meet. For example, in some states, only a supervisor who is licensed as a mental health counselor can supervise a counselor seeking that same license. In other states, any licensed mental health professional (e.g., psychologist or social worker) would be acceptable as a supervisor. Being cognizant of relevant criteria is imperative when selecting a supervisor. A word of caution: Although the amount of overlap among mental health professions is significant, some assumptions about practice can be substantially different. Worldviews among the mental health professions are as compelling as those among different ethnic groups. Choosing a supervisor across professions can be an excellent decision if done deliberately for specific reasons. But assuming that the professional identity of the supervisor does not matter is probably misguided. Finally, some states monitor the supervision process closely and require that supervisors have particular qualifications in supervision (Sutton, 1997). It is relatively easy to determine if a supervisor is on an "approved" list.

This leads to one last essential area to consider in choosing your clinical supervisor. With the exception of a handful of states, to date there is relatively little monitoring of clinical supervision as a distinct professional activity. Therefore, once you have considered your clinical needs and the credentials of potential supervisors, you may want to inquire about the knowledge/training *in clinical supervision per se* of your potential supervisor.

## The Knowledge Base of Clinical Supervision

In the last 25 years, the theory and practice of clinical supervision have been recognized as distinct from counseling and therapy (Bernard & Goodyear, 1998). There is a good deal of consensus about the background knowledge and skills required to be a competently trained supervisor (cf. Borders et al., 1991). In 1998, the National Board for Certified Counselors (NBCC) developed a national credential for approved clinical supervisor (ACS). Among the various requirements for the ACS, NBCC has included nine content areas that must be covered in one's professional education/training. These nine areas, which are very similar to those outlined by Borders and colleagues (1991), are as follows:*

*Note:* NBCC Pub 50 DACS1-5-98. NBCC grants publication rights of this material to Allyn and Bacon. Note that such material is subject to revisions found at ⟨www.nbcc.org⟩. Reprinted by permission of the National Board for Certified Counselors, Inc.

1. *Roles and Functions of Clinical Supervision*—Includes the unique purposes, goals, and foci of supervision, the appropriate conditions for supervision, and the distinction between supervision and other professional roles.
2. *Models of Clinical Supervision*—Includes the major approaches for conceptualizing supervision (e.g., psychotherapy theory-based models of supervision, developmental models, and social models).
3. *Counselor Development*—Includes topics such as individual learning styles, cognitive developmental levels, differences in experience levels, stages of counselor development, and critical transition points, as well as how to create an appropriate educational environment or climate based on developmental differences.
4. *Methods and Techniques in Clinical Supervision*—Includes supervision methods for assessing and intervening with supervisees (e.g., audiotape review, live supervision, self-report), as well as the appropriate use of, and benefits and limitations of, each supervision method.
5. *Supervisory Relationship Issues*—Includes the inter- and intrapersonal variables that affect supervision such as the parameters of a working alliance, conflict within supervision, supervisee anxiety, social influence, and parallel process.
6. *Cultural Issues in Supervision*—Includes the implications of cultural differences and/or similarities between supervisee and supervisor such as race, gender, sexual orientation, and belief systems, and how these impact the process and outcome of supervision.
7. *Group Supervision*—Includes topics such as the structure and processes of group supervision, the unique tasks of the supervisor in the group context, ground rules and stages of group supervision, and the advantages and limitations of the group modality.
8. *Legal and Ethical Issues*—Includes major ethical and legal tenets that affect supervision such as due process, confidentiality, informed consent, dual relationships, competence, duty to warn, and direct and vicarious liability, and the implications of these tenets for supervisees, clients, and the supervisor.
9. *Evaluation*—Includes studies that address the role of evaluation as central to supervision, criteria for evaluation, sources of feedback, the process and outcomes of evaluation, and the role of documentation in evaluation, as well as procedures for the evaluation of the supervision experience.

A supervisor who is knowledgeable in these nine areas will be far better suited to address a variety of supervision challenges than someone who is not. The areas serve as a kaleidoscope of lenses for the supervisor to consider in delivering supervision, thus also serving as some assurance that the supervision being offered is both comprehensive and holistic.

## The Supervision Experience

There are many ways you can influence the supervision process in addition to choosing the right supervisor. Key to influencing a process is understanding it. This section will look at supervision as it is experienced and will highlight areas that can be influenced by the supervisee.

### Organizing Supervision

At some level, supervision is a contract between you and your supervisor, albeit the vast majority of supervision contracts are informal. Even so, the more clarity that can be established going into supervision, the less likelihood there will be for unfortunate misunder-standings or missteps later. Furthermore, some sort of contract or agreement of understanding elevates each person's awareness of his or her duties and responsibilities (Osborn & Davis, 1996).

At the most pragmatic level, contracts should address the frequency of meetings, the methods of supervision that will be used, any fees that might be involved, the types of records that will be kept by both you and the supervisor, and the criteria that will be used for evaluation. Osborn and Davis (1996) suggest a more comprehensive (and thoughtful) contract that includes a written statement of your goals in seeking supervision, a statement of commitment from each of you that describes what you are willing to do to make super-vision successful, and an outline of a procedure to follow if there is a conflict within super-vision that has not been resolved.

Although it is easier if your supervisor approaches supervision with a clear organi-zational plan that includes some of the matters mentioned here, do not be put off if this does not occur. It may even have more impact on the process if you ask about some of these parameters and offer to put some things down on paper. Supervisors can be ener-gized by eager, thoughtful supervisees. In fact, I would hypothesize that *it is the invest-ment of the supervisee in the supervision process that is most predictive of a positive outcome.*

## Supervision Methods

The methods your supervisor uses to gather information about your work will significantly direct your supervision experience. At least three factors will influence your supervisor's choices: the vision of supervision held by your supervisor, institutional constraints, and your individual/developmental needs.

*Supervisor vision* has to do with the ways that supervisors conceptualize counselor growth (Bernard & Goodyear, 1998). If supervisors believe that counselors benefit mostly from examining transference and countertransference issues, they may choose self-report, a method where the counselor reports his or her impressions of each counseling session to the supervisor. If supervisors view counselor growth as a matter of acquiring expert timing in the delivery of well-phrased interventions, they may prefer audio- or videotape or live supervision so that they can observe actual sessions and give specific feedback or, in the case of live supervision, even coach the counselor through a series of interventions. Although many supervisors may not address their visions per se, all supervisors make assumptions about how counselors become more skilled, and these should be consistent with their choice of methods.

*Institutional constraints* may limit method choices. For example, live supervision, which calls for some type of observation room, may be a luxury that a particular agency or school cannot afford. The same may be true for videotape equipment. If the supervisor wants actual samples of the counselor's work, however, the audiotape is a convenient back-up method. If the supervisor believes that live supervision is essential, an inexpensive inter-com system can be used that will relay voices from room to room. As a last resort, the supervisor can engage in cotherapy or direct observation within the counseling room if the supervisor believes that close monitoring is important.

An unfortunate category of institutional constraint has to do with policies rather than physical plant. Occasionally, an agency will have a no-taping policy. Usually, this is a misguided policy that is rationalized as having to do with client privacy (Bernard, 1993). Actually, the underlying motive for such policies may have more to do with the procedure for getting permissions to tape and some free-floating fear of litigation. Unfortunately, these agencies are probably more at risk, not less, because of their fear to track closely the work of their counselors. The vast majority of breaches of confidentiality have been the inappropriate *verbal* sharing of client information, not the passing along of an audiotape. Furthermore, any policy that puts clients at risk by discouraging close supervision is fool-hardy when calls for accountability and competent service are increasing.

Finally, your *individual/developmental needs* may suggest the desirability of a particular supervision method. For example, you may want to increase your skills in family counseling, having had limited opportunity to conduct family sessions during training. If this is so, you will benefit much more from close supervision (e.g., live supervision or cotherapy) until you become adept at maneuvering through what can be a maze of family dynamics within sessions. Once your skills are such that you are relatively sure you could competently conduct a family therapy session, then you might benefit more from taped sessions, allowing you to be more reflective as you and your supervisor watch and discuss your interactions with the family.

## *Focus and Role Possibilities*

Supervisors will target particular aspects of your performance when giving feedback; they will also deliver their feedback in distinct ways. The Discrimination Model of supervision refers to these as the *foci of supervision* and *supervisor roles* (Bernard, 1979; 1997).

### *Supervision Foci*

Although supervision is relatively complex, there is only so much that the supervisor can react to when observing a counselor. Basically, there are four categories of skills that can be addressed in supervision: intervention skills, conceptualization skills, personalization skills, and professional skills (Bernard, 1979, 1997; Lanning, 1986). Understanding these will allow you to put your supervisor's feedback in some context; it will also allow you to communicate with your supervisor in a productive manner.

*Intervention skills* are those overt (in-session) behaviors that distinguish counseling from other social interactions (Bernard, 1999). Intervention skills include all the observable counselor behaviors that define counseling. By contrast, *conceptualization skills* are the cognitive skills that one uses to plan sessions, to react appropriately within sessions, and to process what transpired in each session. Whenever an insight is gleaned or a decision is made about how to proceed, conceptualization skills are being used. Without good conceptualization skills, counseling would be a random activity. *Personalization skills* are skills used to reflect on how well one uses one's *self* in counseling. This includes a host of skills and qualities such as interpersonal strengths, skill at handling transference situations, reaction to supervision, and so no. Finally, *professional skills* consist of behaviors both within and outside the counseling relationship (Lanning, 1986). These include ethical behavior, recordkeeping, and consulting appropriately with other professionals.

Counselors reflect their level of expertise in all four of these areas at all times. It is the responsibility of the supervisor to discriminate among these skill categories when offering feedback. Occasionally, supervisors may discriminate incorrectly. For example, a supervisor may think that a counselor has made an error in judgment (conceptualization issue) when, in fact, the counselor is avoiding an intervention because she is fearful about where it might go (personalization issue). The more insightful and open you are with your supervisor in helping him or her get to the real issue, the more productive will be your supervision.

### Supervisor Roles

The three most common roles that supervisors assume are that of teacher, counselor, and consultant (Bernard, 1979, 1997). Supervisors sometimes choose a role deliberately and with a particular supervisory goal in mind; at other times, the supervisor role may be more reflective of their individual styles. Awareness of these different roles can potentially help you understand and influence the supervision process.

The most directive role for the supervisor to assume is that of *teacher*. When in that role, the supervisor is taking more responsibility and more authority about what the counselor is doing well and what the counselor might need to modify or learn to become more skilled. Any direct suggestion about what to do with a particular client would probably reflect the teacher role. When supervisors are focusing on the interpersonal or intrapersonal dynamics of counselors, they are probably using the *counselor* role (Bernard, 1999). The typical supervisor motive for using this role is to enhance the counselor's personal growth, reflecting an assumption held by many supervisors that growing professionally necessitates some simultaneous personal growth. As counselors progress in their careers, the supervisors' use of the counselor role is more likely to stimulate development than the teacher role (Skovholt & Ronnestad, 1992). Another supervisor role that is highly successful with more seasoned counselors (and can be used selectively and successfully with counselors at all developmental levels) is the *consultant* role. In this role, supervisors are encouraging their supervisees to trust their own insights, thus acting more as a resource than a coach. This role is best used when the supervisor has evidence that the dilemma to be resolved is within the counselor's reach. Otherwise, the counselor might feel "set up" if it *sounds* like the supervisor is extending authority, but this is then reversed when the counselor goes in a direction different from what the supervisor had planned.

Most supervisors draw from all three roles in their work. Occasionally, supervisees encourage a particular role through their own behavior. The questioning, insecure counselor will encourage the supervisor to take on the teacher role; the desperate, overwhelmed counselor will often elicit the counselor role in the supervisor; and the self-assured, contemplative counselor is more likely to bring out the consultant role in a supervisor. Any stereotypic use of roles, however, is likely to stagnate the supervision process.

## Personal and Interpersonal Challenges

It would be hard to conceive of a professional role more personal than that of counselor. As a result, counselors *do* take their work personally. Supervision involves joining with another professional in a very personal endeavor. It is no wonder, then, that supervision encompasses challenges that are experienced as both personal and interpersonal. For these reasons, the supervisory *relationship* (or *environment* created by the supervisor) is central to productive supervision.

Some aspects of this relationship will be determined by individual or developmental differences (Bernard & Goodyear, 1998). For example, the relationship between a seasoned supervisor and a novice counselor will be different from that between the same supervisor and a more experienced counselor. Other relationship issues are less characterized by demographic variables then by interpersonal processes. In other words, you would not expect the same seasoned supervisor to have an identical relationship with you as with a peer of yours. In what must be a cursory fashion, each of these broad relationship dimensions will be reviewed.

### *Individual Differences as a Determinant of the Supervisory Environment*

All other things being equal, each supervision relationship brings together people who must bridge a significant number of individual differences in order to work together. Both you and your supervisor will be unique in how you present yourselves in new situations, how you think and learn, what you believe about the learning process, what larger belief systems you hold as foremost, and how you experience yourselves culturally. All of these and any of these can call on the supervisor to alter the relationship environment.

Let us consider only a few of the ways that individual differences can affect the relationship. Haferkamp (1989) and Haverkamp (1994) studied self-monitoring (the degree of sensitivity about social appropriateness) and found that supervisees differ significantly on this measure. Low self-monitors are much more likely to follow their own instincts; high self-monitors are more likely to follow a supervisor's lead. If not addressed as a supervision issue (or even if it is), this will assuredly influence the supervisor/counselor working relationship, especially if the supervisor and the counselor are significantly different on this variable. Similarly, the Myers-Briggs Type Indicator (Myers, 1962; Myers & McCaulley, 1985) profile of each person has been found to affect supervision (Craig & Sleight, 1990; Swanson & O'Saben, 1993). For example, in terms of the information management scale (*J*udging versus *P*erceiving), supervisors were far more likely to be *J*s than were counselors. This would certainly influence the relationship when necessary paperwork was not completed in a way that met the supervisor's standard. In short, issues as seemingly benign as self-presentation style and cognitive style can complicate (if not compromise) the supervisory relationship, especially if not addressed early in that relationship.

The counseling profession as a whole has made a significant commitment to appreciating the impact of cultural differences within helping relationships. These same cultural issues that modify counseling relationships also influence supervisory relationships. For instance, Sells and associates (1997) say that female supervisors are more likely to focus on the counselor in supervision, whereas male supervisors are more apt to focus on the counselor's client. Such a difference has profound implications for the level of intimacy within the supervisory relationship, as well as for what will be learned within that relationship.

In addition to individual and cultural differences, experience level and developmental level will call for different supervisory environments (Bernard & Goodyear, 1998). Considerable evidence shows that counselors who have accrued greater levels of experience will want and require different types of supervision than counselors of lesser experience (e.g., Borders, 1990; Mallinckrodt & Nelson, 1991; Olk & Friedlander, 1992; Winter & Holloway, 1991). Although there are notable exceptions (e.g., Tracey, Ellickson, & Sherry, 1989; Whisenhunt et al., 1997), most advanced counselors want and need much less structure from the supervisor than counselors-in-training. (In other words, a consultant role would be appropriate more often with advanced counselors than with novice trainees.) There have also been differences noted among counselors of different experience levels in terms of presentation style (e.g., Tracey et al., 1988) and conceptualization of the counseling process (e.g., Cummings et al., 1990). All of these certainly should influence how the supervisor works with the counselor.

As counselors develop their skills, they become less reactive in counseling sessions, process subtle client information more expertly, and challenge themselves at deeper levels. Although experience level is a good indicator of developmental level, it is not assuredly so. Some counselors are more developmentally advanced than their experience would predict; others lag behind. In either case, one can imagine the relationship rub if the supervisor were to assume a direct link between experience and development when this is not the case.

## Processes and Issues within the Supervisory Relationship

Clinical supervision is a context that offers virtually nowhere to hide—at least not for very long. The very work of supervision is challenging and, at times, requires that egos take a back seat. It is no wonder that things do not always go smoothly between counselor and supervisor.

The first interpersonal dilemma that comes to mind is the counselor's anxiety and how this is handled in supervision. Most anxiety stems from a strong need to feel competent (Bordin, 1983). Many counselors harbor a suspicion that they are impostors (Harvey & Katz, 1985) and may eventually be found out. In this case, then, the supervisor is, at some level, the enemy. The dynamics that emerge when this fear of the supervisor's assessment is played out has been chronicled elsewhere as anxiety-avoidant games or maneuvers (Bauman, 1972; Kadushin, 1968; McWilliams, 1994).

It is a psychological assumption that some anxiety motivates us to perform at higher levels. The issue, then, is not how to remove all anxiety from supervision but to address it in a manner that is productive. One supervisee strategy that leads to dubious results is what some authors have referred to as "impression management" (Leary & Kowalski, 1990)—that is, attempting to be perceived in particular ways, especially in light of evaluation. Ronnestad and Skovholt (1993) noted that in some cases, the counselor's attempt at impression management leads to spotty supervision because only success stories are presented or because information is given to the supervisor only in a way that allows the counselor to stay in full control. In this case, the relationship is essentially contrived and superficial.

Although anxiety is a major supervision interpersonal issue, it is not the only one. There are times that conflict occurs, perhaps stemming from some of the individual differences noted earlier. Conflict is also more likely to occur in supervision when the counselor is more experienced (Ronnestad & Skovholt, 1993) or at the time of evaluation (Robiner, Fuhrman, & Ristvedt, 1993). Conflict within supervision may be an indicator that anxiety has not been addressed adequately, or that insufficient time has been spent building a working relationship, including the sharing of assumptions about what can be accomplished as part of supervision.

It is also important to recognize that supervision as a dyad is surrounded by a permeable boundary. The issues of the client can have the strength of affecting the supervisory relationship. In fact, parallel process, a theoretical tenet about the supervision process, holds that occasionally supervisees may unconsciously present themselves to their supervisors as their clients have presented to them. As an example, a counseling session in which the client communicates little affect about his or her situation is followed by a supervision session in which the counselor communicates very little concern about the client's progress.

Whenever parallel process is suspected, transference and/or countertransference may be operating. Grey and Fiscalini (1987) note that transference/countertransference issues often involve the themes of dependency and authority. It makes sense that if either counselor or supervisor enters the relationship with any significant unresolved issues around dependency, authority, power, trust, competence, and/or anxiety, these are likely to manifest themselves in the relationship. Said differently, the supervision relationship can reverberate from dynamics that initiated elsewhere. Learning from these reverberations calls for commitment and compassion from both counselor and supervisor so that the supervisory context becomes a safe haven.

## *Evaluation*

"Evaluation could be viewed as the nucleus of clinical supervision" (Bernard & Goodyear, 1998, p. 152). The gatekeeping function of supervision cannot be accomplished without reliable evaluation. As has been stated already, however, evaluation can also be viewed as the nucleus of counselor anxiety in supervision. Handling this responsibility professionally, with empathy and with integrity, is a major challenge for every clinical supervisor.

Evaluation is sometimes avoided by the supervisor until late in the supervisory relationship. This is always an error and is often paired with an unsatisfactory experience for both you and your supervisor. Instead, as noted earlier, an evaluation plan should be introduced when the initial supervision contract is presented. At the very least, an evaluation plan should include explaining criteria, describing the relationship between supervision method and evaluation, receiving a schedule for formative and summative evaluation and a copy of any evaluation instrument(s) that will be used, and arriving at a mutual understanding of the desired outcome of supervision. For your own protection, if your supervisor does not raise the evaluation topic, then you should.

A good evaluation instrument can be an excellent tool to assist you in understanding the *criteria* by which you will be evaluated. At the same time, criteria that emerge from conversations between you and your supervisor may be equally important. You should also be clear about the ways in which *methods* used for supervision will enhance your development as a counselor. *Formative* evaluation should actually occur as part of each supervision session; that is, you should leave each session with some direction about your next challenge on the learning curve. In other words, when it is time for *summative* (or final) evaluation, you should have a pretty good idea of the progress you have been making all along. If an *evaluation instrument* is used as part of the evaluation plan, you should have some idea of what scores mean (e.g., "Average" compared to what? "Excellent" compared to what standard?). The *outcomes* of evaluation are usually in the form of an endorsement of some sort or a recommendation for additional supervision to achieve particular learning in order to reach a satisfactory level. When the outcomes of evaluation are a surprise (in a negative direction) to the counselor, either the counselor has been in denial or the supervisor has failed to communicate adequately at the formative stages. It is probably these types of outcomes that give evaluation its bad name. On the other hand, when supervision has been productive and dynamic, evaluation is typically an affirming and enhancing experience.

## Professional Issues

The experience of clinical supervision represents the foreground, whereas important professional issues form a stabilizing background. These include ethical and legal issues around supervision as well as the documentation of supervision.

### Legal Issues

The central legal issues for supervisors are *malpractice* and *liability* for harm done to a supervisee or to a client. A supervisor would be vulnerable to malpractice if it could be proved that, within a supervisory relationship, harm was done to a supervisee because of supervision that fell below an acceptable standard of practice. Because a causal relationship must be established between the injury and the negligence (Corey et al., 1993), a high standard is set for plaintiffs to succeed in a malpractice claim. I am unaware of any suits brought against supervisors by their supervisees. It is far more likely that a supervisor would be named as a codefendant in a malpractice suit aimed at the supervisee. This leads us to the core legal issue for supervisors: liability. (Elsewhere in this book, legal and ethical issues pertaining directly to counselors are addressed. But it is important for you to understand your supervisor's vulnerability in order to appreciate the symbiotic relationship between your work and that of your supervisor from a legal standpoint.)

The famous *Tarasoff* case (*Tarasoff* v. *Regents of the University of California,* 1976) was important to supervisors as well as to counselors. As is generally known, this case established within the profession what is referred to as the *duty to warn.* But the case also was a hallmark case because the supervisor was named as a codefendant. Since then, the question has been asked: Under what conditions is a supervisor liable for the negligence of a supervisee?

A supervisor can be accused of either direct or vicarious liability. *Direct* liability would occur if the supervision itself was the cause of the harm (e.g., if a supervisor suggested a strategy to the counselor that was proven to have dire consequences for the client). In general, *vicarious liability* is of greater concern to supervisors—that is, being held responsible for the actions of one's supervisee even if these actions were not known by the supervisor. Disney and Stephens (1994) suggest that establishing the liability of the supervisor might include "whether the supervisor could have reasonably expected the supervisee to commit the act" (p. 16). With this in mind, the forming of a supervisory contract should include some sort of understanding about what you need to share with your supervisor and when. Such an understanding would help protect all parties involved in supervision, including the client.

### Ethical Issues

The ethical issues affecting supervision parallel those of counseling. The mandate, then, is that safeguards offered to clients must be offered to you, as well. Additionally, your supervisor must be assured that you follow ethical guidelines with your clients. Using *informed consent* as an example, the supervisor is required to make certain that (1) you have informed your clients of relevant logistics of counseling, the limits of *confidentiality,* as well as any potential consequences of the treatment they are receiving; (2) you have informed your clients of all relevant supervision procedures (e.g., that taped sessions will be heard by your supervisor); and (3) you are informed of the parameters surrounding supervision, including what kinds of information will be kept confidential, evaluation procedures, and the form that supervision will take. This multilevel responsibility is true for the supervisor in light of any ethical standard. Obviously, a close-working relationship between you and your supervisor will be essential to assure that these ethical mandates are fulfilled.

*Due process* is a critical ethical guideline that offers you some protection around the issue of evaluation. Especially if a counselor's performance has been judged below standard, it is important that the supervisor can document that the counselor's rights, including the right to remediate the situation, have been protected. Any indication that an evaluation was capricious or arbitrary may justify an accusation that the due process standard was violated. This ethical issue has received increasing attention in the literature as the profession struggles with the problem of what to do with impaired counselors (Lamb, Cochran, & Jackson, 1991). At the same time, it serves to remind supervisors that their evaluations, when negative, can have serious consequences and that their contract with you must include steps that alert you if your performance is less than satisfactory.

*Dual relationships* is another ethical standard with a particular complication as it applies to supervision. Obviously, supervisors and counselors must refrain from inappropriate dual relationships just as counselors and clients must. Unlike the situation within counseling, however, often you and your supervisor cannot avoid having *some* kind of dual relationships. It is quite common, for example, within a work setting for your clinical supervisor to be working with you in a variety of ways, some of which may feel far more collaborative than supervisory. In these cases, the supervisor must be particularly cautious that the integrity of the supervisory relationship is maintained. Dual relationships between supervisors and counselors are considered unethical if it is likely that your supervisor's judgment will be impaired or if there is reasonable risk that you will be exploited (Hall, 1988).

Finally, counselors are ethically bound not to practice outside their area(s) or level(s) of *competence.* Being under supervision typically implies that you are not yet ready to practice independently. It is reasonable to assume that it is essentially the supervisor's responsibility to determine whether you are working outside or beyond your competence. Such a judgment call can, in fact, be a *close* call when it is the supervisor's desire to give you more challenging cases specifically to extend your competence. The method of supervision can often be used to balance the difficulty of a case; that is, it is ethical to allow you to work with clients that might be at the very edge of your competence if supervision is closer. In fact, this has been one of the arguments for the desirability of live supervision (Bernard & Goodyear, 1998). It should be noted that the standard of competence can be applied to supervision, as well. In other words, it is becoming more questionable for people to offer clinical supervision without training specific to the supervision process.

Most professional issues have legal and/or ethical implications; this section has reviewed only a sample of these. You should consult more comprehensive reviews of clinical supervision for a thorough investigation of professional issues in the practice of clinical supervision (e.g., Bernard & Goodyear, 1998; Disney & Stephens, 1994). The NBCC Standards for the Ethical Practice of Clinical Supervision (1998) are included in Appendix C.

## *Summary and Conclusion*

Although clinical supervision has traditionally been orchestrated by the supervisor, the educated consumer is more likely to receive greater benefits from the experience. In summary, then, you should consider the following when entering into a supervisory relationship:

1. Have you done the necessary homework to know what qualifications are required of your supervisor for your purposes (e.g., licensure requirements)?
2. Can your supervisor meet your individual professional goals?
3. Is your supervisor adequately trained in clinical supervision?
4. Do you understand the conditions of supervision (contract)?
5. Do you know what methods your supervisor will use? Do you understand the advantages of these methods? Have you discussed a variety of supervision methods?
6. Have you and your supervisor discussed the foci of supervision (interventions, conceptualization, and personalization)? Do you have a sense of your strengths? Your areas for growth?
7. Can you recognize the different roles that your supervisor can assume? Are they in line with your developmental goals?
8. Have you discussed individual differences with your supervisor, including learning styles and cultural differences? Have you addressed these as they might relate to clients?
9. Have you discussed an evaluation plan and are you clear about criteria for evaluation?
10. Finally, have you reviewed pertinent professional issues, most especially relevant ethical tenets?

Clinical supervision is central to a vibrant profession. Most of this chapter has focused on the procedures, or tools, of supervision. Equally important is the spirit that drives supervision. If you have ever watched a professional musician encouraging and delighting in young talent, you have seen supervision at its best. Despite the research, the models, the techniques, and the difficult moments, clinical supervision is ultimately a process of generously handing down the jewels of the profession. Good supervisors are able to engage the excitement of learning. They remain honored to be part of another's professional development.

As this chapter has attempted to communicate, however, the supervisor is only half of the formula for a positive supervision experience. Perhaps more important is the readiness of the supervisee, not only to learn but to engage fully in the supervision process. In so doing, the knowledgeable counselor can look forward to a supervisory experience that will nourish his or her professional development for years to come.

# 10

# Counselor Advocacy

## Promoting the Profession

### Howard B. Smith

*Howard B. Smith is the senior director of professional affairs for the American Counseling Association. He comes to that position with a rich educational, career, and service background in the counseling field. Prior to his present appointment, Smith was professor and department head in the Educational Leadership and Counseling Department at Northeast Louisiana University, and earlier at South Dakota State University. He holds a B.A. in psychology from Sioux Falls College, an M.Div. from Central Baptist Theological Seminary, and M.Ed. in counseling from South Dakota State University, and the doctorate in educational psychology and counseling from the University of South Dakota. Smith has an equally extensive record of service to the profession, including past president of the American Mental Health Counselors Association, member of the Governing Council of the American Counseling Association, Chair of the ACA Government Relations Committee, Chair of the ACA Professionalization Committee, and treasurer of the Southern Association for Counselor Education and Supervision. For relaxation, Smith enjoys escapes and touring on his motorcycle, good mysteries, and cabinetmaking.*

## In This Chapter . . .

- What does Smith consider to be advocacy issues in the "internal domain"?
- What are the advocacy issues of the "external domain"?
- Which of these issues do you consider to be most important to your practice of counseling?

Counselor advocacy is a topic that is little understood, nearly absent in the literature, yet, one of the most vitally needed areas in the profession. This is very difficult to understand, since counselors have little difficulty in advocating for their clients or for social issues that have an impact on society as a whole. However, advocating for counselors and the services they provide has escaped their attention at best or been avoided at worst. At any rate, it has been seriously neglected. Perhaps it is because it appears to be selfish or self-serving. This may be coupled with a quality that often attracts individuals into the counseling profession in the first place—that is, being "others orientated" (desiring to help others). Eriksen (1997) points out that it is only through the advocacy efforts of many counselors that professional counselors are able to practice today. By *practice,* Eriksen is referring to licensed practice in 45 states and the District of Columbia and that the profession as a whole has earned its relative status as a respected profession. This descriptive statement, however, omits certain realities that evolved in mental health care in the recent past.

The mental health provider arena has become very complex and competitive. Evidence of this complexity and competition abounds. As was noted in Chapter 4, there are several separate mental health care provider professions, including (but not necessarily limited to) counseling, marriage and family therapy, psychiatric nursing, psychiatry, psychology, and social work. Most of these professions are further divided into specialties and subspecialties. Further, many of the subspecialties within a given profession have their own unique credential. Within the American Counseling Association, the largest professional counseling association, for example, there are currently 17 divisions, 6 of which have their own special credential through the National Board for Certified Counselors (NBCC). If one adds to this mix the variability among state licensure laws within the profession of counseling described by Sutton in Chapter 5, the complexity becomes self-evident.

Complexity and specialization often lead to divisiveness and competition within the mental health care provider arena. Examples of this can be seen in the reduction of funding for auxiliary or support services in public schools and the outsourcing of counseling services to social workers and marriage and family therapists. The presence of a managed care–driven marketplace in which some professions are recognized across the board as viable providers and others are given only partial recognition with still others not being recognized at all, certainly increases the divisiveness if not the competition. Given this environment, it is little wonder that public policy-makers and the general public often have difficulty with regard to the distinctions (often subtle) between these various groups of providers and what they are qualified to do. This confusion in and of itself serves only to intensify the competition.

Looking specifically and only at the counseling profession, one should not be surprised at either the complexity or the competition, given the history of the profession. As noted in Chapter 2, its path has not been straightforward from some seminal point in history. Its professional roots are intertwined with other mental health provider professions. It remains a conglomerate of ruggedly individualistic specialties amongst and between whom there is much more common ground than they allow themselves to believe.

It would appear that the profession has been struggling with two separate yet equally important issues. On the one hand is the reality of how the various specialties within the counseling profession are alike, and on the other hand is how each of those specialties is very different and unique. Over the years, this struggle has led the profession to abort organized, strategic, and serious attempts at advocacy for the counseling profession as a whole through benign neglect. And yet, there have been attempts on the part of several of the specialties to advocate for that particular specialty. Examples of these efforts abound in brochures and information pieces produced by many of the divisions of ACA (e.g., American School Counselors Association [Henderson and Gysbers, 1998], Association of Counselor Education and Supervision [Griffin, 1993], American Mental Health Counselors Association [Glauser, 1996; Covin, 1994], and American College Counseling Association [1991]. Where does all of this leave the counseling profession (in its entirety and as a whole) regarding the issue of advocacy? The efforts, although numerous, have been largely confined to those of individuals who will advocate for a particular and specific cause or issue, at a particular and specific time, and then return to business as usual. These sorties into advocacy, although admittedly numerous, have extremely limited value when considering the potential of an intentional, strategic, organized, continuous, and strong effort by numerous individuals or by an entire profession.

Liteman and Liteman (1998) note that *turfism,* defined as "loyalty to one's own office, department, division, or section rather than to the association as a whole," can dissipate energy, distort a profession's priorities, and disrupt progress toward meeting overarching goals. Unfortunately, this description describes the counseling profession all too accurately. All is not lost, however, and perhaps the solution to this problem will come from the profession's generation of the future.

In May of 1998, Chi Sigma Iota (CSI), the counseling honor society, instituted an advocacy initiative. An invited group of leaders from within the counseling profession, including current leaders from several specialty areas, met at the University of North Carolina at Greensboro to discuss their respective visions on advocacy with the intent of developing a commitment to promoting the profession. At the conference, participants identified six themes thought to be directly relevant to advocacy: marketplace recognition, interprofessional issues, intraprofessional issues, counselor education, research, and client/constituency welfare. With great respect and gratitude for the efforts of CSI and the participants in this first conference, I carry this concept a bit further.

This chapter will investigate the issue of advocating for the profession of counseling from two different perspectives and offer some specific suggestions for targeting advocacy efforts. Internal and external perspectives or domains will be addressed first. It is helpful to further divide these two perspectives into themes. The themes found in the internal domain, again with gratitude and acknowledgment of the CSI efforts, would be defining the profession, intraprofessional relations, efficacy research based on outcome data, and counselor education. Notice the similarity between the last three themes and the themes identified at the CSI conference. The external domain includes interprofessional relations, marketplace recognition, public policy and legislation efforts, and general public information relative to client welfare. Again, please note that three of these themes are identical to three themes identified at the CSI conference. Each of the eight themes must be addressed if the counseling profession is to be successful in its advocacy efforts.

## *Internal Domain*

The internal domain, which must be addressed first, consists of activities that the counseling profession must do internally prior to being ready to engage in advocacy of any type in the external domain. For example, it is an absolute necessity to have a working and generally agreed upon definition among themselves of who counselors are and what it is that they do. Without this, there is nothing to advocate. Professional counselors (and hence, the profession of counseling) currently suffer from a lack of agreement relative to the necessity of a definition, much less agreement on what that clearly articulated definition is.

This brings us to the second theme of the internal domain: intraprofessional relations. The counseling profession is fragmented. It has divided itself into 17 divisions, many of which have developed a definition of their own special skill bank at the exclusion of the larger profession as a whole. Many of these divisions and/or specialty areas have forgotten the importance of remaining a part of a larger profession. These same divisions would not exist today had they not received the nurturing and care from other divisions as they were getting started. Hence, the term *division* has become all too descriptive, in terms of promoting or advocating for the counseling profession as a whole.

By and large, the profession has survived on anecdotal reports of its effectiveness rather than hard, scientific, data-driven, proof of its efficacy. Counselors have attempted to offer quality assurance with precious little data to prove its presence. Until recently, most of the research has been left up to scholars in this regard. Practitioners have failed in tragic proportions to hold themselves accountable for conducting research, based on the outcomes of their own clients. Therefore, counselors must convince not only the consuming public that their profession is worthy of the trust they expect; they must first convince themselves. It is intellectually dishonest in the environment of today to claim effectiveness with no specific evidence. Managed care organizations and accountability movements in government are forcing the profession to police itself in this regard.

Last, from the internal domain, counselor preparation must teach the necessity of actively promoting the profession. New counselors just entering the profession must know from their own experience as well as what they have learned in the classroom that what they do makes a difference in people's lives. Counselor educators must hold students to the test. They are, after all, the gatekeepers of the profession; allowing poorly prepared individuals to enter the profession not only puts the profession at risk but it may also put some future client at risk.

## Theme 1: Defining the Profession

Simply stated, it is difficult to advocate for something that has no definition. However, defining something as complex as the counseling profession is not an easy task. The definition of who counselors are and what they do has escaped meaningful action until recently. Perhaps this was out of the fear of alienating some of its specialties or the fear of losing the uniqueness of these specialties as a vital part of the larger whole. Stated slightly differently, Liteman and Liteman (1998) imply that loyalty to and of subordinates is a good thing; however, when that loyalty is to one's subgroup, we become blinded to the needs and interests of the whole organization.

The apparent reluctance to deal with the identity issue is still present after nearly 50 years of existence. An example of this recent search for a professional identity was launched by the American Counseling Association (ACA) in November 1995 when Joyce M. Breasure, then president of ACA, charged the Professionalization Committee with developing a definition of professional counseling and its specialties (personal communication, November 13, 1995). That definition was to be presented to the ACA Governing

Council for consideration and adoption. The committee took the charge seriously and made every effort to try to pull this complex and diverse profession together. The issues that faced the committee's efforts were many.

A range of opinions exist within the counseling profession relative to its mission and the level of services it provides. Some counselors, who, because of their education, training, and experience, feel that the services counselors provide should be limited to personal growth, "problems in living," relationship difficulties, and "normal" developmental issues (as opposed to pathological problems). Just as surely, there are other counselors who, because of their education, training, and experience, are of the opinion that this places severe limitations on their practice. They are convinced that counselors can provide a much broader range of services, including the testing and assessment services as well as the diagnosis and treatment planning to individuals who meet diagnostic criteria, and beyond that, to the profoundly and persistently mentally ill client population.

After nearly two years of gathering input from ACA's divisions, state branches, and members at large, the proposed definition represented the best efforts of the Professionalization Committee to be inclusive of these diverse opinions. As evidence of the profession's hesitancy to deal with its own diversity, the definition, placed on the agenda of the April 1997 ACA Governing Council meeting, was moved to the last item of business of the meeting for consideration and action due to other "more pressing" agenda. It was finally considered as several governing council members were literally leaving the room to catch their respective flights home. The proposed definition was as follows:

> The Practice of Professional Counseling: The application of mental health, psychological, and human development principles, through cognitive, affective, behavioral and systemic intervention strategies, that address wellness, personal growth, and career development, as well as pathology. The goals of counseling are to (a) facilitate human development and adjustment throughout the lifespan; (b) prevent, diagnose, and treat mental, emotional, or behavioral disorders or distresses which are associated with or interfere with mental health and a sense of well being; (c) conduct diagnoses or assessments for the purpose of establishing treatment goals and objectives; and (d) plan, implement, and evaluate treatment plans using counseling treatment interventions, in the context of a pluralistic society.

Because of the importance of this issue, even though the motion carried by those governing council members still present, Gail Robinson, then president, in a spirit of fairness, chose not to accept the vote due to a questionable quorum, and put it on the agenda for the next Governing Council meeting in September of 1997.

When the issue of the definition was brought up at the September 1997 meeting, only the first part of the statement was adopted:

> The Practice of Professional Counseling: The application of mental health, psychological, and human development principles, through cognitive, affective, behavioral and systemic intervention strategies, that address wellness, personal growth, and career development, as well as pathology.

The importance of this limited action cannot be overestimated. It was the first time in nearly 50 years of its existence that the governing body of the counseling profession had agreed on a definition of who they are and what they do.

Since the early 1950s, when the American Personnel and Guidance Association was formed by the coming together of four professional associations (the National Career Development Association [NCDA], the Association for Counselor Education and Supervision [ACES], the American School Counselor Association [ASCA] and the American Rehabilitation Counseling Association [ARCA]), the counseling profession has gone through a series of name changes. At times, there has been a confusing shift of emphasis. However, with odds heavily against it, counseling has developed into a profession of high order. If *profession* is defined as a calling or occupation that has a defined knowledge base founded on research, standards of preparation, a code of ethics, members whose training is similar, and so on, then *counseling* is at least a stand-alone profession in the human development and mental health care field.

As this relates to advocacy, it is very difficult to advocate for a profession that has no accepted definition. The struggles over the years, for whatever reasons, failed to yield an acceptable definition of professional counseling that was inclusive of the diversity of specialties and individuals within the profession. The definition of any profession should be a work in progress. That is to say, it must be dynamic. It must reflect the profession as it defines itself through history. That definition must be fine-tuned on a regular basis. The current definition (just discussed) represents a snapshot or a self-portrait at a point in time. This allows the profession to respond to environmental realities. However, the profession must also maintain integrity. It cannot adopt a knee-jerk response to environmental influences. It must have a rudder that allows it to stay the course. The definition, in and of itself, is just such a rudder.

Counseling is a profession that is developing its identity as well as its scope of practice. As history unveils it, counseling will become more clearly defined and more mature, and it will therefore become much easier to advocate for the profession.

## *Theme 2: Intraprofessional Relations*

As the profession evolved, it appeared the better part of wisdom to give some recognition to groups of members who seemed to have a common interest or focus within the practice of counseling. The leaders of the day accomplished this by recognizing what some members thought was important as defined by either particular and specific client population, a particular work setting, or a particular area of interest related to the profession of counseling. In fact, that strategy worked well, as evidenced by the dramatic growth in membership of the American Personnel and Guidance Association from the early 1960s through the early 1980s.

Taking the advantage of looking in retrospect, perhaps rather than focusing on increasing membership, the emphasis should have been on selling the profession or positioning itself in such a way that the general public would know what the profession was about and what members were able to do. Had it engaged in its own advocacy, it would have garnered the support from the general public that would sustain it through societal changes that were about to occur.

A growing sense of frustration is evolving over what many counselors see as an overemphasis on the uniqueness of the specialties within the counseling profession. Such an emphasis, according to them, serves only to divide the profession and confuse the public policy-makers and the potential consumers of counseling services. This emphasis on uniqueness comes at a time when unity and focus are needed to help the counseling profession with its definition and recognition problems. Care providers would point out that the public is more concerned about the competency of care providers than what they call themselves.

Liteman and Liteman (1998) point out that in Dumas's classic *The Three Muskateers,* the motto was clearly "All for one and one for all." That was the only way they could survive. The polar opposite of that is "Every man (person) for himself (self)"—a cry of desperation blurted out when the ship is about to go down. It is the fear of many counselors that the latter is more descriptive of the counseling profession at this point in its history than the former. If this is the case, counseling will be seen as disorganized and appear foolish to the average person.

The marketplace will tolerate no such foolishness; the harsh reality is that any profession that allows this to happen does not deserve to be recognized as a profession. To avoid this catastrophe, unity must be the order of the day. Similarities must be emphasized over differences. As an absolute minimum response, the profession as a whole must engage in advocacy on its own behalf.

As stated earlier, the divisiveness that exists in the mental health care professions (note the plural) is devastating. The situation is only exacerbated further when one of the major players divides itself as a profession. This is not to say that specialization within the profession has no place. Rather, ACA must somehow find a way to pull its factions together and develop meaningful ways to relate to each other in presenting a united front to the public. It is absolutely critical that the specialty areas work collaboratively and cooperatively to develop and implement a unified advocacy plan for the promotion and advancement of the counseling profession as a whole. There would be no worse fate than to lose the profession at its own hand.

## Theme 3: Outcome Research on Efficacy

Counselors, in general, have avoided conducting research based on hard, scientific data necessary to prove that their individual services bring about positive results in the lives of their clients. Although there has been research toward this end, it has primarily been conducted by scholars rather than practitioners themselves (e.g., Johnson & Shaha, 1996; Lambert & Cattani-Thompson, 1996; Nelson and Neufeldt, 1996; Sexton, 1996; Sexton et al., 1997; Steenbarger & Smith, 1996; Whiston, 1996). We are very fortunate to have those scholars just mentioned and many more like them, but the point is this: We live in a day of increasing accountability, positive results, and a demand for impressive outcomes. This is especially true in a managed care-driven marketplace where results and bottom-line mentality dominate the world of practice. This is no less true of teaching, administrative, and, yes, counseling services being provided in our schools, or select any other area of specialty in which professional counseling is practiced. Data-driven research results must be gathered, interpreted, and utilized to hold the counseling profession accountable, just as it is for any other mental health profession.

Beyond that, counseling could move into the forefront if we were to promote outcome research with children, adults, families, and groups on an individual practitioner basis. This requires much deeper scrutiny than simply adding a course to the curriculum of counselor education programs. This issue will be addressed more directly in the next section of this chapter.

There needs to be a new paradigm in the way we practice counseling. Every practitioner, regardless of specialty area, must hold himself or herself accountable to a high standard of excellence. This cannot be done without assessing the results of one's practice with one's own clients. There is no shortcut or easy alternative to the security, the absolute certainty, that counseling efforts are of benefit to clients, other than through the hard data generated by good research methodology on those specific and particular clients. The old approach of spending time listening to clients as they give an oral rendition of their particular problematic life circumstance, offering a suggestion here or there, and throwing out a challenge now and then is simply inadequate and unacceptable in this day and age. Counselors, as well as other mental health care provider groups, have been guilty of taking their effectiveness for granted in applying the knowledge, techniques, and intervention strategies learned in their training programs.

Other skills have been slow to enter the repertoire of professional counselors. For example, the counseling profession generally has been slow to implement diagnosis and treatment planning into its training programs over the years. The counseling profession must now prove to the consuming public, the public policy-makers, and third parties (be they the managed care organization, the insurance company, or the local school board,) that there is strong and hard data supporting the effectiveness of counseling services. Beyond that, and perhaps even more importantly, individual counselors must prove it to themselves.

Imagine the increase in integrity and the sense of pride felt by a counselor who has conducted longitudinal, outcome research on his or her own clients. Outcome research must be conducted on other topics within the counseling profession, as well. For example, do we know that counselor education programs that have stood the test of accreditation by the Council for Accreditation of Counseling and Related Educational Programs (CACREP), produce better and more effective graduates than nonaccredited programs? The underlying issue here is one of truth in packaging. We claim that having graduated from an accredited program is a badge of honor. Is that claim supported by research or is it only believed to be true?

In summary, our advocacy efforts must be based on scientific evidence as opposed to heart-warming testimonies by a few brave souls who have been helped by a competent professional counselor. The profession must have conclusive results that prove the efficacy of their services. Then, and only then, can we stand toe to toe with the other mental health care providers and have the assurance that we are, in fact, a force to be dealt with. Our training prepares us to prove our effectiveness in working with people.

## *Theme 4: Counselor Education*

Counselor education programs must be prepared to train graduates whose clear identity and level of competence is worthy of a sense of pride necessary to support advocacy. As Cummings (1995) points out, to succeed as a prime provider in the mental health care arena, a fundamental and pervasive shift is essential. Cummings was referring primarily to psychologists and their training, but the statement is no less true of counselor education.

The counseling profession has come a long way in a relatively short period of time regarding its development as a profession. It was only in 1976 that the first state passed licensure for counselors. Since that time, national certification has become established, accreditation for its training programs has become accepted, and licensure legislation in 45 states plus the District of Columbia has been passed. In spite of odds stacked heavily against it by competitors in the mental health care provider arena, the counseling profession has done its homework in getting its house in order.

However, as good as that sounds, there is still much need for improvement on several fronts. Although we are now prepared to govern the profession by the standards that are in place, we have not yet developed the commitment nor the skills necessary to engage in the aggressive advocacy for the profession to claim our place as a major provider of quality mental health care services.

Very few counselor education programs adequately prepare their graduates to be advocates for the profession. Such advocacy, if it is covered at all, is treated as a topic within a course on professional issues. What is needed is a complete and total integration of the necessity of advocating for the profession throughout the entire curriculum. Advocacy should not be treated as a separate topic but rather as a meta-topic—a backdrop to all courses. Advocacy for the profession itself must be covered as well as advocacy for our clients or certain other populations that need recognition.

The fact that many counselor educators are individuals who identify primarily with the field of psychology rather than counseling, and who refer to themselves as psychologists as opposed to counselors, puts counseling graduate students in the throes of an identity crisis. The lines between the two professions are blurred by virtue of the similarities (e.g., having common elements in their historical development, both being mental health care provider professions, etc.). To expect entry-level graduate students to have a clear understanding of the subtle distinctions is unrealistic. The fact that there are self-identified "psychologists" teaching students to be "counselors" implies that psychology is the higher-level profession.

It also follows that if the higher-achieving students are to reach their individual potential, they should also become identified as psychologists rather than counselors. How are students to develop a clear sense of identity when the professional loyalty of the faculty members sends a very different message of professionalism? How does one explain this phenomenon in any serious advocacy attempts? Are counselors to use this fact (that they have been trained by psychologists) as evidence that they are therefore worthy of competing in the marketplace? That, by definition, would be demeaning and counterproductive.

This leads us to promoting membership in the professional association(s). Counselor educators need to be clear about the value of belonging to the appropriate professional association. Neophyte counselors can be easily confused in this regard if they look to their faculty members for role models and are told that although the American Psychological Association is the association of choice for the faculty member, the American Counseling Association is more appropriate for the student. Counselors new to the profession need nurturing and mentoring into the professional association by faculty members whom they have come to know, trust, and respect. Hesitation on the faculty member's part can be interpreted as lack of certainty or clarity in the mind of the student or new professional. Hence, faculty must not only teach advocacy of the profession but they must also model it both in the internal and external domains.

Among the several provider groups, the counseling profession has some distinct advantages and unique features. In a recent survey of counselor education programs, Smith (1999) finds, that these unique features, according to the respondents, can be gathered under three general headings: (1) prevention focus, (2) problems-in-living orientation (i.e., normal developmental problems as well as pathology), and (3) collaborative approaches. This list is not exhaustive by any means.

The prevention focus should place counselors in a highly advantageous position in working with clients across the age span in the eyes of schools, agencies, and third-party payers, since prevention is cost effective. Not only is it less costly to prevent behavioral problems before they occur but there are also instances where more serious pathologies can be dealt with effectively. For example, suppose a counselor provides group therapy to a group of individuals or perhaps to a family who is having difficulty with grief issues surrounding the loss of a significant other. Such therapy may well head off a much more serious, unresolved grief that could contribute to, or even cause, a depressive condition that would interfere with work, family, or school.

Another example might be a school counselor who develops an Alternatives to Violence program in his or her school. By increasing the response alternatives for adolescents who find themselves in anger- or frustration-producing situations, the local Board of Education can begin to appreciate counseling as a profession for its uniqueness among other mental health care provider groups. With the alarming increase in violence in the schools (e.g., shootings, teachers and students being physically assaulted, break-ins and vandalism, etc.), prevention programs are seen as a cost-effective method to reduce litigation, damage repair, and disruption of the learning environment.

Counselors have a long-standing tradition of addressing the normal, day-to-day problems faced by virtually everyone. They have operated from a wellness orientation, believing that a person does not have to be "sick" before getting better. Simply stated, if a client can be brought to the understanding that what he or she is feeling, thinking, or experiencing at the moment, although uncomfortable, is not necessarily abnormal, but rather it is the situation of the moment that is abnormal, it can have great therapeutic value.

More recently, counselor education programs have begun preparing counselors to address more "pathological" difficulties. This is especially appropriate for graduates going into the clinically oriented specialties within the counseling profession, (e.g., clinical mental health, marriage and family, rehabilitation counseling, etc.). A school counselor who has coursework in mental pathology is better prepared to do his or her job than one who has not taken the coursework. All of this is to say that counselors respond to a broad range of services along the mental health continuum.

The fact that counselors engage in collaborative approaches a bit more readily than other provider groups may well be a function of being the newest of the mental health care professions. Counselors have had to collaborate and cooperate with other provider groups to promote their skills and to gain recognition and appreciation of these other groups who, by virtue of their having arrived a bit earlier in history, already have the recognition needed to survive as a profession. Also, in struggling for recognition by other professions such as medicine and law, counselors have become very creative in finding their niche in providing mental health services by collaboration in these environments.

Finally, the curriculum must be worthy of advocacy in terms of being pertinent to society and the marketplace. Many, if not most, counselor education programs still teach a broad-based approach to counseling theory that relegates the more contemporary, time-sensitive, solution-focused modalities to a "one-of-many" approach. If counselors are to be able to promote the profession in a market-driven fashion, these brief therapies must dominate the theoretical component of the curriculum.

# External Domain

Professional counselors are obligated to be advocates for their profession to the general public, public policy-makers, other health care professions, and other entities in society such as business and industry from which our clients may come. If we do not market (advocate for) our profession in an effective and convincing manner to individuals and groups outside of the profession, if we fail to convince the public and the public policy-makers of the value of our services, we have no future. No one is looking for an additional provider of services such as what we offer. We must promote the profession and be so convincing in doing it that we become a sought-after provider (i.e., the provider of choice) of services among other providers of very similar, and in many cases, identical services. Counselors must be self-promoters and sales representatives of the services they provide in a highly competitive market if they are to survive, much less thrive.

## Theme 5: Interprofessional Relations

We must learn to deal effectively with our competitors. This does not mean that we must beat them at competing or be combative with them. It does mean, very simply, that we must learn how to work with the reality of a competitive marketplace. We are but one of many professions who, based on our training and preparation, are capable of providing quality mental health care services to the public—often the very same people to whom our competitors are already providing many if not all of these same services.

Aubrey (1986) states that counseling is not a long-established profession but rather one that, in many ways, is just emerging from being an occupation to being a full-fledged profession. We were preceded in providing mental health care by psychiatry, psychology, social work, and psychiatric nursing, to name some of the major players. When considered with the likes of these groups, we are the new kids on the block. Being relatively new as a profession has both positive and negative aspects.

The positive aspect is that the other professions have proven the value of mental health care services in general terms as well as in terms of their unique contributions. That has opened the minds of society to see the value of mental health care in addition to physical health care; this is one battle counselors do not need to fight. These other professions have been fairly successful at opening the door for the concept of mental health care in general.

However, there are also several negative aspects in being relatively new on the scene. The other professions have been doing advocacy on their own behalf for a number of years. They have the contacts and connections to be more effective than someone just getting started. They have the recognition we so vitally need. It also gives these other professions an advantage in that the various publics to which we must advocate our profession already trust them and often listen to them as they describe or define counselors. Unfortunately, this is most often done without any particular knowledge about our preparation and training, what is required to become a counselor, or what type of services we have to offer. Because we have not had their training (with which they are obviously very familiar), naturally, we are thereby different and unfamiliar to them. The assumption embodied in this benign ignorance is that we must also be inferior to them in many important ways.

This means that often, when we go before these external audiences to promote our profession, the first order of the day is to deny the less than complimentary, inaccurate concepts of ourselves that have been left with the audience by our competitors. It is rarely the case that members of these other professions are intentionally ill-willed or even necessarily opposed to counselors or the profession of counseling. It is a form of innocent ignorance that can be addressed only by aggressive advocacy for counselors by counselors.

Once our competition knows who we are by our own definition, and respect who we are, based on an intimate knowledge of our curriculum, knowledge base, and supervised clinical training, then and only then can we have an intelligent conversation about the virtues and frailties of their training and ours. However, educating them as to who we are is very definitely a slow process. Their resistance to learning has its roots in their emotional and uninformed opinions. Emotionally, they react to the financial threat that we pose for them. We may take away some of their livelihood. This emotion has been fanned over the years by our own less-than-certain identity. They have a clear and concise definition of who they are; counselors, however, mumble through a rendition of being similar in this regard and different in that regard, which quite frankly, is boring and casts doubts about our confidence as professionals if not our competence.

Counselors need to be careful not to fall into the same trap (i.e., discussing the other professions and what they are about). Therefore, it is vitally important that counselors know exactly how the counseling profession is similar and exactly how it is different from these other professions. To do that, we must get acquainted with them individually and collectively. The importance of this cannot be overemphasized. In any given community, there will be members of these other professions with whom the counselor must interact daily on a professional level. To ensure the best care to the client, which is what both professions want, they must understand each other and the training and expertise that each has.

Counselors must come to know the competition on a personal and professional basis. We gain nothing by throwing rocks at the competition in the same fashion we accuse them of throwing rocks at us. It behooves us to take the high road. We must engage the other provider professions in dialogue about our mutual concerns. We must ask questions that enable us to show them that we are invested. We must find ways to show them that we have appropriate professional humility and know that we are not always the best provider for every type of client. We must acknowledge that there are certain areas of their training that we may approach a bit differently. Just as in marriage, we must give of ourselves but not give ourselves away.

The truth of the matter is that there are far more similarities than differences between the various mental health care providing professions. Each has a similar knowledge base and each operates under a strict Code of Ethics, and, in most instances, state laws define the parameters of practice for each profession even though there is tremendous overlap. If one were to observe a counselor, a social worker, a psychologist, and perhaps a psychiatric nurse through a window as they applied their professional expertise with a client, one would be hard-pressed to tell the difference between them. Effective psychologists, social workers, marriage and family therapists, and counselors have much more in common with each other than do effective and ineffective practitioners of the same provider group.

This is not to say that there are not some unique differences that are rightfully claimed by each of these groups. Generally speaking, these differences are minimal in terms of quality of service. However, there are often differences in terms of levels of education in professional identity. Psychologists, for example, require a doctoral degree. Social workers, marriage and family therapists, and counselors alike may practice with either a doctorate or a master's degree. In some states, one cannot engage in independent practice or provide unsupervised service unless one has a doctorate in psychology. Master's-level professions often must have psychiatrists or psychologists sign off on their work for reimbursement. This fact seriously curtails efforts at private and independent practice.

Counselors must understand precisely what it is that their training prepares them to do. Then they must advocate with the other professions regarding those competencies. In this way, professional counselors define who they are and exactly what they are prepared to do. The ignorance of other professions loses its innocence once we have done this. The open battles between the professions serves no useful purpose; it only wastes limited resources and confuses the public and public policy-makers. This type of behavior is unprofessional and harms the good standing of all parties involved. It is the counseling profession's obligation and responsibility to avoid being pulled into these quagmires.

In the best of all worlds, the professions would work cooperatively between groups and focus on informing the public as practitioners of the mental health professions instead of playing verbal games or engaging in verbal rock throwing at each other. When economic survival is thought to be at stake, however, reason and high-mindedness are typically the first fatalities. Advocating for one's own profession in a complex and competitive marketplace with the very people with whom one is in competition is always difficult. It is nonetheless of critical importance to the ongoing existence and health of the profession.

## *Theme 6: Marketplace Recognition*

As mentioned earlier, recognition in the marketplace must be accomplished by each profession on its own behalf. Unfortunately, since the counseling profession is the more recent arrival and has been busy getting its own house in order by establishing its credentials, much of the marketplace has already been claimed by our predecessors. The tragedy, once again, is that the decisions have been made and precedents have been set based on academic discipline rather than competency. These decisions were made by well-intentioned (if naive) noncounseling individuals in the personages of politicians and insurance providers. It is easier to carve up the mental health pie if the players have certain things that they, and only they, are allowed to do. However, that is a terribly simplistic approach, given the complexity of the mental health care field today. Since much of what any of the particular provider group offers as service overlaps with what one or more other provider group offers, it becomes difficult if not impossible to approach the problem in this way.

This means that counselors must advocate (lobby, promote, and otherwise "sell") their profession diligently in the arenas of these important decision makers and stakeholders. In the final analysis, it is a primarily a matter of educating the marketplace regarding who counselors are and what they are prepared to do. To do this, these decision makers need to know what skills counselors have that are unique to them, which skills are common among and between counselors and other master's-level mental health care providers, and what skills counselors have in common with the doctoral-level providers, as well.

The end goal of the marketplace recognition efforts is for decision makers to establish parity with counselors and other providers, including a full scope of practice within their areas of competence. To achieve this end, counselors must be accepted for payment of employment in any service area for which they have competence. They need broad recognition through media and elsewhere for clients found in the marketplace to begin requesting the services of counselors. Advocacy to this end is multifaceted and involves one-to-one education as well as a Madison Avenue approach in public relations on behalf of the profession. Counselors need a media campaign that presents their case, including a definition, knowledge, and skills that constitute a guaranteed minimal level of competence in a wide variety of specifically named services, and they must do this in a style that acknowledges the state-of-the art advertising skills. This material must literally flood the marketplace—insurance companies, managed care organizations, health maintenance organizations, medical and legal communities, businesses and industries who might be self-insured, and others.

## *Theme 7: Public Policy and Legislators*

In addition to achieving recognition in the marketplace by third-party payers (managed care organizations, insurance companies, etc.), it is of vital importance that counselors promote their profession in the public policy arena. State legislators make decisions regarding the practice of many professions within their state's boundaries. They do their best to assure the citizens of their states a certain quality of life. Regulating physical and mental health care, along with other professions and trades within their respective state, is one way they do that.

Since psychologists and social workers were among the first mental health care providers to become recognized by state legislative bodies, counselors are now held to the standard that these other groups have already set. Most elected officials do not understand the subtle differences between the various provider groups. Hence, counselors need to engage in advocacy efforts with public policy-makers at the state level. The opposition is often present in the form of other provider groups. Therefore, it is essential for the counseling profession to have its own definition clearly in mind and to understand and be able to articulate the uniqueness and similarities between itself and the other providers. It must also possess a razor-sharp grasp of the minimum competencies that can be guaranteed every client who seeks the services of a counselor.

Beyond that, counselors cannot afford the luxury of getting pulled into a public battle with other providers who have already gained the recognition and respect of the policymakers. It goes without saying that counselors cannot afford careless public fighting within the counseling profession itself. School counselors, clinical mental health counselors, career counselors, college campus counselors, rehabilitation counselors, and all other specialty areas must do their advocacy work in locked-arm style.

Public policy-makers become annoyed at the trivial games played by professional groups, especially when it is obvious that they would never be satisfied with whatever the policy-makers might do on their behalf. The profession cannot waste resources by spending advocacy time foolishly. If there are differences between members of the counseling family, these differences should be worked out in private before presenting the profession publicly.

At the federal level, the stakes are often higher. Whereas states give the scope of practice to licensed professional counselors (LPCs), it is the federal government that often gives the right or privilege to practice and sets the overall recognition standards. This is true not only for state governments but also for third-party payers. Both groups usually follow the federal government's lead. If counselors are not recognized at the federal level, they will have an uphill battle in gaining recognition at either the state level or among insurance carriers. Thus, advocacy for the counseling profession at the federal government level is of critical importance.

Engaging in advocacy, even at the federal level, involves very few rules. Most often, counselors will say that they have never engaged in formal advocacy of any kind at any level. As pointed out in the American Counseling Association's brochure titled "Effective Advocacy and Communication with Legislators" (1997), even if one has never talked or written to a legislator before, one probably already has all the skills needed to advocate effectively for one's self and the counseling profession. Being effective at communication, and this includes listening as well as being able to articulate one's thoughts, is extremely important. The brochure, which is available through the American Counseling Association, goes on to list several basic principles. Included in the list are such things as being specific with one's request, having one's thoughts organized and coordinated, keeping the message simple, staying flexible, being prepared to compromise, and anticipating and dealing with one's opposition—all rather simple, basic rules of good communication.

Without being included in state and federal legislative language, professional counselors are condemned to being second-class providers. Legislation sets the standards regarding which of the provider professions are automatically reimbursable for services to people who benefit in one way or another from governmental programs.

All too often, those few brave counselors who engage in advocacy and get legislation passed that provides them the privilege of practice in either state or federal legislation then feel that the job is done. Advocacy in any arena is an ongoing responsibility that does not go away after the licensure, the inclusion battle, or any other specific recognition battle has been won. Advocacy, especially at the state level with public policy-makers, must be continued in the form of monitoring the legislation. Other provider groups or well-meaning citizen groups (e.g., the National Alliance for the Mentally Ill [NAMI]) will attempt to exclude counselors from the qualified provider lists. These groups often are misinformed or only partially informed about what professional counselors are trained to do.

An important component of advocacy is simply to stay informed and remain watchful over the process. When the state legislature is in session, anything can (and does) happen. Counselors must maintain vigilance on the legislative process. The vigil need not be only protective of what recognition they do have; it can also provide an early alert for advocacy

on behalf of different client groups who are mentioned in or affected by proposed legislation. Whenever the legislature is dealing with education issues, issues of the aging, issues
surrounding the family or underrepresented groups, the counseling profession must be
present to influence that legislation.

## Theme 8: Client/Constituency Wellness

The proceedings of the May 1998 Chi Sigma Iota meeting define the goal of the client/con-
stituency wellness theme as the identification of the needs of those whom professional
counselors serve in such a manner that others can appreciate their unique role in service to
society. In essence, this theme speaks to the importance of results. When counselors have
proved themselves to have been effective with a client population—either through direct
one-on-one counseling, group counseling, or preventive, developmentally based, or wellness programs in which counselors have played key roles in the development and implementation—this needs to be presented to the consuming public.

Due to the confidential nature of counseling, there are ethical issues that surround a
counselor asking clients directly to refer other clients to him or her. Admittedly, many clients
do, in fact, refer others to their counselor, but it is often difficult to do because of the private
nature of the counseling process. It would involve the client stating to an acquaintance that
he or she had received mental health counseling, thereby suffering the consequences of the
stereotyped image of being weak or somewhat less than capable of dealing with life issues.
However, there are other ways of implementing advocacy around this particular theme.

For example, let's say that Mark Brown is a counselor who has a contract with the
Johnson Corporation to provide an employee assistance program (EAP). In addition to the
one-on-one and family counseling services provided in the contract, Mr. Brown has developed an effective management training component. He sees this as an opportunity to build
some clientele as well as give evidence to the wellness and preventative orientation of the
counseling profession. The Johnson Corporation sees it as good business. This management training program (the training of employees who have been recommended by their
supervisor to participate) has several components. Included in its curriculum are such topics as stress management, supervising former fellow employees, leadership development,
and identification and referral procedures for troubled employees. The purpose of such a
training program is that when supervisory- or management-level positions become available within the Johnson Corporation, whether through natural attrition or expansion, a pool
of applicants are already familiar with company policies and procedures and have proven
themselves to be good employees. The program has been of great bottom-line benefit for
the Johnson Corporation.

Mr. Brown could ask the CEO of the Johnson Corporation to write a letter of recommendation, based on this success, that he could present to other businesses or industries as he
discusses the benefits of providing such a service to *their* employees. Beyond that, some of
the trainees might be willing to provide their comments and attest to the value of their participation. Success breeds success. This is a form of advocacy for the business and industry
client.

A counselor who works closely with a physician could serve as another example. Part
of this working relationship involves the physician making referrals of a particular diagno-

sis (e.g., dysthymic disorder) to the counselor. If, over the course of time, the physician is convinced that the counselor is effective and that the working together has provided high-quality health care for their mutual clients, the M.D. could be asked to advocate on the counselor's behalf with other physicians.

These are simple marketing strategies. Much of advocacy is just that: simple marketing strategy. The problem is that many, if not most, counselors fail to recognize the importance of advocating for the profession of counseling. They hesitate to engage in what could be considered good business practices for fear of appearing to be callused to the nature of their work or the needs of their clients. The point here is that counselors miss many opportunities that appear to be routine business procedures to advocate, promote, and otherwise "sell" their wares. This timidity, cumulatively and collectively, can have a devastating effect on the profession, much less a single practitioner's practice.

## Summary and Conclusions

The counseling profession has paid its dues. It has developed a knowledge base and a clinical application component that needs no apology. Throughout the last 20 to 25 years, it has put into place the credentials (in the form of licensure and national certification), the accreditation of its preparation and training programs, and its reputation for being able to deliver quality services. Based on this knowledge base, skills package, credentialing process, and reputation, the profession must now move on to the advocacy responsibility. Stated slightly differently, it has developed a product for which it need not be ashamed nor embarrassed to offer the public. It is in fact, of high quality. Yet, there is still work to be done to assure continuous quality improvement of that product.

Now the counseling profession must promote, advertise, and sell the product. Without attention to all of the themes mentioned in this chapter, internal and external in perspective, all of the good effort of this rich history will be lost. Professional counseling must be more realistic than to believe that advocacy is any easier a challenge than any of the other tasks it has already accomplished. There were times when obtaining licensure in a majority of states was seen as an impossible task. There were times when agreement on the qualifications of either certification or accreditation was thought to be impossible to obtain. These hurdles have been overcome.

The next logical step in the developmental process for the counseling profession is to accept the challenge of advocacy—not only for its clients but also for its own right to exist and compete in the marketplace. To fail at this step would render its own history a less than worthy cause. Arrival at full recognition among ourselves, other professions, the general public, public policy-makers, and marketplace stakeholders will not be easy. It necessitates that all professional counselors maintain their personal and professional integrity, believe in their abilities, and promote their identity and professional stature.

# 11

# *Counseling and Spirituality*

## Oliver J. Morgan

*Oliver (Ollie) J. Morgan* *is a professor of counselor education and chair of the Department of Human Services at the University of Scranton, a Jesuit university in northeast Pennsylvania. He received the M.F.T. degree from Hahnemann Medical University in Philadelphia and the Ph.D. degree in pastoral psychology from Boston University. His scholarly pursuits include family studies, addictions counseling, and aspects of human spirituality. He has recently coedited a book titled* Addiction and Spirituality: A Multidisciplinary Approach *(Chalice Press). Morgan serves on the Board of Directors for the Council for Accreditation of Counseling and Related Educational Programs (CACREP) and is on the editorial boards of the* Journal of Addictions and Offender Counseling *and the* Journal of the Pennsylvania Counseling Association. *In addition, he is book review editor for the* Journal of Ministry in Addiction and Recovery. *Morgan enjoys long dinners and conversations with friends. His two passions are pistol shooting and playing with his 2-year-old goddaughter, Sierra.*

## In This Chapter . . .

- Why do you suppose spirituality has become such a contemporary topic of interest among counseling professionals?
- What are the perceived obstacles to responding to client spirituality issues?
- What is involved in being sensitive to a client's spirituality?
- What kinds of countertransference issues might arise in a counselor/client exploration of the client's spirituality?
- To what extent might a client's religious orientation contribute to or complicate the process of change?
- What are the psychological ramifications of *healing,* as contrasted with *remediation?*
- Must one be a spiritually oriented counselor to work with clients whose problems involve a spiritual dimension?

... to pay attention to another at the place where his or her soul is on the line. (O'Reilley, 1998, p. 24)

An emerging awareness exists among professional counselors about the potential role of spirituality in counseling practice. Attendees at national and regional conferences sponsored under the auspices of the American Counseling Association (ACA) have seen an explosion of presentation topics that delve into spiritual issues, and the number of publications addressing spirituality and counseling continues to grow (see Burke & Miranti, 1992, 1995; Hinterkopf, 1998; Kelly, 1995; and Richards & Bergen, 1997). Morgan and Jordan (1999) address these issues from multiple counseling-related perspectives.

Counseling and other mental health journals are accepting and publishing articles on a variety of spiritually related topics, while some produce "special issues" on spirituality by guest editors. Examples of the latter include Vash and McCarthy (1995), a special double issue on "Spirituality, Disability and Rehabilitation" by *Rehabilitation Education,* and a special issue of the *American Journal of Health Promotion,* edited by Underwood and associates. Journal articles that provide a more thorough understanding of the topic include Chandler, Holden, and Kolander (1992), Goodwin (1996), Hinterkopf (1994), Kelly (1994), and Witmer and Sweeney (1992).

The newest standards for counselor education, currently under revision by the Council for Accreditation of Counseling and Related Educational Programs (CACREP), list spiritual concerns as an important topic in a holistic understanding of persons, in appreciating the diverse cultural backgrounds and resources of clients, and in assessment of client needs (CACREP, 1998).

This emerging interest in spirituality by professional counselors is mirrored by similar interests in other domains, including counseling psychology, addiction studies, medicine, physical and mental health, pastoral care, and even business, to name only a few. The National Institute for Healthcare Research (NIHR) has published a state-of-the-art report entitled *Scientific Research on Spirituality and Health: A Consensus Report* (1998), edited by Larsen, Swyers, and McCullough. Chapters examine in detail what is known about the role and value of spirituality within each discipline and the prospects for future research within the context of physical health, mental health, neuroscience, and addictions.

Although attention to spiritual concerns is a noticeable phenomenon in contemporary thought and culture (Bergin, 1992), it is also consistent with the history and self-identity of counseling as a profession. For example, the American Counseling Association has a long-standing relationship with one of its own divisions, currently called the Association for Spiritual, Ethical and Religious Values in Counseling (ASERVIC).

Many of the chapters in this book have pointed out the roots and values that are unique to professional counseling. The holistic, developmental, relational, preventive, and resource-oriented stance of counseling helps keep the profession open to consideration of spiritual concerns. Greater appreciation of diversity (Pate & Bondi, 1992) and a concern for social improvement, as seen in the origins of vocational counseling (Kelly, 1995), also aid in sensitizing counselors to the spiritual needs and values of those with whom they work. In addition, Chandler and colleagues (1992) and Witmer and Sweeney (1992) have related growing interest in spirituality to foundational themes in counseling as a profession and field of study. These themes include a holistic view of the person, human development over the life span, a concern for wellness and prevention, and a resource-oriented (as opposed to pathological) view of the counseling process. Growing out of the modern situation just described, and consistent with the historical identity of counseling as a profession, it is imperative that today's counseling practitioner be attentive to spiritual issues.

## A Stance of Practicality

Many people who come for counseling today bring with them a spiritual or religious world-view of some kind; many find involvement in a religious tradition or practice meaningful. This has been consistently demonstrated over the years in survey research (Greer, 1988; Wills, 1990), particularly in a string of Gallup polls beginning in the 1950s. For instance, two-thirds of respondents to the 1992 Gallup survey, when faced with a serious problem in living, would prefer to be counseled by someone who personally holds spiritual values and beliefs. Additionally, 81 percent of respondents preferred some integration of their beliefs and values into the counseling process (Kelly, 1995, p. 34). This leads a noted author in the counseling field to state that, in relation to critical life issues (e.g., depression and suicide, anxiety, stress and coping, self-esteem, well being, facing death, struggling with addiction, and the like),

> counselors can expect that at least for some clients spirituality and religion play a part in how the client feels and thinks about these issues and problems. As counselors explore the cognitive, affective and unconscious elements of issues such as these, they can help clients by an alert openness to how spiritual and religious threads may be woven into such concerns and used in their resolution. (Kelly, 1995, p. 36)

Many counseling professionals themselves have beliefs and engage in practices of a spiritual or religious kind. Kelly (1995, p. 37) reports that 64 percent of those responding to a recent ACA survey believe in a personal God, and another 25 percent believe in a transcendent or spiritual dimension to reality. Almost 45 percent reported active affiliation with an organized religion.

With some variation, these patterns of interest, affiliation, and practice involving spirituality and religion are consistent with the attitudes of a variety of mental health practitioners and those who might come to them for help (Kelly, 1995; National Institute for Healthcare Research [NIHR], 1998). Many mental health workers, including counselors, believe that "seeking a spiritual understanding of one's place in the universe" is important in overall health and well being (Kelly, 1995, p. 38). Kelly (1995) reports on a number of research projects that highlight the role of spirituality in the general population and among counselors and other mental health workers. Significant studies in these areas include Gallup and Castelli (1989), Jensen and Bergin (1988), and Shafranske and Malony (1990).

In addition, recent research presents mounting evidence that "religious and spiritual factors may play a more direct role in affecting physical and mental health," not only in prevention but in enhancing traditional treatments and in persons' ability to cope with illnesses of different kinds (NIHR, 1998, p. 2). Yet, for a long time, it was accepted that counselors and other mental health practitioners ought not to bring discussion of spiritual matters into the consulting room. This position is being modified today. An informed discussion of these issues is contained in Richards and Bergin (1997).

Clearly, it is a matter of practical sense for counselors to pay attention to the spiritual concerns that clients may bring to counseling. Many counselors and their clients appear to believe that this is an important area of living. It is increasingly a matter of theoretical sense, as well, for spirituality—as thoughtful research increasingly demonstrates—may be understood as a critical element in the holistic consideration of persons, the nature of human development, the effectiveness of prevention, and the usefulness of resources available for health and well-being (Chandler et al., 1992; NIHR, 1998; Witmer & Sweeney, 1992).

This is not to say that some of the traditional cautions or concerns about addressing spirituality or religion in counseling are groundless. Counseling practitioners must pay attention to the context or setting in which they practice. Sensitivity to clients' spiritual concerns may be appropriate for holistic practice, but counselors must also be sensitive to the "secular" leanings of many practice settings and integrate spirituality in a nonthreatening way (Kelly, 1995, pp. 41–43). In proposing that spirituality be properly considered in counseling practice, there is no suggestion that there be a return to unscientific or magical thinking, or the establishment of certain dogmas, or a naive acceptance of clients' unhealthy attitudes, or the imposition of counselors' views and values on unsuspecting and vulnerable clients (Bergin, 1992; Kelly, 1995). Several publications that show interest in exploring spiritual topics are also appreciative of the cautions and respectful of reasons why the social and clinical sciences have traditionally been wary of spirituality (e.g., Kelly, 1995; McCarthy, 1995a, 1995b).

Rather, the movement and theme of this chapter is both simpler and more far-reaching. This chapter suggests that all involved—counselors, counselees, and the profession as a whole—will benefit from counselors (1) becoming more sensitive and attentive to spiritual and religious elements in their practice, (2) becoming better informed about these matters generally and in the lives of their clients, and (3) learning how to integrate spirituality and religious sensibilities into effective counseling practice.

## Dimensions of Spirituality

Currently, there is no commonly accepted definition of *spirituality,* particularly as it relates to counseling. Yet, informed conversation with a variety of professionals and lay people reveals that there is interest in spirituality and, in fact, there exist a variety of spiritualities that persons find meaningful and helpful. Each of the great religious traditions has a spiritual view and discipline shaped by its communal experience and sacred literature, and within these traditions are believers and spiritual seekers of various stripes (e.g., liberal, fundamentalist, etc.). The ethnic and cultural experiences of people often incorporate spiritual beliefs (e.g., Native American and other indigenous spiritualities), while it is also true that there are contemporary spiritual movements (e.g., twelve-step programs, New Age, etc.) to be accounted for (Kelly, 1995).

None of this diversity in spirituality should be surprising. As Sheldrake (1991) and others have reminded us, spirituality is not a single, transcultural or transhistorical phenomenon. Rather, it is decisively shaped by culture, the network of relationships, and the experiences of individuals who encounter God's presence in their lives (p. 41).

For counselors today, the task is to understand the particular experiences, communal contexts, and historical-cultural elements that shape a client's spiritual perspective and practice. How does this person experience transcendence, or a higher power, or ultimacy in his or her life? What attitudes and values are important for him or her to live by, in order to feel connected with the spiritual realm? What practices keep the client "on track" in his or her search for meaning?

Among the growing cadre of researchers into spirituality, this variety is a rich source of data, yet for practicing counselors, the variety can become a confusing welter of beliefs, values, attitudes, and practices that tax the counselor's ability to understand and respond. The important thing to remember is that, although the counselor cannot have in-depth knowledge about all the possible spiritualities to which clients adhere, it is possible to have an informed sensitivity to the notion of spiritual beliefs and needs and a base from which to respond flexibly to clients' concerns (Kelly, 1995).

For the purpose of this discussion, the notions of *spirituality* and *religiousness* will be used interchangeably. Although there is an entire and ongoing academic discussion about the distinctions among terms such as *spirituality, religion, religiousness,* and the like, the practicing counselor may approach the practical issues more simply. *Spirituality* may be seen—from the human point of view—as a personal affirmation of transcendence, whereas *religion* constitutes the institutional, ritual, and creedal expressions of this affirmation. Kelly (1995) gives a more extensive consideration of this issue.

Across a number of disciplines looking at spirituality, there is a growing sense of common *themes* or *dimensions* that, when taken together, reveal the outlines of spirituality as it relates to human growth and development (NIHR, 1998). Understanding these dimensions may help counselors in the practical task of listening to their clients attentively and sensitively: "The human being needs a framework of values, a philosophy of life, a religion or religion-surrogate to live by and understand by in about the same sense that he [sic] needs sunlight, calcium or love" (Maslow, 1968, p. 206).

Distinctive to spirituality is the notion of a *sacred core,* the sense of a divine being or the ultimate truth or reality. It is the perception, however dim, of divine ultimacy and a desire to align oneself with what is sacred and therefore worthy of devotion and commitment (NIHR, 1998, p. 20). It is related to the notion of the transcendent or transpersonal (Miller, 1997, 1998; Miranti & Burke, 1992), a sensitivity for "depth of life" (Chandler et al., 1992). Burke (1998) describes it this way: "Spirituality refers to a way of being in the world that acknowledges the existence of a transcendent dimension in a person's life, while religion refers to the social or organized means by which persons express spirituality. In general, spirituality is less formal and more encompassing than religion" (p. 2).

Not unlike the counseling process itself, spirituality also involves a *quest* or *active search* for something beyond the self that can lead to greater knowledge and love (Chandler et al., 1992; Miller, 1997). Often likened to a "journey of discovery" (Barret, 1995; Nosek, 1995), the search is envisioned as an essential aspect of being human that includes a yearning for connectedness, belonging, and fullness of living (Kelly, 1995; LaPierre, 1994; May, 1982; NIHR, 1998; Shafranske & Gorsuch, 1984).

This search is, of course, a personal endeavor that is understood to lead in developmental fashion to an experience often described as transformative. Chandler and colleagues (1992) provide a model of spiritual wellness that is based on developmental principles and oriented around the integration of spiritual experiences into the process of personal transformation. This *experiential dimension* of spirituality has cognitive, affective, and behavioral components. The panel of experts for NIHR's scientific study of spirituality and health took these elements to be their primary criterion and common denominator for both spirituality and religion: "Both spirituality and religion involve the subjective feelings, thoughts, and behaviors that arise from a search for the sacred. The term "search" refers to attempts to identify, articulate, maintain, or transform. The term "sacred" refers to a divine being or Ultimate Reality or Ultimate Truth as perceived by the individual" (NIHR, 1998, p. 22).

Awareness of, or openness to, a transcendent dimension and having a worldview based on it and an imagination excited or awed by it (cognitive dimension); feelings of connectedness among self, others, nature, and the social world, along with a sense of belonging and "at-homeness" (affective dimension); practicing those values, attitudes, and rituals (e.g., prayer, examination of conscience, etc.) that help one to live in the world with integrity, that keep one in harmonious and vital contact with the spiritual (behavioral dimension)—all these are dimensions of spirituality. Morgan (1992, 1995a) provides a sense of how these dimensions may work together to create a sense of the spiritual and to bring healing to those in recovery from alcoholism.

Counselors need not be fully informed about all these dimensions as they relate to a host of spiritualities, nor need they be masters of many spiritual practices. Rather, in working with clients, counselors ought to (1) be able to affirm the importance of the client's spirituality; (2) value understanding of the spiritual dimension, so that they attempt to enter the world and imagination of the client in formulating problems and strategies of helping; and (3) be willing, as Ingersoll (1995) suggests, to consult with other "healers" in clients' lives who may be important in their spiritual worldview.

## Spirituality and Counseling

Recently, a number of leading counseling professionals met for a Summit on Spirituality, endorsed by ASERVIC. They developed a number of competencies in counseling practice related to spirituality, utilizing the CACREP core area training standards as a format. Their report identifies a set of spiritual competencies that would equip the counselor to work with clients who experience spiritual issues or emergencies:

> In order to be competent to help clients address the spiritual dimension of their lives, a counselor needs to be able to 1) explain the relationship between religion and spirituality, including similarities and differences, 2) describe religious and spiritual beliefs and practices in a cultural context, 3) engage in self-exploration of his/her religious and spiritual beliefs in order to increase sensitivity, understanding and acceptance of his/her belief system, 4) describe one's religious and/or spiritual belief system and explain various models of religious/spiritual development across the lifespan, 5) demonstrate sensitivity to and accep-

tance of a variety of religious and/or spiritual expressions in the client's communication, 6) identify the limits of one's understanding of a client's spiritual expression, and demonstrate appropriate referral skills and general possible referral sources, 7) assess the relevance of the spiritual domains in the client's therapeutic issues, 8) be sensitive to and respectful of the spiritual themes in the counseling process as befits each client's expressed preference, and 9) use a client's spiritual beliefs in the pursuit of the client's therapeutic goals as befits the client's expressed preference. (*CACREP Connection,* Winter 1998, p. 2)

It will be useful to demonstrate how some of these competencies are related in practical ways to the intersection of counseling and spirituality.

## *Identity, Attitude, and Attentive Listening*

This chapter has focused on the counselor's sensitivity to and acceptance of his or her client's spirituality (competencies 5 and 8). The ability to do this is directly related to the counselor's professional identity and clinical attitude (see Schafer, 1983; Schlauch, 1995).

*Identity* and *attitude* have to do with the counselor's fundamental stance toward the practice of counseling and toward those to be served. The counselor expresses his or her personality, history, education and training, commitments, and primary beliefs in professional identity and clinical attitude; they are essential elements in the counselor's quality of presence and in the healing process. All counselors have a professional identity and a basic attitude or stance toward their work. These function as "a gyroscope or lens through which a person guides and shapes his [sic] characteristic way of experiencing" (Schlauch, 1995, p. 77). An attitude of deep respect for, and attentive listening to, clients and their stories can be bolstered by openness to spirituality as a dimension of the whole person:

> In the spiritual perspective, respect in the human and counseling relationship is an in-depth attitude, a qualitative orientation toward human mutuality and serious care for positive human development. A spiritually imbued respect on the part of the counselor acts to enlarge the sphere of caring safety for the client within the demands of the counseling effort and to help the counselor and client believe in, search for, call forth, and activate the positive life energies that will enliven the client's growth and improvement (Kelly, 1995, p. 93).

Just as the counselor's attitude of openness and sensitivity toward clients' cultural or racial diversity is a critical element in the quality of care, so too is his or her sensitivity and willingness to listen to clients' spiritual concerns and beliefs (Kelly, 1995). The counselor's attitude toward spirituality will govern whether, and how well, he or she can attentively listen to these concerns from the client.

Attention to the spiritual dimension of a person leads to an attitude of respect for the whole person, a valuing of his or her beliefs and meaning making, a visioning of the counseling room as a sacred space in which life stories are told, authentic encounter is encouraged, and change—even transformation—is facilitated (Barret, 1995; Kopp, 1972). Particularly in relation to critical life issues, sensitivity to the spiritual dimension allows the counselor "to pay attention to another at the place where his or her soul is on the line" (O'Reilley, 1998, p. 4). An informed openness to spirituality will lead to cultivating more specific attitudes that can be helpful in the overall counseling process. Attitudes of confidence, receptivity, patience, welcoming, and expectation toward all dimensions of clients' lives, including the spiritual, can only enhance the counseling encounter. Hinterkopf (1998) provides a discussion of these attitudes in relation to spirituality and counseling.

Addressing the identity and attitude of counselors is an important task in counselor education and in the ongoing development of counselors as professional practitioners. Helping counselors examine their own attitudes and guiding perspectives and assumptions is an important undertaking for supervision and overall counselor development. For counselors-in-training, facilitating an appreciation for and an openness to the spiritual dimension as integral to holistic understanding of people and as important for the counseling process is a critical "growing edge" in counselor education.

## *Assessment*

Openness to spirituality and a religious perspective in counseling may be made concrete in a number of ways. For the counseling professional, the impact on assessment and building the therapeutic relationship is an important area to consider (competencies 5 and 7).

Assessment in counseling is oriented toward increased and mutual understanding, treatment planning, and action taking for both client and counselor (Kelly, 1995). Within this overall orientation, consideration of spiritual and religious dimensions can serve four basic purposes: building and enhancing the counseling relationship, accurate diagnosis, understanding the role of spirituality in development and personality, and discovering information useful for treatment.

*Purposes.*    One goal of assessment is to begin the construction of a healing relationship, a working alliance, between counselor and client. Eliciting information in a matter-of-fact and open way about a client's and family's religious background and practice, spiritual beliefs, and observance—much as one might do with an educational, vocational, or medical history—communicates to clients the counselor's openness to discuss such issues. Inquiring about the client's understanding of his or her presenting problem, and including (potential) philosophical beliefs or religious perspectives on understanding the problem and the healing process in general also communicates the counselor's open attitude and commitment to listening attentively. For many clients, this will be a refreshing and liberating experience, allowing them to pursue counseling with confidence that these concerns will be addressed.

In the process, counselors will begin to learn the client's language, symbol, and value systems. Listening attentively to how clients frame their concerns and speak about them, and openness to spiritual ways of perceiving and narrating their concerns, can help construct a common language between counselor and client that aids in the healing process.

Accurate diagnosis consists of understanding the client and his or her presenting problem in all its dimensions. Openness to the spiritual allows the counselor to assess whether, and how much, the problem is related to the client's spirituality. For some clients, their spiritual or religious backgrounds are clearly part of the problem, as they struggle with how to make sense of their lives in the face of failure or disappointment, guilt, or shame (Denton, 1998; Pruyser, 1976). Are their spiritual beliefs implicated in the etiology or maintenance of the problem? Are their beliefs or a religious network available for support and help with their problem (Pruyser, 1976; Worthington, 1989)?

Just as some understanding of a client's psychosocial development and basic personality is essential for assessment purposes, so too is a sense of the client's spiritual development and religious background. Historically and dynamically, this will be intimately tied to the family of origin experience of the client, and may be more easily pursued in this connection. The counselor may want to inquire here about early experiences with church, nature, or a sense of community; the counselor may also wish to explore the religiosity of parents or others, the role of peak experiences in the clients' lives, the sense of nourishment or depletion, of belonging or isolation, and of "rightness" or exclusion that clients experience today in regard to the religious tradition of their youth. All these inquiries may help to flesh out a sense of the strengths and potential weaknesses in the client's spiritual and/or religious experience.

Attentive listening to these matters may help convey a sense of the maturity of the client's religiosity, and the current state of his or her spirituality along a continuum between wellness and distress (Kelly, 1995; Malony, 1985, 1993). Understanding such issues may help guide the counselor's further inquiries and shape potential interventions.

Finally, attention to spiritual and religious views and language may help the counselor gather information that will be useful for more general treatment. An understanding of the client's typical ways of understanding the self and the world, of articulating resources and deficits, and of describing situations and perceptions through use of metaphor may provide clues to the client's inner and relational world. In turn, this may potentially allow the counselor to support or intervene in harmony with the client's own life and values. Such attention may also reveal clues to potential sources of support and care in the client's relational world (e.g., family, church, neighborhood, and spiritual traditions and practices) that the counselor might otherwise miss (Pruyser, 1976).

Pruyser's use of biblical metaphors, for example, are so deeply embedded in the common cultural heritage of clients that they will be used to frame problems or experiences and are available as avenues to explore a more healthy way forward. It is not uncommon for clients to resonate to the story of the prodigal son, or the good Samaritan, or Israel's long desert sojourn as capturing something of their own experience. Counselors who are aware and informed about such stories may be able to guide clients' usage of them in more helpful ways (Morgan, 1998). These four purposes or goals of the assessment process can help in understanding the potential value of conversation about spiritual and religious experience early on in the counseling process.

Kelly (1995) offers an extended discussion of differing types of individuals who come to counseling with varying commitments to the spiritual/religious dimension. He provides a typology of eight categories of individuals, ranging from those who are "religiously committed" to those who are "hostile to religion" (1995, pp. 136–142). In addition, he presents four problem categories that involve varying degrees of spiritual/religious involvement, from "predominantly or specifically spiritual/religious issue/problem" to problems with "little apparent or close connection with the spiritual/religious dimension" (1995, pp. 142–152). Some assessment of client and presenting problem with such typologies in mind will help the counselor choose the most therapeutic course of action.

*Procedures.*    Two procedures for facilitating these conversations with clients—interview procedures and instruments measuring aspects of spirituality—will now be discussed.

**1.** *Interviews*.  Midelfort (1962) utilizes an interviewing process in family therapy that can be integrated into counseling assessment. He asks family members about their ethnic origins and religious affiliations. Inquiry is also made into the belief systems that provide meaning to their life perspectives and views of healing. The counselor then attempts to work in ways that allow clients to utilize their own ethnic, religious, and spiritual resources (Kelly, 1995). Also from family therapy, discussion of a family genogram or a life-span developmental time line, with attention to patterns of spiritual belief and religious affiliation, may be useful (Gladding, 1998; McGoldrick, 1995). These approaches may have positive benefits, since they use values within the client's and family's own heritage. In this regard, discussion of the latest research information about "healthy families," conducted in an accessible way in counseling sessions, may also help to open up the religious/spiritual area for conversation (Curran, 1983; Stinnett & DeFrain, 1986).

From the field of pastoral counseling, Pruyser (1976) and Denton (1998) have each contributed texts that can assist counselors in thinking and interviewing a variety of clients about spiritual beliefs, perspectives, and resources. Both texts suggest a "translation" of the client's presentation in terms of religious themes and symbols (e.g., conversion, redemption, death-resurrection; prodigal son, good samaritan; and the cross) that may shed light on the problem and may connect with the client's worldview.

Another form of interviewing might utilize the models of spiritual wellness and development that are beginning to appear in the counseling literature. Witmer and Sweeney's (1992) *wheel of wellness* or the *model of spiritual assessment and intervention* by Farran and associates (1989) might be presented and briefly explained to clients with an invitation to apply them to their own life situations and current problems for which counseling is sought. Discussion could then pursue important and relevant themes as they present themselves in conversation.

**2.** *Instruments*.  As research and clinical experience begin to take spirituality more seriously as an important dimension that may be measured (at least in part), assessment instruments will continue to make their appearance for use in counseling situations. Several of these are already available and may prove to be of benefit to counselors willing to explore their uses. Ellison's (1994) Spiritual Well-Being Scale (SWBS) is one such instrument. The Family Environment Scale, or FES (Moos & Moos, 1981), used in family therapy to measure the psychosocial attributes of family networks, contains a number of items that are sensitive to spiritual factors and yields a Moral-Religion Emphasis subscale. In the field of addictions counseling, the Spiritual Health Inventory (SHI) constructed by Veach and Chappel (1992) and the Brown-Peterson Recovery Progress Inventory (B-PRPI), a 53-item inventory designed to give the counselor a sense of the spiritual cognitions, beliefs, and practices of those seeking addiction recovery, may be useful (Brown & Peterson, 1991).

A remarkable listing of spiritual assessment instruments and scales for assessing religious/spiritual phenomena is included in Appendix A of the consensus report on *Scientific Research on Spirituality and Health* (NIHR, 1998).

## The Healing Process

As the counseling process unfolds and the helping relationship between counselor and client(s) deepens, opportunities will arise for exploring the spiritual dimension more fully (competencies 8 and 9). This is true across a variety of counseling modalities, from more long-term individual, family, and group approaches to the brief and solution-focused methods, from the humanistic to the more behavioral ways of proceeding. Richards and Bergen (1997) discuss the relationship of various spiritual practices (e.g., prayer, meditation, reading sacred writings, forgiveness and repentance, and ritual) to numerous treatment approaches, such as cognitive restructuring, bibliotherapy, journal keeping, and guided imagery. The use and usefulness of such practices have been studied and are presented with empirical validation. In addition, they provide numerous case reports in the use of such interventions. If you are interested in pursuing this area of counseling practice in more detail, consult Hinterkopf (1998), Kelly (1995), Richards and Bergin (1997) and others for more in-depth information and guidance.

When counselors adopt an open and listening stance toward their clients and their work, and when clients begin to share their stories of pain, confusion, hurt, resentment, recrimination, shame, and the like with a real desire to move beyond their present state, an interactive kind of encounter and energy opens up between the counselor and client and can become a catalyst for growth in *both* of them (Kopp, 1972; May, 1982). This is especially true when openness to the spiritual dimension is added to the mix. The counselor, no less than the client, is challenged to grow: "Counselors' caring and competent attention to spirituality and religion opens *them* to a dimension of being, thinking, feeling, and living that for many clients is not only important in itself but may also be interwoven with the issues and concerns that clients bring to counseling" (Kelly, 1995, p. 245; italics added).

Artistic productions such as *Ordinary People, Equus,* and *Good Will Hunting* have acquainted a wide audience with the human and spiritual struggles that confront both clients and their counselors. It is not uncommon to see authentic encounters in the healing process lead to deep and life-giving growth for those involved; the counselor brings skill, experience, and empathy to the encounter, and often experiences personal growth, as well. As clients learn to befriend various aspects of themselves and their histories, and make peace with people in their relationship networks, so too do counselors often experience a deeper level of connectedness and empathy. This is to be expected, but it can also be energizing—and sometimes uncomfortable.

Sensitivity to spiritual concerns and ways of thinking, as well as the use of spiritual techniques and interventions, open *both* client and counselor to powerful forces for growth. Whether one chooses to ascribe these forces to resiliency, or to an innate drive for health, or to the intervention and care of a higher power, *something* operates in the healing encounter for the betterment of all concerned. For the counselor-in-training, the counselor educator, and the experienced practitioner, this mutual growth process demands openness to personal and relational development and a welcoming receptivity to one's own "growing edges." It also calls forth in *each person* a patient confidence in the power of the spiritual to bring good out of the chaotic, the confusing, and the hurtful.

In addition, as clients and counselors encounter each other, one must be aware that each may be dealing with different spiritual issues and challenges, or working at different levels or stages of spiritual development. Spirituality is not a univocal or static concept (e.g., a light switch that is either on or off); rather, spirituality is a developmental and energizing experience, with varying gradations of presence and growth (e.g., a rheostat). Moreover, this is true for both counselor and client. As the counseling relationship develops, the counselor must be aware and respectful of these potential developmental differences.

Differences can often arise most clearly in the face of critical life issues (discussed previously). The developmental disparity between counselor and client can be a source of help or difficulty, depending on the sensitivity of the counselor. For example, how does a counselor who is struggling with the meaning of multiple losses in her own life assist a client who is coming to discuss the impending loss of a loved one or his own terminal illness? Clearly, a spiritual worldview and sense of divine care or presence may be helpful in confronting situations of loss. As counselor and client face these issues together, they may discover both a difference in spiritual maturity *and* the potential for mutual growth because of their deep encounter. In any case, sensitivity to differences in this regard is important to acknowledge and work through. These challenging elements in the intersection of counseling and spirituality call the counselor to attend to his or her own growth and development.

## *The Counselor's Own Spirituality*

Spirituality is a participative discipline and perspective (Schneiders, 1986, 1990). This means that, in order to be sensitive to its meaning and contours, counselors will also need to be somewhat engaged in it themselves (competencies 3 and 4).

As the information at the beginning of this chapter suggests, many counseling professionals already do have some religious affiliation and/or spiritual beliefs and engage in a variety of spiritual practices. These may be related to traditional religious traditions or denominations or to those "spiritual" disciplines that are available in the wider culture, such as twelve-step practices, Eastern forms of meditation or "mindfulness," yoga, and the like. Many counselors find these practices and their underlying spirituality to be nourishing and helpful.

Continued growth in areas related to professional practice is an ongoing objective of counselor education, supervision, and certification. Development of knowledge and skill is encouraged through recertification procedures such as continuing education credits for NBCC certification. Counselors may also wish to consider ways in which they can keep their spiritual sensitivities open and available for use in the practice of counseling. Certainly, developing some sense of the counselor's own religious or spiritual history, background, beliefs, and the like—as well as formulating a personal working philosophy on the relationship of counseling and spirituality—is an important element in the counselor's professional stance and ongoing personal development.

## *Collaboration*

There is no doubt that the emergence of spirituality as a topic for consideration in the practice of professional counseling presents a number of challenges. An important challenge worth mentioning at the close of this chapter is the increased need for counselors to be interdisciplinary and collaborative in their practice (competency 6).

While maintaining openness and sensitivity to a number of concerns in clients' lives, including the dimension of spirituality, counselors may be more effective if they are willing to collaborate with others in the client's network or within the healing professions. One clear example of this is the cooperation that many counselors foster with a recovering client's twelve-step sponsor and recovery group. Counselors might also consider some cooperative work with the client's clergyperson, spiritual director, or shaman (Morgan, 1995b).

This is but an extension of the traditional collaborative role between counselors and physicians, and between counselors and other mental health practitioners (e.g., psychologists and psychiatrists). Here, however, the focus is on maintaining and enhancing spiritual well-being and development. Accurate and sensitive assessment of the client's needs and psychosocial network will provide information about appropriate spiritual resources within the client's worldview; such information may provide clues about an appropriate collaborative partner in the overall process of promoting healing and growth.

## *Summary*

This chapter briefly touched on the importance and usefulness of a sensitive appreciation of clients' spiritual perspectives. It advocates renewed consideration of spirituality by professional counselors and suggests several ways in which counselors might integrate spiritual concerns into practice. It suggests the development of a meaningful perspective on the inclusion of spirituality within counseling practice and attempts to highlight some of the challenging aspects of this inclusion.

Ongoing research into this topic is an important challenge to the counseling field in years to come. Conceptual clarity, more thorough assessment procedures, development of helpful instruments, and sensitive treatment of this topic within counselor preparation will aid in integrating this "emerging issue" into professional practice and informed counselor education.

# 12

# *Technology and Web Counseling*

## John W. Bloom

***John W. Bloom*** *received a B.A. in English and an M.Ed. in guidance and counseling, both from Miami University of Ohio, and then took a Ph.D. in counselor education from Purdue University. He is presently the coordinator of the school counseling program at Butler University in Indianapolis. Prior to this appointment, he was a professor of counselor education at Northern Arizona University. Bloom has served on the boards of the National Board for Certified Counselors, the American Counseling Association, and the American School Counselors Association. His interests include geneology, stamp collecting, clowns, humor, and particularly computers and the Internet. Bloom is currently researching Hoosier role models from all walks of life.*

## In This Chapter . . .

- What are the various activities that could be included under the concept of *web counseling?*
- What exactly is the "web counseling debate"?
- What are the potential obstacles to successful counseling on the Internet?
- What are the potential ethical issues related to counseling on the Internet?
- IF web counseling successfully negotiates these obstacles and ethical issues, what is the potential for using the Internet for counseling purposes?

For many counselors and counselor educators, the growing practice of counseling individuals at remote sites using electronic means is the most perplexing aspect of the technological revolution. The practice of *web counseling,* or *on-line therapy,* is defined as "the practice of professional counseling and information delivery that occurs when client(s) and counselor are in separate or remote locations and utilize electronic means to communicate over the Internet" (NBCC, 1997). This chapter will examine many of the consumer concerns and professional issues surrounding the practice of web counseling.

## Consumer Concerns

Among the many concerns shared by consumers are the following:

- Many potential clients have no idea that web counseling is available to them.
- Many potential clients do not have personal computers, Web access, or the knowledge to use the Web to obtain web counseling services.
- Many potential clients do not know how to identify qualified on-line practitioners.
- Many potential clients do not know how to check on-line practitioner credentials.
- Many potential clients do not understand the web counseling process.
- Many potential clients are unaware of on-line confidentiality issues.
- Many potential clients fear revealing credit card information to any on-line entity.

## Professional Concerns

Counseling professionals, educated to believe that the relationship between client and therapist is paramount, quickly question the wisdom and the efficacy of placing an electronic device, with or without visual input, between client and therapist. The bygone phrase of the 1980s, *High tech, high touch,* was but one way traditionalists sought to remind counselors of their responsibility to maintain human touch and eye contact in the counseling relationship. Although there is ample evidence of ethical, questionably ethical, and clearly unethical counseling practices on the Internet (Sampson, Kolodinsky, & Greeno, 1997), their growing presence suggests that more, not fewer, sites and practices will be created in the future. However, that growth appears to be more gradual than originally anticipated—perhaps an indication that counselors and clients alike are proceeding with due caution and will strive constantly to maintain the intimacy and closeness inherent in face-to-face counseling (Bloom & Sampson, 1998a). Among those concerns that have been voiced by professional counselors, the following are noted:

- Some web counselors experience difficulty obtaining liability insurance.
- Some web counselors are waiting until empirical research documents the efficacy of web counseling.
- Some web counselors live in jurisdictions that have determined the practice of web counseling to be unethical.
- Some web counselors live in jurisdictions where the legality of working with clients across state or international borders is uncertain.
- Some web counselors are waiting for more advanced video technology or encryption methodologies.

- Some web counselors do not know how to access information about establishing legal, ethical, and professional practices.
- Some web counselors are concerned about the legality of working with children and teenagers.

# The Web Counseling–Telehealth Link

When trying to understand how the Internet can affect the delivery of all professional services, web counselors would do well to follow progress made by counterparts in the medical professions, as the medical community seeks to apply its knowledge and skills with technological acumen. In the medical community, the on-line service delivery phenomenon is called *telehealth*. State and national telehealth legislation can serve as a model for the counseling profession.

## Telehealth

Senator Kent Conrad introduced the Comprehensive Telehealth Act of 1997 (S. 385) to help put a range of health care services within reach of people living in small and rural communities through telecommunication links to distant hospitals, clinics, and specialized health care services by July 1, 1998 (Arent et al., 1997). This legislation is designed to promote the development and use of advanced telecommunication and diagnostic technology in health care. Telehealth includes a wide variety of applications, such as interactive consultations between a patient and a distant physician, the transfer of X-rays, or continuing education classes for health professionals.

Conrad claims that technological advances and the development of a national information infrastructure give telehealth the potential to overcome barriers to health care services long experienced by rural Americans. The senator is convinced that our nation needs to do more to integrate telehealth into our overall health care delivery system. I believe counseling professionals need to feel as strongly about integrating ethical on-line therapy services into that same system. While Conrad imagines a patient in a small town in North or South Dakota receiving consultation services from a specialist in Bismarck or Grand Forks without leaving home, I imagine an isolated client in Los Angeles or in Hong Kong accessing similar expertise over the Internet. Conrad's bill takes four steps to develop the potential of telehealth in the United States:

1. The bill makes telehealth services eligible for Medicare reimbursement.
2. It asks the Secretary of Health and Human Services to study state-to-state licensure barriers for health professionals who provide services through telehealth.
3. The legislation requires annual telehealth reports to Congress from the Federal Joint Working Group on Telehealth.
4. Finally, it provides grants and loans to rural hospitals, clinics, universities, libraries, and other organizations to develop local telehealth networks and to foster rural economic development.

### *Medicare Considerations*

Thanks to Conrad's legislation, telehealth services are now eligible for Medicare reimbursement. Medicare must cover telehealth services in rural areas that the federal government has determined to have a shortage of health professionals. The legislation is expected to benefit Medicare patients in 745 counties around the country. Fee schedules for telehealth services will be the same as for traditional office visits.

### *Credentialing and Telemedicine*

Since 29 percent of the nation's rural hospitals already practice telemedicine, but the jury is still out as to how precise credentialing of off-site practitioners should be (Opus Communications, cited in Arent et al., 1997). At the very least, a facility must "make sure that the person [it is] talking to on the phone or communicating with through video is a qualified health care provider," explains R. Peter Ericson, JD, assistant counsel and chief of litigation and employment law services for PHICO Group in Mechanicsburg, PA.

The details about documentation are far from clear. Ericson encourages credentialers to use common sense. For example, if a facility uses a physician for telemedicine consultations on a regular basis, it may need to set up a comprehensive credentials file for that practitioner. But for those clinicians the facility contacts less frequently, a quick, documented call to the physician's affiliated hospital for credentialing and privileging information may be enough.

Erickson also advises credentialers to be aware that the consulting physician may not hold a license to practice in the home state of the patient. As of yet, there are no clear licensing laws or regulations. However, the American Medical Association House of Delegates officially recommended that physicians seek licensing in every state where their patients are located, not just the state where the physician practices.

Mahue (1997, February 9) has noted that there are a number of nationwide trends in telehealth that have been developing rapidly, and without psychologists' participation. The legal race among states wanting to pass telemedicine acts has already been won by California. Its Telemedicine Development Act of 1996 was signed into law in September 1995 and enacted in July 1996. The California law defines and regulates the practice of telemedicine on a statewide level for the first time. It not only restricts California telemedicine services to practitioners licensed in California but it also requires insurance carriers to reimburse providers for its delivery, including HMOs and Medi-Cal. It amends four major state codes to add telemedicine as a normal part of health care services. The California Telemedicine Development Act of 1996 and the Federal Telehealth Act (1997) appear on the World Wide Web at www.cybertowers.com/ct/dlc/

## *The Web Counseling Debate: To Counsel On-Line or Not to Counsel On-Line?*

Critics of web counseling primarily appear to be those who have yet to try on-line therapy for one or more of the reasons previously mentioned. Aside from the possibility of censure or mockery by hesitant colleagues, trying web counseling is an arduous and risky task. The first-time web counselor must have the necessary hardware and software, have in hand appropriate standards to guide practice, have liability insurance and be assured that insurance will cover on-line therapy, be aware of exactly how all state and professional certification and licensure boards will react if a complaint is filed, and so on. The first-timer must still find willing clients with compatible hardware, software, and so on as well as the computer literacy to take a risk. Advocates of web counseling are those who have jumped into the fray, oblivious to professional concerns, or those who believe that professionals can be addressed efficaciously.

## Concerns about Web Counseling

Those concerned about the practice of web counseling often cite real or imagined legal, ethical, or professional concerns. Murphy and Mitchell (1998) report that the advantages of conducting counseling via the Internet are mitigated by numerous concerns. In a recent survey of 38 counselors, counseling students, and counselor educators (Kirk, 1997), more than one-third of the respondents said they would not use the Internet for counseling or counselor education. The reasons for this cautious stance include the lack of security for confidential material, including the difficulty of verifying the identity of the client and counselor; lack of visual cues; and the negative impact of physical absence on relationship formation. Related to security is a concern that clients receiving services via the Internet have to manage their own privacy on their computer and their immediate surroundings (Murphy & Mitchell, 1998).

Can one do psychotherapy by telephone, teleconferencing, or the Internet? Some argue that, by definition of the word *counseling* or *psychotherapy,* the answer is *absolutely not!* Consider the following definition:

> Psychotherapy is conducted by trained and qualified therapists and consists of diagnosing and treating mental disorders. This includes using psychological techniques to help a client or patient to develop and achieve goals, objectives, and strategies which will ameliorate problems with behavior, mood, thought processes, or psychosomatic disorders. (Nagy, 1997, p. 7)

Holmes (1997) adds that psychotherapy is not yet possible on the Internet because of unresolved ethical issues, problems related to current "bandwidth" of the Net, and unresolved regulatory and licensing issues. Davis (1997), however, suggests there is nothing to debate: "Conspicuously absent from all of these definitions of counseling, whether in text or statute, and from the descriptions of effective counseling practice is the concept that counseling is performed solely in a face to face manner" (p. 1).

## Legal Issues

Although many questions have been raised about the legality of on-line counseling, little precedent has been established in state or federal law that specifically relates to such practice. Love (1998) mentions problems associated with counselors practicing across state (or national) lines, something often done by the unscrupulous in other professions. The state of

Minnesota (Minnesota Attorney General, 1998), for example, not only is concerned about the welfare of its residents but also about the loss of revenue when such activities go untaxed. Thus, the Attorney General's office in Minnesota has begun to clamp down on on-line scams such as individuals placing a bet through Internet gambling organizations.

Web counselors, particularly those who practice across state lines, must keep in mind that there is no one set of national standards to govern the practice of on-line therapy (Love, 1998). They must bear the responsibility of knowing and adhering to the statutes of both the state they practice in and the state (or country) where their client or clients live (NBCC, 1997).

## *Ethical Issues*

The last years of the 1990s witnessed tremendous growth in the amount of attention being paid to ethical issues surrounding the practice of web counseling. Peterson, Murray, and Chan (1998) have written the most comprehensive examination of ethical, legal, and professional issues to date. They address topics such as the ethical management of electronic media, on-line forums of counseling, computer-assisted assessment, computer-assisted–counselor-assisted counselor education, ethical use of software, technological counseling interventions for people with disabilities, and a four-level model of ethical practice and technology. (Firsthand information from over 90 on-line therapists concerning their experience with web counseling can be found at Dr. Marlene Mahue's Online Ethics Survey Project at www.cybertowers.com/cgibin/ethics_forum.cgi)

Hughs and Ruiz (1998), members of the Ethics Committee of the American Counseling Association, suggest the following considerations when using the Internet to provide counseling services: services and products, competence and credentials, security, damage to operations and contact, intellectual property infringement, flow over, username, therapy limitations, and informed consent. Those wishing to offer comments on these matters can contact the American Counseling Association's Center for Effective Counseling Practice at www.cecp@counseling.org

Counseling professionals are also addressing ethical concerns by conducting research (see the findings of Murphy and Mitchell [1998] and Cohen and Kerr [in press] mentioned later). In addition, counseling associations are developing standards of practice and preparation, which are also included later in this chapter.

Trailblazing web counselors in the mid-1990s were forced to travel many unmarked roads along the information highway, but the dawn of the new millennium sees those roads becoming better marked with informational signage addressing some of the myriad of professional concerns one is likely to encounter along the way. Clearly, however, there is no one central repository and distribution point of technological information as it applies to the helping professions. The traveler of the information highway is still urged to exercise caution and to search vigorously for the latest information from other web counselors, from professional associations and licensure boards, and from the World Wide Web itself.

A concrete example of these concerns is relevant to Texas licensed professional counselors or counselors from Brisbane or Biloxi who wish to counsel Texans. Holland (1998), of the Texas Counseling Association, observes that as with every ethical standard, there are still gray areas and conflicts with other ethical codes and licensing rules. The counselor will have to make decisions based on the individual client and what the counselor believes is right. Web counseling is one of those situations. Holland cites a conflict with the Texas licensed professional counselor rule 681.32g, which states, "A licensee shall provide counseling treatment intervention only in the context of a professional relationship, and shall not provide counseling treatment intervention by means of newspaper or magazine articles, radio or television programs, mail or means of a similar nature, electronic media, or telephonic media when that is the primary vehicle for maintaining the counseling relationship."

Meyers (1998), also of the Texas Counseling Association, further outlines five counselor implications of the NBCC WebCounseling Standards:

1. Counselors need to be familiar with encryption methodology or at least know that the broken key at the bottom of the computer screen means that the current communication is not secure.
2. Formal steps must be taken to secure Web communications.
3. Web counselors must be thoroughly knowledgeable of transmission procedures, lest a confidential communication be sent worldwide.
4. Web counseling requires clarity and precision of thought (e.g., both the client and the counselor can differentiate when the word *swell* means good or great and when a sarcastic *swell* means quite the opposite).
5. Web-informed consent must include procedures to be taken if technology fails or nature intercedes.

Wilson, Jencius, and Duncan (1997) have written an introduction to the Internet and about the opportunities and dilemmas it presents the counseling profession. In it, they list a number of dangers and ethical pitfalls, including the following:

1. Assessment, diagnosis, and screening issues
2. Forming a legal contract with a client
3. Disclosure to clients
4. Inability to give consent
5. Issues related to clients served by others
6. Issues related to personal needs, nondiscrimination, and respecting differences
7. Protecting clients and the client relationship
8. Confidentiality and the right to privacy, the respect for privacy, and confidentiality of records.

## *The Case for Web Counseling*

Dan Mitchell and Lawrence Murphy, master's-level counselors in Vancouver, British Columbia, investigated the possibility of offering counseling services on the Internet in September 1995 (Mitchell & Murphy, 1998). They created three services: the Virtually Solve It worksheet (VSI), a form consisting of several questions carefully designed to help clients gain a fresh understanding of their concerns and develop potential solutions;

Therap-e-mail, a therapeutic e-mail communication between client and counselor; and Ask PATtY Q, an acronym for a Professional Answer To Your Question.

In May 1996, Mitchell and Murphy began offering counseling services on the World Wide Web under the name of Therapy Online (www.therapyonline.ca). The website consists of information regarding the services offered, the qualifications of and professional information about the therapists, advantages of and precautions about on-line counseling, and a Conditions of Service consent form.

In July 1998, the authors interviewed, by e-mail, a client (SW) who participated in an exchange of more than 100 Therap-e-mail messages between March and August 1997. Most of the Therap-e-mail messages involved SW as an individual. On a few occasions, her husband was invited to read and reply to the therapist's e-mail. The follow-up interviews consisted of a series of e-mails presenting SW with several of the concerns raised by the profession and asking for her perspective of the concerns.

Murphy (personal communication, December 2, 1998) further explained that SW lived a considerable distance from the counselor and that the relationship between counselor and client was entirely virtual. Through the client's work with the counselor, SW developed the courage to confront her husband on a number of issues that were making her miserable and, as a result, SW and her husband agreed to seek face-to-face marital counseling.

The concerns raised by the profession, SW's perspective on those concerns, and discussion procedures developed by Murphy and Mitchell to alleviate or reduce each concern include the following:

> ***Security Issues.*** To address the concern of the security of e-mail, we [Murphy and Mitchell] encourage all clients to use encryption software. This reduces the risks associated with the transmission and storage of confidential counseling material. However, we recognize that clients may not have appropriate software and/or the skill to encrypt their e-mail. If they do not have suitable software, free software, available on the Web, is recommended. Therapy Online's website also states a recognition that some clients will feel more distressed if they are asked to acquire and learn how to use encryption software. These clients are welcome to use the services without e-mail encryption, provided they are willing to accept full responsibility for the risks of using nonencrypted e-mail.
>
> Verifying the identity of clients remains a challenge. To reduce the likelihood of clients using false identities, Therapy Online asks clients who are registering for services to make a declaration that they are, in fact, the person they are claiming to be. As a further precaution, we ask clients for certain pieces of personal information that would likely be known only by the client. Clients can verify therapists' identities if the therapists register with a third party who confirms their credentials and makes that information available on a secured server. Clients can click on a link to the secured server to verify the identity of the therapist. One such service is available at www.cmhc.com/check/clinicians We are currently exploring similar procedures for clients. (*Note:* Sampson and associates (1997) suggest that as biometric technology [e.g., voiceprints or thumbprints] becomes more reliable and cost effective, it will likely be used to control users at the receiving end of the information highway.)
>
> ***Physical Absence.*** Counselors who are blind cannot see their clients' nonverbal behavior. They must attend closely to tone of voice, volume, choice of words, and changes in speech patterns. Text-based counselors must develop similar compensatory skills. It is our experi-

ence that careful attention to basic counseling skills, in written form, is highly effective in establishing and maintaining a therapeutic relationship. The liberal use of empathy, warmth, paraphrasing, interpretation, and immediacy seem especially important to clients. When interviewed about the impact of the lack of visual cues and the physical absence of the counselor, SW reports a surprisingly positive experience: "I learned to become more aware of the feelings I was expressing, and to emphasize them (e.g., being attentive to explaining how I feel, sending hugs, etc., that I could then imagine). I think this is a great skill to learn—to become more conscious of one's behavior. It's useful all the time in life. Impact suggests something negative, but I don't think it was negative at all. I learned a new and useful skill."

At another point in the interview process, SW wrote, "I felt that there was someone out there who cared about me and would help me." Her choice of words *out there* is interesting. They suggest that the physical presence of the counselor may not be necessary in order to communicate warmth and caring that characterize a healthy therapeutic relationship. In fact, physical absence appears to have encouraged her to deal with sensitive topics. She writes: "It was less embarrassing to write it down than to talk to someone face to face." Writing allowed SW a means of confronting her concerns in an emotionally safe manner. "I was so distressed I couldn't tell someone without becoming hysterical, so writing it down allowed me to say it all, without showing someone how distressed I was."

***Emergency Situations.*** SW's mention of distress points to the responsibilities of on-line counselors to help their clients manage emotional crises. In advance of participating in on-line counseling, we ask our clients to read a page on our website www.therapyonline.ca/crisis that advises them on how to mange an emotional crisis. In addition, Therapy Online provides clients with a toll-free number that can connect them with a crisis center in the counselor's city. In the eventuality of more serious emergencies—such as suicide, homicide, or children at risk of harm—it is important that on-line counselors follow procedures that are consistent with face-to-face procedures. In the case of an imminent emergency, appropriate authorities in the client's locale need to be contacted by telephone. This points to the importance of collecting client addresses and telephone numbers at intake. As an additional precaution, Therapy Online asks clients for the name and telephone number of an emergency contact person who does not live in the client's household.

***Technological Failure.*** Therapy Online's website states that clients can expect their counselor to reply to the e-mails within a specified time frame. The website also notes that Therapy Online's technological equipment or the client's equipment could fail unexpectedly at any time. Clients are advised to send their latest e-mail again if they suspect the latter. The same advice is given if they think there has been an unwarranted delay in the counselor's response. As a fail-safe measure, clients can use the toll-free telephone number if they have concerns of this nature.

***Therapeutic Relationship.*** Regarding the question of whether therapy is possible via e-mail, SW shares that she felt personal caring from the counselor: "I was helped a lot! I went from hardly able to think coherently to being able to tell my whole story, express my feelings, and identify ways I've grown."

Regarding the use of Therap-e-mail for couples and/or families, SW had this to say: "I think Therap-e-mail could work well for a family/couple. It can be less painful to write things down, and have time to consider rather than getting angry and saying something you later regret. I think it can be a good environment to learn to respect the other person's feelings and think of the implications of what you say."

***Access.*** We expect e-mail counseling services to be especially valuable to people with disabilities and illnesses. Some studies are beginning to support this assertion. In one such instance, an interactive computer system was placed in the homes of people with HIV. Part of the system provided opportunities for patients with HIV to connect with one another via e-mail. Although numerous other services were provided on the computer system, by far the most widely used service was the e-mail Discussion Group, which was used by 73 percent of the patients. Forty-one percent of these patients used the Discussion Group more often than once a day. Focus groups revealed that "Discussion Group allowed far more and varied contact with others than [patients] had managed previously through other means."

SW also makes an interesting point about accessibility of on-line services: "It's not just physical handicaps that prevent people from getting to a counselor. For some people, seeing a counselor is a stigma. Many people don't want to ask for help. Perhaps for these people, on-line help is a little easier. I guess this was somewhat the case for me too." (Murphy, personal communication, December 2, 1998)

Murphy further clarified (personal communication, December 7, 1998), "The relationship was entirely virtual.... Essentially, [face-to-face] couldn't happen because SW lives a long way from either of us. However, I believe that through her work... she developed the courage to confront her husband on a number of issues that were making her miserable and, as a result, the two of them agreed to seek face-to-face marital counseling. Extremely positive outcome in my mind."

Mitchell added, "Lawrence and I do not expect to be able to provide face-to-face counseling very often because of distance. However, we have often referred people to face-to-face counselors for a variety of reasons, such as high risk for suicide, age (client seeking on-line counseling is under age 14 and has no parental consent), and so on. The client in the case study sought face-to-face marital counseling on her own accord as the process moved from personal work to couples work. We experimented with asynchronous on-line couples work, but it seemed a little cumbersome and didn't last long."

From a technology perspective, text-only communication soon may become a relic of the past, but from a consumer perspective, it may be years before every client and counselor has video capabilities. Murphy and Mitchell (1998) present strong arguments that suggest that regardless of the technology available, text-only communication may be appropriate for years to come. Therap-e-mail—involving an asynchronous exchange of e-mail messages after the client has completed an intake form, called a Virtually Solve It worksheet, and provided informed consent—works.

Further, Murphy and Mitchell mention the work of Walther and Burgoon (1992) who compared a face-to-face (FTF) group with a computer mediated e-mail communication group (CMC). Walther and Burgoon found that relationships did evolve in a positive direction in the CMC group and that the effects of time were stronger than the effects of the medium in general. So, given adequate time, they believe on-line therapists can overcome any possible negative effective of not having visual input.

Murphy and Mitchell also cite Colon (1996), who conducted two therapy groups via a commercial on-line e-mail service. Clients were expected to post messages to the group at least three times a week, but most posted an e-mail every day. Colon sensed fewer emotional distractions in the on-line group than exist in off-line therapies, and noticed that on-line group members were more willing to disclose, thus making therapy more comprehensive. Murphy and Mitchell also refer to their own work with clients as evidence that caring professionals can convey their care without visual input. One client of theirs wrote of Murphy:

In just our brief exchange of messages you have left me with the sense that you are a caring, creative, helpful, hopeful soul. This is hard enough to achieve in person, let alone in the impersonal world of electronic communication. Your warmth and your humanity shine through the pixels on my screen, and come at a time when I need them most. For this I thank you and congratulate you. The irony is not lost on me that I find a True Person in a virtual void at the same time the doctor in my own home country has given me short shrift. (Murphy & Mitchell, 1998, p. 24)

## *Computer-Mediated Counseling versus Face-to-Face Counseling*

Cohen (Cohen & Kerr, in press), a recent graduate of the master's-degree program in counseling at Arizona State University (ASU), investigated the effects of computer-mediated versus traditional face-to-face counseling. Clients, 24 undergraduates at ASU, were told that different counseling methods were being studied in the treatment of anxiety and were randomly assigned to receive either computer-mediated counseling or face-to-face counseling. The computer-mediated counseling was synchronous and text based, meaning that counselors were present and followed a standardized protocol of questions in a semistructured interview format, which was the same for both counseling conditions. Clients experienced a uniform decrease in state anxiety and rated their counselors equally on expertness, attractiveness, and trustworthiness, regardless of the mode of delivery they received. Cohen and Kerr (in press) offer a number of thought-provoking suggestions regarding the outcomes of this study, including the following:

> Many people who are suffering are unable or unwilling to present themselves for FTF counseling; and the perceived anonymity of CM counseling may aid clients in disclosing sensitive information and lowering their defenses enough to benefit from therapy. Introverts, for example, might appreciate the slower, more thoughtful process offered by CM counseling. Beauvois and Eledge (1996) found that introverts reacted positively to computer-mediated communication because it allowed them more time to think before responding. Therapists can also take advantage of the time delay to consciously convey main points they want to communicate. Several counselors in this study reported appreciating the extra time they had to construct better responses. (p. 13)

## *Web Counseling and Necessary Conditions for Counseling Success*

Robson and Robson (1998) address the question of whether intimacy, considered by most to be an essential component of the counseling process, can be achieved via computer communication. The researchers first examined the definition of *intimacy*. They found little research and even less consensus as to the essential elements of intimacy, but did discover some factors, such as self-disclosure and emotional expressiveness, that are possible in on-line relationships. They also mention that some authors suggest that it is the lack of visual stimulation that increases self-disclosure by others.

Other factors are mentioned by Robson and Robson (1998), such as physical contact and even sex, as not possible in on-line therapy, even though virtual reality systems may eventually approximate human touch and cybersex is indeed feasible and widely practiced in an age of AIDS and herpes. These authors question if the client-centered counselor can offer and the client can accept the core conditions of counseling if that counseling is provided on-line. For example, can the on-line therapist listen to the feelings behind a client's words? They conclude by saying that they feel on-line therapy would be a barrier in being allowed to get so close to a human soul and that the uniqueness of humanity will always be limited by transmission through the wires.

It must be pointed out that the article mentions the affiliate of one author with the Department of Computer Science, University of Durham (UK) and the other with the School of Education at the same institution. It does not mention that either has attempted to offer Web-based counseling services. Although observations or data from those who have actually provided or received such services is limited, it tends to present a very different picture.

### Selecting a Web Counselor

Ainsworth (1999)—a self-described computer communications consultant, an electronic publisher, an apostle of cyberspace, and a community builder—offers many web counseling resources at her Metanoia website (www.metanoia.org), including the Metanoia Guide to Internet Therapists and Counselors. By clicking on the directory, one accesses the Directory of Internet Psychotherapists, which was prepared in partnership with Dr. John Grohol's Mental Health Net (www.metanoia.org/imhs/directry.htm). Directory resources listed are links to individuals or organizations that provide psychological counseling or give advice on the Internet, generally through e-mail. Most charge per question or e-mail, are usually around $20 to $25. The directory is an independent consumer guide, not an advertisement of services. Some of the sites have star ratings, which reflect the opinions of Mental Health Net colleagues who have visited each of the sites and are more a statement regarding consumer issues (i.e., confidentiality, credentials, etc.) than the therapist's ability to counsel.

Metanoia.org also provides an informative introduction and discussion of issues surrounding on-line therapy services. Particularly helpful are links to the following: Is This Therapy, Ethics, Confidentiality, Legal Issues, and Fees & Payment. If there is one negative associated with this site, it is that the concerned consumer who wishes to be a thoroughly informed client must wade through a lot of information, much of it more important to the on-line therapist than to the client, before arriving at a final decision. The positives, which certainly outweigh the negative, is that the information is conveniently assembled at one site and can be accessed any time the client wants more facts or informed opinions about the process.

### Web Counselor Credential Check

Credential Check is accessible either through Ainsworth's Metanoia webpage (www.metanoia.org) or directly through Dr. John Grohol's Mental Health Net (1999) (www.cmhc.com/check) and is a voluntary process for on-line therapists who choose to have their credentials independently verified. Thus far, about 30 on-line therapists from a variety of behavioral health professions have taken advantage of the Ainsworth and Grohol collaborative venture. Conversely, many unscrupulous on-line therapists have not taken advantage of this service and are unlikely to do so in the future.

Therapists provide Credential Check with information about their highest academic degrees, their licenses or certifications, and other professional data. In return for this and an annual renewal fee of $19.95, therapists are authorized to display the Credential Check symbol at their websites.

As of December 1998, 36 on-line therapists had submitted their credentials and had those credentials posted at the Credential Check site. A review of the 14 females and 22 males who submitted credentials shows that most, if not all, of those so registered held master's degrees ($n = 13$) or doctorates ($n = 16$). The 7 who did not indicate a degree at the site could be assumed to have at least a master's on the basis of the certification or licensure they held.

The location of the on-line therapists' practice indicates the interstate and international nature of such Internet communication. Four therapists were from outside the United States (Guam, British Columbia, Germany, and Korea) and several therapists indicated being licensed in more than one state. States in which more than one on-line therapist are located include California (7), New York (4), and Texas, Florida, and Arizona (3 each). Credentials held by the 36 ranged from ACSW, SW, LCSW, CSW, LISW social worker (10); psychologist (9); California marriage, family and child counselor (5); CPC, LPC professional counselors (4); clinical psychologist (4); CMHC, LPMHC, LMHC mental health counselors (3); national certified counselor (2); RD, LD (dietician) (1); RPN (nurse) (1); chemical dependence (1); CMAC addictions counselor (1); certified rehabilitation counselor (1); and three who appear to be uncredentialed because they live in jurisdictions that do not credential their profession.

## *Technology Standards*

Several professional organizations have developed standards for the delivery of counseling services using technology (NBCC, 1997; NCDA, 1997; ASCA, 1998; Academic Senate for California Community Colleges, 1997). The Association for Counselor Education and Supervision (ACES) is developing two sets of standards, one to address technology in counselor education courses and one to address technology skills needed by counselor education students and graduates. Program accreditation standards likewise must consider the constantly evolving role of technology in graduate training programs. Others, such as the American Psychological Association, point to already existing documents as standards to which web counselors must adhere (APA, 1995).

## *WebCounseling Practice Standards*

The first Standards for the Ethical Practice of WebCounseling Standards were developed by the National Board for Certified Counselors (1997) (www.nbcc.org/ethics/wcstandards. htm). In addition, the National Career Development Association Ethics Committee (NCDA, 1997) has developed guidelines for the use of the Internet for Provision of Career Information and Planning Services.

## *Internet for Provision of Career Information and Planning Services*

Sampson (1998) makes a case for delivery of career counseling services, stating:

> There are several potential benefits resulting from the use of the Internet in delivering career resources and services. Individuals in geographically remote, currently underserved locations can receive resources and services from a wider range of practitioners with specialized expertise. Individuals with physical disabilities can choose to access resources and counseling services at their residence. Also, the anonymity possible with the Internet may encourage some individuals to seek services who would not have done so in the past. For the general population, the Internet provides an expanded array of options for accessing guidance resources and services. (p. 2)

## *Technology and School Counseling Standards*

Hartman (1998) offered a course, Using Technology in School Counseling, at the University of Delaware, Summer Session I, 1998, which provided school counselors with 10 technical skills and theoretical knowledge necessary to integrate technology into their work with students, parents, and colleagues, in accordance with the ASCA National Standards for School Counseling Programs. The standards, which emphasize asynchronous Internet-based activities, were authored for the Education Trust and the American School Counselor Association. The syllabus for this course is available on the Internet (www.garcon. education. louisville.edu/~rasabe01/technology.html). Technical skills referred to in the course are available also (www.udel.edu/~khartman/page25.html).

## *Community College Counseling Standards*

The Academic Senate for California Community Colleges (1997) has created a set of technology standards for practice within California Community College Counseling Programs. The standards implore counseling faculty, who perform core functions (academic counseling, career counseling, personal counseling, crisis intervention, multicultural counseling, outreach, consultation, research, and training), to take advantage of new technologies in doing their jobs.

The Senate states that counseling is by nature an interpersonal activity rather than an interaction between human and machine, and that although computers will never replace the skills of a counseling professional, computers nevertheless have the capacity to dramatically improve the access and accuracy in the delivery of information. Counseling programs that do not take advantage of emerging technologies will eventually be unable to meet the needs or expectations of students. Therefore, counseling faculty need to take the initiative to develop technology that adds to the counseling relationship rather than detracts from it. Counseling faculty should neither resist nor blindly accept technology use plans imposed on them. The Academic Senate for California Community Colleges (1997) recommends that technology use practices should incorporate the following principles:

1. Counseling programs should select only those technologies which enhance the delivery of services to students. Electronic access to student educational plans, articulation information, transcripts, petitions, and the like should be encouraged.
2. Counseling programs should use technologies to enhance communications within the counseling department, as well as to the college and to the community.
3. Counseling programs should use technologies to document accurately and efficiently the student use of services.
4. Counseling technology plans should be developed with significant input from users of the plans—counseling faculty and personnel, counseling administrators, and students—in addition to technology experts.
5. Counseling technology plans should be closely integrated with college and district technology plans.
6. There should be adequate technical support services for maintenance of current technologies and installation of new technologies.
7. Policies and procedures to maximize technology use and access, while ensuring safety of records and appropriate confidentiality, should be developed and implemented.
8. As programs begin to include greater use of technologies, adequate time and training for personnel to learn and maintain skills in using these technologies should be provided.
9. Many of the new technologies give college information directly to students (e.g., web home pages, kiosks). To prevent confusion and misinformation, counseling faculty should be involved in ensuring that the information provided is accurate and up-to-date.
10. All students should have access to counseling faculty when they need counseling, rather than mere information. Access to technology should not replace access to counseling.
11. Students enrolled through distance learning should be afforded the same level of counseling and support services made available to other students. The services made available should adhere to all the standards contained in this document. (pp. 15–16)

## Guidelines for On-Line Instruction in Counselor Education

Counselor educators have a responsibility to present on-line courses in an ethical and legal manner, but guidelines for doing so have not been adopted. However, the ACES Technology Interest Network, under the leadership of Scott Christie (Oregon State University), Michael Tyler (Florida Gulf Coast University), Harry Daniels (University of Florida), and Network Chair Thomas Hohenshil (Virginia Tech), has developed the Proposed ACES Guidelines for Online Instruction in Counselor Education (Morrisey, 1998) (www.chre.vt.edu/thohen/ACESWEB.htm). At the time of this book's publication, the guidelines have been reviewed by counselor education groups, revised as appropriate, and submitted for formal adoption by the ACES Executive Committee.

## Technical Competencies for Counselor Education Students

The Association for Counselor Education and Supervision (Morrisey, 1998, thohen @vt.edu) has drafted Technical Competencies for Counselor Education Students to propel graduate students into the new millennium.

### *Program Accreditation Standards*

Program accreditation standards heavily influence, if not dictate, professional practice in counselor education. In the counseling profession, those standards are the standards of the Council for Accreditation of Counseling and Related Educational Programs (CACREP, 1998). Standards developed in 1994 must be revised for the year 2001, with technological advancements clearly in focus. Carol L. Bobby, Executive Director, CACREP (Memorandum, December 3, 1998) states:

> [CACREP] must ensure through a systematic standards revision schedule that our accreditation criteria remain relevant and useful. Because technology has enhanced the ability of programs to deliver education from a distance, it is very important to revise our standards in a manner that allows for new technological advances in training while not compromising quality in counselor preparation. In addition, the increased use of technology for delivering education may affect how we define a program, what we mean by a site visit, and how self-studies can be constructed and submitted.

### *American Psychological Association*

The American Psychological Association cautions psychologists about providing on-line "therapy" services (APA, 1995) saying many of the enforceable ethical standards are, in fact, relevant to such services (Internet services), and based on these standards it could be difficult for a psychologist to demonstrate that it is ethical to conduct therapy solely by telephone, teleconferencing, Internet, or similar methods.

## *Core Standards*

On January 9, 1998, a Bilateral Forum on Internet Mental Health Practice was convened in Bethesda, MD at the invitation of the National Board for Certified Counselors and the Center for Credentialing and Education (CCE) (Bloom & Sampson, 1998b). Twenty-one representatives of mental health professional membership associations as well as individuals from key federal agencies attended. Participants shared information on current developments in Internet practice and began to clarify opportunities for future consideration. Two areas designated for such collaboration were the development and dissemination of interim "core standards" and the gathering of information related to organizational certificant/ member experiences with what was termed *Internet mental health services.*

Existing codes of ethics and standards of practice have been developed as a result of experiences with face-to-face interactions between client and therapist; few such codes exist for remote interactions. In recognition that Internet mental health services are occurring and that this practice may be growing across professions, Bilateral Forum representatives agreed that there exists a need for broader standards.

Efforts to date to provide standards of practice for Internet mental health services include the WebCounseling Standards developed by the National Board for Certified Counselors and adopted by the NBCC Board of Directors (www.nbcc.org) and the Core Principles resulting from the May 1997 Inter-Professional Meeting on Standards of Practice in Telehealth, hosted by the American Nursing Association (ANA). These core principles were developed by a workgroup of an interprofessional meeting cochaired by the ANA and the American Psychological Association.

The Bilateral Forum Core Standards presented here are adaptations of the deliberations of that workgroup. Its work, the work of NBCC, and the work of the larger Inter-Professional Telehealth Meeting is graciously acknowledged. Efforts to have all professions involved in the practice of Internet mental health services approve the following standards continues. The Bilateral Internet Mental Health Care Practice Forum's Core Standards are intended to

- Protect clients receiving mental health services on the Internet
- Give mental health care professions a common ground
- Provide a basis for review of professional standards, clinical standards, and the need for Internet mental health practice guidelines by professions and government agencies

The basic standards of professional conduct governing each mental health care profession are not altered by the use of Internet technologies to deliver mental health care, conduct research, or provide education. Developed by each profession, these standards focus in part on the practitioner's responsibility to provide ethical and high-quality care on the Internet. A mental health care system or mental health care practitioner cannot use the Internet as a vehicle for providing services that are not otherwise legally or professionally authorized. For example, the practitioner should be credentialed (licensed, certified, or registered) by an appropriate entity or organization prior to offering Internet-based services. The use of Internet technologies does not require additional licensure; however, special care should be taken to avoid licensing issues regarding jurisdiction, both national and global.

Services provided via the Internet must adhere to basic assurance of quality and professional health care in accordance with each mental health care discipline's clinical standards. Each mental health care discipline must examine how Internet mental health practice affects and/or changes its patterns of care delivery and how this may require modifications of existing clinical standards.

Each mental health care profession is responsible for developing its own processes for assuring competencies in the delivery of health care through the use of Internet mental health practice. The National Board for Certified Counselors has taken the following position on such practice:

I. Internet mental health practice guidelines should be based upon consensus among the mental health care professions, empirical evidence when available, and collaboration with government agencies.
II. The integrity and therapeutic value of the client-mental health care professional relationship should be maintained, not diminished by the use of Internet mental health technology.
III. Confidentiality of client diagnosis, treatment, and consultation records, Internet mental health contacts, and mental health care information systems is essential.
IV. Informed consent documents need to incorporate concerns unique to Internet mental health practice.

    **V.** The safety of clients and practitioners involved in Internet mental health practice must be ensured. Appropriate hardware and valid software, combined with demonstrated user competency and readiness, are essential components.

   **VI.** A systematic and comprehensive research agenda must be developed and supported by government agencies and the mental health care professions for the ongoing assessment of Internet mental health practices.

 **VII.** Geographically remote mental health care professionals must be aware of location-specific conditions, events, and cultural issues that may limit credibility or lead to inappropriate interventions.

**VIII.** The mental health professional has an obligation to be aware of free public access points to the Internet within the client's community, such as public libraries, so that a lack of financial resources does not create a significant barrier to clients accessing resources and services.

  **IX.** Geographically remote mental health care professionals shall provide potential clients with appropriate backup measures such as the name and phone number of a local on-call professional, a local crisis intervention number, or a reminder about calling 911 in emergency situations. (Approved by the NBCC Board of Directors, March 1998)

## The Web Counseling Process

Sommers (1998) offers four main mental/behavioral health resources at his Mental Health Cyber-Clinic site (www.nicom.com/~davids/pageone.htm#tableofcontents). These are opportunities for ongoing helping dialog (also called *interactive therapeutic consultation* here) using e-mail; information and links to other mental/behavioral health and Internet-based communication resources; some attempts to provide a little humor and fun based on the idea that laughter helps, heals, and promotes wellness; and exercises and simple tasks intended to promote balance and well-being. Sommers suggests:

> As far as getting direct interactive help goes, (my) site may appeal if the potential client has economic barriers to traditional psychotherapy, wants a little distance in any sort of therapeutic relationship, lives in a remote area where therapists are not readily accessible, has a physical disability which makes getting to traditional therapy too difficult, is thinking about entering traditional therapy but first wants to get a sense of what therapy might be like. (www.nicom.com/~davids/pageone.htm)

## Web Counseling Skills

It is quite reasonable to expect that new skills ought to follow new technology. Murphy and Mitchell (1998) discuss two skills they have developed to help overcome possible negative factors involved in text-only (e-mail) on-line therapy.

    The first of these is *emotional bracketing,* which involves the inclusion of relevant emotional material in brackets in their e-mail exchanges. For example, they might write, "It has been several weeks since I have heard from you, John [concern, worry] and I would very much appreciate it if you could at least acknowledge this e-mail [feeling pushy, demanding]." Emotional bracketing would also be beneficial to the on-line therapist as a mechanism for keeping in touch with one's own emotions, much as is done in counselor education programs when students reviewing audio- or videotapes of their work are asked to identify how they were feeling when they made certain interventions.

The second skill is called *textual visualization* or *descriptive immediacy*. This involves putting into e-mail text what the counselor believes the eyes of the on-line client would be seeing if he or she were actually participating in a face-to-face counseling session. Consider the following example:

> If you were standing beside me as I write this, Tanya, you would notice me stopping often, falling back against the back of my chair saying, "That's incredible!" to myself. Your recent successes against guilt are so wonderful that even now I find myself (right now!) stopping in the middle of my sentence, my hands toward the computer screen, my mouth wide open as if to say, "This is amazing. How did she defeat guilt?" (Murphy & Mitchell, 1998, p. 24)

## *Web Counseling Research*

John J. Schmidt, professor and chair of the Counselor and Adult Education Department at East Carolina University in Greenville, interviewed Garry R. Walz, director of the Educational Resources Information Center/Counseling and Student Services Clearinghouse at the University of North Carolina at Greensboro, to gain counseling research insights—past, present, and future—from this highly regarded researcher and former president of the American Counseling Association (Schmidt, 1998). A portion of that interview, which addresses technology issues, is included here as a prelude to an exploration of what research is already telling us about our rapidly changing profession.

> **JS (John Schmidt):** Given these issues for counseling research, are there new areas that you feel ERIC/CASS should prioritize in the future?
>
> **GW (Garry Walz):** The Internet has revolutionized how we share information and communicate over the network with one another. More people can be reached, faster, over great distances, and at less cost than ever before. It is only logical that we would take the next step—counseling over the Internet or "cyber-counseling" as it is called by some. It offers intriguing possibilities but also some predictable problems. In consort with other groups, such as NBCC [National Board for Certified Counselors], we want to explore the legal and professional ramifications of these innovations and offer helpful resources as they expand (as they surely will!).

## *Summary*

Worldwide, the use of computer technology exploded during the last half of the twentieth century—so much so that the United States Postal Service has issued a 32-cent commemorative stamp in recognition of the completion of the world's first true computer, the ENIAC, in 1946 (USPS, 1966). Only 50 or so years later, professional counselors are taking a leadership role in finding new ways to utilize technology for the betterment of the profession and the enhancement of the counseling relationship.

The future of technology and counseling is bright, exciting, and limitless. We are on the brink of affordable technology to make visual communication possible on our office computers and home television sets. We will be reading about technological advancements in electronic journals in cyberspace, not hard-copy texts and journals. We will find new and exciting ways to simulate counseling relationships and counseling situations for students in counselor education programs. To the twenty-first century: Here comes the counseling profession!

## *Issues to Consider and Discuss*

When the day arrives that web counselors and clients have ready access to visual as well as auditory input, then counseling purists may begin to claim that although the face-to-face issue has been solved, there still remains an issue of touch; counselors need to be able to reach out and physically touch their clients. Exactly what are the necessary conditions for counseling to take place? Is it time to redefine *counseling?*

At what point should counselor educators begin to teach web counseling skills such as emotional bracketing and descriptive immediacy described by Murphy and Mitchell (1998)? And because it is more likely that web counselors having these skills are behavioral health practitioners than university professors, who will provide such instruction?

A world that always has had cops and robbers surely will always have both cyber cops and cyber robbers. Cyber robbers will always try to steal cyber information, alter cyber information, and use cyber information inappropriately. Professional associations are developing codes, but who are the cyber cops? Who is to do the enforcing of these standards?

State and professional licensing boards are, first and foremost, responsible for protecting the public. Denying the public access to counseling services on the Web—if those services are beneficial, affordable, convenient, and therapeutic—is not "protecting the public." Will credentialing bodies come together to address web counseling issues in the least restrictive manner? Will those same bodies realize that international trade agreements will eventually make arbitrary and capricious restrictions on professional practice across state and international boundaries a moot point?

Research such as that advocated by Walz (Schmidt, 1998) is being conducted as I write, but until the results of such research are published on-line, practical applications of research findings will always lag behind our knowledge base. Will the profession move swiftly to report research results in an expedient, cyber manner?

# Appendix A

# American Counseling Association Code of Ethics and Standards of Practice

## As Approved by Governing Council April 1997 (Effective July 1, 1997)

## Preamble

The American Counseling Association is an educational, scientific and professional organization whose members are dedicated to the enhancement of human development throughout the life span. Association members recognize diversity in our society and embrace a cross-cultural approach in support of the worth, dignity, potential, and uniqueness of each individual.

The specification of a code of ethics enables the association to clarify to current and future members, and to those served by members, the nature of the ethical responsibilities held in common by its members. As the code of ethics of the association, this document establishes principles that define the ethical behavior of association members. All members of the American Counseling Association are required to adhere to the Code of Ethics and the Standards of Practice. The Code of Ethics will serve as the basis for processing ethical complaints initiated against members of the association.

## Section A: The Counseling Relationship

### A.1. Client Welfare

#### a. Primary Responsibility.
The primary responsibility of counselors is to respect the dignity and to promote the welfare of clients.

#### b. Positive Growth and Development.
Counselors encourage client growth and development in ways that foster the clients' interest and welfare; counselors avoid fostering dependent counseling relationships.

#### c. Counseling Plans.
Counselors and their clients work jointly in devising integrated, individual counseling plans that offer reasonable promise of success and are consistent with abilities and circumstances of clients. Counselors and clients regularly review counseling plans to ensure their continued viability and effectiveness respecting clients' freedom of choice. (See A.3.b.)

### d. Family Involvement.

Counselors recognize that families are usually important in clients' lives and strive to enlist family understanding and involvement as a positive resource when appropriate.

### e. Career and Employment Needs.

Counselors work with their clients in considering employment in jobs and circumstances that are consistent with the clients' overall abilities, vocational limitations, physical restrictions, general temperament, interest and aptitude patterns, social skills, education, general qualifications, and other relevant characteristics and needs. Counselors neither place nor participate in placing clients in positions that will result in damaging the interest and the welfare of clients, employers, or the public.

## A.2. Respecting Diversity

### a. Nondiscrimination.

Counselors do not condone or engage in discrimination based on age, color, culture, disability, ethnic group, gender, race, religion, sexual orientation, marital status, or socioeconomic status. (See C.5.a., C.5.b., and D.1.i.)

### b. Respecting Differences

Counselors will actively attempt to understand the diverse cultural backgrounds of the clients with whom they work. This includes, but is not limited to, learning how the counselor's own cultural/ethnic/racial identity impacts her/his values and beliefs about the counseling process. (See E.8. and F.2.i.)

## A.3. Client Rights

### a. Disclosure to Clients.

When counseling is initiated, and throughout the counseling process as necessary, counselors inform clients of the purposes, goals, techniques, procedures, limitations, potential risks, and benefits of services to be performed, and other pertinent information. Counselors take steps to ensure that clients understand the implications of diagnosis, the intended use of tests and reports, fees, and billing arrangements. Clients have the right to expect confidentiality and to be provided with an explanation of its limitations, including supervision and/or treatment team professionals; to obtain clear information about their case records; to participate in the ongoing counseling plans; and to refuse any recommended services and be advised of the consequences of such refusal. (See E.5.a. and G.2.)

### b. Freedom of Choice.

Counselors offer clients the freedom to choose whether to enter into a counseling relationship and to determine which professional(s) will provide counseling. Restrictions that limit choices of clients are fully explained. (See A.1.c.)

### c. Inability to Give Consent.

When counseling minors or persons unable to give voluntary informed consent, counselors act in these clients' best interests. (See B.3.)

## A.4. Clients Served by Others

If a client is receiving services from another mental health professional, counselors, with client consent, inform the professional persons already involved and develop clear agreements to avoid confusion and conflict for the client. (See C.6.c.)

## A.5. Personal Needs and Values

### a. Personal Needs.

In the counseling relationship, counselors are aware of the intimacy and responsibilities inherent in the counseling relationship, maintain respect for clients, and avoid actions that seek to meet their personal needs at the expense of clients.

### b. Personal Values.

Counselors are aware of their own values, attitudes, beliefs, and behaviors and how these apply in a diverse society and avoid imposing their values on clients. (See C.5.a.)

## A.6. Dual Relationships

### a. Avoid When Possible.

Counselors are aware of their influential positions with respect to clients, and they avoid exploiting the trust and dependency of clients. Counselors make every effort to avoid dual relationships with clients that could impair professional judgment or increase the risk of harm to clients. (Examples of such relationships include, but are not limited to, familial, social, financial, business, or close personal relationships with clients.) When a dual relationship cannot be avoided, counselors take appropriate professional precautions, such as informed consent, consultation, supervision, and documentation to ensure that judgment is not impaired and no exploitation occurs. (See F.1.b.)

### b. Superior/Subordinate Relationships.

Counselors do not accept as clients superiors or subordinates with whom they have administrative, supervisory, or evaluative relationships.

## A.7. Sexual Intimacies with Clients

### a. Current Clients.

Counselors do not have any type of sexual intimacies with clients and do not counsel persons with whom they have had a sexual relationship.

### b. Former Clients.

Counselors do not engage in sexual intimacies with former clients within a minimum of two years after terminating the counseling relationship. Counselors who engage in such relationship after two years following termination have the responsibility to thoroughly examine and document that such relations did not have an exploitative nature, based on factors, such as duration of counseling, amount of time since counseling, termination circumstances, client's personal history and mental status, adverse impact on the client, and actions by the counselor suggesting a plan to initiate a sexual relationship with the client after termination.

## A.8. Multiple Clients

When counselors agree to provide counseling services to two or more persons who have a relationship (such as husband and wife, or parents and children), counselors clarify at the outset which person or persons are clients and the nature of the relationships they will have with each involved person. If it becomes apparent that counselors may be called upon to perform potentially conflicting roles, they clarify, adjust, or withdraw from roles appropriately. (See B.2. and B.4.d.)

## A.9. Group Work

### a. Screening.

Counselors screen prospective group counseling/therapy participants. To the extent possible, counselors select members whose needs and goals are compatible with goals of the group, who will not impede the group process, and whose well-being will not be jeopardized by the group experience.

### b. Protecting Clients.

In a group setting, counselors take reasonable precautions to protect clients from physical or psychological trauma.

## A.10. Fees and Bartering
## (See D.3.a. and D.3.b.)

### a. Advance Understanding.

Counselors clearly explain to clients, prior to entering the counseling relationship, all financial arrangements related to professional services including the use of collection agencies or legal measures for nonpayment. (A.11.c.)

### b. Establishing Fees.

In establishing fees for professional counseling services, counselors consider the financial status of clients and locality. In the event that the established fee structure is inappropriate for a client, assistance is provided in attempting to find comparable services of acceptable cost. (See A.10.d., D.3.a., and D.3.b.)

### c. Bartering Discouraged.

Counselors ordinarily refrain from accepting goods or services from clients in return for counseling services because such arrangements create inherent potential for conflicts, exploitation, and distortion of the professional relationship. Counselors may participate in bartering only if the relationship is not exploitive, if the client requests it, if a clear written contract is established, and if such arrangements are an accepted practice among professionals in the community. (See A.6.a.)

### d. Pro Bono Service.

Counselors contribute to society by devoting a portion of their professional activity to services for which there is little or no financial return (pro bono).

## A.11.  Termination and Referral

### a.  Abandonment Prohibited.
Counselors do not abandon or neglect clients in counseling. Counselors assist in making appropriate arrangements for the continuation of treatment, when necessary, during interruptions, such as vacations, and following termination.

### b.  Inability to Assist Clients.
If counselors determine an inability to be of professional assistance to clients, they avoid entering or immediately terminate a counseling relationship. Counselors are knowledgeable about referral resources and suggest appropriate alternatives. If clients decline the suggested referral, counselors should discontinue the relationship.

### c.  Appropriate Termination.
Counselors terminate a counseling relationship, securing client agreement when possible, when it is reasonably clear that the client is no longer benefiting, when services are no longer required, when counseling no longer serves the client's needs or interests, when clients do not pay fees charged, or when agency or institution limits do not allow provision of further counseling services. (See A.10.b. and C.2.g.)

## A.12.  Computer Technology

### a.  Use of Computers.
When computer applications are used in counseling services, counselors ensure that (1) the client is intellectually, emotionally, and physically capable of using the computer application; (2) the computer application is appropriate for the needs of the client; (3) the client understands the purpose and operation of the computer applications; and (4) a follow-up of client use of a computer application is provided to correct possible misconceptions, discover inappropriate use, and assess subsequent needs.

### b.  Explanation of Limitations.
Counselors ensure that clients are provided information as a part of the counseling relationship that adequately explains the limitations of computer technology.

### c.  Access to Computer Applications.
Counselors provide for equal access to computer applications in counseling services. (See A.2.a.)

## Section B: Confidentiality

## B.1.  Right to Privacy

### a.  Respect for Privacy.
Counselors respect their clients' right to privacy and avoid illegal and unwarranted disclosures of confidential information. (See A.3.a. and B.6.a.)

### b.  Client Waiver.
The right to privacy may be waived by the client or their legally recognized representative.

### c.  Exceptions.
The general requirement that counselors keep information confidential does not apply when disclosure is required to prevent clear and imminent danger to the client or others or when legal requirements demand that confidential information be revealed. Counselors consult with other professionals when in doubt as to the validity of an exception.

### d.  Contagious, Fatal Diseases.
A counselor who receives information confirming that a client has a disease commonly known to be both communicable and fatal is justified in disclosing information to an identifiable third party, who by his or her relationship with the client is at a high risk of contracting the disease. Prior to making a disclosure the counselor should ascertain that the client has not already informed the third party about his or her disease and that the client is not intending to inform the third party in the immediate future. (See B.1.c and B.1.f.)

### e.  Court Ordered Disclosure.
When court ordered to release confidential information without a client's permission, counselors request to the court that the disclosure not be required due to potential harm to the client or counseling relationship. (See B.1.c.)

### f.  Minimal Disclosure.
When circumstances require the disclosure of confidential information, only essential information is revealed. To the extent possible, clients are informed before confidential information is disclosed.

### g.  Explanation of Limitations.
When counseling is initiated and throughout the counseling process as necessary, counselors inform clients

of the limitations of confidentiality and identify fore-seeable situations in which confidentiality must be breached. (See G.2.a.)

### h. Subordinates.
Counselors make every effort to ensure that privacy and confidentiality of clients are maintained by subordinates including employees, supervisees, clerical assistants, and volunteers. (See B.1.a.)

### i. Treatment Teams.
If client treatment will involve a continued review by a treatment team, the client will be informed of the team's existence and composition.

## B.2. Groups and Families

### a. Group Work.
In group work, counselors clearly define confidentiality and the parameters for the specific group being entered, explain its importance, and discuss the difficulties related to confidentiality involved in group work. The fact that confidentiality cannot be guaranteed is clearly communicated to group members.

### b. Family Counseling.
In family counseling, information about one family member cannot be disclosed to another member without permission. Counselors protect the privacy rights of each family member. (See A.8., B.3., and B.4.d.)

## B.3. Minor or Incompetent Clients

When counseling clients who are minors or individuals who are unable to give voluntary, informed consent, parents or guardians may be included in the counseling process as appropriate. Counselors act in the best interests of clients and take measures to safeguard confidentiality. (See A.3.c.)

## B.4. Records

### a. Requirement of Records.
Counselors maintain records necessary for rendering professional services to their clients and as required by laws, regulations, or agency or institution procedures.

### b. Confidentiality of Records.
Counselors are responsible for securing the safety and confidentiality of any counseling records they create,

maintain, transfer, or destroy whether the records are written, taped, computerized, or stored in any other medium. (See B.1.a.)

### c. Permission to Record or Observe.
Counselors obtain permission from clients prior to electronically recording or observing sessions. (See A.3.a.)

### d. Client Access.
Counselors recognize that counseling records are kept for the benefit of clients and, therefore, provide access to records and copies of records when requested by competent clients unless the records contain information that may be misleading and detrimental to the client. In situations involving multiple clients, access to records is limited to those parts of records that do not include confidential information related to another client. (See A.8., B.1.a., and B.2.b.)

### e. Disclosure or Transfer.
Counselors obtain written permission from clients to disclose or transfer records to legitimate third parties unless exceptions to confidentiality exist as listed in Section B.1. Steps are taken to ensure that receivers of counseling records are sensitive to their confidential nature.

## B.5. Research and Training

### a. Data Disguise Required.
Use of data derived from counseling relationships for purposes of training, research, or publication is confined to content that is disguised to ensure the anonymity of the individuals involved. (See B.1.g. and G.3.d.)

### b. Agreement for Identification.
Identification of a client in a presentation or publication is permissible only when the client has reviewed the material and has agreed to its presentation or publication. (See G.3.d.)

## B.6. Consultation

### a. Respect for Privacy.
Information obtained in a consulting relationship is discussed for professional purposes only with persons clearly concerned with the case. Written and oral reports present data germane to the purposes of the con-

sultation, and every effort is made to protect client identity and avoid undue invasion of privacy.

### b. Cooperating Agencies.

Before sharing information, counselors make efforts to ensure that there are defined policies in other agencies serving the counselor's clients that effectively protect the confidentiality of information.

## Section C: Professional Responsibility

### C.1. Standards Knowledge

Counselors have a responsibility to read, understand, and follow the Code of Ethics and the Standards of Practice.

### C.2. Professional Competence

#### a. Boundaries of Competence.

Counselors practice only within the boundaries of their competence, based on their education, training, supervised experience, state and national professional credentials, and appropriate professional experience. Counselors will demonstrate a commitment to gain knowledge, personal awareness, sensitivity, and skills pertinent to working with a diverse client population.

#### b. New Specialty Areas of Practice.

Counselors practice in specialty areas new to them only after appropriate education, training, and supervised experience. While developing skills in new specialty areas, counselors take steps to ensure the competence of their work and to protect others from possible harm.

#### c. Qualified for Employment.

Counselors accept employment only for positions for which they are qualified by education, training, supervised experience, state and national professional credentials, and appropriate professional experience. Counselors hire for professional counseling positions only individuals who are qualified and competent.

#### d. Monitor Effectiveness.

Counselors continually monitor their effectiveness as professionals and take steps to improve when necessary. Counselors in private practice take reasonable steps to seek out peer supervision to evaluate their efficacy as counselors.

#### e. Ethical Issues Consultation.

Counselors take reasonable steps to consult with other counselors or related professionals when they have questions regarding their ethical obligations or professional practice. (See H.1.)

#### f. Continuing Education.

Counselors recognize the need for continuing education to maintain a reasonable level of awareness of current scientific and professional information in their fields of activity. They take steps to maintain competence in the skills they use, are open to new procedures, and keep current with the diverse and/or special populations with whom they work.

#### g. Impairment.

Counselors refrain from offering or accepting professional services when their physical, mental or emotional problems are likely to harm a client or others. They are alert to the signs of impairment, seek assistance for problems, and, if necessary, limit, suspend, or terminate their professional responsibilities. (See A.11.c.)

### C.3. Advertising and Soliciting Clients

#### a. Accurate Advertising.

There are no restrictions on advertising by counselors except those that can be specifically justified to protect the public from deceptive practices. Counselors advertise or represent their services to the public by identifying their credentials in an accurate manner that is not false, misleading, deceptive, or fraudulent. Counselors may only advertise the highest degree earned which is in counseling or a closely related field from a college or university that was accredited when the degree was awarded by one of the regional accrediting bodies recognized by the Council on Postsecondary Accreditation.

#### b. Testimonials.

Counselors who use testimonials do not solicit them from clients or other persons who, because of their particular circumstances, may be vulnerable to undue influence.

#### c. Statements by Others.

Counselors make reasonable efforts to ensure that statements made by others about them or the profession of counseling are accurate.

### d. Recruiting through Employment.

Counselors do not use their places of employment or institutional affiliation to recruit or gain clients, supervisees, or consultees for their private practices. (See C.5.e.)

### e. Products and Training Advertisements.

Counselors who develop products related to their profession or conduct workshops or training events ensure that the advertisements concerning these products or events are accurate and disclose adequate information for consumers to make informed choices.

### f. Promoting to Those Served.

Counselors do not use counseling, teaching, training, or supervisory relationships to promote their products or training events in a manner that is deceptive or would exert undue influence on individuals who may be vulnerable. Counselors may adopt textbooks they have authored for instruction purposes.

### g. Professional Association Involvement.

Counselors actively participate in local, state, and national associations that foster the development and improvement of counseling.

## C.4. Credentials

### a. Credentials Claimed.

Counselors claim or imply only professional credentials possessed and are responsible for correcting any known misrepresentations of their credentials by others. Professional credentials include graduate degrees in counseling or closely related mental health fields, accreditation of graduate programs, national voluntary certifications, government-issued certifications or licenses, ACA professional membership, or any other credential that might indicate to the public specialized knowledge or expertise in counseling.

### b. ACA Professional Membership.

ACA professional members may announce to the public their membership status. Regular members may not announce their ACA membership in a manner that might imply they are credentialed counselors.

### c. Credential Guidelines.

Counselors follow the guidelines for use of credentials that have been established by the entities that issue the credentials.

### d. Misrepresentation of Credentials.

Counselors do not attribute more to their credentials than the credentials represent and do not imply that other counselors are not qualified because they do not possess certain credentials.

### e. Doctoral Degrees from Other Fields.

Counselors who hold a master's degree in counseling or a closely related mental health field but hold a doctoral degree from other than counseling or a closely related field do not use the title "Dr.," in their practices and do not announce to the public in relation to their practice or status as a counselor that they hold a doctorate.

## C.5. Public Responsibility

### a. Nondiscrimination.

Counselors do not discriminate against clients, students, or supervisees in a manner that has a negative impact based on their age, color, culture, disability, ethnic group, gender, race, religion, sexual orientation, or socioeconomic status, or for any other reason. (See A.2.a.)

### b. Sexual Harassment.

Counselors do not engage in sexual harassment. Sexual harassment is defined as sexual solicitation, physical advances, or verbal or nonverbal conduct that is sexual in nature, that occurs in connection with professional activities or roles, and that either (1) is unwelcome, is offensive, or creates a hostile workplace environment, and counselors know or are told this; or (2) is sufficiently severe or intense to be perceived as harassment to a reasonable person in the context. Sexual harassment can consist of a single intense or severe act or multiple persistent or pervasive acts.

### c. Reports to Third Parties.

Counselors are accurate, honest, and unbiased in reporting their professional activities and judgments to appropriate third parties including courts, health insurance companies, those who are the recipients of evaluation reports, and others. (See B.1.g.)

### d. Media Presentations.

When counselors provide advice or comment by means of public lectures, demonstrations, radio or television programs, prerecorded tapes, printed articles, mailed material, or other media, they take reasonable precautions to ensure that (1) the statements are based on appropriate professional counseling literature and practice; (2) the statements are otherwise consistent with the Code of Ethics and the Standards of Practice; and (3) the recipients of the information are not encouraged to infer that a professional counseling relationship has been established. (See C.6.b.)

### e. Unjustified Gains.

Counselors do not use their professional positions to seek or receive unjustified personal gains, sexual favors, unfair advantage, or unearned goods or services. (See C.3.d.)

## C.6. Responsibility to Other Professionals

### a. Different Approaches.

Counselors are respectful of approaches to professional counseling that differ from their own. Counselors know and take into account the traditions and practices of other professional groups with which they work.

### b. Personal Public Statements.

When making personal statements in a public context, counselors clarify that they are speaking from their personal perspectives and that they are not speaking on behalf of all counselors or the profession. (See C.5.d.)

### c. Clients Served by Others.

When counselors learn that their clients are in a professional relationship with another mental health professional, they request release from clients to inform the other professionals and strive to establish positive and collaborative professional relationships. (See A.4.)

## Section D: Relationships with Other Professionals

### D.1. Relationships with Employers and Employees

### a. Role Definition.

Counselors define and describe for their employers and employees the parameters and levels of their professional roles.

### b. Agreements.

Counselors establish working agreements with supervisors, colleagues, and subordinates regarding counsel-

ing or clinical relationships, confidentiality, adherence to professional standards, distinction between public and private material, maintenance and dissemination of recorded information, workload, and accountability. Working agreements in each instance are specified and made known to those concerned.

### c. Negative Conditions.

Counselors alert their employers to conditions that may be potentially disruptive or damaging to the counselor's professional responsibilities or that may limit their effectiveness.

### d. Evaluation.

Counselors submit regularly to professional review and evaluation by their supervisor or the appropriate representative of the employer.

### e. In-Service.

Counselors are responsible for in-service development of self and staff.

### f. Goals.

Counselors inform their staff of goals and programs.

### g. Practices.

Counselors provide personnel and agency practices that respect and enhance the rights and welfare of each employee and recipient of agency services. Counselors strive to maintain the highest levels of professional services.

### h. Personnel Selection and Assignment.

Counselors select competent staff and assign responsibilities compatible with their skills and experiences.

### i. Discrimination.

Counselors, as either employers or employees, do not engage in or condone practices that are inhumane, illegal, or unjustifiable (such as considerations based on age, color, culture, disability, ethnic group, gender, race, religion, sexual orientation, or socioeconomic status) in hiring, promotion, or training. (See A.2.a. and C.5.b.)

### j. Professional Conduct.

Counselors have a responsibility both to clients and to the agency or institution within which services are performed to maintain high standards of professional conduct.

### k. Exploitive Relationships.

Counselors do not engage in exploitive relationships with individuals over whom they have supervisory, evaluative, or instructional control or authority.

### l. Employer Policies.

The acceptance of employment in an agency or institution implies that counselors are in agreement with its general policies and principles. Counselors strive to reach agreement with employers as to acceptable standards of conduct that allow for changes in institutional policy conducive to the growth and development of clients.

## D.2. Consultation (See B.6.)

### a. Consultation as an Option.

Counselors may choose to consult with any other professionally competent persons about their clients. In choosing consultants, counselors avoid placing the consultant in a conflict of interest situation that would preclude the consultant being a proper party to the counselor's efforts to help the client. Should counselors be engaged in a work setting that compromises this consultation standard, they consult with other professionals whenever possible to consider justifiable alternatives.

### b. Consultant Competency.

Counselors are reasonably certain that they have or the organization represented has the necessary competencies and resources for giving the kind of consulting services needed and that appropriate referral resources are available.

### c. Understanding with Clients.

When providing consultation, counselors attempt to develop with their clients a clear understanding of problem definition, goals for change, and predicted consequences of interventions selected.

### d. Consultant Goals.

The consulting relationship is one in which client adaptability and growth toward self-direction are consistently encouraged and cultivated. (See A.1.b.)

## D.3. Fees for Referral

### a. Accepting Fees from Agency Clients.

Counselors refuse a private fee or other remuneration for rendering services to persons who are entitled to such services through the counselor's employing agency or institution. The policies of a particular agency may make explicit provisions for agency clients to receive counseling services from members of its staff in private practice. In such instances, the clients must be informed of other options open to them should they seek private counseling services. (See A.10.a., A.11.b., and C.3.d.)

### b. Referral Fees.

Counselors do not accept a referral fee from other professionals.

## D.4. Subcontractor Arrangements

When counselors work as subcontractors for counseling services for a third party, they have a duty to inform clients of the limitations of confidentiality that the organization may place on counselors in providing counseling services to clients. The limits of such confidentiality ordinarily are discussed as part of the intake session. (See B.1.e. and B.1.f.)

# Section E: Evaluation, Assessment, and Interpretation

## E.1. General

### a. Appraisal Techniques.

The primary purpose of educational and psychological assessment is to provide measures that are objective and interpretable in either comparative or absolute terms. Counselors recognize the need to interpret the statements in this section as applying to the whole range of appraisal techniques including test and nontest data.

### b. Client Welfare.

Counselors promote the welfare and best interests of the client in the development, publication, and utilization of educational and psychological assessment techniques. They do not misuse assessment results and interpretations and take reasonable steps to prevent others from misusing the information these techniques provide. They respect the client's right to know the results, the interpretations made, and the bases for their conclusions and recommendations.

## E.2. Competence to Use and Interpret Tests

### a. Limits of Competence.

Counselors recognize the limits of their competence and perform only those testing and assessment services for which they have been trained. They are familiar with reliability, validity, related standardization, error of measurement, and proper application of any technique utilized. Counselors using computer-based test interpretations are trained in the construct being measured and the specific instrument being used prior to using this type of computer application. Counselors take reasonable measures to ensure the proper use of psychological assessment techniques by persons under their supervision.

### b. Appropriate Use.

Counselors are responsible for the appropriate application, scoring, interpretation, and use of assessment instruments, whether they score and interpret such tests themselves or use computerized or other services.

### c. Decisions Based on Results.

Counselors responsible for decisions involving individuals or policies that are based on assessment results have a thorough understanding of educational and psychological measurement including validation criteria, test research, and guidelines for test development and use.

### d. Accurate Information.

Counselors provide accurate information and avoid false claims or misconceptions when making statements about assessment instruments or techniques. Special efforts are made to avoid unwarranted connotations of such terms as IQ and grade equivalent scores. (See C.5.c.)

## E.3. Informed Consent

### a. Explanation to Clients.

Prior to assessment, counselors explain the nature and purposes of assessment and the specific use of results in language the client (or other legally authorized person on behalf of the client) can understand unless an explicit exception to this right has been agreed upon in advance. Regardless of whether scoring and interpretation are completed by counselors, by assistants, or by computer or other outside services, counselors take rea-

sonable steps to ensure that appropriate explanations are given to the client.

### b. Recipients of Results.

The examinee's welfare, explicit understanding, and prior agreement determine the recipients of test results. Counselors include accurate and appropriate interpretations with any release of individual or group test results. (See B.1.a. and C.5.c.)

## E.4. Release of Information to Competent Professionals

### a. Misuse of Results.

Counselors do not misuse assessment results, including test results, and interpretations and take reasonable steps to prevent the misuse of such by others. (See C.5.c.)

### b. Release of Raw Data.

Counselors ordinarily release data (e.g., protocols, counseling or interview notes, or questionnaires) in which the client is identified only with the consent of the client or the client's legal representative. Such data are usually released only to persons recognized by counselors as competent to interpret the data. (See B.1.a.)

## E.5. Proper Diagnosis of Mental Disorders

### a. Proper Diagnosis.

Counselors take special care to provide proper diagnosis of mental disorders. Assessment techniques (including personal interview) used to determine client care (e.g., locus of treatment, type of treatment, or recommended follow-up) are carefully selected and appropriately used. (See A.3.a. and C.5.c.)

### b. Cultural Sensitivity.

Counselors recognize that culture affects the manner in which clients' problems are defined. Clients' socioeconomic and cultural experience is considered when diagnosing mental disorders.

## E.6. Test Selection

### a. Appropriateness of Instruments.

Counselors carefully consider the validity, reliability, psychometric limitations, and appropriateness of instruments when selecting tests for use in a given situation or with a particular client.

### b. Culturally Diverse Populations.
Counselors are cautious when selecting tests for culturally diverse populations to avoid inappropriateness of testing that may be outside of socialized behavioral or cognitive patterns.

## E.7. Conditions of Test Administration

### a. Administration Conditions.
Counselors administer tests under the same conditions that were established in their standardization. When tests are not administered under standard conditions or when unusual behavior or irregularities occur during the testing session, those conditions are noted in interpretation, and the results may be designated as invalid or of questionable validity.

### b. Computer Administration.
Counselors are responsible for ensuring that administration programs function properly to provide clients with accurate results when a computer or other electronic methods are used for test administration. (See A.12.b.)

### c. Unsupervised Test-Taking.
Counselors do not permit unsupervised or inadequately supervised use of tests or assessments unless the tests or assessments are designed, intended, and validated for self-administration and/or scoring.

### d. Disclosure of Favorable Conditions.
Prior to test administration, conditions that produce most favorable test results are made known to the examinee.

## E.8. Diversity in Testing

Counselors are cautious in using assessment techniques, making evaluations, and interpreting the performance of populations not represented in the norm group on which an instrument was standardized. They recognize the effects of age, color, culture, disability, ethnic group, gender, race, religion, sexual orientation, and socioeconomic status on test administration and interpretation and place test results in proper perspective with other relevant factors. (See A.2.a.)

## E.9. Test Scoring and Interpretation

### a. Reporting Reservations.
In reporting assessment results, counselors indicate any reservations that exist regarding validity or reliability because of the circumstances of the assessment or the inappropriateness of the norms for the person tested.

### b. Research Instruments.
Counselors exercise caution when interpreting the results of research instruments possessing insufficient technical data to support respondent results. The specific purposes for the use of such instruments are stated explicitly to the examinee.

### c. Testing Services.
Counselors who provide test scoring and test interpretation services to support the assessment process confirm the validity of such interpretations. They accurately describe the purpose, norms, validity, reliability, and applications of the procedures and any special qualifications applicable to their use. The public offering of an automated test interpretations service is considered a professional-to-professional consultation. The formal responsibility of the consultant is to the consultee, but the ultimate and overriding responsibility is to the client.

## E.10. Test Security

Counselors maintain the integrity and security of tests and other assessment techniques consistent with legal and contractual obligations. Counselors do not appropriate, reproduce, or modify published tests or parts thereof without acknowledgement and permission from the publisher.

## E.11. Obsolete Tests and Outdated Test Results

Counselors do not use data or test results that are obsolete or outdated for the current purpose. Counselors make every effort to prevent the misuse of obsolete measures and test data by others.

## E.12. Test Construction

Counselors use established scientific procedures, relevant standards, and current professional knowledge for test design in the development, publication, and utilization of educational and psychological assessment techniques.

# Section F: Teaching, Training, and Supervision

## F.1. Counselor Educators and Trainers

### a. Educators as Teachers and Practitioners.
Counselors who are responsible for developing, implementing, and supervising educational programs are skilled as teachers and practitioners. They are knowledgeable regarding the ethical, legal, and regulatory aspects of the profession, are skilled in applying that knowledge, and make students and supervisees aware of their responsibilities. Counselors conduct counselor education and training programs in an ethical manner and serve as role models for professional behavior. Counselor educators should make an effort to infuse material related to human diversity into all courses and/or workshops that are designed to promote the development of professional counselors.

### b. Relationship Boundaries with Students and Supervisees.
Counselors clearly define and maintain ethical, professional, and social relationship boundaries with their students and supervisees. They are aware of the differential in power that exists and the student's or supervisee's possible incomprehension of that power differential. Counselors explain to students and supervisees the potential for the relationship to become exploitive.

### c. Sexual Relationships.
Counselors do not engage in sexual relationships with students or supervisees and do not subject them to sexual harassment. (See A.6. and C.5.b)

### d. Contributions to Research.
Counselors give credit to students or supervisees for their contributions to research and scholarly projects. Credit is given through coauthorship, acknowledgment, footnote statement, or other appropriate means in accordance with such contributions. (See G.4.b. and G.4.c.)

### e. Close Relatives.
Counselors do not accept close relatives as students or supervisees.

### f. Supervision Preparation.
Counselors who offer clinical supervision services are adequately prepared in supervision methods and techniques. Counselors who are doctoral students serving as practicum or internship supervisors to master's level students are adequately prepared and supervised by the training program.

### g. Responsibility for Services to Clients.
Counselors who supervise the counseling services of others take reasonable measures to ensure that counseling services provided to clients are professional.

### h. Endorsement.
Counselors do not endorse students or supervisees for certification, licensure, employment, or completion of an academic or training program if they believe students or supervisees are not qualified for the endorsement. Counselors take reasonable steps to assist students or supervisees who are not qualified for endorsement to become qualified.

## F.2. Counselor Education and Training Programs

### a. Orientation.
Prior to admission, counselors orient prospective students to the counselor education or training program's expectations including but not limited to the following: (1) the type and level of skill acquisition required for successful completion of the training, (2) subject matter to be covered, (3) basis for evaluation, (4) training components that encourage self-growth or self-disclosure as part of the training process, (5) the type of supervision settings and requirements of the sites for required clinical field experiences, (6) student and supervisee evaluation and dismissal policies and procedures, and (7) up-to-date employment prospects for graduates.

### b. Integration of Study and Practice.
Counselors establish counselor education and training programs that integrate academic study and supervised practice.

### c. Evaluation.
Counselors clearly state to students and supervisees, in advance of training, the levels of competency expected, appraisal methods, and timing of evaluations for both didactic and experiential components. Counselors pro-

vide students and supervisees with periodic performance appraisal and evaluation feedback throughout the training program.

### d. Teaching Ethics.

Counselors make students and supervisees aware of the ethical responsibilities and standards of the profession and the students' and supervisees' ethical responsibilities to the profession. (See C.1. and F.3.e.)

### e. Peer Relationships.

When students or supervisees are assigned to lead counseling groups or provide clinical supervision for their peers, counselors take steps to ensure that students and supervisees placed in these roles do not have personal or adverse relationships with peers and that they understand they have the same ethical obligations as counselor educators, trainers, and supervisors. Counselors make every effort to ensure that the rights of peers are not compromised when students or supervisees are assigned to lead counseling groups or provide clinical supervision.

### f. Varied Theoretical Positions.

Counselors present varied theoretical positions so that students and supervisees may make comparisons and have opportunities to develop their own positions. Counselors provide information concerning the scientific bases of professional practice. (See C.6.a.)

### g. Field Placements.

Counselors develop clear policies within their training program regarding field placement and other clinical experiences. Counselors provide clearly stated roles and responsibilities for the student or supervisee, the site supervisor, and the program supervisor. They confirm that site supervisors are qualified to provide supervision and are informed of their professional and ethical responsibilities in this role.

### h. Dual Relationships as Supervisors.

Counselors avoid dual relationships, such as performing the role of site supervisor and training program supervisor in the student's or supervisee's training program. Counselors do not accept any form of professional services, fees, commissions, reimbursement, or remuneration from a site for student or supervisee placement.

### i. Diversity in Programs.

Counselors are responsive to their institution's and program's recruitment and retention needs for training program administrators, faculty, and students with diverse backgrounds and special needs. (See A.2.a.)

## F.3. Students and Supervisees

### a. Limitations.

Counselors, through ongoing evaluation and appraisal, are aware of the academic and personal limitations of students and supervisees that might impede performance. Counselors assist students and supervisees in securing remedial assistance when needed and dismiss from the training program supervisees who are unable to provide competent service due to academic or personal limitations. Counselors seek professional consultation and document their decision to dismiss or refer students or supervisees for assistance. Counselors assure that students and supervisees have recourse to address decisions made, to require them to seek assistance, or to dismiss them.

### b. Self-Growth Experiences.

Counselors use professional judgment when designing training experiences conducted by the counselors themselves that require student and supervisee self-growth or self-disclosure. Safeguards are provided so that students and supervisees are aware of the ramifications their self-disclosure may have on counselors whose primary role as teacher, trainer, or supervisor requires acting on ethical obligations to the profession. Evaluative components of experiential training experiences explicitly delineate predetermined academic standards that are separate and not dependent on the student's level of self-disclosure. (See A.6.)

### c. Counseling for Students and Supervisees.

If students or supervisees request counseling, supervisors or counselor educators provide them with acceptable referrals. Supervisors or counselor educators do not serve as counselor to students or supervisees over whom they hold administrative, teaching, or evaluative roles unless this is a brief role associated with a training experience. (See A.6.b.)

### d. Clients of Students and Supervisees.

Counselors make every effort to ensure that the clients at field placements are aware of the services rendered and the qualifications of the students and supervisees rendering those services. Clients receive professional disclosure information and are informed of the limits of confidentiality. Client permission is obtained in order for the students and supervisees to use any information concerning the counseling relationship in the training process. (See B.1.e.)

### e. Standards for Students and Supervisees.
Students and supervisees preparing to become counselors adhere to the Code of Ethics and the Standards of Practice. Students and supervisees have the same obligations to clients as those required of counselors. (See H.1.)

## Section G: Research and Publication

### G.1. Research Responsibilities

#### a. Use of Human Subjects.
Counselors plan, design, conduct, and report research in a manner consistent with pertinent ethical principles, federal and state laws, host institutional regulations, and scientific standards governing research with human subjects. Counselors design and conduct research that reflects cultural sensitivity appropriateness.

#### b. Deviation from Standard Practices.
Counselors seek consultation and observe stringent safeguards to protect the rights of research participants when a research problem suggests a deviation from standard acceptable practices. (See B.6.)

#### c. Precautions to Avoid Injury.
Counselors who conduct research with human subjects are responsible for the subjects' welfare throughout the experiment and take reasonable precautions to avoid causing injurious psychological, physical, or social effects to their subjects.

#### d. Principal Researcher Responsibility.
The ultimate responsibility for ethical research practice lies with the principal researcher. All others involved in the research activities share ethical obligations and full responsibility for their own actions.

#### e. Minimal Interference.
Counselors take reasonable precautions to avoid causing disruptions in subjects' lives due to participation in research.

#### f. Diversity.
Counselors are sensitive to diversity and research issues with special populations. They seek consultation when appropriate. (See A.2.a. and B.6.)

### G.2. Informed Consent

#### a. Topics Disclosed.
In obtaining informed consent for research, counselors use language that is understandable to research participants and that (1) accurately explains the purpose and procedures to be followed; (2) identifies any procedures that are experimental or relatively untried; (3) describes the attendant discomforts and risks; (4) describes the benefits or changes in individuals or organizations that might be reasonably expected; (5) discloses appropriate alternative procedures that would be advantageous for subjects; (6) offers to answer any inquiries concerning the procedures; (7) describes any limitations on confidentiality; and (8) instructs that subjects are free to withdraw their consent and to discontinue participation in the project at any time. (See B.1.f.)

#### b. Deception.
Counselors do not conduct research involving deception unless alternative procedures are not feasible and the prospective value of the research justifies the deception. When the methodological requirements of a study necessitate concealment or deception, the investigator is required to explain clearly the reasons for this action as soon as possible.

#### c. Voluntary Participation.
Participation in research is typically voluntary and without any penalty for refusal to participate. Involuntary participation is appropriate only when it can be demonstrated that participation will have no harmful effects on subjects and is essential to the investigation.

#### d. Confidentiality of Information.
Information obtained about research participants during the course of an investigation is confidential. When the possibility exists that others may obtain access to such information, ethical research practice requires that

the possibility, together with the plans for protecting confidentiality, be explained to participants as a part of the procedure for obtaining informed consent. (See B.1.e.)

### e. Persons Incapable of Giving Informed Consent.
When a person is incapable of giving informed consent, counselors provide an appropriate explanation, obtain agreement for participation and obtain appropriate consent from a legally authorized person.

### f. Commitments to Participants.
Counselors take reasonable measures to honor all commitments to research participants.

### g. Explanations After Data Collection.
After data are collected, counselors provide participants with full clarification of the nature of the study to remove any misconceptions. Where scientific or human values justify delaying or withholding information, counselors take reasonable measures to avoid causing harm.

### h. Agreements to Cooperate.
Counselors who agree to cooperate with another individual in research or publication incur an obligation to cooperate as promised in terms of punctuality of performance and with regard to the completeness and accuracy of the information required.

### i. Informed Consent for Sponsors.
In the pursuit of research, counselors give sponsors, institutions, and publication channels the same respect and opportunity for giving informed consent that they accord to individual research participants. Counselors are aware of their obligation to future research workers and ensure that host institutions are given feedback information and proper acknowledgment.

## G.3. Reporting Results

### a. Information Affecting Outcome.
When reporting research results, counselors explicitly mention all variables and conditions known to the investigator that may have affected the outcome of a study or the interpretation of data.

### b. Accurate Results.
Counselors plan, conduct, and report research accurately and in a manner that minimizes the possibility that results will be misleading. They provide thorough discussions of the limitations of their data and alternative hypotheses. Counselors do not engage in fraudulent research, distort data, misrepresent data, or deliberately bias their results.

### c. Obligation to Report Unfavorable Results.
Counselors communicate to other counselors the results of any research judged to be of professional value. Results that reflect unfavorably on institutions, programs, services, prevailing opinions, or vested interests are not withheld.

### d. Identity of Subjects.
Counselors who supply data, aid in the research of another person, report research results, or make original data available take due care to disguise the identity of respective subjects in the absence of specific authorization from the subjects to do otherwise. (See B.1.g. and B.5.a.)

### e. Replication Studies.
Counselors are obligated to make available sufficient original research data to qualified professionals who may wish to replicate the study.

## G.4. Publication

### a. Recognition of Others.
When conducting and reporting research, counselors are familiar with and give recognition to previous work on the topic, observe copyright laws, and give full credit to those to whom credit is due. (See F.1.d. and G.4.c.)

### b. Contributors.
Counselors give credit through joint authorship, acknowledgment, footnote statements, or other appropriate means to those who have contributed significantly to research or concept development in accordance with such contributions. The principal contributor is listed first and minor technical or professional contributions are acknowledged in notes or introductory statements.

### c. Student Research.

For an article that is substantially based on a student's dissertation or thesis, the student is listed as the principal author. (See F.1.d. and G.4.a.)

### d. Duplicate Submission.

Counselors submit manuscripts for consideration to only one journal at a time. Manuscripts that are published in whole or in substantial part in another journal or published work are not submitted for publication without acknowledgment and permission from the previous publication.

### e. Professional Review.

Counselors who review material submitted for publication, research, or other scholarly purposes respect the confidentiality and proprietary rights of those who submitted it.

## Section H: Resolving Ethical Issues

### H.1.  Knowledge of Standards

Counselors are familiar with the Code of Ethics and the Standards of Practice and other applicable ethics codes from other professional organizations of which they are member or from certification and licensure bodies. Lack of knowledge or misunderstanding of an ethical responsibility is not a defense against a charge of unethical conduct. (See F.3.e.)

### H.2.  Suspected Violations

#### a. Ethical Behavior Expected.

Counselors expect professional associates to adhere to Code of Ethics. When counselors possess reasonable cause that raises doubts as to whether a counselor is acting in an ethical manner, they take appropriate action. (See H.2.d. and H.2.e.)

#### b. Consultation.

When uncertain as to whether a particular situation or course of action may be in violation of Code of Ethics, counselors consult with other counselors who are knowledgeable about ethics, with colleagues, or with appropriate authorities.

### c. Organization Conflicts.

If the demands of an organization with which counselors are affiliated pose a conflict with Code of Ethics, counselors specify the nature of such conflicts and express to their supervisors or other responsible officials their commitment to Code of Ethics. When possible, counselors work toward change within the organization to allow full adherence to Code of Ethics.

### d. Informal Resolution.

When counselors have reasonable cause to believe that another counselor is violating an ethical standard, they attempt to first resolve the issue informally with the other counselor if feasible providing that such action does not violate confidentiality rights that may be involved.

### e. Reporting Suspected Violations.

When an informal resolution is not appropriate or feasible, counselors, upon reasonable cause, take action, such as reporting the suspected ethical violation to state or national ethics committees, unless this action conflicts with confidentiality rights that cannot be resolved.

### f. Unwarranted Complaints.

Counselors do not initiate, participate in, or encourage the filing of ethics complaints that are unwarranted or intend to harm a counselor rather than to protect clients or the public.

### H.3.  Cooperation with Ethics Committees

Counselors assist in the process of enforcing Code of Ethics. Counselors cooperate with investigations, proceedings, and requirements of the ACA Ethics Committee or ethics committees of other duly constituted associations or boards having jurisdiction over those charged with a violation. Counselors are familiar with the ACA Policies and Procedures and use it as a reference in assisting the enforcement of the Code of Ethics.

## Standards of Practice

All members of the American Counseling Association (ACA) are required to adhere to the Standards of Practice and the Code of Ethics. The Standards of Practice represent minimal behavioral statements of the Code of

Ethics. Members should refer to the applicable section of the Code of Ethics for further interpretation and amplification of the applicable Standard of Practice.

## Section A: The Counseling Relationship

### Standard of Practice One (SP-1) Nondiscrimination

Counselors respect diversity and must not discriminate against clients because of age, color, culture, disability, ethnic group, gender, race, religion, sexual orientation, marital status, or socioeconomic status. (See A.2.a.)

### Standard of Practice Two (SP-2) Disclosure to Clients

Counselors must adequately inform clients, preferably in writing, regarding the counseling process and counseling relationship at or before the time it begins and throughout the relationship. (See A.3.a.)

### Standard of Practice Three (SP-3) Dual Relationships

Counselors must make every effort to avoid dual relationships with clients that could impair their professional judgment or increase the risk of harm to clients. When a dual relationship cannot be avoided, counselors must take appropriate steps to ensure that judgment is not impaired and that no exploitation occurs. (See A.6.a. and A.6.b.)

### Standard of Practice Four (SP-4) Sexual Intimacies with Clients

Counselors must not engage in any type of sexual intimacies with current clients and must not engage in sexual intimacies with former clients within a minimum of two years after terminating the counseling relationship. Counselors who engage in such relationship after two years following termination have the responsibility to thoroughly examine and document that such relations did not have an exploitative nature.

### Standard of Practice Five (SP-5) Protecting Clients during Group Work

Counselors must take steps to protect clients from physical or psychological trauma resulting from interactions during group work. (See A.9.b.)

### Standard of Practice Six (SP-6) Advance Understanding of Fees

Counselors must explain to clients, prior to their entering the counseling relationship, financial arrangements related to professional services. (See A.10. a.-d. and A.11.c.)

### Standard of Practice Seven (SP-7) Termination

Counselors must assist in making appropriate arrangements for the continuation of treatment of clients, when necessary, following termination of counseling relationships. (See A.11.a.)

### Standard of Practice Eight (SP-8) Inability to Assist Clients

Counselors must avoid entering or immediately terminate a counseling relationship if it is determined that they are unable to be of professional assistance to a client. The counselor may assist in making an appropriate referral for the client. (See A.11.b.)

## Section B: Confidentiality

### Standard of Practice Nine (SP-9) Confidentiality Requirement

Counselors must keep information related to counseling services confidential unless disclosure is in the best interest of clients, is required for the welfare of others, or is required by law. When disclosure is required, only information that is essential is revealed and the client is informed of such disclosure. (See B.1. a.-f.)

*Standard of Practice Ten (SP-10)*
*Confidentiality Requirements*
*for Subordinates.*

Counselors must take measures to ensure that privacy and confidentiality of clients are maintained by subordinates. (See B.1.h.)

*Standard of Practice Eleven (SP-11)*
*Confidentiality in Group Work*

Counselors must clearly communicate to group members that confidentiality cannot be guaranteed in group work. (See B.2.a.)

*Standard of Practice Twelve (SP-12)*
*Confidentiality in Family Counseling*

Counselors must not disclose information about one family member in counseling to another family member without prior consent. (See B.2.b.)

*Standard of Practice Thirteen (SP-13)*
*Confidentiality of Records*

Counselors must maintain appropriate confidentiality in creating, storing, accessing, transferring, and disposing of counseling records. (See B.4.b.)

*Standard of Practice Fourteen (SP-14)*
*Permission to Record or Observe*

Counselors must obtain prior consent from clients in order to electronically record or observe sessions. (See B.4.c.)

*Standard of Practice Fifteen (SP-15)*
*Disclosure or Transfer of Records*

Counselors must obtain client consent to disclose or transfer records to third parties unless exceptions listed in SP-9 exist. (See B.4.e.)

*Standard of Practice Sixteen (SP-16) Data*
*Disguise Required*

Counselors must disguise the identity of the client when using data for training, research, or publication. (See B.5.a.)

## Section C: Professional Responsibility

*Standard of Practice Seventeen (SP-17)*
*Boundaries of Competence*

Counselors must practice only within the boundaries of their competence. (See C.2.a.)

*Standard of Practice Eighteen (SP-18)*
*Continuing Education*

Counselors must engage in continuing education to maintain their professional competence. (See C.2.f.)

*Standard of Practice Nineteen (SP-19)*
*Impairment of Professionals*

Counselors must refrain from offering professional services when their personal problems or conflicts may cause harm to a client or others. (See C.2.g.)

*Standard of Practice Twenty (SP-20)*
*Accurate Advertising*

Counselors must accurately represent their credentials and services when advertising. (See C.3.a.)

*Standard of Practice Twenty-One (SP-21)*
*Recruiting through Employment*

Counselors must not use their place of employment or institutional affiliation to recruit clients for their private practices. (See C.3.d.)

*Standard of Practice Twenty-Two*
*(SP-22) Credentials Claimed*

Counselors must claim or imply only professional credentials possessed and must correct any known misrepresentations of their credentials by others. (See C.4.a.)

*Standard of Practice Twenty-Three*
*(SP-23) Sexual Harassment*

Counselors must not engage in sexual harassment. (See C.5.b.)

### Standard of Practice Twenty-Four (SP-24) Unjustified Gains

Counselors must not use their professional positions to seek or receive unjustified personal gains, sexual favors, unfair advantage, or unearned goods or services. (See C.5.e.)

### Standard of Practice Twenty-Five (SP-25) Clients Served by Others

With the consent of the client, counselors must inform other mental health professionals serving the same client that a counseling relationship between the counselor and client exists. (See C.6.c.)

### Standard of Practice Twenty-Six (SP-26) Negative Employment Conditions

Counselors must alert their employers to institutional policy or conditions that may be potentially disruptive or damaging to the counselor's professional responsibilities or that may limit their effectiveness or deny clients' rights. (See D.1.c.)

### Standard of Practice Twenty-Seven (SP-27) Personnel Selection and Assignment

Counselors must select competent staff and must assign responsibilities compatible with staff skills and experiences. (See D.1.h.)

### Standard of Practice Twenty-Eight (SP-28) Exploitive Relationships with Subordinates

Counselors must not engage in exploitive relationships with individuals over whom they have supervisory, evaluative, or instructional control or authority. (See D.1.k.)

## Section D: Relationship with Other Professionals

### Standard of Practice Twenty-Nine (SP-29) Accepting Fees from Agency Clients

Counselors must not accept fees or other remuneration for consultation with persons entitled to such services through the counselor's employing agency or institution. (See D.3.a.)

### Standard of Practice Thirty (SP-30) Referral Fees

Counselors must not accept referral fees. (See D.3.b.)

## Section E: Evaluation, Assessment, and Interpretation

### Standard of Practice Thirty-One (SP-31) Limits of Competence

Counselors must perform only testing and assessment services for which they are competent. Counselors must not allow the use of psychological assessment techniques by unqualified persons under their supervision. (See E.2.a.)

### Standard of Practice Thirty-Two (SP-32) Appropriate Use of Assessment Instruments

Counselors must use assessment instruments in the manner for which they were intended. (See E.2.b.)

### Standard of Practice Thirty-Three (SP-33) Assessment Explanations to Clients

Counselors must provide explanations to clients prior to assessment about the nature and purposes of assessment and the specific uses of results. (See E.3.a.)

### Standard of Practice Thirty-Four (SP-34) Recipients of Test Results

Counselors must ensure that accurate and appropriate interpretations accompany any release of testing and assessment information. (See E.3.b.)

### Standard of Practice Thirty-Five (SP-35) Obsolete Tests and Outdated Test Results

Counselors must not base their assessment or intervention decisions or recommendations on data or test results that are obsolete or outdated for the current purpose. (See E.11.)

## Section F: Teaching, Training, and Supervision

### Standard of Practice Thirty-Six (SP-36) Sexual Relationships with Students or Supervisees

Counselors must not engage in sexual relationships with their students and supervisees. (See F.1.c.)

### Standard of Practice Thirty-Seven (SP-37) Credit for Contributions to Research

Counselors must give credit to students or supervisees for their contributions to research and scholarly projects. (See F.1.d.)

### Standard of Practice Thirty-Eight (SP-38) Supervision Preparation

Counselors who offer clinical supervision services must be trained and prepared in supervision methods and techniques. (See F.1.f.)

### Standard of Practice Thirty-Nine (SP-39) Evaluation Information

Counselors must clearly state to students and supervisees in advance of training, the levels of competency expected, appraisal methods, and timing of evaluations. Counselors must provide students and supervisees with periodic performance appraisal and evaluation feedback throughout the training program. (See F.2.c.)

### Standard of Practice Forty (SP-40) Peer Relationships in Training

Counselors must make every effort to ensure that the rights of peers are not violated when students and supervisees are assigned to lead counseling groups or provide clinical supervision. (See F.2.e.)

### Standard of Practice Forty-One (SP-41) Limitations of Students and Supervisees

Counselors must assist students and supervisees in securing remedial assistance, when needed, and must dismiss from the training program students and super-visees who are unable to provide competent service due to academic or personal limitations. (See F.3.a.)

### Standard of Practice Forty-Two (SP-42) Self-Growth Experiences

Counselors who conduct experiences for students or supervisees that include self-growth or self disclosure must inform participants of counselors' ethical obligations to the profession and must not grade participants based on their nonacademic performance. (See F.3.b.)

### Standard of Practice Forty-Three (SP-43) Standards for Students and Supervisees

Students and supervisees preparing to become counselors must adhere to the Code of Ethics and the Standards of Practice of counselors. (See F.3.e.)

## Section G: Research and Publication

### Standard of Practice Forty-Four (SP-44) Precautions to Avoid Injury in Research

Counselors must avoid causing physical, social, or psychological harm or injury to subjects in research. (See G.1.c.)

### Standard of Practice Forty-Five (SP-45) Confidentiality of Research Information

Counselors must keep confidential information obtained about research participants. (See G.2.d.)

### Standard of Practice Forty-Six (SP-46) Information Affecting Research Outcome

Counselors must report all variables and conditions known to the investigator that may have affected research data or outcomes. (See G.3.a.)

### Standard of Practice Forty-Seven (SP-47) Accurate Research Results

Counselors must not distort or misrepresent research data nor fabricate or intentionally bias research results. (See G.3.b.)

### Standard of Practice Forty-Eight (SP-48) Publication Contributors

Counselors must give appropriate credit to those who have contributed to research. (See G.4.a. and G.4.b.)

## Section H: Resolving Ethical Issues

### Standard of Practice Forty-Nine (SP-49) Ethical Behavior Expected

Counselors must take appropriate action when they possess reasonable cause that raises doubts as to whether counselors or other mental health professionals are acting in an ethical manner. (See H.2.a.)

### Standard of Practice Fifty (SP-50) Unwarranted Complaints

Counselors must not initiate, participate in, or encourage the filing of ethics complaints that are unwarranted or intended to harm a mental health professional rather than to protect clients or the public. (See H.2.f.)

### Standard of Practice Fifty-One (SP-51) Cooperation with Ethics Committees

Counselors must cooperate with investigations, proceedings, and requirements of the ACA Ethics Committee or ethics committees of other duly constituted associations or boards having jurisdiction over those charged with a violation. (See H.3.)

## References

The following documents are available to counselors as resources to guide them in their practices. These resources are not a part of the Code of Ethics and the Standards of Practice.

American Association for Counseling and Development/ Association for Measurement and Evaluation in Counseling and Development. (1989). The responsibilities of users of standardized tests (revised). Washington, DC: Author.

American Counseling Association. (1988). American Counseling Association Ethical Standards. Alexandria, VA: Author.

American Psychological Association. (1985). Standards for educational and psychological testing (revised). Washington, DC: Author.

American Rehabilitation Counseling Association, Commission on Rehabilitation Counselor Certification, and National Rehabilitation Counseling Association. (1995). Code of professional ethics for rehabilitation counselors. Chicago, IL: Author.

American School Counselor Association. (1992). Ethical standards for school counselors. Alexandria, VA: Author.

Joint Committee on Testing Practices. (1988). Code of fair testing practices in education. Washington, DC: Author.

National Board for Certified Counselors. (1989). National Board for Certified Counselors Code of Ethics. Alexandria, VA: Author.

Prediger, D. J. (Ed.). (1993, March). Multicultural assessment standards. Alexandria, VA: Association for Assessment in Counseling.

## Policies and Procedures for Responding to Members' Requests for Interpretations of the Ethical Standards

### Section A: Appropriate Requests

1. ACA members may requests that the Committee issue formal interpretations of the ACA Code of Ethics for the purpose of guiding the member's own professional behavior.

2. Requests for the interpretations will not be considered in the following situations:

   a. The individual requesting the interpretation is not an ACA member, or

   b. The request is intended to determine whether the behavior of another mental health professional is unethical. In the event an ACA member believes the behavior of another mental health professional is unethical, the ACA member should resolve the issue directly with the professional, if possible, and should file an ethical complaint if appropriate.

### Section B: Procedures

1. Members must send written requests for interpretations to the Committee at ACA Headquarters.

**2.** Questions should be submitted in the following format: "Does (counselor behavior) violate Sections _____ or any other sections of the ACA Ethical Standards?" Questions should avoid unique details, be general in nature to the extent possible, and be brief.

**3.** The Committee staff liaison will revise the question, if necessary, and submit it to the Committee Co-Chair for approval.

**4.** The question will be sent to Committee members who will be asked to respond individually.

**5.** The Committee C-Chair will develop a consensus interpretation on behalf of the Committee.

**6.** The consensus interpretation will be sent to members of the Committee for final approval.

**7.** The formal interpretation will be sent to the member who submitted the inquiry.

**8.** The question and the formal interpretation will be published in the ACA newsletter, but the identity of the member requesting the interpretation will not be disclosed.

# Policies and Procedures for Processing Complaints of Ethical Violations

## Section A: General

**1.** The American Counseling Association, hereafter referred to as the "Association" or "ACA," is dedicated to enhancing human development throughout the life span and promoting the counseling profession.

**2.** The Association, in furthering its objectives, administers the Code of Ethics and Standards of Practice developed and approved by the ACA Governing Council.

**3.** The purpose of this document is to facilitate the work of the ACA Ethics Committee ("Committee") by specifying the procedures for processing cases of alleged violations of the ACA Code of Ethics, codifying options for sanctioning members, and stating appeals procedures. This document is to be used as a supplement to the ACA Code of Ethics, not as a substitute. The intent of the Association is to monitor the professional conduct of its members to promote sound

ethical practices. ACA does not, however, warrant the performance of any individual.

## Section B: Ethics Committee Members

**1.** The Ethics Committee, a standing committee of the Association, consists of six (6) appointed members including two (2) Co-Chairs whose terms overlap. Two members are appointed annually for three (3) year terms by the President-Elect; appointments are subject to confirmation by the ACA Governing Council. Any vacancy on the Committee will be filled by the President in the same manner, and the person appointed shall serve the unexpired term of the member whose place he or she took. Committee members may be reappointed to not more than one (1) additional consecutive term.

**2.** One (1) of the Committee Co-Chairs is appointed annually by the President-Elect from among the Committee members who have two (2) years of service remaining and serves as Co-Chair for two (2) years, subject to confirmation by the ACA Governing Council.

## Section C: Role and Function

**1.** The Ethics Committee is responsible for
   **a.** Educating the membership as to the Association's Code of Ethics;
   **b.** Periodically reviewing and recommending changes in the Code of Ethics of the Association, as well as Policies and Procedures for Processing Complaints of Ethical Violations;
   **c.** Receiving and processing complaints of alleged violations of the Code of Ethics of the Association; and,
   **d.** Receiving and processing requests for interpretations.

**2.** The Committee shall meet in person or by telephone conference a minimum of three (3) times per year for processing complaints.

**3.** In processing complaints about alleged ethical misconduct, the Committee will compile an objective, factual account of the dispute in question and make the best possible recommendation for the resolution of the case. The Committee, in taking any action, shall do so only for cause, shall only take a reasonable degree of disciplinary action, shall utilize these procedures with objectivity and fairness, and in general shall act only to further the interests and objectives of the Association and its membership.

**4.** Of the six (6) voting members of the Committee, a vote of four (4) is necessary to conduct business. In the event a Co-Chair or any other member of the Committee has a personal interest in the case, he or she shall withdraw from reviewing the case.

**5.** In the event Committee members recuse themselves from a complaint and insufficient voting members are available to conduct business, the President shall appoint former ACA Committee members to decide the complaint.

## Section D: Responsibilities of the Committee Members

**1.** The Committee members have an obligation to act in an unbiased manner, to work expeditiously, to safeguard the confidentiality of the Committee's activities, and to follow procedures established to protect the rights of all individuals involved.

## Section E: Responsibilities of the Co-Chairs Administering the Complaint

**1.** In the event that one of the Co-Chairs administering the complaint has a conflict of interest in a particular case, the other Co-Chair shall administer the complaint. The Co-Chair administering the compliant shall not have a vote in the decision.

**2.** In addition to the above guidelines for members of the Committee, the Co-Chairs, with the assistance of the Headquarters staff liaison (and legal counsel where necessary), have the responsibilities of

    **a.** Receiving, via ACA Headquarters, complaints that have been certified for membership status of the charged member;

    **b.** Determining whether the alleged behavior(s), if true, would violate ACA's Code of Ethics and whether the Committee should review the complaint under these rules;

    **c.** Notifying the complainant and the charged member of receipt of the case by certified mail return receipt requested;

    **d.** Notifying the members of the Committee of the case;

    **e.** Requesting additional information from complainants, charged members and others;

    **f.** Presiding over the meetings of the Committee;

    **g.** Preparing and sending, by certified mail, communications to the complainant and charged member on the recommendations and decisions of the Committee; and

    **h.** Arranging for legal advice with assistance and financial approval of the ACA Executive Director.

## Section F: Jurisdiction

**1.** The Committee will consider whether individuals have violated the ACA Code of Ethics if those individuals

    **a.** Are current members of the American Counseling Association or

    **b.** Were ACA members when the alleged violations occurred.

**2.** Ethics committees of divisions, branches, corporate affiliates, or other ACA entities must refer all ethical complaints involving ACA members to the Committee.

## Section G: Eligibility to File Complaints

**1.** The Committee will receive complaints that ACA members have violated one or more sections of the ACA Code of Ethics from the following individuals:

    **a.** Any individuals who have reason to believe that ACA members have violated the ACA Code of Ethics.

    **b.** ACA members, or members of other helping professions, who have reason to believe that other ACA members have violated the ACA Code of Ethics.

    **c.** The Co-Chair of the Committee on behalf of the ACA membership when the Co-Chair has reason to believe through information received by the Committee that ACA members have violated the ACA Code of Ethics.

    **d.** Ethics committees of divisions, branches, corporate affiliates, or other ACA entities as provided for in Section F.2. above.

**2.** If possible, individuals should attempt to resolve complaints directly with charged members before filing ethical complaints.

## Section H: Time Lines

**1.** The time lines in these standards are guidelines only and have been established to provide a reasonable time framework for processing complaints.

**2.** Complainants or charged members may request extensions of deadlines when appropriate. Extensions of deadlines will be granted by the Committee only when justified by unusual circumstance.

## Section I: Nature of Communication

**1.** Only written communications regarding ethical complaints against members will be acceptable. If telephone inquiries are received regarding the filing of complaints, responding to complaints, or providing information regarding complaints, the individuals will be informed of the written communication requirement and asked to comply.

**2.** All correspondence related to an ethical complaint must be addressed to the Ethics Committee, ACA Headquarters, 5999 Stevenson Avenue, Alexandria, VA 22304 and must be marked "confidential." This process is necessary to protect the confidentiality of the complainant and the charged member.

## Section J: Filing Complaints

**1.** Only written complaints, signed by complainants, will be considered.

**2.** Individuals eligible to file complaints will send a letter outlining the nature of the complaint to the Committee at the ACA Headquarters. The complaint should include, if possible, (a) the name and address of the complainant, (b) the name and address of the charged member, (c) the names and addresses of any other persons who have knowledge of the facts involved, and (d) a brief description of the reason why the complaint is being filed.

**3.** The ACA staff liaison to the Committee will communicate in writing with complainants. Receipt of complaints and confirmation of membership status of charged members as defined in Section F.1 above will

be acknowledged to the complainant. Proposed formal complaints will be sent to complainants after receipt of complaints have been acknowledged.

**4.** If the complaint does not involve a member as defined in Section F.1. above the staff liaison shall inform the complainant.

**5.** The ACA staff liaison shall assign the complaint to a Co-Chair to determine whether the complaint, if true, would violate one or more sections of the Code of Ethics or if the complaint could be properly decided if accepted. If not, the complaint will be forwarded to the other Co-Chair for review, as if a new complaint. If both Co-Chairs determine that a complaint would not violate one or more sections of the Code of Ethics or if the complaint could not be properly decided if accepted, then the complaint will not be accepted and the complainant shall be notified.

**6.** If the Committee Co-Chair administering the complaint determines that there is insufficient information to make a fair determination of whether the behavior alleged in the complaint would be cause for action by the Committee, the ACA staff liaison may request further information from the complainant or others. They shall be given thirty (30) working days from receipt of the request to respond.

**7.** When complaints are accepted, complainants will be informed that copies of the formal complaints plus evidence and documents submitted in support of the complaint will be provided to the charged member and that the complainant must authorize release of such information to the charged member before the complaint process may proceed.

**8.** The ACA staff liaison, after receiving approval of the Committee Co-Chair administering a complaint, will formulate a formal complaint which will be presented to the complainant for his or her signature.

    **a.** The correspondence from complainants will be received, and the staff liaison and Committee Co-Chair administering the complaint will identify all ACA Code of Ethics that might have been violated if the accusations are true.

    **b.** The formal complaint will be sent to complainants with a copy of these Policies and Procedures, a copy of the ACA Code of Ethics, a verification affidavit form and an authorization and release of information form. Complainants will be asked to sign and return the completed complaint, verification affidavit and authorization and release of information forms. It will be explained to complainants that sections of the codes that might have been violated may be added or deleted by the complainant before signing the formal statement.

**c.** If complainants elect to add or delete sections of the Code of Ethics in the formal complaint, the unsigned formal complaint shall be returned to ACA Headquarters with changes noted, and a revised formal complaint will be sent to the complainants for their signature.

9. When the completed formal complaint, verification affidavit form and authorization and release of information form are presented to the complainant for signature, he or she will be asked to submit all evidence and documents he or she wishes to be considered by the Committee in reviewing the complaint. The complainant shall submit all evidence and documentation in support of the claim within thirty (30) days of filing the formal complaint. The Committee may accept, at its discretion, evidence or documentation submitted late if good cause is shown.

## Section K: Notice to Charged Members

1. Once signed formal complaints have been received, charged members will be sent a copy of the formal complaint by U.S. mail, certified, with return-receipt requested, a copy of these Policies and Procedures, a copy of the Code of Ethics, notification of their right to request a hearing, (including the time limit within which to request the hearing, and that the failure to request a hearing within the time limit constitutes a waiver of the hearing), ACA's policy of disclosing adverse actions to its members and/or informing state and national licensure boards of a member's suspension or expulsion, and copies of all evidence and documents submitted in support of the complaint.

2. Charged members will be asked to respond to the complaint against them by addressing each section of the ACA Code of Ethics they have been accused of having violated. They will be informed that if they wish to respond they must do so in writing within sixty (60) working days.

3. Charged members will be informed that they must submit all evidence and documents they wish to

be considered by the Committee in reviewing the complaint within sixty (60) working days.

4. After charged members have received notification that a complaint has been brought against them, they will be given sixty (60) working days to notify the Committee Co-Chair (via ACA Headquarters) in writing, by certified mail, if they wish to request a formal face-to-face hearing before the Committee. Charged members may waive their right to a formal hearing before the Committee and shall sign a waiver of the right to a hearing. (See Section O: Hearings).

5. If the Committee Co-Chair determines that there is insufficient information to make a fair determination of whether the behavior alleged in the complaint would be cause for action by the Committee, the ACA staff liaison to the Committee may request further information from the charged member or others. They shall be given thirty (30) working days from receipt of the request to respond.

6. All requests for additional information from others will be accompanied by a verification affidavit form which the information provider will be asked to complete and return.

7. The Committee may, in its discretion, delay or postpone its review of the case with good cause including if the Committee wishes to obtain additional information. The charged member may request in writing that the Committee delay or postpone its review of the case for good cause.

## Section L: Disposition of Complaints

1. After receiving the responses from charged members, Committee members will be provided copies of (a) the complaint, (b) supporting evidence and documents sent to charged members, (c) the response, and (d) supporting evidence and documents provided by charged members and others.

2. Decisions will be rendered based on the evidence and documents provided by the complainant and charged member or others.

3. The Committee Co-Chair administering a complaint will not participate in deliberations or decisions regarding that particular complaint.

4. At the next meeting of the Committee held no sooner than fifteen (15) working days after members

received copies of documents related to a complaint, the Committee will discuss the complaint, response, and supporting documentation, if any, and determine the outcome of the complaint.

**5.** The Committee will determine whether each Code of Ethics the member has been accused of having violated was violated based on the information provided.

**6.** After deliberations, the Committee may decide to dismiss the complaint or to dismiss charges within the complaint.

**7.** In the event it is determined that any of the ACA Codes of Ethics have been violated, the Committee will impose for the entire complaint one or a combination of the possible sanctions allowed.

## Section M: Withdrawal of Complaints

**1.** If the complainant and charged member both agree to discontinue the complaint process, the Committee may, at its discretion, complete the adjudication process if available evidence indicates that this is warranted. The Co-Chair of the Committee, on behalf of the ACA membership, shall act as complainant.

## Section N: Possible Sanctions

**1.** Remedial requirements may be stipulated by the Committee.

**2.** Probation for a specified period of time subject to Committee review of compliance. Remedial requirements may be imposed to be completed within a specified period of time.

**3.** Suspension from ACA membership for a specified period of time subject to Committee review of compliance. Remedial requirements may be imposed to be completed within a specified period of time.

**4.** Permanent expulsion from ACA membership. This sanction requires a unanimous vote of those voting.

**5.** The penalty for failing to satisfactorily fulfill a remedial requirement imposed by the Committee as a result of a probation sanction will be automatic suspension until the requirement is met unless the Committee determines that the remedial requirement should be modified based on good cause shown prior to the end of the probationary period.

**6.** The penalty for failing to satisfactorily fulfill a remedial requirement imposed by the Committee as a result of a suspension sanction will be automatic permanent expulsion unless the Committee determines that the remedial requirement should be modified based on good cause shown prior to the end of the suspension period.

**7.** Other corrective action.

## Section O: Hearings

**1.** At the discretion of the Committee, a hearing may be conducted when the results of the Committee's preliminary determination indicate that additional information is needed.

**2.** When charged members, within sixty (60) working days of notification of the complaint, request a formal face-to-face or telephone conference hearing before the Committee a hearing shall be conducted. (See Section K.6.)

**3.** The charged member shall bear all their expenses associated with attendance at hearings requested by the charged member.

**4.** The Committee Co-Chair shall schedule a formal hearing on the case at the next scheduled Committee meeting and notify both the complainant and the charged member of their right to attend the hearing in person or by telephone conference call.

**5.** The hearing will be held before a panel made up of the Committee and, if the charged member chooses, a representative of the charged member's primary Division. This representative will be identified by the Division President and will have voting privileges.

## Section P: Hearing Procedures

**1. Purpose.**
   **a.** A hearing will be conducted to determine whether a breach of the Code of Ethics has occurred and, if so, to determine appropriate disciplinary action.
   **b.** The Committee will be guided in its deliberations by principles of basic fairness and professionalism and will keep its deliberations as

confidential as possible except as provided herein.

**2. Notice.**

**a.** The charged members shall be advised in writing by the Co-Chair administering the complaint of the time and place of the hearing, the list of any witnesses expected to testify at the hearing against the charged member (which list may not be complete), and the charges involved at least forty-five (45) working days before the hearing. A copy of the notification shall be sent to the complainant. Notice shall include a formal statement of the complaints lodged against the charged member and supporting evidence.

**b.** The charged member is under no duty to respond to the notice, but the Committee will not be obligated to delay or postpone its hearing unless the charged member so requests in writing with good cause received at least fifteen (15) working days in advance. In the absence of such 15-day advance notice and postponement by the Committee, if the charged member fails to appear at the hearing, the Committee shall decide the complaint on record. Failure of the charged member to appear at the hearing shall not be viewed by the Committee as sufficient grounds alone for taking disciplinary action.

**3. Conduct of the Hearing.**

**a.** Accommodations. The location of the hearing shall be determined at the discretion of the Committee. The Committee shall provide a private room to conduct the hearing, and no observers or recording devices other than a recording device used by the Committee shall be permitted.

**b.** Presiding Officer. The Co-Chair in charge of the case shall preside over the hearing and deliberations of the Committee. At the conclusion of the hearing and deliberations, the Co-Chair shall promptly notify the charged member and complainant of the Committee's decision in writing as provided in Section Q., Paragraphs 1 and 2, below.

**c.** Record. A record of the hearing shall be made and preserved, together with any documents presented in evidence, at ACA Headquarters for a period of three (3) years or until the complaint process is final, whichever is longer.

The record shall consist of a summary of testimony received or a verbatim transcript at the discretion of the Committee.

**d.** Right to Counsel. The charged member shall be entitled to have legal counsel present to advise and represent him or her throughout the hearing. Legal counsel for ACA shall also be present at the hearing to advise the Committee and shall have the privilege of the floor.

**e.** Witnesses. Either party shall have the right to call witnesses to substantiate his or her version of the case.

**f.** The Committee shall have the right to call witnesses it believes may provide further insight into the matter. ACA shall, in its sole discretion, determine the number and identity of witnesses to be heard.

**g.** Witnesses shall not be present during the hearing except when testifying and shall be excused upon completion of their testimony and any cross-examination.

**h.** The Co-Chair administering the complaint shall allow questions of any witness by the opposition or members of the Committee if such questions and testimony are relevant to the issues in the case.

**i.** The Co-Chair administering the complaint will determine what questions and testimony are relevant to the case. Should the hearing be disturbed by irrelevant testimony, the Co-Chair administering the complaint may call a brief recess to restore order.

**j.** All expenses associated with counsel on behalf of the parties shall be borne by the respective parties. All expenses associated with witnesses on behalf of the charged member shall be borne by the charged member when the charged member requests a hearing. If the Committee requests the hearing, all expenses associated with witnesses shall be borne by ACA.

**4. Presentation of Evidence.**

**a.** The staff liaison or the Co-Chair administering the complaint shall be called upon first to present the charge(s) against the charged member and to briefly describe the supporting evidence. The person presenting the charges shall also be responsible for examining and cross-examining witnesses on behalf of the complainant and for otherwise presenting the matter during the hearing.

**b.** The complainant or the staff liaison or the Committee Co-Chair administering the complaint shall then present the case against the charged member. Witnesses who can substantiate the case may be called upon to testify and answer questions of the charged member and the Committee.

**c.** If the charged member is present at the hearing, he or she shall be called upon after the case has been presented against the charged member to present any evidence which refutes the charges against him or her. This includes witnesses as in Subsection (3) above. The charged member and the complainant may submit a written statement at the close of the hearing.

**d.** The charged member will not be found guilty simply for refusing to testify. Once the charged member chooses to testify, however, he or she may be cross-examined by the complainant and members of the Committee.

**e.** The Committee will endeavor to conclude the hearing within a period of approximately three (3) hours. The parties will be requested to be considerate of this time frame in planning their testimony. If it appears that additional time will be needed to develop the issues adequately, an extension of time may be granted.

**f.** Testimony that is merely cumulative or repetitious may, at the discretion of the Co-Chair administering the complaint, be excluded.

**g.** At any time during the presentation of evidence, the presiding members of the Committee may ask pertinent questions.

5. **Relevancy of Evidence.**

   **a.** The Hearing Committee is not a court of law and is not required to observe formal rules of evidence. Evidence inadmissible in a court of law may be admissible in the hearing before the Committee if it is relevant to the case. That is, if the evidence offered tends to explain, clarify, or refute any of the important facts of the case, it should generally be considered.

   **b.** The Committee will not consider evidence or testimony for the purpose of supporting any charge that was not set forth in the notice of the hearing or that is not relevant to the issues of the case.

6. **Burden of Proof.**

   **a.** The burden of proving a violation of the Code of Ethics is on the complainant and/or the Committee. It is not up to the charged member to prove his or her innocence of any wrongdoing.

   **b.** Although the charge(s) need not be proved "beyond a reasonable doubt," the Committee will not find the charged member guilty in the absence of substantial, objective, and believable evidence to sustain the charge(s).

7. **Deliberation of the Committee.**

   **a.** After the hearing is completed, the Committee shall meet in a closed session to review the evidence presented and reach a conclusion. ACA legal counsel may attend the closed session to advise the Committee if the Committee so desires.

   **b.** The Committee shall be the sole trier of the facts and shall weigh the evidence presented and assess the credibility of the witnesses. The act of a majority of the members of the Committee present shall be the decision of the Committee. A unanimous vote of those voting is required for permanent expulsion from ACA membership.

   **c.** Only members of the Committee who were present throughout the entire hearing shall be eligible to vote.

8. **Decision of the Committee.**

   **a.** The Committee will first resolve the issue of the guilt or innocence of the charged member on each charge. Applying the burden of proof in subsection (5) above, the Committee will vote by secret ballot unless the members of the Committee consent to an oral vote.

   **b.** In the event a majority of the members of the Committee do not find the charged member guilty, the charges shall be dismissed. If the Committee finds the charged member has violated the Code of Ethics, it must then determine what sanctions, in accordance with Section N: Possible Sanctions, shall be imposed.

   **c.** As provided in Section Q below, the Co-Chair administering the complaint shall notify the charged member and complainant of the Committee's decision and rights to appeal in writing.

## Section Q: Notification of Results

**1.** Charged members shall be notified of Committee decisions regarding complaints against them. Within thirty (30) days after the hearing, charged members shall be notified of the Committee's decisions and their right to appeal. The Committee's decision shall be sent by U.S. mail, certified, with return-receipt requested.

**2.** After the deadline for filing an appeal, or in the event an appeal is filed, after a decision on appeals has been rendered, and if a violation has been found and charged members have been suspended or expelled, counselor licensure, certification, or registry boards, other mental health licensure, certification, or registry boards, voluntary national certification boards, and appropriate professional associations will also be notified of the results. In addition, ACA divisions, state branches, the ACA Insurance Trust, and other ACA-related entities will also be notified of the results.

**3.** After the deadline for filing an appeal, or in the event an appeal is filed, after a decision on appeals has been rendered, and if a violation has been found and charged members have been suspended or expelled, a notice of the Committee's action that includes the sections of the ACA Code of Ethics that were found to have been violated and the sanctions imposed will be published in the ACA newsletter.

## Section R: Appeals

**1.** Decisions of the ACA Ethics Committee may be appealed by the member found to have been in violation based on one or both of the following grounds:

    **a.** The Committee violated its policies and procedures for processing complaints of ethical violations; and/or

    **b.** The decision of the Committee was arbitrary and capricious and was not supported by the materials provided by the complainant and charged member.

**2.** After members have received notification that they have been found in violation of one or more ACA Codes of Ethics, they will be given thirty (30) working days to notify the Committee in writing by certified mail that they are appealing the decision. If an appeal is not requested, the Committee shall issue its decision as the final decision as soon as the time during which an appeal may be filed expires.

**3.** An appeal may consist only of a letter stating one or both of the grounds of appeal listed in subsection 1 above and the reasons for the appeal. The filing of an appeal automatically stays the execution of a decision by the Committee until the appeal is completed.

**4.** The appealing member will be asked to identify the primary ACA division to which he or she belongs. The ACA President will appoint a three (3) person appeals panel consisting of two (2) former ACA Ethics Committee Chairs (neither of whom served on the Committee during the hearings on the matter) and the President of the identified division. The ACA attorney shall serve as legal advisor and have the privilege of the floor.

**5.** The three (3) member appeals panel will be given copies of the materials available to the Committee when it made its decision, a copy of the hearing record if a hearing was held, plus a copy of the letter filed by the appealing member.

**6.** The appeals panel will not consider evidence that was not presented to the Committee.

**7.** The appeals panel generally will render its decision regarding an appeal requiring a majority vote within sixty (60) working days of their receipt of the above materials

**8.** The decision of the appeals panel is limited to
    **a.** Upholding the decision of the Committee, or
    **b.** Upholding the decision of the Committee on the finding of an ethical violation but reversing and remanding the Committee's decision on sanctions, or
    **c.** Recommending reconsideration by the Committee of the decision providing guidance to the Committee in detail in writing for considering a new decision on remand.

**9.** The decision of the appeals panel need not be unanimous.

**10.** When a Committee decision is reversed and remanded, the complainant and charged member will be informed in writing, and additional information may be requested first from the complainant and then from the charged member. The Committee will then render another decision without a hearing.

**11.** Decisions of the appeals panel to uphold the Committee decision are final and binding and not subject to further hearings or appellate review.

### Section S: Substantial New Evidence

**1.** In the event substantial new evidence is presented in a case in which an appeal was not filed, or in a case for which a final decision has been rendered, the case may be reopened by the Committee.

**2.** The Committee will consider substantial new evidence and if found to be substantiated and capable of exonerating a member who was expelled, the Committee will reopen the case and go through the entire complaint process again.

### Section T: Records

**1.** The records of the Committee regarding complaints are confidential except as provided herein.

**2.** Original copies of complaint records will be maintained in locked files at ACA Headquarters or at an off-site location chosen by ACA.

**3.** Members of the Committee will keep copies of complaint records confidential and will destroy copies of records after a case has been closed or when they are no longer a member of the Committee.

### Section U: Legal Actions Related to Complaints

**1.** Complainants and charged members are required to notify the Committee if they learn of any type of legal action (civil or criminal) being filed related to the complaint.

**2.** In the event any type of legal action is filed regarding an accepted complaint, all actions related to the complaint will be stayed until the legal action has been concluded. The Committee will consult with legal counsel concerning whether the processing of the complaint will be stayed if the legal action does not involve the same complainant and the same facts complained of.

**3.** If actions on a complaint are stayed, the complainant and charged member will be notified.

**4.** When actions on a complaint are continued after a legal action has been concluded, the complainant and charged member will be notified.

# Appendix B

# National Board for Certified Counselors Code of Ethics

## Preamble

The National Board for Certified Counselors (NBCC) is a professional certification board which certifies counselors as having met standards for the general and specialty practice of professional counseling established by the Board. The counselors certified by NBCC may identify with different professional associations and are often licensed by jurisdictions which promulgate codes of ethics. The NBCC code of ethics provides a minimal ethical standard for the professional behavior of all NBCC certificants. This code provides an expectation of and assurance for the ethical practice for all who use the professional services of an NBCC certificant. In addition, it serves the purpose of having an enforceable standard for all NBCC certificants and assures those served of some resource in case of a perceived ethical violation.

The NBCC Ethical Code applies to all those certified by NBCC regardless of any other professional affiliation. Persons who receive professional services from certified counselors may elect to use other ethical codes which apply to their counselor. Although NBCC cooperates with professional associations and credentialing organizations, it can bring actions to discipline or sanction NBCC certificants only if the provisions of the NBCC Code are found to have been violated.

The National Board for Certified Counselors, Inc. (NBCC) promotes counseling through certification. In pursuit of this mission, the NBCC:

- Promotes quality assurance in counseling practice
- Promotes the value of counseling
- Promotes public awareness of quality counseling practice
- Promotes professionalism in counseling
- Promotes leadership in credentialing

## Section A: General

**1.** Certified counselors engage in continuous efforts to improve professional practices, services, and research. Certified counselors are guided in their work by evidence of the best professional practices.

**2.** Certified counselors have a responsibility to the clients they serve and to the institutions within which the services are performed. Certified counselors also strive to assist the respective agency, organization, or institution in providing competent and ethical professional services. The acceptance of employment in an institution implies that the certified counselor is in agreement with the general policies and principles of the institution. Therefore, the professional activities of the certified counselor are in accord with the objectives of the institution. If the certified counselor and the employer do not agree and cannot reach agreement on policies that are consistent with appropriate counselor ethical practice that is conducive to client growth and development, the employment should be terminated. If the situation warrants further action, the certified counselor should work through professional organizations to have the unethical practice changed.

**3.** Ethical behavior among professional associates (i.e., both certified and non-certified counselors) must be expected at all times. When a certified counselor has doubts as to the ethical behavior of professional colleagues, the certified counselor must take action to attempt to rectify this condition. Such action uses the respective institution's channels first and then uses procedures established by the NBCC or the perceived violator's profession.

**4.** Certified counselors must refuse remuneration for consultation or counseling with persons who are entitled to these services through the certified counselor's employing institution or agency. Certified counselors must not divert to their private practices, without the mutual consent of the institution and the client, legitimate clients in their primary agencies or the institutions with which they are affiliated.

**5.** In establishing fees for professional counseling services, certified counselors must consider the financial status of clients. In the event that the established fee status is inappropriate for a client, assistance must be provided in finding comparable services at acceptable cost.

**6.** Certified counselors offer only professional services for which they are trained or have supervised experience. No diagnosis, assessment, or treatment should be performed without prior training or supervision. Certified counselors are responsible for correcting any misrepresentations of their qualifications by others.

**7.** Certified counselors recognize their limitations and provide services or use techniques for which they are qualified by training and/or supervision. Certified counselors recognize the need for and seek continuing education to assure competent services.

**8.** Certified counselors are aware of the intimacy in the counseling relationship and maintain respect for the client. Counselors must not engage in activities that seek to meet their personal or professional needs at the expense of the client.

**9.** Certified counselors must insure that they do not engage in personal, social, organizational, financial, or political activities which might lead to a misuse of their influence.

**10.** Sexual intimacy with clients is unethical. Certified counselors will not be sexually, physically, or romantically intimate with clients, and they will not engage in sexual, physical, or romantic intimacy with clients within a minimum of two years after terminating the counseling relationship.

**11.** Certified counselors do not condone or engage in sexual harassment, which is defined as unwelcome comments, gestures, or physical contact of a sexual nature.

**12.** Through an awareness of the impact of stereotyping and unwarranted discrimination (e.g., biases based on age, disability, ethnicity, gender, race, religion, or sexual orientation), certified counselors guard the individual rights and personal dignity of the client in the counseling relationship.

**13.** Certified counselors are accountable at all times for their behavior. They must be aware that all actions and behaviors of the counselor reflect on professional integrity and, when inappropriate, can damage the public trust in the counseling profession. To protect public confidence in the counseling profession, certified counselors avoid behavior that is clearly in violation of accepted moral and legal standards.

**14.** Products or services provided by certified counselors by means of classroom instruction, public lectures, demonstrations, written articles, radio or television programs or other types of media must meet the criteria cited in this code.

**15.** Certified counselors have an obligation to withdraw from the practice of counseling if they violate the Code of Ethics, or if the mental or physical condition of the certified counselor renders it unlikely that a professional relationship will be maintained.

# Section B: Counseling Relationship

**1.** The primary obligation of certified counselors is to respect the integrity and promote the welfare of clients, whether they are assisted individually, in family units, or in group counseling. In a group setting, the certified counselor is also responsible for taking reasonable precautions to protect individuals from physical and/or psychological trauma resulting from interaction within the group.

**2.** Certified counselors know and take into account the traditions and practices of other professional disciplines with whom they work and cooperate fully with such. If a person is receiving similar services from another professional, certified counselors do not offer their own services directly to such a person. If a certified counselor is contacted by a person who is already receiving similar services from another professional, the certified counselor carefully considers that professional relationship as well as the client's welfare and proceeds with caution and sensitivity to the therapeutic issues. When certified counselors learn that their clients are in a professional relationship with another counselor or mental health professional, they request release from the clients to inform the other counselor or mental health professional of their relationship with the client and strive to establish positive and collaborative professional relationships that are in the best interest of the client. Certified counselors discuss these issues with clients and the counselor or professional so as to minimize the risk of confusion and conflict and encourage clients to inform other professionals of the new professional relationship.

**3.** Certified counselors may choose to consult with any other professionally competent person about a client and must notify clients of this right. Certified counselors avoid placing a consultant in a conflict-of-interest situation that would preclude the consultant serving as a proper party to the efforts of the certified counselor to help the client.

**4.** When a client's condition indicates that there is a clear and imminent danger to the client or others, the certified counselor must take reasonable action to inform potential victims and/or inform responsible authorities. Consultation with other professionals must be used when possible. The assumption of responsibility for the client's behavior must be taken only after careful deliberation, and the client must be involved in the resumption of responsibility as quickly as possible.

**5.** Records of the counseling relationship, including interview notes, test data, correspondence, audio or visual tape recordings, electronic data storage, and other documents are to be considered professional information for use in counseling. Records should contain accurate factual data. The physical records are property of the certified counselors or their employers. The information contained in the records belongs to the client and therefore may not be released to others without the consent of the client or when the counselor has exhausted challenges to a court order. The certified counselors are responsible to insure that their employees handle confidential information appropriately. Confidentiality must be maintained during the storage and disposition of records. Records should be maintained for a period of at least five (5) years after the last counselor/client contact, including cases in which the client is deceased. All records must be released to the client upon request.

**6.** Certified counselors must ensure that data maintained in electronic storage are secure. By using the best computer security methods available, the data must be limited to information that is appropriate and necessary for the services being provided and accessible only to appropriate staff members involved in the provision of services. Certified counselors must also ensure that the electronically stored data are destroyed when the information is no longer of value in providing services or required as part of clients' records.

**7.** Any data derived from a client relationship and used in training or research shall be so disguised that the informed client's identity is fully protected. Any data which cannot be so disguised may be used only as expressly authorized by the client's informed and uncoerced consent.

**8.** When counseling is initiated, and throughout the counseling process as necessary, counselors inform clients of the purposes, goals, techniques, procedures, limitations, potential risks and benefits of services to be performed, and clearly indicate limitations that may affect the relationship as well as any other pertinent information. Counselors take reasonable steps to ensure that clients understand the implications of any diagnosis, the intended use of tests and reports, methods of treatment and safety precautions that must be taken in their use, fees, and billing arrangements.

**9.** Certified counselors who have an administrative, supervisory and/or evaluative relationship with individuals seeking counseling services must not serve as the counselor and should refer the individuals to other professionals. Exceptions are made only in instances where an individual's situation warrants counseling intervention and another alternative is unavailable. Dual relationships that might impair the certified counselor's objectivity and professional judgment must be avoided and/or the counseling relationship terminated through referral to a competent professional.

**10.** When certified counselors determine an inability to be of professional assistance to a potential or existing client, they must, respectively, not initiate the counseling relationship or immediately terminate the relationship. In either event, the certified counselor must suggest appropriate alternatives. Certified counselors must be knowledgeable about referral resources so that a satisfactory referral can be initiated. In the event that the client declines a suggested referral, the certified counselor is not obligated to continue the relationship.

**11.** When certified counselors are engaged in intensive, short-term counseling, they must ensure that professional assistance is available at normal costs to clients during and following the short-term counseling.

**12.** Counselors using electronic means in which counselor and client are not in immediate proximity must present clients with local sources of care before establishing a continued short or long-term relationship. Counselors who communicate with clients via Internet are governed by NBCC standards for Web Counseling.

**13.** Counselors must document permission to practice counseling by electronic means in all governmental jurisdictions where such counseling takes place.

**14.** When electronic data and systems are used as a component of counseling services, certified counselors must ensure that the computer application, and any information it contains, is appropriate for the respective needs of clients and is non-discriminatory. Certified counselors must ensure that they themselves have acquired a facilitation level of knowledge with any system they use including hands-on application, and understanding of the uses of all aspects of the computer-based system. In selecting and/or maintaining computer-based systems that contain career information, counselors must ensure that the system provides current, accurate, and locally relevant information. Certified counselors must also ensure that clients are intellectually, emotionally, and physically compatible with computer applications and understand their purpose and operation. Client use of a computer application must be evaluated to correct possible problems and assess subsequent needs.

**15.** Certified counselors who develop self-help/stand-alone computer software for use by the general public, must first ensure that it is designed to function in a stand-alone manner that is appropriate and safe for all clients for which it is intended. A manual is required. The manual must provide the user with intended outcomes, suggestions for using the software, descriptions of inappropriately used applications, and descriptions of when and how other forms of counseling services might be beneficial. Finally, the manual must include the qualifications of the developer, the development process, validation date, and operating procedures.

**16.** The counseling relationship and information resulting from it remains confidential, consistent with the legal and ethical obligations of certified counselors. In group counseling, counselors clearly define confidentiality and the parameters for the specific group being entered, explain the importance of confidentiality, and discuss the difficulties related to confidentiality involved in group work. The fact that confidentiality cannot be guaranteed is clearly communicated to group members. However, counselors should give assurance about their professional responsibility to keep all group communications confidential.

**17.** Certified counselors must screen prospective group counseling participants to ensure compatibility with group objectives. This is especially important when the emphasis is on self-understanding and growth through self-disclosure. Certified counselors must maintain an awareness of the welfare of each participant throughout the group process.

## Section C: Measurement and Evaluation

**1.** Because many types of assessment techniques exist, certified counselors must recognize the limits of their competence and perform only those assessment functions for which they have received appropriate training or supervision.

**2.** Certified counselors who utilize assessment instruments to assist them with diagnoses must have appropriate training and skills in educational and psychological measurement, validation criteria, test research, and guidelines for test development and use.

**3.** Certified counselors must provide instrument specific orientation or information to an examinee prior to and following the administration of assessment instruments or techniques so that the results may be placed in proper perspective with other relevant factors. The purpose of testing and the explicit use of the results must be made known to an examinee prior to testing.

**4.** In selecting assessment instruments or techniques for use in a given situation or with a particular client, certified counselors must carefully evaluate the specific theoretical bases and characteristics, validity, reliability and appropriateness of the instrument.

**5.** When making statements to the public about assessment instruments or techniques, certified counselors must provide accurate information and avoid false claims or misconceptions concerning the meaning of the instrument's reliability and validity terms.

**6.** Counselors must follow all directions and researched procedures for selection, administration and interpretation of all evaluation instruments and use them only within proper contexts.

**7.** Certified counselors must be cautious when interpreting the results of instruments that possess insufficient technical data, and must explicitly state to examinees the specific limitations and purposes for the use of such instruments.

**8.** Certified counselors must proceed with caution when attempting to evaluate and interpret performances of any person who cannot be appropriately compared to the norms for the instrument.

**9.** Because prior coaching or dissemination of test materials can invalidate test results, certified counselors are professionally obligated to maintain test security.

**10.** Certified counselors must consider psychometric limitations when selecting and using an instrument, and must be cognizant of the limitations when interpreting the results. When tests are used to classify clients, certified counselors must ensure that periodic review and/or retesting are made to prevent client stereotyping.

**11.** An examinee's welfare, explicit prior understanding, and consent are the factors used when determining who receives the test results. Certified counselors must see that appropriate interpretation accompanies any release of individual or group test data (e.g., limitations of instrument and norms).

**12.** Certified counselors must ensure that computer-generated test administration and scoring programs function properly thereby providing clients with accurate test results.

**13.** Certified counselors who develop computer-based test interpretations to support the assessment process must ensure that the validity of the interpretations is established prior to the commercial distribution of the computer application.

**14.** Certified counselors recognize that test results may become obsolete, and avoid the misuse of obsolete data.

**15.** Certified counselors must not appropriate, reproduce, or modify published tests or parts thereof without acknowledgment and permission from the publisher, except as permitted by the fair educational use provisions of the U.S. copyright law.

## Section D: Research and Publication

**1.** Certified counselors will adhere to applicable legal and professional guidelines on research with human subjects.

**2.** In planning research activities involving human subjects, certified counselors must be aware of and responsive to all pertinent ethical principles and ensure that the research problem, design, and execution are in full compliance with any pertinent institutional or governmental regulations.

**3.** The ultimate responsibility for ethical research lies with the principal researcher, although others involved in the research activities are ethically obligated and responsible for their own actions.

**4.** Certified counselors who conduct research with human subjects are responsible for the welfare of the subjects throughout the experiment and must take all reasonable precautions to avoid causing injurious psychological, physical, or social effects on their subjects.

**5.** Certified counselors who conduct research must abide by the basic elements of informed consent:

    **a.** fair explanation of the procedures to be followed, including an identification of those which are experimental

    **b.** description of the attendant discomforts and risks

    **c.** description of the benefits to be expected

    **d.** disclosure of appropriate alternative procedures that would be advantageous for subjects with an offer to answer any inquiries concerning the procedures

    **e.** an instruction that subjects are free to withdraw their consent and to discontinue participation in the project or activity at any time

**6.** When reporting research results, explicit mention must be made of all the variables and conditions known to the investigator that may have affected the outcome of the study or the interpretation of the data.

**7.** Certified counselors who conduct and report research investigations must do so in a manner that minimizes the possibility that the results will be misleading.

**8.** Certified counselors are obligated to make available sufficient original research data to qualified others who may wish to replicate the study.

**9.** Certified counselors who supply data, aid in the research of another person, report research results, or make original data available, must take due care to disguise the identity of respective subjects in the absence of specific authorization from the subjects to do otherwise.

**10.** When conducting and reporting research, certified counselors must be familiar with and give recognition to previous work on the topic, must observe all copyright laws, and must follow the principles of giving full credit to those to whom credit is due.

**11.** Certified counselors must give due credit through joint authorship, acknowledgment, footnote statements, or other appropriate means to those who have contributed to the research and/or publication, in accordance with such contributions.

**12.** Certified counselors should communicate to other counselors the results of any research judged to be of professional value. Results that reflect unfavorably on institutions, programs, services, or vested interests must not be withheld.

**13.** Certified counselors who agree to cooperate with another individual in research and/or publication incur an obligation to cooperate as promised in terms of punctuality of performance and with full regard to the completeness and accuracy of the information required.

**14.** Certified counselors must not submit the same manuscript, or one essentially similar in content, for simultaneous publication consideration by two or more journals. In addition, manuscripts that have been published in whole or substantial part should not be submitted for additional publication without acknowledgment and permission from any previous publisher.

## Section E: Consulting

Consultation refers to a voluntary relationship between a professional helper and a help-needing individual, group, or social unit in which the consultant is providing help to the client(s) in defining and solving a work-related problem or potential work-related problem with a client or client system.

**1.** Certified counselors, acting as consultants, must have a high degree of self awareness of their own values, knowledge, skills, limitations, and needs in entering a helping relationship that involves human and/or organizational change. The focus of the consulting relationship must be on the issues to be resolved and not on the person(s) presenting the problem.

**2.** In the consulting relationship, the certified counselor and client must understand and agree upon the problem definition, subsequent goals, and predicted consequences of interventions selected.

**3.** Certified counselors acting as consultants must be reasonably certain that they, or the organization represented, have the necessary competencies and resources for giving the kind of help that is needed or that may develop later, and that appropriate referral resources are available.

**4.** Certified counselors in a consulting relationship must encourage and cultivate client adaptability and growth toward self-direction. Certified counselors must maintain this role consistently and not become a decision maker for clients or create a future dependency on the consultant.

## Section F: Private Practice

**1.** In advertising services as a private practitioner, certified counselors must advertise in a manner that accurately informs the public of the professional services, expertise, and techniques of counseling available.

**2.** Certified counselors who assume an executive leadership role in a private practice organization do not permit their names to be used in professional notices during periods of time when they are not actively engaged in the private practice of counseling unless their executive roles are clearly stated.

**3.** Certified counselors must make available their highest degree (described by discipline), type and level of certification and/or license, address, telephone number, office hours, type and/or description of services,

and other relevant information. Listed information must not contain false, inaccurate, misleading, partial, out-of-context, or otherwise deceptive material or statements.

**4.** Certified counselors who are involved in a partnership/corporation with other certified counselors and/or other professionals, must clearly specify all relevant specialties of each member of the partnership or corporation.

## Appendix: Certification Examination

Applicants for the NBCC Certification Examinations must have fulfilled all current eligibility requirements, and are responsible for the accuracy and validity of all information and/or materials provided by themselves or by others for fulfillment of eligibility criteria.

Approved on July 1, 1982

Amended on February 21, 1987, January 6, 1989, and October 31, 1997

### Acknowledgment

Reference documents, statements, and sources for the development of the NBCC Code of Ethics were as follows: The Ethical Standards of the American Counseling Association (ACA), Responsible Uses for Standardized Testing (AMECD), codes of ethics for the American Psychological Association, and the National Career Development Association, Handbook of Standards for Computer-Based Career Information Systems (ACSCI); and Guidelines for the Use of Computer-Based Career Information and Guidance Systems (ACSCI).

# Appendix C

# National Board for Certified Counselors Standards for the Ethical Practice of Clinical Supervision

In addition to following the NBCC Code of Ethics pertaining to the practice of professional counseling, clinical supervisors shall:

1. Ensure that supervisees inform clients of their professional status (e.g., intern) and of all conditions of supervision.

   Supervisors need to ensure that supervisees inform their clients of any status other than being fully qualified for independent practice or licensed. For example, supervisees need to inform their clients if they are a student, intern, trainee or, if licensed with restrictions, the nature of those restrictions (e.g., associate or conditional). In addition, clients must be informed of the requirements of supervision (e.g., the audiotaping of all counseling sessions for purposes of supervision).

2. Ensure that clients have been informed of their rights to confidentiality and privileged communication when applicable. Clients also should be informed of the limits of confidentiality and privileged communication.

   The general limits of confidentiality are when harm to self or others is threatened; when the abuse of children, elders or disabled persons is suspected and in cases when the court compels the counselor to testify and break confidentiality. These are generally accepted limits to confidentiality and privileged communication, but they may be modified by state or federal statute.

3. Inform supervisees about the process of supervision, including supervision goals, case management procedures, and the supervisor's preferred supervision model(s).

4. Keep and secure supervision records and consider all information gained in supervision as confidential.

5. Avoid all dual relationships with supervisees that may interfere with the supervisor's professional judgment or exploit the supervisee.

   Although all dual relationships are not in of themselves inappropriate, any sexual relationship is considered to be a violation. Sexual relationship means sexual contact, sexual harassment, or sexual bias toward a supervisee by a supervisor.

6. Establish procedures with their supervisees for handling crisis situations.

7. Provide supervisees with adequate and timely feedback as part of an established evaluation plan.

8. Render assistance to any supervisee who is unable to provide competent counseling services to clients.

9. Intervene in any situation where the supervisee is impaired and the client is at risk.

10. Refrain from endorsing an impaired supervisee when such impairment deems it unlikely that the supervisee can provide adequate counseling services.

11. Refrain from offering supervision outside of their area(s) of competence.

12. Ensure that supervisees are aware of the current ethical standards related to their professional practice, as well as legal standards that regulate the practice of counseling.

Current ethical standards would mean standards published by the National Board for Certified Counselors (NBCC) and other appropriate entities such as the American Counseling Association (ACA). In addition, it is the supervisor's responsibility to ensure that the supervisee is aware that state and federal laws might regulate the practice of counseling and to inform the supervisee of key laws that affect counseling in the supervisee's jurisdiction.

13. Engage supervisees in an examination of cultural issues that might affect supervision and/or counseling.

14. Ensure that both supervisees and clients are aware of their rights and of due process procedures.

Adopted by the NBCC Board of Directors: June 12, 1998.

## Appendix D

# *National Board for Certified Counselors Standards for the Ethical Practice of WebCounseling*

The relative newness of the use of the Internet for service and product delivery leaves authors of standards at a loss when beginning to create ethical practices on the Internet. This document, like all codes of conduct, will change as information and circumstances not yet foreseen evolve. However, each version of this code of ethics is the current best standard of conduct passed by the NBCC Board of Directors. As with any code, and especially with a code such as this, created for an evolving field of work, NBCC and CCE welcome comments and ideas for further discussion and inclusion.

Further, the development of these WebCounseling standards has been guided by the following principles:

These standards are intended to address practices which are unique to WebCounseling and WebCounselors,

These standards are not to duplicate non-Internet-based standards adopted in other codes of ethics,

Recognizing that significant new technology emerges continuously, these standards should be reviewed frequently,

WebCounseling ethics cases should be reviewed in light of delivery systems existing at the moment rather than at the time the standards were adopted.

WebCounselors who are not National Certified Counselors may indicate at their WebSite their adherence to these standards, but may not publish these standards in their entirety without written permission of the National Board for Certified Counselors.

The *Practice of WebCounseling* shall be defined as "the practice of professional counseling and information delivery that occurs when client(s) and counselor are in separate or remote locations and utilize electronic means to communicate over the Internet".

In addition to following the NBCC Code of Ethics pertaining to the practice of professional counseling, WebCounselors shall:

1. review pertinent legal and ethical codes for possible violations emanating from the practice of WebCounseling and supervision.

   Liability insurance policies should also be reviewed to determine if the practice of Web-Counseling is a covered activity. Local, state, provincial, and national statutes as well as the codes of professional membership organizations, professional certifying bodies and state or provincial licensing boards need to be reviewed. Also, as no definitive answers are known to questions pertaining to whether WebCounseling takes place in the WebCounselor's location or the WebClient's location, WebCounselors should consider carefully local customs regarding age of consent and child abuse reporting.

2. inform WebClients of encryption methods being used to help insure the security of client/counselor/supervisor communications.

   Encryption methods should be used whenever possible. If encryption is not made available to clients, clients must be informed of the potential hazards of unsecured communication on the Internet. Hazards may include authorized or unauthorized monitoring of transmissions and/or records of WebCounseling sessions.

3. inform clients if, how and how long session data are being preserved.

   Session data may include WebCounselor/WebClient e-mail, test results, audio/video session recordings, session notes, and counselor/supervisor communications. The likelihood of electronic sessions being preserved is greater because of the ease and decreased costs involved in recording. Thus, its potential use in supervision, research and legal proceedings increases.

4. in situations where it is difficult to verify the identity of WebCounselor or WebClient, take steps to address impostor concerns, such as by using code words, numbers, or graphics.

5. when parent/guardian consent is required to provide WebCounseling to minors, verify the identity of the consenting person.

6. follow appropriate procedures regarding the release of information for sharing WebClient information with other electronic sources.

   Because of the relative ease with which e-mail messages can be forwarded to formal and casual referral sources, WebCounselors must work to insure the confidentiality of the Web-Counseling relationship.

7. carefully consider the extent of self disclosure presented to the WebClient and provide rationale for WebCounselor's level of disclosure.

   WebCounselors may wish to ensure that, minimally, the WebClient has the same data available about his/her service provider as would be available if the counseling were to take place face to face (i.e., possibly ethnicity, gender, etc.). Compelling reasons for limiting disclosure should be presented. WebCounselors will remember to protect themselves from unscrupulous users of the Internet by limiting potentially harmful disclosure about self and family.

8. provide links to websites of all appropriate certification bodies and licensure boards to facilitate consumer protection.

9. contact NBCC/CEE or the WebClient's state or provincial licensing board to obtain the name of at least one Counselor-On-Call within the WebClient's geographical region.

   WebCounselors who have contacted an individual to determine his or her willingness to serve as a Counselor-On-Call (either in person, over the phone or via e-mail) should also ensure that the WebClient is provided with Local crisis intervention hotline numbers, 911 and similar numbers in the event that the Counselor-On-Call is unavailable.

10. discuss with their WebClients procedures for contacting the WebCounselor when he or she is off-line.

    This means explaining exactly how often e-mail messages are to be checked by the WebCounselor.

11. mention at their websites those presenting problems they believe to be inappropriate for Web-Counseling.

    While no conclusive research has been conducted to date, those topics might include: sexual abuse as a primary issue, violent relationships, eating disorders, and psychiatric disorders that involve distortions of reality.

12. explain to clients the possibility of technology failure.

The WebCounselor

- gives instructions to WebClients about calling if problems arise,

- discusses the appropriateness of the client calling collect when the call might be originating from around the world,

- mentions differences in time zones,

- talks about dealing with response delays in sending and receiving e-mail messages

13. explain to clients how to cope with potential misunderstandings arising from the lack of visual cues from WebCounselor or WebClient.

> For example, suggesting the other person simply say, "Because I couldn't see your face or hear your tone of voice in your e-mail message, I'm not sure how to interpret that last message."

# Appendix E

# Important Websites

**Codes of Ethics**
**American Counseling Association (ACA)—Code of Ethics and Standards of Practice**
www.counseling.org/resources/codeofethics.htm

**American School Counselor Association (ASCA)—Code of Ethics**
www.schoolcounselor.org/ethicsmain.html
www.schoolcounselor.org/ethicstd.html

**National Association of Social Workers (NASW)—Code of Ethics**
www.naswdc.org/code.htm

**National Board for Certified Counselors (NBCC)**
www.nbcc.org/ethics/wcstandards.htm

**National Career Development Association (NCDA)**
ncda.org/polethic.html

**National Career Development Association (NCDA) Guidelines for the Use of the Internet for Provision of Career Information and Planning Services**
ncda.org/polweb.html

**State Licensure**
**State Credentialing Boards**
www.nbcc.org/states/boards.htm

**National Counselor Certification**
**National Board for Certified Counselors (NBCC)**
www.nbcc.org

**Spirituality**
**Center for Spirituality & Psychotherapy**
www.psychospiritualtherapy.com

**National Institute for Healthcare Research (NIHR)**
www.nihr.org

**Psychotherapy & Spirituality Institute**
www.mindspirit.org

**Training Program Accreditation**
**American Association for Marriage and Family Therapy (AAMFT) Program Accreditation**
www.aamft.org

**Council for Accreditation of Counseling and Related Educational Programs (CACREP)**
couseling.org/CACREP/main.htm

**CACREP Directory of Accredited Preparation Programs**
www.counseling.org/CACREP/directory/htm

**Council on Social Work Education (CSWE)—MSW Program Accreditation**
www.cswe.org/mswcps.htm

**Graduate Psychology Program Accreditation**
www.apa.org/ed/accrfaq.htm

# References

Academic Senate for California Community Colleges. (1997). *Standards of practice for California Community College Counseling Programs.* Sacramento, CA: Author.

Ainsworth, M. (1997, April). *Metanoia Guide to Internet Mental Health Services.* www.metanoia.org/imhs

Ainsworth, M. (1999). *Choose a competent counselor: A consumer's guide.* www.metanoia.org/imhs/gethelpl.htm

American Association of Counseling and Development (AACD). (1980). Licensure committee action packet. Falls Church, VA: APGA Publications.

American College Counseling Association. (1991). *Advocating for college counseling: A public service announcement providing information about college counseling.* [Brochure]. Alexandria, VA: Author.

American Counseling Association. (1995). *Code of ethics and standards of practice.* Alexandria, VA: Author.

American Counseling Association. (1997). *Effective advocacy and communication with legislators.* [Brochure]. Office of Public Policy and Information. Alexandria, VA: Author.

American Psychological Association. (1995, July). *Services by telephone, teleconferences, and Internet.* A statement by the ethics committee of the American Psychological Association. www.apa.org/ethics/stmnt01.html Also published in *APA Monitor,* July 16, 1995.

American School Counselor Association (ASCA). (1981). The practice of guidance and counseling by school counselors. *School Counselor, 29,* 7–12.

American School Counselor Association (ASCA). (1998). *Ethical standards for school counselors,* revised June 25, 1998. www.schoolcounselor.org/Ethics/ethicstd.html

Arambula, D., DeKraai, M., & Sales, B. (1993). Law, children, and therapists. In T. R. Kratochwill & R. J. Morris (Eds.), *Handbook of psychotherapy with children and adolescents* (pp. 583–619). Boston: Allyn and Bacon.

Arent, Fox, Kintner, Plotkin, & Kahn (1997, August). *State telemedicine legislation* [Annotated bibliography of World Wide Web links to state legislation]. www.arentfox.com/telemed/telemed.sta.html

Arthur, G. L., & Swanson, C. D. (1993). In T. P. Remley, Jr. (Ed.), *Confidentiality and privileged communication. The ACA legal series: Vol. 6.* Alexandria, VA: American Counseling Association.

Aubrey, R. F. (1977). Historical development of guidance and counseling and implications for the future. *Personnel and Guidance Journal, 55,* 288–295.

Aubrey, R. F. (1986). The professionalization of counseling. In M. D. Lewis, R. L. Hayes, & J. A. Lewis (Eds.), *An introduction to the counseling profession.* Itasca, IL: Peacock.

Baker, S. (1996). Recollections of the boom era in school counseling. *The School Counselor, 43,* 163–164.

Barret, R. L. (1995). The spiritual journey: Explorations and implications for counselors. In M. T. Burke & J. G. Miranti (Eds.), *Counseling: The spiritual dimension* (pp. 103–111). Alexandria, VA: ASERVIC/ACA. [Originally published in *Journal of Humanistic Education and Development, 26,* 154–163.]

Baruth, L. G., & Robinson, E. H., III (1987). *An introduction to the counseling profession.* Upper Saddle River, NJ: Prentice Hall.

Bauman, W. F. (1972). Games counselor trainees play: Dealing with trainee resistance. *Counselor Education and Supervision, 11,* 251–256.

Beauchamp, T. L., & Childress, J. F. (1995). *Principles of biomedical ethics* (4th ed.). New York: Oxford University Press.

Beers, C. (1908). *A mind that found itself.* New York: Longman Green.

Brueske, L. E. (1998, Winter). Specialties: A growing issue. *The National Certified Counselor, 15,* 1, 3.

Belger, A. L. (1997). Legal issues in professional practice with families. In D. T. Marsh & R. D. Magee (Eds.), *Ethical and legal issues in professional practice with families* (pp. 27–49). New York: Wiley.

Bergin, A. E. (1992). Three contributions of a spiritual perspective to counseling, psychotherapy, and behavior change. Reprinted in M. T. Burke & J. G. Miranti (Eds.), *Ethical and spiritual values in counseling* (pp. 5–15). Alexandria, VA: ARVIC/AACD.

Bernard, J. M. (1979). Supervisor training: A discrimination model. *Counselor Education and Supervision, 19*, 60–68.

Bernard, J. M. (1993). Why tape? *Dialog*, pp. 5–12.

Bernard, J. M. (1997). The discrimination model. In C. E. Watkins, Jr. (Ed.), *Handbook of psychotherapy supervision* (pp. 310–327). New York: Wiley.

Bernard, J. M. (1999). Receiving and using supervision. In H. Hackney & L. S. Cormier, *Counseling strategies and interventions* (5th ed., pp. 163–180). Boston: Allyn and Bacon.

Bernard, J. M., & Goodyear, R. K. (1998). *Fundamentals of clinical supervision* (2nd ed.). Boston: Allyn and Bacon.

Bersoff, D. N. (1996). The virtue of principle ethics. *The Counseling Psychologist, 24* (1), 86–91.

Bertalanffy, L. von (1968). *General systems theory: Foundations, development, application*. New York: Braziller.

Bertram, B., & Wheeler, A. M. (1995). *Legal aspects of counseling: Avoiding lawsuits and legal problems.* Materials presented at ACA seminar. Alexandria, VA: American Counseling Association.

Berube, M. S., et al. (Eds.). (1982). *American heritage dictionary* (2nd college ed.). Boston: Houghton Mifflin.

Bloom, J. W., & Sampson, J. P., Jr. (1998a). *Preliminary results of an Internet mental health practice survey.* Unpublished paper, Bilateral Forum on Internet Mental Health Practice. www.nbcc.org

Bloom, J. W., & Sampson, J. P., Jr. (1998b). *Core standards for Internet mental health practice.* Unpublished paper, National Board for Certified Counselors. www.nbcc.org

Bongar, B., Berman, A. L., Maris, R. W., Silverman, M. M., Harris, E. A., & Packman, W. L. (Eds.). (1998). *Risk management with suicidal patients.* New York: Guilford.

Borders, L. D. (1990). Developmental changes during supervisees' first practicum. *The Clinical Supervisor, 8* (2), 157–167.

Borders, L. D., Bernard, J. M., Dye, H. A., Fong, M. L., Henderson, P., & Nance, D. W. (1991). Curriculum guide for training counseling supervisors: Rationale, development, and implementation. *Counselor Education and Supervision, 31,* 58–82.

Borders, L. D., Cashwell, C. S., & Rotter, J. C. (1995). Supervision of counselor licensure applicants: A comparative study. *Counselor Education and Supervision, 35,* 54–69.

Borders, L. D., & Usher, C. H. (1992). Post-degree supervision: Existing and preferred practices. *Journal of Counseling and Development, 70,* 594–599.

Bordin, E. S. (1983). A working alliance model of supervision. *The Counseling Psychologist, 11,* 35–42.

Breasure, J. (1995, November 13). Personal communication.

Brewer, J. M. (1932). *Education as guidance.* New York: Macmillan.

Brief of Amicus Curiae American Counseling Association in Support of Respondents, *Jaffee* v. *Redmond*, 518 U.S. 1 (1996). No. 95-266.

Brooks, D. K., Jr. (1986). Credentialing of mental health counselors. In A. J. Palmo & W. J. Weikal (Eds.), *Foundations of mental health counselings* (pp. 243–262). Springfield, IL: Charles Thomas.

Brooks, D. K., Jr., & Gerstein, L. H. (1990). Counselor credentialing and interprofessional collaboration. *Journal of Counseling and Development, 68* (5), 477–484.

Brown, D., & Srebalus, D. J. (1996). *Introduction to the counseling profession* (2nd ed.). Boston: Allyn and Bacon.

Brown, H. P., Jr., & Peterson, J. H., Jr. (1991). Assessing spirituality in addiction treatment and follow-up: Development of the Brown-Peterson Recovery Progress Inventory (B-PRPI). *Alcoholism Treatment Quarterly, 8* (2), 21–50.

Brown, N. W. (1997). Report on hearings of ethical and legal violations for licensed professional counselors and certified substance abuse counselors, 1994–1996. *Virginia Counselors Journal, 25,* 72–80.

Bryson, M. B. (1997). Note: Protecting confidential communications between a psychotherapist and patient: *Jaffee* v. *Redmond. Catholic University Law Review, 46,* 963–1004.

Buffone, G. W. (1991). Understanding and managing the litigious patient. *Psychotherapy in Private Practice, 9* (2), 27–45.

Burke, M. T. (1998, Winter). From the Chair. *CACREP Connection,* p. 2.

Burke, M. T., & Miranti, J. G. (Eds.). (1992). *Ethical and spiritual values in counseling.* Alexandria, VA: ARVIC.

Burke, M. T., & Miranti, J. G. (Eds.). (1995). *Counseling: The spiritual dimension.* Alexandria, VA: ASERVIC/ACA.

*Canterbury* v. *Spence*, 464 F.2d 772 (D.C. Cir. 1972), *cert. denied*, 409 U.S. 1064 (1972).

Cayne, B. S., et al. (Eds.). (1987). *Encyclopedia Americana, international edition* (Vol. 14). Danbury, CT: Grolier.

Chandler, C. K., Holden, J. M., & Kolander, C. A. (1992). Counseling for spiritual wellness: Theory and practice. *Journal of Counseling and Development, 71,* 168–175.

Chauvin, J. C., & Remley, T. P. (1996). Responding to allegations of unethical conduct. *Journal of Counseling and Development, 74,* 563–568.

Cohen, E. D. (1990). Confidentiality, counseling and clients who have AIDS: Ethical foundations of a model rule. *Journal of Counseling and Development, 68,* 282–286.

Cohen, G., & Kerr, B. (in press). Computer-mediated counseling: An empirical study of a new mental health treatment. *Computers in Human Services.*

Colon, Y. (1996). Chatter(er)ing through the fingertips: Doing group therapy online. *Women and Performance: A Journal of Feminist Theory, 9,* 205–215.

Colorado State University, Department of Human Development and Family Studies. (1998). Graduate Sample Programs. Fort Collins, CO.www.colostate. edu/Depts/HDFS/admiss/grad/samples. html#therapy

Commission on Rehabilitation Counselor Certification. (1995). *Code of professional ethics for certified rehabilitation counselors.* Chicago, IL: Author.

Committee on Psychiatry and Law, Group for the Advancement of Psychiatry. (1991). *The mental health professional and the legal system.* New York: Brunner/Mazel.

*Consumer Reports.* (1996, January). Letter to the editor, p. 4.

Cook, D. A. (1994). Racial identity in supervision. *Counselor Education and Supervision, 34,* 132–141.

Cook, E. P. (1993). The gender context of life: Implications for women's and men's career-life plans. *Career Development Quarterly, 41,* 227–237.

Corey, G., Corey, M. S., & Callahan, P. (1993). *Issues and ethics in the helping professions* (4th ed.). Pacific Grove, CA: Brooks/Cole.

Corey, G., Corey, M. S., & Callahan, P. (1998). *Issues and ethics in the helping profession* (5th ed.). Pacific Grove, CA: Brooks/Cole.

Corey, G., Williams, G. T., & Moline, M. E. (1995). Ethical and legal issues in group counseling. *Ethics & Behavior, 5* (2), 161–183.

Cormier, W. H., & Cormier, L. S. (1985). *Interviewing strategies for helpers* (2nd ed.). Monterey, CA: Brooks/Cole.

Cottone, R. R., & Tarvydas, V. (1998). *Ethical and professional issues in counseling.* Upper Saddle River, NJ: Merrill.

Council for Accreditation of Counseling and Related Educational Programs. (1996). *CACREP accreditation standards and procedures manual* (rev. ed.). Alexandria, VA: Author.

Council for Accreditation of Counseling and Related Educational Programs. (1998). *The 2001 standards—Draft 2.* Alexandria, VA: Author.

Council on Social Work Education Accreditation Standards. (1998). *Standards, curriculum policy, fees and dues, resources.* Alexandria, VA. www.cswe.org

Covin, T. M. (1994, February). Freedom of choice and advocacy. *AMHCA Advocate.* Alexandria, VA.

Craig, C. H., & Sleight, C. C. (1990). Personality relationships between supervisors and students in communication disorders as determined by the Myers-Briggs Type Indicator. *The Clinical Supervisor, 8* (1), 41–51.

Crawford, R. L. (1994). In T. P. Remley, Jr. (Ed.), *Avoiding counselor malpractice. The ACA legal series: Vol. 12.* Alexandra, VA: American Counseling Association.

Crenshaw, W. B., Lichtenberg, J. W., & Bartell, P. A. (1993). Mental health providers and child sexual abuse: A multivariate analysis of the decision to report. *Journal of Child Sexual Abuse, 2* (4), 19–42.

Cummings, A. L., Hallberg, E. T., Martin, J., Slemon, A., & Hiebert, B. (1990). Implications of counselor conceptualizations for counselor education. *Counselor Education and Supervision, 30,* 120–134.

Cummings, N. A. (1995). Impact of managed care of employment and training: A primer for survival. *Professional Psychology: Research and Practice, 26,* 10–15.

Curran, D. (1983). *Traits of a healthy family.* New York: Ballantine Books.

Davis, H. V. (1988). *Frank Parsons: Prophet, innovator, counselor.* Carbondale: University of Southern Illinois Press.

Davis, M. S. (1997). *Telecounseling: The use of computer mediated communication in the counseling process.* Unpublished report.

Denton, D. D., Jr. (1998). *Religious diagnosis in a secular society: A staff for the journey.* Lanham, MD: University Press of America.

Disney, M. J., & Stephens, A. M. (1994). *Legal issues in clinical supervision.* Alexandria, VA: ACA Press.

Drummond, R. J., & Ryan, C. W. (1995). *Career counseling: A developmental approach.* Upper Saddle River, NJ: Prentice Hall.

Egan, G. (1990). *The skilled helper: A systematic approach to effective helping* (4th ed.). Pacific Grove, CA: Brooks/Cole.

Ellison, C. W. (1994). *Spiritual Well-Being Scale.* Nyack, NY: Life Advance.

Emerson, P. (1996). Will other state boards accept my counseling credential?: Reciprocity revisited. (CASS Capsule CG-96-4). Greensboro, NC: ERIC Clearinghouse on Counseling and Student Services. (ERIC Document Reproduction Service No. ED 399498)

Erickson, S. H. (1993). Ethics and confidentiality in AIDS counseling: A professional dilemma. *Journal of Mental Health Counseling, 15,* 118–131.

Eriksen, K. (1997). *Making an impact: A handbook on counselor advocacy.* Washington, DC: Accelerated Development.

Fall, M., & Sutton, J. M., Jr. (1999). *Current practices of the supervision of conditionally licensed counselors.* Manuscript in preparation.

Family Educational Rights and Privacy Act, 20 U.S.C. □ 1232g (1974).

Farran, C. J., Fitchett, G., Quiring-Emblen, J. D., & Burck, R. (1989). Development of a model for spiritual assessment and intervention. *Journal of Religion and Health, 28,* 185–194.

Fine, S. F., & Glasser, P. H. (1996). *The first helping interview: Engaging the client and building trust.* Thousand Oaks, CA: Sage.

Fordham University Graduate School of Social Service. (1998). *Plans of study—Two year plan of study.* New York. www.fordham.edu/gss/POS.html#2yps

Forester-Miller, H., & Davis, T. E. (1995). *A practitioner's guide to ethical decision making.* Alexandria, VA: American Counseling Association.

Forester-Miller, H., & Shumate, S. (1998). Report of the ACA Ethics Committee: 1996–1997. *Journal of Counseling and Development, 76,* 231–234.

Frankl, V. (1969). *The will to meaning: Foundations and applications of logotherapy.* New York: New American Library.

Freidson, E. (1994). *Professionalism reborn: Theory, prophecy, and policy.* Chicago: University of Chicago Press.

Furrow, B. R., Greaney, T. L., Johnson, S. H., Jost, T. S., & Schwartz, R. L. (1995). *Health law.* St. Paul, MN: West.

Gallup, G., Jr., & Castelli, J. (1989). *The people's religion: American faith in the 90s.* New York: Macmillan.

Gibson, R. L., & Mitchell, M. H. (1995). *Introduction to counseling and guidance* (4th ed.). Englewood Cliffs, NJ: Merrill/Prentice Hall.

Gilligan, C. (1982). *In a different voice.* Cambridge, MA: Harvard University Press.

Gladding, S. T. (1996). *Counseling: A comprehensive profession* (3rd ed.). Englewood Cliffs, NJ: Prentice Hall.

Gladding, S. T. (1998). *Family therapy: History, theory, and practice* (2nd ed.). Upper Saddle River, NJ: Prentice Hall.

Gladding, S. T. (2000). *Counseling: A comprehensive profession* (4th ed.). Upper Saddle River, NJ: Prentice Hall.

Glauser, A. (1996). A hub for mental health counselor practitioners: The untapped potential. *Journal of Mental Health Counseling, 18* (4), 312–315.

Glosoff, H. L., & Rockwell, P. J. (1997). The counseling profession: A historical perspective. In D. Capuzzi & D. R. Gross (Eds.), *Introduction to the counseling profession* (pp. 3–47). Boston: Allyn and Bacon.

Goldberg, R. (1997). Ethical dilemmas in working with children and adolescents. In D. T. Marsh & R. D. Magee (Eds.), *Ethical and legal issues in professional practice with families* (pp. 97–111). New York: Wiley.

Goodwin, L. R. (1986). A holistic perspective for the provision of rehabilitation counseling services. *Journal of Applied Rehabilitation Counseling, 17* (2), 29–36.

Goodyear, R. K. (1984). On our journal's evolution: Historical developments, transitions, and future directions. *Journal of Counseling and Development, 63,* 3–9.

Greer, K. (1988, January). Are American families finding new strength in spirituality? *Better Homes and Gardens,* pp. 16, 19, 21, 23, 25–27.

Grey, A. L., & Fiscalini, J. (1987). Parallel process as transference-countertransference interaction. *Psychoanalytic Psychology, 4,* 131–144.

Griffin, B. (1993). ACES: Promoting professionalism, collaboration, and advocacy. *Counselor Education and Supervision, 33,* 2–9.

Grohol, J. (1998). Psych Central: Dr. John Grohol's Mental Health Page. www.psychcentral.com and www.grohol.com

Gross, S. J. (1977). Professional disclosure: An alternative to licensing. *The Personnel and Guidance Journal, 55,* 586–588.

Gross, S. J. (1978). The myth of professional licensing. *American Psychologist, 33,* 1109–1116.

Gummere, R. M., Jr. (1988). The counselor as prophet: Frank Parsons, 1854–1908. *Journal of Counseling and Development, 66,* 402–405.

Haferkamp, C. J. (1989). Implications of self-monitoring theory for counseling supervision. *Counselor Education & Supervision, 28,* 290–298.

Hall, J. E. (1988). Dual relationships in supervision. *Register Report, 15* (1), 5–6.

Harding, A. K., Gray, L. A., & Neal, M. (1993). Confidentiality limits with clients who have HIV: A review of ethical and legal guidelines and professional policies. *Journal of Counseling and Development, 71* (3), 297–305.

Harold, M. (1985). Council's history examined after 50 years. *Guidepost, 27* (10), 4.

Hartman, K. (1998). Technology and the school counselor. *Education Week, 18* (9), 40, 43.

Harvey, C., & Katz, C. (1985). *If I'm so successful, why do I feel like a fake: The impostor phenomenon.* New York: St. Martin's Press.

Haverkamp, B. E. (1994). Using assessment in counseling supervision: Individual differences in self-monitoring. *Measurement & Evaluation in Counseling & Development, 27,* 316–324.

Hedges, L. E. (1983). *Listening perspectives in psychotherapy.* Northvale, NJ: Jason Aronson.

Henderson, P., & Gysbers, N. C. (1998). *Leading and managing your school guidance program staff: A manual for school administrators and directors of guidance.* Alexandria, VA: American Counseling Association.

Herlihy, B., & Corey, G. (1992). *Dual relationships in counseling.* Alexandria, VA: American Association for Counseling and Development.

Herlihy, B., & Corey, G. (1996). *ACA ethical standards casebook* (5th ed.). Alexandria, VA: American Counseling Association.

Herlihy, B., & Remley, T. P. (1995). Unified ethical standards: A challenge for professionalism. *Journal of Counseling and Development, 74,* 130–133.

Herr, E. L. (1985). AACD: An association committed to unity through diversity. *Journal of Counseling and Development, 63,* 395–404.

Hiatt, J. F. (1986). Spirituality, medicine, and healing. *Southern Medical Journal, 79,* 736–743.

Higgins, T. J. (1958). *Man as man: The science and art of ethics.* Milwaukee, IL: Bruce.

Hinterkopf, E. (1994). Integrating spiritual experiences in counseling. *Counseling and Values, 38,* 165–175.

Hinterkopf, E. (1998). *Integrating spirituality in counseling: A manual for using the experiential focusing method.* Alexandria, VA: American Counseling Association.

Hogan, D. B. (1983). The effectiveness of licensing: History, evidence, and recommendations. *Law and Human Behavior, 7* (2/3), 117–138.

Holland, J. A. (1998, February). Editor's note. *TCA Guidelines (Official Publication of the Texas Counseling Association), 49* (6), 3.

Holland, J. L. (1973). *Making vocational choices: A theory of careers.* Upper Saddle River, NJ: Prentice Hall.

Holmes, L. (1997). You can't do psychotherapy on the net (yet). Paper presented at the meeting of the American Psychological Association. www.mentalhealth.tqn.com/library/weekly/aa010499.htm

Hosie, T. W. (1991). Historical antecedents and current status of counselor licensure. In F. O. Bradley (Ed.), *Credentialing in counseling* (pp. 23–52). Alexandria, VA: Association for Counselor Education and Supervision.

Hughes, R. B., & Friedman, A. L. (1994). AIDS-related ethical and legal issues for mental health professionals. *Journal of Mental Health Counseling, 16* (4), 445–458.

Hughs, A. L., & Ruiz, N. J. (1998, April). Cyberspace and the counseling practice. *Counseling Today,* p. 16.

Ingersoll, R. E. (1995). Spirituality, religion and counseling: Dimensions and relationships. In M. T. Burke & J. G. Miranti (Eds.), *Counseling: The spiritual dimension* (pp. 5–18). Alexandria, VA: ASERVIC/ACA.

Intelitrak. (1999, January 6). *Voice authentification.* www.intelitrak.com

Ivey, A. E., Ivey, M. B., & Simek-Morgan, L. (1997). *Counseling and psychotherapy: A multicultural approach* (4th ed.). Boston: Allyn and Bacon.

Jacob-Timm, S., & Hartshorne, T. S. (1998). *Ethics and law for school psychologists* (3rd ed.). New York: Wiley.

*Jaffee* v. *Redmond,* 518 U.S. 1 (1996).

Janofsky, J. S. (1996). The mental health system and the law. In W. R. Breakey (Ed.), *Integrated mental health services* (pp. 175–191). New York: Oxford University Press.

Jensen, J. P., & Bergin, A. E. (1988). Mental health values of professional therapists: A national interdisciplinary survey. *Professional Psychology: Research and Practice, 19,* 290–297.

Johnson, L. D., & Shaha, S. (1996). Improving the quality of psychotherapy. *Psychotherapy, 33,* 225–236.

Kadushin, A. (1968). Games people play in supervision. *Social Work, 13,* 23–32.

Kelly, E. W., Jr. (1994). The role of religion and spirituality in counselor education: A national survey. *Counselor Education and Supervision, 33,* 227–237.

Kelly, E. W., Jr. (1995). *Spirituality and religion in counseling and psychotherapy: Diversity in theory and practice.* Alexandria, VA: American Counseling Association.

Kidder, R. M. (1995). *How good people make tough choices: Resolving the dilemmas of ethical living.* New York: Fireside.

Kirk, M. A. (1997, January). Current perceptions of counseling and counselor education in cyberspace. *Counseling Today, 39,* 17–18.

Kitchner, K. S. (1984). Intuition, critical evaluation and ethical principles: The foundation for ethical decisions in counseling psychology. *The Counseling Psychologist, 12* (3), 43–55.

Kitchner, K. S. (1988). Dual role relationships: What makes them so problematic? *Journal of Counseling and Development, 67,* 217–221.

Knapp, S. (1997). Professional liability and risk management in an era of managed care. In D. T. Marsh & R. D. Magee (Eds.), *Ethical and legal issues in professional practice with families* (pp. 271–288). New York: Wiley.

Knapp, S., & VanderCreek, L. (1997). Ethical and legal aspects of clinical supervision. In C. E. Watkins, Jr. (Ed.), *Handbook of psychotherapy supervision* (pp. 589–602). New York: Wiley.

Kopp, S. B. (1972). *If you meet the Buddha on the road, kill him!* New York: Bantam Books.

Lamb, D. H., Cochran, D. J., & Jackson, V. R. (1991). Training and organizational issues associated with identifying and responding to intern impairment. *Professional Psychology Research and Practice, 22,* 291–296.

Lambert, M. J., & Cattani-Thompson, K. (1996). Current findings regarding the effectiveness of counseling: Implications for practice. *Journal of Counseling and Development, 74,* 601–608.

Lanning, W. (1986). Development of the supervisor emphasis rating form. *Counselor Education and Supervision, 25,* 191–196.

LaPierre, L. L. (1994). A model for describing spirituality. *Journal of Religion and Health, 33,* 153–161.

Lazarus, A. A. (1967). In support of technical eclecticism. *Psychological Bulletin, 21,* 415–416.

Leary, M. R., & Kowalski, R. M. (1990). Impression management: A literature review and two-component model. *Psychological Bulletin, 107,* 34–47.

Lee, J. M. (1966). Issues and emphases in guidance: A historical perspective. In J. M. Lee & N. J. Pallone (Eds.), *Readings in guidance and counseling.* New York: Sheed & Ward.

Lewis, R., & Maude, A. (1952). *Professional people.* London: Phoenix.

Liteman, M., & Liteman, J. (1998, December). Turf battles. *Executive Update.* Entire issue.

Locke, D. C., & Faubert, M. (1993). Getting on the right track: A program for African American high school students. *The School Counselor, 41,* 129–133.

Love, J. (1998, January). *Regulation of online counseling services.* Paper presented at the meeting of the American Association of State Counseling Boards, Tucson, AZ. Also published in the *Proceeds of the Annual Conference of the American Association of State Counseling Boards,* John M. Sutton, Jr. (Ed.).

Mahue, M. (1997). *Telehealth: A call to action.* www.telehealth.net/articles/action.html

MacNair, R. R. (1992). Ethical dilemmas of child abuse reporting: Implications for mental health counselors. *Journal of Mental Health Counseling, 14,* 127–136.

Maine Board of Counseling Professionals Licensure. (1998, January). *Rules and regulations.* Augusta, ME: State of Maine.

Mallinckrodt, B., & Nelson, M. L. (1991). Counselor training level and the formation of the psychotherapeutic working alliance. *Journal of Counseling Psychology, 38,* 133–138.

Malony, H. N. (1985). Assessing religious maturity. In E. M. Stern (Ed.), *Psychotherapy and the religiously committed patient* (pp. 25–33). New York: Haworth.

Malony, H. N. (1993). The uses of religious assessment in counseling. In L. B. Brown (Ed.), *Religion, personality, and mental health* (pp. 16–28). New York: Plenum.

Maslow, A. (1968). *Toward a psychology of being* (2nd ed.). New York: Van Nostrand.

May, G. G. (1982). *Will and spirit: A contemplative psychology.* San Francisco: Harper and Row.

McCarthy, H. (1995a). Integrating spirituality into rehabilitation in a technocratic society. *Rehabilitation Education, 9* (2), 87–95.

McCarthy, H. (1995b). Understanding and reversing rehabilitation counseling's neglect of spirituality. *Rehabilitation Education, 9* (2), 187–199.

McGoldrick, M. (1995). *You can go home again: Reconnecting with your family.* New York: Norton.

McLeod, J. (1990). The client's experience of counseling and psychotherapy: A review of the research literature. In D. Mearns & W. Dryden (Eds.), *Experience of counseling in action* (pp. 1–20). London: Sage.

McWilliams, N. (1994). *Psychoanalytic diagnosis: Understanding personality structure in the clinical process.* New York: Guilford.

Mental health: Does therapy work? (1995, November). *Consumer Reports.*

Meyer, R. G., Landis, E. R., & Hays, J. R. (1988). *Law for the psychotherapist.* New York: Norton.

Meyers, H. (1998, February). NBCC Ethical Standards for WebCounseling. *TCA Guidelines (Official Publication of the Texas Counseling Association), 49* (6), 1, 3.

Midelfort, C. F. (1962). Use of members of the family in the treatment of schizophrenia. *Family Process, 1,* 114–118.

Miller, W. R. (1997). Spiritual aspects of addictions treatment and research. *Mind/Body Medicine, 2* (1), 37–43.

Miller, W. R. (1998). Researching the spiritual dimensions of alcohol and other drug problems. *Addiction, 93* (7), 971–982.

Minnesota Attorney General. (1998). *Warning to all Internet users and providers.* www.ag.state.mn.us/consumer/news/OnlineScams/memo.txt

Miranti, J., & Burke, M. T. (1992). Ethics and spirituality: The prevailing forces influencing the counseling profession. In M. T. Burke & J. G. Miranti (Eds.), *Ethical and spiritual values in counseling* (pp. 1–4). Alexandria, VA: ARVIC/AACD.

Mitchell, R. W. (1991). In T. P. Remley, Jr. (Ed.), *Documentation in counseling records. The ACA legal series: Vol. 2.* Alexandria, VA: American Counseling Association.

Moos, R. H., & Moos, B. S. (1981). *Manual for the Family Environment Scale.* Palo Alto, CA: Consulting Psychologist Press.

Morgan, O. J. (1992). In a sober voice: A psychological study of long-term alcoholic recovery with attention to spiritual dimensions. *Dissertation Abstracts International, 52* (11), 6069–B. (University Microfilms No. 92-10480)

Morgan, O. J. (1995a). Extended length of sobriety: The missing variable. *Alcoholism Treatment Quarterly, 12* (1), 59–71.

Morgan, O. J. (1995b). Recovery-sensitive counseling in the treatment of alcoholism. *Alcoholism Treatment Quarterly, 13* (4), 63–73.

Morgan, O. J. (1998). Practical theology, alcohol abuse and alcoholism: Methodological and biblical considerations. *Journal of Ministry in Addiction and Recovery, 5* (2), 33–64.

Morgan, O. J., & Jordan, M. R. (Eds.). (1999). *Addiction and spirituality: A multidisciplinary approach.* St. Louis: Chalice Press.

Morrisey, M. (1998, May). *ACES Technology Interest Network drafts technology competencies for students.* www.counseling.org/ctonline/archives/ct0598/aces.htm

Murphy, J. W., & Pardeck, J. T. (1986). The "burnout syndrome" and management style. *The Clinical Supervisor, 4* (4), 35–44.

Murphy, L., & Mitchell, D. (1998). When writing helps to heal: E-mail as therapy. *British Journal of Guidance & Counselling, 26* (1), 21–32.

Myers, I. B. (1962). *The Myers-Briggs Type Indicator.* Palo Alto, CA: Consulting Psycholgist Press.

Myers, I. B., & McCaulley, M. H. (1985). *Manual: A guide to the development and use of the Myers-Briggs Type Indicator.* Palo Alto, CA: Consulting Psychologists Press.

Myers, J. E. (1995). Specialties in counseling: Rich heritage or force for fragmentation? *Journal of Counseling and Development, 74,* 115–116.

Nagy, T. (1997). *Definition of psychotherapy.* www.cybertowers.com/ct/dlc/apa97/psytx/tsld007.htm

National Association of Social Workers. (1996). *Code of ethics.* Washington, DC: Author.

National Board for Certified Counselors. (1997). *Code of ethics.* Greensboro, NC: Author.

National Board for Certified Counselors and the Council for Credentialing and Education. (1997). *Standards for the ethical practice of WebCounseling.* Greensboro, NC: Author. www.nbcc.org/ethics/wcstandards.htm

National Career Development Association. (1991). *Code of ethics.* Alexandria, VA. www.ncda.org/polethic.html

National Career Development Association. (1997). *Guidelines for the use of the Internet for provision of career information and planning services.* Alexandria, VA. www.ncda.org/polweb.html

National Institute for Healthcare Research. (1998). *Scientific research on spirituality and health: A consensus report.* Washington, DC: Author.

Nelson, M. L., & Neufeldt, S. A. (1996). Building on an empirical foundation. *Journal of Counseling and Development, 74,* 609–615.

Neukrug, E. (1999). *The world of the counselor: An introduction to the counseling profession.* Pacific Grove, CA: Brooks/Cole.

Neukrug, E., Lovell, C., & Parker, R. J. (1996). Employing ethical codes and decision-making models: A developmental process. *Counseling and Values, 40,* 98–106.

Nosek, M. A. (1995). The defining light of Vedanta: Personal reflections on spirituality and disability. *Rehabilitation Education, 9,* 171–182.

Nugent, F. A. (1994). *An introduction to the profession of counseling* (2nd ed.). Upper Saddle River, NJ: Prentice Hall.

Nurcombe, B., & Partlett, D. F. (1994). *Child mental health and the law.* New York: Free Press.

Ohlsen, M. M. (1983). *Introduction to counseling.* Itasca, IL: Peacock.

Olk, M. E., & Friedlander, M. L. (1992). Trainees' experiences of role conflict and role ambiguity in supervisory relationships. *Journal of Counseling Psychology, 39,* 389–397.

O'Reilley, M. R. (1998). *Radical presence: Teaching as contemplative practice.* New York: Boynton/Cook.

Osborn, C. J., & Davis, T. E. (1996). The supervision contract: Making it perfectly clear. *The Clinical Supervisor, 14* (2), 121–134.

Osborne, J. O., & Collison, B. B. (1998). School counselors and external providers: Conflict or complement. *Professional School Counseling, 1,* 7–11.

Parsons, F. (1909). *Choosing a vocation.* Boston: Houghton Mifflin.

Pate, R. H., & Bondi, A. M. (1992). Religious beliefs and practice: An integral aspect of multicultural awareness. *Counselor Education and Supervision, 32,* 108–115.

Perlin, M. L. (1997). The "duty to protect" others from violence. In *The Hatherleigh guide to ethics in therapy* (pp. 127–146). New York: Hatherleigh Press.

Peterson, D., Murray, G., & Chan, F. (1998). Ethics and technology. In R. R. Cottone & V. M. Tarvydas (Eds.), *Ethical and professional issues in counseling* (pp. 196–235). Upper Saddle River, NJ: Merrill.

Peterson, J. V., & Nisenholz, B. (1999). *Orientation to counseling.* Boston: Allyn and Bacon.

Peterson, P. B. (1997). The cultural context of the American Counseling Association Code of Ethics. *Journal of Counseling and Development, 76,* 23–28.

Ponterotto, J. G., & Casas, J. M. (1987). In search of multicultural competence within counselor education programs. *Journal of Counseling and Development, 65,* 430–434.

Pruyser, P. W. (1976). *The minister as diagnostician.* Philadelphia: Westminster.

Quinn, K. M., & Weiner, B. A. (1993). Legal rights of children. In B. A. Weiner & R. M. Wettstein (Eds.), *Legal issues in mental health care* (pp. 309–347). New York: Plenum.

Rae, W. A., Worchel, F. F., & Brunnquell, D. (1995). Ethical and legal issues in pediatric psychology. In M. C. Roberts (Ed.), *Handbook of pediatric psychology* (2nd ed., pp. 19–36). New York: Guilford.

Reisner, R., & Slobogin, C. (1990). *Law and the mental health system: Civil and criminal aspects* (2nd ed.). St. Paul, MN: West.

Remley, T. P. (1991). An argument for credentialing. In F. O. Bradley (Ed.), *Credentialing in counseling* (pp. 81–84). Alexandria, VA: Association for Counselor Education and Supervision.

Remley, T. P., Jr., Herlihy, B., & Herlihy, S. B. (1997). The U.S. Supreme Court decision in *Jaffee* v. *Redmond:* Implications for counselors. *Journal of Counseling and Development, 75* (3), 213–218.

Richards, P. S., & Bergin, A. E. (1997). *A spiritual strategy for counseling and psychotherapy.* Washington, DC: American Psychological Association.

Ritchie, M. H. (1990). Counseling is not a profession—yet. *Counselor Education and Supervision, 29,* 220–227.

Robiner, W. N., Fuhrman, M., & Ristvedt, S. (1993). Evaluation difficulties in supervising psychology interns. *The Clinical Psychologist, 46,* 3–13.

Robson, D., & Robson, M. (1998). Intimacy and computer communication. *British Journal of Guidance & Counselling, 26* (1), 33–41.

Rogers, C. (1973). Some new challenges. *The American Psychologist, 28,* 379–388.

Rogers, C. R. (1942). *Counseling and psychotherapy: Newer concepts in practice.* Boston: Houghton Mifflin.

Rogers, C. R. (1951). *Client-centered therapy.* Boston: Houghton Mifflin.

Ronnestad, M. H., & Skovholt, T. M. (1993). Supervision of beginning and advanced graduate students of counseling and psychotherapy. *Journal of Counseling and Development, 71,* 396–405.

Salo, M. M., & Shumate, S. G. (1993*).* In T. P. Remley, Jr. (Ed.), *Counseling minor clients. The ACA legal series: Vol. 4.* Alexandria, VA: American Counseling Association.

Sampson, J. P., Jr. (1998). *Integrating Internet-based distance guidance with services provided in career centers.* (Based on a paper presented in a seminar entitled, "Guidance in Open Learning Environments in the Finnish Polytechnics" at Espoo-Vantaa Polytechnic, Vantaa, Finland, March 12, 1998.)

Sampson, J. P., Jr., Kolodinsky, R. W., & Greeno, P. B. (1997). Counseling on the information highway: Future possibilities and potential problems. *Journal of Counseling and Development, 75,* 203–212.

Sattem, L. (1997). *Mandatory continuing professional education in an emerging field: A perspective on the counseling profession.* Doctoral dissertation, The Ohio State University.

Sattem, L. (1998). Counselor professional continuing education requirements for the new millennium. *Proceedings of the Annual Conference of the American Association of State Counseling Boards,* pp. 36–51.

Schafer, R. (1983). *The analytic attitude.* New York: Basic Books.

Schlauch, C. R. (1995). *Faithful companioning: How pastoral counseling heals.* Minneapolis, MN: Fortress.

*Schloendorff* v. *Society of New York Hospital, 105* N.E. 92 (N.Y. 1914), *overruled on other grounds* by *Bing* v. *Thunig, 143* N.E.2d 3 (N.Y. 1957).

Schmidt, J. J. (1998). Perspectives and projections in counseling research: An interview with Garry R. Walz. *Journal of Counseling and Development, 76,* 483–489.

Schmitt, K. (1995). What is licensure? In J. C. Impara (Ed.), *Licensure testing: Purposes, procedures, and practices* (pp. 3–32). Lincoln, NE: Buros Institute of Mental Measurement.

Schneiders, S. M. (1986). Theology and spirituality: Strangers, rivals, or partners? *Horizons, 13* (2), 253–274.

Schneiders, S. M. (1990). Spirituality in the academy. In B. C. Hanson (Ed.), *Modern Christian spirituality: Methodological and historical essays* (pp. 15–37). Atlanta, GA: Scholars Press.

Schon, D. (1987). *Educating the reflective practitioner.* San Francisco: Jossey-Bass.

Scott, G. S. (1998). *Making ethical choices, resolving ethical dilemmas.* St. Paul, MN: Paragon.

Sells, J. N., Goodyear, R. K., Lichtenberg, J. W., & Polkinghorne, D. E. (1997). Relationship of supervisor and trainee gender and client severity to in-session verbal behavior, session, impact, trainee ratings. *Journal of Counseling Psychology, 44,* 1–7.

Sexton, T. L., Montgomery, D., Goff, K., & Nugent, W. (1993). Ethical, therapeutic, and legal considerations in the use of paradoxical techniques: The emerging debate. *Journal of Mental Health Counseling, 15* (3), 260–277.

Sexton, T. L., Whiston, S. C., Bleuer, J. C., & Walz, G. R. (1997). *Integrating outcome research into counseling practice and training.* Alexandria, VA: American Counseling Association.

Shafranske, E. P., & Gorsuch, R. L. (1984). Factors associated with the perception of spirituality in psychotherapy. *Journal of Transpersonal Psychology, 16,* 231–241.

Shafranske, E. P., & Malony, H. N. (1990). Clinical psychologists' religious and spiritual orientation and their practice of psychotherapy. *Psychotherapy, 27,* 72–78.

Sheldrake, P. (1991). *Spirituality and history: Questions of interpretation and method.* London: SPCK.

Shimberg, B. (1981). Testing for licensure and certification. *American Psychologist, 36* (10), 1138–1146.

*Simmons* v. *United States,* 805 f, 2nd 1363 (9th Cir. 1986).

Skovholt, T. M., & Ronnestad, M. H. (1992). *The evolving professional self: Stages and themes in therapist and counselor development.* Chichester, England: Wiley.

Smith, H. B. (1999). Managed care: A survey of counselor educators and practitioners. *Journal of Mental Health Counseling,* in press.

Smith, S. R. (1996). Malpractice liability of mental health professionals and institutions. In B. D. Sales & D. W. Shuman (Eds.), *Law, mental health and mental disorder* (pp. 76–98). Pacific Grove, CA: Brooks/Cole.

Smith-Bell, M., & Winslade, W. J. (1996). Confidentiality in the psychotherapeutic relationship. In B. D. Sales & D. W. Shuman (Eds.), *Law, mental health and mental disorder* (pp. 62–75). Pacific Grove, CA: Brooks/Cole.

Sommers, D. L. (1998, October 18). Mental health cyberclinic thoughts on all topics. www.nicom.com/~davids/wordresu.htm

Spann, M. G., & Nickles, N. B. (Eds.). (1992). *Counseling & spiritual issues: An annotated bibliography.* Alexandria, VA: ARVIC/AACD.

Stamm, M. L., & Nissman, B. S. (1979). *Improving middle school guidance.* Boston: Allyn and Bacon.

Stanard, R., & Hazler, R. (1995). Legal and ethical implications of HIV and duty to warn for counselors: Does *Tarasoff* apply? *Journal of Counseling and Development, 73* (4), 397–400.

Steenbarger, B. N., & Smith, H. B. (1996). Assessing the quality of counseling services: Developing accountable helping systems. *Journal of Counseling and Development, 75,* 145–148.

Steinhauser, L., & Bradley, R. (1983). Accreditation of counselor education programs. *Counselor Education and Supervision, 25,* 98–108.

Stinnett, N., & DeFrain, J. (1986). *Secrets of strong families.* Boston: Little, Brown.

Stripling, R. O. (1978). ACES guidelines for doctoral preparation in counselor education. *Counselor Education and Supervision, 17,* 163–166.

Super, D. E. (1955). Transition: From vocational guidance to counseling psychology. *Journal of Counseling Psychology, 2,* 3–9.

Super, D. E. (1957). *The psychology of careers.* New York: Harper.

Sutton, J. M., Jr. (1997). *A descriptive study of the supervision of counselors as mandated by state statutes and rules.* Paper presented at the meeting of the American Association of State Counseling Boards, Hot Springs, AR.

Sutton, J. M., Jr., Nielsen, R., & Essex, M. (1998). A descriptive study of the ethical standards related to supervisory behavior employed by counselor licensure boards. *Proceedings of the Annual Conference of the American Association of State Counseling Boards,* pp. 52–70.

Swanson, J. L., & O'Saben, C. L. (1993). Differences in supervisory needs and expectations by trainee experience, cognitive style, and program membership. *Journal of Counseling and Development, 71,* 457–464.

Sweeney, T. J. (1998). Counselor advocacy leadership conference. *Proceedings of the Chi Sigma Iota Meeting, University of North Carolina at Greensboro,* May 1998.

Swenson, L. C. (1993). *Psychology and law for the helping professions.* Pacific Grove, CA: Brooks/Cole.

Swenson, L. C. (1997). *Psychology and law for the helping professions* (2nd ed.). Pacific Grove, CA: Brooks/Cole.

*Tarasoff* v. *Regents of the University of California.* 118 Cal. Rptr. 129, 529 P 2d 533 (1974).

*Tarasoff* v. *Regents of the University of California.* 551 P.2d 334, (Cal., 1976).

Tracey, T. J., Ellickson, J. L., & Sherry, P. (1989). Reactance in relation to different supervisory environments and counselor development. *Journal of Counseling Psychology, 36,* 336–344.

Tracey, T. J., Hays, K. A., Malone, J., & Herman, B. (1988). Changes in counselor response as a function of experience. *Journal of Counseling Psychology, 35,* 119–126.

*United States Fidelity & Guaranty Co.* v. *Guenther,* 281 U.S. 34 (1930).

Vacc, N. A., & Loesch, L. C. (1994). *A professional orientation to counseling* (2nd ed.). Bristol, PA: Accelerated Development.

VanZandt, C. E. (1990). Professionalism: A matter of personal initiatives. *Journal of Counseling and Development, 68,* 243–245.

Vash, C. L., & McCarthy, H. (Eds.). (1995). *Rehabilitation counseling: Special double issue: Spirituality, disability and rehabilitation.* Athens, GA: National Council on Rehabilitation Education.

Veach, T. L., & Chappel, J. N. (1992). Measuring spiritual health: A preliminary study. *Substance Abuse, 13,* 139–147.

Walther, J. B., & Burgoon, J. K. (1992). Relational communication in computer mediated interaction. *Relational Communication, 19,* 50–58.

Wedding, D. (1995). Current issues in psychotherapy. In R. J. Corsini & D. Wedding (Eds.), *Current psychotherapies* (5th ed., pp. 419–432). Itasca, IL: Peacock.

Weiner, B. A., & Wettstein, R. M. (1993). *Legal issues in mental health care.* New York: Plenum.

Welfel, E. R. (1998). *Ethics in counseling and psychotherapy: Standards, research and emerging issues.* Pacific Grove, CA: Brooks/Cole.

Wettstein, R. M. (1994). Legal and ethical issues. In M. Hersen, R. T. Ammerman, & L. A. Sisson (Eds.), *Handbook of aggressive and destructive behavior in psychiatric patients* (pp. 113–128). New York: Plenum.

Whisenhunt, B. J., Romans, J. S. C., Boswell, D. L., & Carlozzi, A. F. (1997). Counseling students' perceptions of supervisory modalities. *The Clinical Supervisor, 15* (2), 79–90.

Whiston, S. C. (1996). Accountability through action research: Research methods for practitioners. *Journal of Counseling and Development, 74,* 616–623.

Williams, S. Y. (1998). Where is the performance in our assessments of counselor readiness to practice? *Proceedings of the Annual Conference of the American Association of State Counseling Boards,* pp. 71–90.

Williamson, E. G. (1939). *How to counsel students: A manual of techniques for clinical counselors.* New York: McGraw-Hill.

Williamson, E. G., & Biggs, D. A. (1979). Trait-factor theory and individual differences. In H. M. Burks, Jr., & B. Stefflre (Eds.), *Theories of counseling* (3rd ed., pp. 91–131). New York: McGraw-Hill.

Wills, G. (1990). *Under God: Religion and American politics.* New York: Simon and Schuster.

Wilson, F. R., Jencius, M., & Duncan, D. (1997). *Introduction to the Internet: Opportunities and dilemmas.* Denver, CO: Love.

Winter, M., & Holloway, E. L. (1991). Relation of trainee experience, conceptual level, and supervisor approach to selection of audiotaped counseling passages. *Clinical Supervisor, 9* (2), 87–103.

Witmer, J. M. (1978). Professional disclosure in licensure. *Counselor Education and Supervision, 18* (1), 71–73.

Witmer, J. M. (1980). Professional disclosure in licensure: In R. W. Warner, Jr., D. K. Brooks, Jr., & J. A. Thompson (Eds.), *Counselor licensure: Issues and perspectives* (pp. 52–54). Falls Church, VA: American Personnel and Guidance Association.

Witmer, J. M., & Sweeney, T. J. (1992). A holistic model of wellness and prevention over the life span. *Journal of Counseling and Development, 71,* 140–148.

Worthington, E. L., Jr. (1989). Religious faith across the life span: Implications for counseling and research. *The Counseling Psychologist, 17,* 555–612.

WWW document. *www.geocities.com/RainForest/1801/gethelp8.htm#reprint*

Zytowski, D. (1985). Frank! Frank! Where are you now that we need you? *Counseling Psychologist, 13,* 129–135.

# *Index*